Ancient Civilizations

CHINA

THE WORLD'S OLDEST LIVING CIVILIZATION REVEALED

Ancient Civilizations

CHINA

THE WORLD'S OLDEST LIVING CIVILIZATION REVEALED

With over 510 illustrations, 480 in colour

CHIEF CONSULTANT **Dr John Makeham**

Thames & Hudson

First published in the United Kingdom in 2008 by
Thames & Hudson Ltd, 181A High Holborn,
London WC1V 7QX

www.thamesandhudson.com

Conceived and produced by
Global Book Publishing
Level 8, 15 Orion Road,
Lane Cove, NSW 2066, Australia
Ph: (612) 9425 5800   Fax: (612) 9425 5804
Email: rightsmanager@globalpub.com.au

British Library Cataloguing-in-Publication Data
A catalogue record for this book is available from the British Library

ISBN: 978-0-500-25142-3

Printed and bound in China by SNP Leefung Printers Limited
Color separation Pica Digital Pte Ltd, Singapore

Contributors

CHIEF CONSULTANT

Dr John Makeham is a specialist in Chinese philosophy and Chinese intellectual history. Although trained in classical and medieval Chinese philosophy, in recent years his research interests have embraced twentieth-century Chinese philosophy, especially New Confucianism; the formation and development of Chinese philosophy as an academic discipline; and, more recently, Yogācāra or Weishi Buddhism. His most important research monograph is *Transmitters and Creators: Chinese Commentators and Commentaries on the Analects,* for which he was awarded the 2005 Joseph Levenson Book Prize (pre-1900 category) by the Association for Asian Studies. His most significant recent contribution is a study of how "Confucianism" has been understood by contemporary Chinese intellectuals, *Lost Soul: "Confucianism" in Contemporary Chinese Academic Discourse.*

CONTRIBUTORS

Dr Paul D. Buell holds a Masters in Chinese and a PhD in history, both from the Western Washington University, United States. He is the author of more than 120 books, book chapters, and articles and specializes in the political and cultural history of the Mongolian Empire and of the Mongols in China, including medical history. He is currently completing his translation of the surviving chapters of the *Huihui yaofang*, "Muslim Medicinal Recipes," an encyclopedia of Islamic medicine from Mongol China.

Duncan Campbell is a Senior Lecturer in Chinese language and literature, modern and classical, at Victoria University of Wellington, New Zealand. He first visited China in the mid-1970s. His present research focuses on aspects of the literary and material culture of late imperial China.

Dr Rafe de Crespigny is Adjunct Professor of Asian Studies at the Australian National University. A Fellow of the Australian Academy of the Humanities, he has written many books and articles on the history, geography, and literature of China, specializing on early imperial and modern periods. His most recent publication is *A Biographical Dictionary of Later Han to the Three Kingdoms (23–220 AD).* He is currently working on a biography of third-century warlord Cao Cao, founder of the state of Wei which succeeded the Han dynasty.

Associate Professor Paola Demattè is Associate Professor of Chinese Art and Archaeology at the Rhode Island School of Design, Providence, United States. She holds a Laurea in Chinese Language and Literature from the Università degli Studi di Venezia, and a PhD in archaeology from the University of California, Los Angeles. She specializes in Neolithic and Bronze Age archaeology of China and has written on the origins of Chinese writing, pre-dynastic urbanism, archaic jades, and funerary art, and on East–West contacts and exchanges.

Professor Edward L. Farmer is Professor of History at the University of Minnesota, United States. His research has concentrated on Chinese history of the Ming period (1368–1644). He is active in the Society for Ming Studies, and serves as the Managing Editor of the Society's journal, *Ming Studies.* In addition, he is Editor of the Ming Studies Research Series. He has published three books and a number of articles on Ming history. His recent writing and research has focused on representations of the Ming Empire in gazetteer maps and the place of the Ming Empire in early modern world history.

Associate Professor Tze-ki Hon is Associate Professor of History at State University of New York at Geneseo, United States. He is the author of *The Yijing and Chinese Politics: Classical Commentary and Literati Activism in the Northern Song Period, 960–1127,* and Co-Editor of *The Politics of Historical Production in Late Qing and Republican China* and *Beyond the May Fourth Paradigm: In Search of Chinese Modernity.* He is completing a book on the *Guocui xuebao.*

Professor Anne Behnke Kinney is Professor of Chinese and Chair of the Department of East Asian Languages, Literatures, and Cultures at the University of Virginia, United States. She received her PhD in Chinese Language and Literature from the University of Michigan, and spent six years studying in Beijing at Peking University, and in Taiwan at the Inter-University program for Chinese Language Studies in Taiwan. Her books include *Representations of Childhood and Youth in Early China,* and she is currently at work on a large publicly accessible digital resource for the study of women in early China.

Associate Professor Tracey Lie-Dan Lu is at the Anthropology Department, Chinese University of Hong Kong, China. She obtained her undergraduate and Masters degrees on archaeology from Zhongshan and Beijing Universities of China respectively, and her PhD from the Australian National University. She has been working on prehistoric archaeology of mainland China and Hong Kong since 1994, focusing on the transition from hunting–gathering to agriculture, and the impact of agriculture on prehistoric cultural developments and human diaspora in East Asia and the Pacific. She is also working on heritage conservation.

Jeffrey Moser is a Harvard Fulbright Scholar and specializes in the art and intellectual history of Tang and Song dynasty China. He is currently a PhD candidate at Harvard University, United States, where he is completing a dissertation on the changing conceptualizations of antiquities and recreation of archaistic rituals during the eleventh–thirteenth centuries.

Associate Professor Scott Pearce is Associate Professor of Liberal Studies and East Asian Studies, Western Washington University, Washington, United States. He received his PhD from Princeton. In 1996, he organized a conference held in Bellingham on "Dialogue with the Ancients: New Perspectives on Thought and Action in Early Medieval China," which resulted in publication by Harvard University Press of *Culture and Power in the Reconstitution of the Chinese Realm, 200-600*. He has since written a number of articles on China's Period of Division, and is currently at work on a study of Emperor Xiaowen of the Northern Wei dynasty.

Professor Yuri Pines, born in Ukraine (1964), is a Michael W. Lipson Chair of Chinese Studies in the Hebrew University of Jerusalem, Israel. His major fields of research are ancient Chinese political thought, traditional Chinese political culture, Chinese historiography, and sociopolitical history of early China. His major publications include *Foundations of Confucian Thought: Intellectual Life in the Chunqiu Period, 722-453 BCE* and *Envisioning Eternal Empire: Chinese Political Thought of the Warring States Period*, in addition to over 40 scholarly articles.

Associate Professor N. Harry Rothschild is an Associate Professor of Asian History at the University of North Florida, United States. He completed his dissertation, "Rhetoric, Ritual, and Support Constituencies in the Political Authority of Wu Zhao, China's Only Woman Emperor" and earned his PhD in History at Brown. He recently published his first book, *Wu Zhao, China's Only Woman Emperor,* in Longman's World Biography series. Professionally, he is a member of the T'ang Studies Society, the Association of Asian Studies, the Southeast Early China Roundtable, and the International Board of the Wu Zetian Research Association.

Professor Gideon Shelach is the Louis Frieberg Chair of East Asian Studies at the Hebrew University of Jerusalem, Israel. He received his PhD from the Department of Anthropology, University of Pittsburgh in 1996 and has conducted, since 1994, archaeological fieldwork projects in northeastern China. His research addresses the archaeology of northeastern China from the Neolithic to the end of the Bronze Age, gender archaeology, and the formation of local identities during the Chinese Bronze age. His most recent book is titled *Prehistoric Societies on the Northern Frontiers of China: Archaeological Perspectives on Identity Formation and Economic Change during the First Millennium BCE.*

Professor Richard von Glahn is Professor of History at the University of California, Los Angeles, United States. Trained in Chinese economic history at UC Berkeley and Yale, he has taught Chinese history and world history at UCLA since 1987. He is the author of *The Country of Streams and Grottoes: Expansion, Settlement, and the Civilizing of the Sichuan Frontier in Song Times; Fountain of Fortune: Money and Monetary Policy in China, 1000-1700;* and *The Sinister Way: The Divine and the Demonic in Chinese Religious Culture;* and is Co-Editor of *The Song-Yuan-Ming Transition in Chinese History.*

Professor Victor Cunrui Xiong is Professor of Chinese History at Western Michigan University, United States. He is the author of *Sui-Tang Chang'an: A Study in the Urban History of Medieval China; Emperor Yang of the Sui Dynasty: His Life, Times, and Legacy;* and *A Historical Dictionary of Medieval China*. He has also been the Editor of the academic journals *Early Medieval China* (1994–1999) and *Chinese Historians* (1995–1999).

Dr Xiaoqing Ye is a Senior Lecturer in Chinese at Macquarie University, Australia. She was a research fellow at the Institute of History of the Academy of Social Sciences in Shanghai before coming to Australia in 1986 to study for her PhD at the Australian National University. She has wide interests in Chinese history, including Qing history, the history of Chinese medicine, Shanghai history, and Peking Opera. She is currently working on a book on Imperial Institutions and Drama in the Qing Court.

CONTENTS

INTRODUCING
CHINA

Geography of China

From its original home in the North China Plain, the Chinese empire steadily expanded outward over a vast territory. In adapting their way of life to a wide variety of landscapes, the Chinese people have profoundly transformed the natural environment.

ABOVE **Guangxi Zhuang Autonomous Region** is a mountainous, coastal province in southern China, through which rivers have cut deep valleys.

The Chinese people inhabit remarkably diverse landscapes, ranging from windblown deserts to lush tropical forests. Sharp contrasts can be seen almost everywhere. Gently rolling hills and broad plains are rare; instead, flat alluvial valleys, teeming with villages and cultivated fields, end abruptly at the feet of steep, rugged mountains.

China's climate exhibits extreme variations as well. Monsoon winds, which shift direction with the season, have the most pronounced effect on climate and habitat. In winter, strong winds sweep southward across the whole country, bringing dry weather and filling cities such as Beijing with choking sandstorms. The summer monsoon, carrying moisture from the Indian Ocean, is weaker. Southern China, especially south of the Yangzi River, receives heavy rainfall from April to September, while the massive Tibetan Plateau, with an average elevation of more than 14,800 ft (4,500 m) above sea level,

shields the interior of northern China from the monsoonal rains. The land becomes progressively more arid as one moves toward the northwest, where the vast Taklamakan and Gobi Deserts separate China from the grasslands of Mongolia and central Asia.

Mountains and Rivers

Belts of mountain ranges running west to east divide China into three large river valleys: the Yellow River in the north, the Yangzi River in the center, and the Pearl River in the south. All of China's major rivers flow eastward to the sea. However, folding of the earth's crust from tectonic action has also thrust up a series of mountain ranges stretching in a northeast–southwest direction from the Pacific coast to Sichuan in the west and these obstruct the flow of the great rivers. The Yellow River must bend around the Taihang Mountains before reaching the North China Plain, while the Yangzi River has gouged out spectacular gorges as it bores through the mountains ringing the Sichuan basin.

China's landscape thus resembles a checkerboard with mountain belts running both east–west and north–south, and dividing the river valleys into a series of basins. The Yangzi River, fourth among the world's rivers in the volume of water discharged into the ocean, pools into several large, shallow lakes in these inland basins before resuming its eastward march to the sea.

The middle course of the Yellow River passes through thick deposits of loamy yellow soil known as loess. The Yellow River carries great quantities of loess soil—which gives the river its name—downstream as silt. The North China Plain was formed by the annual floods of the Yellow River, which spread this silt over a large area. The earliest records of attempts to control the channel of the Yellow River by human engineering date back to the seventh century BCE. However, over many centuries of levee-building the silt had built up in the riverbed, making the threat of flood ever more perilous. On at least five occasions, most recently in 1897, the river breached its levees and took a new course to the sea. While the surface layer of loess has made the North China Plain fertile for agriculture, the Yellow River's devastating floods have earned it the name "China's Sorrow."

Wet and Dry Regions

Rainfall is not only more infrequent in the north, but also more variable from year to year. In the past, years of prolonged drought turned large areas of north China into dustbowls. By contrast, the heaviest rainfall occurs in the mountainous areas of south China where rain has severely weathered the mountains, creating the fantastic limestone spires of Guilin, and the equally dramatic granite canyons and peaks of Huang Shan, in southern Anhui Province.

Woodlands of pine and oak that once covered eastern China from Manchuria to the Yangzi valley have disappeared, largely due to human activity. In the south, too, settlers cut down the forests of broadleaf evergreen oaks for building materials and firewood, leaving barren hills vulnerable to erosion. Only in the rugged southwestern highlands of Guizhou and Yunnan and in the interior of Hainan Island do large swaths of original forest still stand.

In many parts of southern China, farmers also cleared hillsides to plant tea, a crop that requires frequent rainfall and well-drained soils, or to construct terraced fields suitable for rice cultivation. The largest diversity of vegetation can be found in the Sichuan basin where the great variation in climate and elevation supports many tropical species such as longan, bamboo, lychee, and Chinese olive, as well as broadleaf evergreens and Chinese firs.

The Human Impact on Nature

The landscape of China today has been transformed over thousands of years by human habitation. At the end of the last Ice Age, China, which was never covered by glaciers, had the richest variety of flora and fauna among the temperate zones of the world. However, the ingenuity that enabled Chinese to shape their environment to support a population that had surpassed 100 million people as early as the twelfth century has exacted a significant ecological toll. The need to feed a huge human population led to highly specialized agriculture, especially in areas where rice was grown, and the disappearance of many animal and plant species. The elephants and tigers that once roamed much of China are long gone. One of the great challenges facing China today is to protect its land and waters in the face of the mounting demands of a rapidly industrializing society.

ABOVE **The Zhangjiang (Xiaoqikong) rain forest in Guizhou Province** is one of the few natural areas still in pristine condition. This is due to the slow progress of industrialization in the area.

BELOW **Xinjiang Uighur Autonomous Region** is a large, sparsely populated area in the northwest of China. It takes up about one-sixth of China's territory.

Cultural Treasures

From Peking Opera to the music of ancient chimes, from temple architecture to the murals of Dunhuang, it is difficult to take full account of China's cultural treasures. However, three achievements that have had a lasting influence on both Chinese and world culture are porcelain, silk, and paper.

ABOVE **The caves situated at Dunhuang, Gansu Province,** contain some of the finest examples of Buddhist art and span a period of 1,000 years. This mural illustrates Parables of the Sacred Way.

of ceramics in China, beginning in the Neolithic period with simple kiln-fired pots. Glazed wares, known as "primitive porcelain," first emerged in the late Shang dynasty. They were distinguished from more ordinary glazed pots by the use of white kaolin clay, improved glazes, and increased firing temperature. It was the development of a variety of colored glazes, slightly higher firing temperatures, and improved kiln ventilation, that allowed the Chinese to be able, finally, to produce true porcelain with its eggshell thinness, smooth, glass-like surface, and brilliant colors.

Porcelain, lacquerware, silk, and paper were developed and valued by the Chinese, long before the West knew of their existence. When these products first became available in the West, they were viewed with wonder.

Porcelain

Europeans imported porcelain of astonishing beauty and fineness from China for centuries. However, they had no idea how it was made. English author and physician, Thomas Browne, theorized in *Pseudodoxia Epidemica*, published in 1646, that these exquisite pieces of china were made of eggshells, lobster carapaces, and gypsum that had been hardened and aged underground. In 1708, the German alchemist, Johann Böttger, finally unlocked the mysteries of porcelain production.

Even in China, the creation of true porcelain was relatively late—one of the earliest surviving examples dates to about CE 99. Porcelain is, however, the culmination of a long tradition

Lacquer

Like porcelain, the development of lacquer was a triumph of chemical engineering. It is anti-corrosive, durable, light, waterproof, and beautiful in appearance. Joseph Needham, the great historian of Chinese science, called lacquer China's first plastic. Lacquer was at first produced only in China for the simple reason that the lacquer tree, *Rhus vernicifera,* was found only in East Asia. Early Chinese artisans made lacquerware with the sap of lacquer trees that had first been exposed to the air to evaporate excess moisture and then combined with tong oil and pigment. Thousands of these vessels have been excavated from tombs, many still in pristine condition.

Silk

Pliny, the Roman encyclopedist, believed that silk cloth was the product of moths that wove webs like spiders. Like porcelain, silk-producing techniques were a mystery to Europeans and did not become known in Europe until the fifth or sixth century CE. However, there is little evidence of sophisticated silk-producing machinery in Europe until the thirteenth century. On the other hand, fragments of Chinese silk were found in a German tomb dated to the fifth or sixth century BCE, and elsewhere in Europe at a very early date, demonstrating that silk fabrics entered Europe well before the official opening of the Silk Road by Zhang Qian in the Former Han dynasty.

Within China, however archaeologists have discovered fragments of silk fabric dating from between 2850 and 2650 BCE, and the earliest written records concerning silk are found in Shang oracle-bone inscriptions which mention a silkworm spirit to whom prayers were directed and human beings sacrificed.

At first, the Chinese produced silk using wild silkworms, but gradually, after much trial and error, they were able to domesticate silkworms for large-scale textile production. Somewhat later, Han-dynasty improvements in spindle-wheel and loom technology not only allowed women to triple their output of fabric, but also to weave silk as fine as the full-length robe found in the tombs at Mawangdui that weighs a mere 1.7 ounces (50 g).

In premodern China, taxes were often paid in silk, so that out of necessity a huge percentage of the female population was engaged in silk production. Cloth of profuse variety and astonishing beauty emerged from the production of silken fabrics over four millennia. Some of the finest examples of Chinese textiles are the imperial robes worn by emperors and their families and officials. The silks, satins, and brocades used for their garments were also further refined with exquisite embroidery, culminating in the needlework commissioned in the reign of the Qing emperor Qianlong (reigned 1736–1795).

Works on Paper

The centrality of the written word in Chinese culture generated the invention of paper and movable-type printing, as well as the development of the art of calligraphy, and the Chinese preference for relatively abstract artistic expression using brush and ink on silk or paper.

Historians believe that printing developed from the Chinese use of both inscribed seals and stele inscriptions. In the fourth century CE, print copies of the Chinese classics were made by pressing thin wet paper onto stone tablets inscribed with text, allowing it to dry, and then applying ink. When the paper was removed from the tablet, the incised characters showed up in white against the black inked background.

Woodblock printing probably developed from this process around the sixth century CE. One of China's earliest extant woodblock texts is an edition of the Buddhist *Diamond Sutra*, dated to 868. In 971, the entire Buddhist canon, a labor of 12 years, consisting of 1,076 volumes, became available in a woodblock edition. Finally, in the years 1041–1048, Bi Sheng, a woodblock printer, invented the world's first movable-type printing press. The speed and ease with which books could now be mass produced placed books within the reach of ordinary people. A further refinement, the world's first block-printing with color was developed at least as early the fourteenth century, and by the seventeenth century, printers were able to make multi-colored, subtly shaded woodblock illustrations.

LEFT **Lacquer** was often applied to bases of hemp, wood, and metal to make anything from towering sculptures to small exquisite jewelry boxes.

LEFT **It took an average of eight years** to complete a robe like this embroidered silk Twelve Symbol Dragon Robe from the Qianlong period. Such robes incorporated more than six million stitches.

Agriculture and Economy

China was one of the first regions of the world to develop agriculture. Since antiquity, diverse natural resources and political unity have fostered economic innovation, regional specialization, and long-distance trade.

ABOVE **Filial piety (love and respect for one's parents and ancestors)**, as shown in this idealized twelfth-century scene, ensured that all worked harmoniously on the family's small farm.

The Rice Economy and Household Labor

Rice cultivation was heavily labor intensive. Wet-rice agriculture required the flooding and draining of fields at precise times, and thus sophisticated methods of irrigation. Rice cultivation also demanded enormous effort during the transplanting and harvest seasons, when all members of the family—young and old—worked in the fields. At other times, however, household labor could be spared for other tasks such as raising silkworms, breeding fish, fowl and pigs, and handicrafts. The nature of wet-rice farming—small, enclosed fields worked by hand and the alternation between periods of intense and slack labor—made it more suitable for a household scale of production rather than large farms worked with hired or slave labor. The family farm emerged as the mainstay of the Chinese economy at the beginning of the imperial era and remained the primary form of livelihood for much of the population down to modern times.

A long with Mesopotamia, New Guinea, Mesoamerica, and the Andes highlands, China ranks among the few places where agriculture developed independently. Recent archaeological finds indicate that wild plants, such as millet and rice, were domesticated before 7000 BCE. Millet, which is a hardy, drought-resistant cereal, was the staple crop of the dry loess soil region of the Yellow River valley, while the wet, humid climate of southern China was more favorable to rice. For this reason, from earliest times to the present, China has been divided into two distinct agricultural zones.

In the north of China, farmers have grown dryland crops such as millet, wheat (introduced from West Asia), sorghum, and soybeans. In the south, by contrast, rice prevails as the single dominant crop. In the tropical zone, rice can be harvested twice or even three times a year, while in more temperate areas, in addition to the summer rice crop, farmers plant winter crops, including wheat and soybeans.

Handicrafts and Industries

Silkworm raising and silk weaving are nearly as old as agriculture in China. In early times, it was only the upper classes who could afford silk clothing. The clothes of ordinary people were woven from coarse hemp fibers. The introduction of cotton from India in the thirteenth century brought radical changes to the division of labor within the household, as well as to the economy as a whole. Cotton cloth quickly replaced hemp for everyday clothing. Moreover, while silk manufacture became concentrated in urban workshops employing skilled male artisans, cotton spinning and weaving were performed by rural women working at home, and household work became increasingly segregated by gender. It was only in the late imperial period that the ancient Chinese saying "men till while women weave" actually described the social reality.

The First Emperor (reigned 221–210 BCE) was deeply suspicious of private wealth and was intent on putting industry and commerce under the control of the state. He established uniform weights and uniform measures, a unified currency system based on bronze coins, and tight state regulation of the marketplaces. In the second century BCE, a Han emperor imposed government monopolies on iron and salt, which were the most lucrative industries of the time. But strict state control of the economy on the huge scale of the Chinese empire proved impossible. The Han court relinquished control over the iron industry in the first century CE, although the salt monopoly remained a major source of government revenue.

The Song Economic Revolution

The most dramatic changes in the Chinese economy came in the Song dynasty (960–1279). The Song period marked the ascendancy of the southern rice economy over the less productive dryland agriculture of the north, the heartland of the early empires. By 1100, two-thirds of the Chinese population lived in the rice-growing regions of the south, a ratio that has remained constant to the present. At the same time, advances in metallurgy and kiln technology vastly increased the output of iron and bronze foundries and led to the invention of porcelain. Printing, which was developed during the Tang (618–907), became widespread in the Song, thus broadening access to knowledge and new technologies.

South China had other advantages in natural resources—the climate was well suited to valuable cash crops such as tea, sugar, and later cotton; its numerous navigable rivers and lakes facilitated transport and trade; and its abundant forests supplied timber for shipbuilding.

Commercial expansion spurred innovations in business organization and finance. Demand for money became so acute that the Song government introduced the world's first successful paper money. Commercial prosperity also drew artisans, laborers, and entrepreneurs to the cities. It then became increasingly difficult for the state to control the size and complexity of the urban economy.

The Song dynasty also witnessed a major shift in China's international trade. From the beginning of the Han dynasty (206 BCE–CE 220), caravans crossing the Silk Road through Central Asia carried silk and other goods to India and the Roman Empire. During the Song dynasty, the overland Silk Road was eclipsed by maritime routes that linked the robust economy of south China to markets in Southeast Asia and the Islamic world, and those around the Indian Ocean. Porcelain surpassed silk as China's main export, while war horses from Central Asia remained the most significant import. China also played a major role in the global economy created by the European conquests in the New World. By the sixteenth century the Chinese economy, hungry for money, had become the

LEFT **Wu Zhu coins** minted from the second to the seventh century are unlike earlier coins, as they had a raised rim to prevent filing. They bear no reign titles and, so, are difficult to date.

BELOW **Marco Polo** is illustrated on this Catalan World Map of 1375 as he travels on the Silk Road. Polo was one of the first Westerners to travel to China along this route.

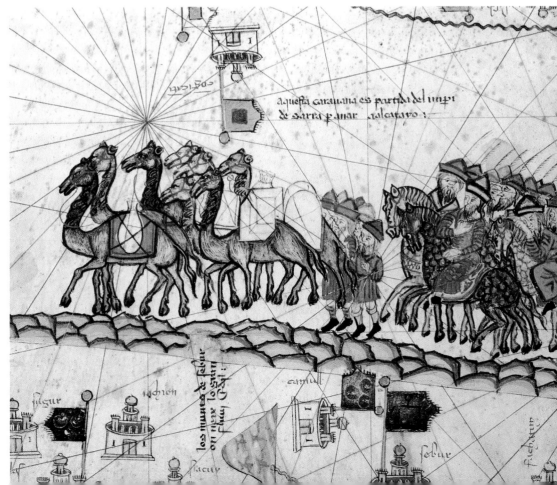

Science and Technology

Premodern China was the world's leading economy, with a large population and a highly productive agriculture. It was also a leader in science and technology and provided key innovations to the rest of the world.

By the Qin dynasty (221–206 BCE), China was already significantly in advance of the rest of the world in such areas as metal casting. During the Qin, progress accelerated. The Qin led the world in the standardization of weights and measures, while a similar standardization of China's written language greatly facilitated communication. Even the axle lengths of carts were controlled to limit road wear.

Han Dynasty

Under the Han (206 BCE–CE 220), the invention of paper further improved communication. Among other innovations of the Han were standardized weapons with replaceable parts, the introduction of the world's first "dog tags", the earliest known use of the crank, outside calipers measuring to the thousandth of an inch, advanced bellows, and the world's first controlled experimentation with crop plants to improve agricultural productivity. Another Han innovation was the sternpost rudder, and Chinese ships were already being built with watertight compartments.

The crossbow, while not a Han invention, was disseminated by them, including to the Roman West. A few centuries later, the Romans also received more efficient harnesses and stirrups from China. Another Chinese invention was the wheelbarrow, a more efficient device than that used in the West. In addition, the Han created the first truly scientific medicine based on the interpretation of materialistic principles, though older views emphasizing supernatural forces persisted.

Period of Disunity

Although disunity in China from the fall of the Han to the establishment of the Sui in 581 was a time of political weakness, this period witnessed the arrival in China of Buddhism and many other Indian ideas.

Among other Buddhist influences to reach China were the first systematic linguistics; the introduction of Indian medicine, which was then combined with Chinese medicine to produce a new synthesis; and an entirely new art form and architecture. There was also experimentation with the distillation of alcohol.

China's period of disunity saw, also, a first flowering of its systematic herbal literature, which included its first regional botany, and the invention of doufu, or tofu.

Sui and Tang

The Sui and Tang dynasties (581–907) saw the reunification China after centuries of division. China's scientific and technology progress was accelerated once more. Achievements included the first printing of whole books—at first Buddhist texts and then others; the first experimentation with gunpowder—including the first pyrotechnical weapons; and China's first mechanical clocks. Tang scholars also made strenuous efforts to systematize knowledge of the past. The use of waterpower expanded and intensified.

Five Dynasties and the Song

There followed, after the Tang, a golden age for science and technology. Under the Northern Song (960–1127), Chinese production of iron, steel, and coal attained a level not achieved in Europe until the nineteenth century. The compass appeared, and Song multi-masted ships were among the largest and most sophisticated ships in the world. The Song also had paddle-wheel driven warships,

BELOW **The trigger mechanism used on crossbows** depended on advanced bronze technology. The Han exported this technology to warring states beyond China's borders.

advanced mechanical clocks, sophisticated building techniques, and even building codes to encourage the construction of healthful and environmentally sound buildings.

Northern Song intellectuals were among the world's first archaeologists, publishing major catalogs of artifacts. They also made major contributions in the field of botany. In war, the Song became the first to shoot handguns, and hurl bombs, as well as employ flamethrowers and similar weapons. Song astronomy and mathematics were among the most advanced in the world, as was Song mapmaking, which was based upon mathematical modeling. The first forensics manual was a product of Song times, although the Chinese had been a leader in forensics since the Qin.

Above all else, however, the greatest Song achievement was its extensive use of printing. Under the Song, books on every topic—including standard editions of scientific works as well as the Confucian classics—were mass produced and disseminated throughout the empire. Hitherto, learning had been the right of the privileged, and a matter of family inheritance, but now it was different, to the great advantage of all literate people in China, many of whom could now afford to buy books. The Song also used printing for

another purpose—to introduce the first paper money as the preferred medium of exchange.

The first systematic acupuncture treatises date from Song and toward the end of the period a major effort was made to produce a single theoretical system to encompass all medicine.

The Mongols and After

The Mongol Yuan dynasty (1279–1368) continued the advance of science and technology, but also imported it from the Islamic world. Furthermore, the Yuan transmitted Chinese achievements to the West in bulk. Gunpowder weapons spread to the Islamic world and the West, and the West began its own serious experiments with printing, soon producing its first printed books. Even the idea of paper money, though unsuccessful at first, traveled west.

Although major new advances in both science and technology were made under Mongol rule, assisted by new inputs from outside the empire and official patronage at the highest level, Europe benefited even more from the great exchanges taking place. As time went on, Europe gradually pulled ahead. At first the differences were not great, and the Ming (1368–1644) and, initially, the Qing (1644–1911) dynasties held their own. However, by the early nineteenth century Europe and not China was in the forefront of economic, scientific, and technological advancement. China, as a consequence, was almost carved up into colonies and its progress stymied until today, when a new China has begun to absorb new stimulus from the West and to develop it.

LEFT **The Astrological Observatory at Dengfeng, Henan,** was built in 1276 and was used to observe the movement of the sun and stars, and to develop a calendar of 364.25 days.

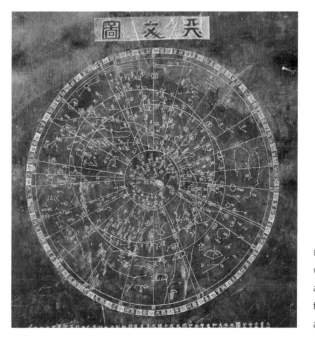

LEFT **Astronomical maps** were created in China from about the sixth century BCE, for both timekeeping and astrological divination.

Archaeology in China

While archaeology may be playing a role in shaping national identity in contemporary China, the discipline has, in fact, a much longer history. Since antiquity, Chinese scholars and rulers have been concerned with the study of the past and have collected ancient artifacts.

ABOVE **Bronze Age artifacts** were uncovered at a site in Sanxingdui, Sichuan, in 1986. The site is considered by some to be a more out-standing find than the terracotta army at Xi'an.

Archaeological research, influenced by the antiquarian tradition, took shape during the Tang dynasty (618–906), and bloomed during the Song (960–1279). Two archaeological catalogs from the Song—the *Kaogutu* and the *Xuanhe bogutu*—recorded, with woodcut images and text, the antiquities that were then being excavated and collected. Notwithstanding their limitations, both works remained the standard antiquarian publications for scholars to imitate right up to the eighteenth century, when the Qing emperor ordered the compilation of the *Four Mirrors* in order to document the imperial collection of ancient bronzes.

In the nineteenth century, Chinese scholars began to move away from antiquarianism with its detailed recordings of objects detached from an archaeological context, and became increasingly interested in more scientific approaches to the investigation of the past, like site documentation and philological research (the study of language and its connection to history).

The Beginning of Modern Archaeology

The first systematic archaeological studies began in the early twentieth century when foreign scientists arrived in China and started excavations under the auspices of Chinese agencies. These early Sino-Western archaeological interventions peaked in the 1920s with the discoveries by Swedish geologist Gunnar Andersson of the Peking Man *Homo erectus* site at Zhoukoudian, near Beijing, and the Neolithic Yangshao culture of the middle Yellow River valley.

Between 1928–1937, while Zhoukoudian was being excavated by an international team led by Chinese paleoanthropologist Jia Lanpo, the first solely Chinese excavation took place at Anyang (Henan) under the direction of archaeologist Li Ji. Retrieved from this site were inscribed oracle bones, objects which had caught scholars' atten-tion since the late nineteenth century. These finds proved that the area had been Yin, the last capital of the Bronze Age Shang dynasty (*c*. 1600–1046 BCE), and thus confirmed the existence of Shang, a dynasty which had hitherto been consi-dered legendary. Shortly thereafter, Li Ji and other Chinese archaeologists excavated at Chengziyai, in Longshan, an urban settlement characterized by the presence of fine black pottery, which defined the late Neolithic Longshan culture.

Legislation

While there was serious research carried out by well qualified international investigators in China in the early twentieth century, the country also suffered plundering by foreign adventurers and scholars who removed frescoes, documents, and artifacts from ancient Silk Road sites, causing incalculable damage to the local cultural heritage.

With the establishment of the People's Republic of China in 1949, archaeology received government support, and foreign participation in excavations was halted. In the 1950s, laws were issued to protect the national cultural heritage. The Ministry of Culture established the State Bureau of Cultural Relics, and the Chinese Academy of Social Sciences set up the Institute of Archaeology which was, for a long time, directed by archaeologist Xia Nai.

Archaeological research slowed during the Cultural Revolution (1966–1976), but the situation improved in the 1980s. At that time, the Institute of Archaeology was decentralized and provincial branches in charge of research and excavations were established in each province. In the 1990s, the State Bureau of Cultural Relics changed its policy on international cooperation, thus removing the ban on Chinese archaeologists collaborating with foreign entities. As a result, there are several international archaeological projects active in China today.

Although Chinese archaeology is entering a brilliant phase, new threats are looming. Economic development and building expansion leave little time to study threatened sites which, like those in the Three Gorges Dam area, are often destroyed before they have been fully documented.

Outstanding Archaeological Sites

Beyond the sites mentioned already, several other noteworthy discoveries have taken place in China since the 1950s.

Excavations in the Nihewan basin, in northern China, document early humans in East Asia, while early Neolithic sites, such as Jiahu, have highlighted the origins of agriculture in the region. Sites like the Niuheliang ceremonial center in Liaoning, the Xishuipo burial with human sacrifices in Henan, and the jade-rich Fanshan necropolis in Zhejiang, record late Neolithic social complexity.

The sacrificial pits at Sanxingdui, Sichuan, document a previously unknown Bronze Age culture in southwest China, while investigations in Zhouyuan, Shaanxi, shed light on the origins of the founders of the Zhou dynasty. In addition, the discovery of European-looking mummies in the western province of Xinjiang, some dating as early as 1800 BCE, has reopened the debate on East–West contacts.

The site of the First Emperor's mausoleum at Lintong near Xi'an in Shaanxi continues to be investigated for evidence of the early empire. Apart from the terracotta army, the tomb site is unexcavated. Also continuing are the excavations of Han dynasty sites and burials, such as the tomb of Lady Dai at Mawangdui, Hunan, where the preserved corpses of the deceased, as well as silks, books, and paintings, have been unearthed.

LEFT **This bronze hand** was found at Anyang, the capital of the Bronze Age Shang dynasty (1600–1046 BCE). The archaeological site at Anyang, Henan Province, is one of China's largest.

BELOW **The oasis city of Gaochang,** which is now in ruins, was built in the first century BCE as a stopping point for merchants who traveled the Silk Road.

METHODS OF DATING

Recently, archaeologists and historians have switched to a new dating terminology, particularly when discussing non-Christian cultures. Today, rather than using the Christian form BC (before Christ), scholars prefer the more secular BCE, which means "before the common era." Likewise, the Christian form AD (*anno Domini*, in the year of our Lord) is replaced by the secular counterpart CE, a term meaning "common era." Beyond the change of these two forms, archaeologists and other specialists working in the prehistoric period adopt other technical dating terms. One of the most common is BP, meaning "before the present," if the date in question was obtained with radiocarbon dating. The "present" is understood as the year CE 1950, the year when the radiocarbon parameters were set. In cases in which the date is very ancient, scientists tend to prefer the acronym MYA (million years ago).

Origins:
Prehistoric China

Introduction

Recent archaeological discoveries have led to a greater understanding of Chinese prehistory, a previously little-known era in China's past. These new archaeological advances are contributing information on such topics as the origins of modern humans, the development of agriculture, and the beginnings of social organization.

Recent discoveries of stone tools at early Pleistocene sites in the Nihewan basin (Hebei) have pushed the date for the early human occupation of East Asia to at least 1.7 million years ago. Remains relating to the hominid *Homo erectus* (dating to the middle Pleistocene) have been discovered at Lantian (Shaanxi), Yuanmou (Yunnan), Yunxian (Hubei), and Tangshan (Nanjing).

Evidence relating to archaic modern humans has also been found in China, at sites such as Dali (Shaanxi), Jinniushan (Liaoning), Maba (Guangdong), and Xujiayao (Shanxi). Upper Paleolithic materials and tools as well as fossil remains of archaic modern humans have been discovered in the area of the Peking Man site at Zhoukoudian (Beijing), specifically in the Tianyuan Cave and in the Upper Cave. No Paleolithic cave art is known from the Chinese continent, but a bone tool with carved designs dating to *c.* 30,000 BP was recovered at Shiyu (Shanxi).

The Neolithic Era

The end of the Pleistocene glacial period around 10,000 BP signaled a transition from the Paleolithic to the Neolithic and ushered in momentous changes in China. The concept of a "Neolithic revolution" well describes these transformations. With the improved climatic conditions of the Holocene period, the population started to rely more on food production and less on foraging activities. The demands of agriculture in turn caused the population to expand and become more sedentary. As a result, villages came into being and new technologies developed.

The thousands of Chinese Neolithic sites so far discovered in China have been organized and analyzed in terms of regional cultures and chronological stages. Archaeologists have defined regional cultures (or horizons of influence) by the specific characters of their material culture, such as types

SITES OF PALEOLITHIC AND NEOLITHIC CHINA

MONGOLIA

Xinglongwa, Xinglonggou

Niuheliang · Jinniushan

Yellow · Nihewan basin

Zhoukoudian

NORTH KOREA

CHINA

Xujiayao

Taosi Cishan · Changziyai
Dawenkou Necropolis

Yellow River valley

SOUTH KOREA

Dadiwan · Dali · Yellow

Wei River valley

Zaojiaoshu

Wei · Banpo · Peiligang

Jiahu
Guchengzhai

Yunxian

Yangzi River valley

Yangzi

Longqiuzhuang

Caoxieshan

Yellow Sea

JAPAN

Yangzi

Hemudu

East China Sea

Bashidang
Chengtoushan
Pengtoushan · Lake Dongting · Xianrendong Cave

Yuanmou

Zengpiyan · Yuchanyan Cave
Maba

VIETNAM

LAOS

South China Sea

KEY
- ■ Paleolithic site
- ▫ Neolithic site
- — International border

N

0 ———— 400 km
0 ———— 400 miles

of Hebei and Xianrendong in the southern province of Guangxi. Somewhat later (7000–5000 BCE), the sites of Hemudu (Zhejiang) and Jiahu (Henan) show a fully agricultural society.

Archaeological research indicates that various middle Neolithic regional cultures were highly sophisticated. Insights into village structure, ritual activities, and burial practices have come from the Yangshao, Hongshan, and Dawenkou cultures, particularly the Yangshao villages of Banpo and Jiangzhai (Shaanxi), the Hongshan ceremonial center at Niuheliang (Liaoning), and the Dawenkou necropolis.

Late Neolithic Cultures

Recent research on the origins of Chinese civilization, social complexity, and state formation has involved a thorough investigation of the late Neolithic Longshan culture. Several walled cities have been excavated in northern China, particularly in the provinces of Henan and Shandong, and in Inner Mongolia. Large settlements once occupied by the late Neolithic Shijiahe and Liangzhu have also been investigated in the area of the middle and lower Yangzi River valley.

of pottery and their decoration. In terms of chronological development, in addition to the transition from the Paleolithic to the Neolithic, archaeologists have identified three Neolithic phases: early, middle, and late. The early Neolithic marks the development of agricultural villages, the middle Neolithic shows the diversification of material culture, and the late Neolithic sees the rise of social inequality.

Food Production, Settlement, and Civilization

Archaeological discoveries in both northern and southern China have shown that agricultural development in China occurred independently from other parts of Asia, placing the first agricultural experiments at *c.* 8000 BCE. The excavation of several early Neolithic villages shows that agriculture began in south central China with the domestication of the wild ancestors of rice (*Oryza sativa*) in the Yangzi River valley. In northern China it began with the domestication of millet (*Setaria italica* and *Panicum miliaceum*) in the Yellow River valley and surrounding areas. Some of the earliest sites with evidence of a transition to agriculture include Nanzhuangtou in the northern province

NEOLITHIC TECHNOLOGIES

China's Neolithic cultures are distinguished by varied technological advances. Pottery was developed very early in the Neolithic and possibly even in the late Paleolithic period. The earliest pottery was made using the coil method and was decorated with cord or incised designs. Later, painted motifs appeared and in the late Neolithic a very fine wheel-made pottery emerged. Rather than being painted, this ceramic was mostly monochrome.

Jade working, used to manufacture ritual items and ornaments, was another key technology of this period. Silk production and wood lacquering also began in the Neolithic period: archaeologists have found silk remains and representations of the silk-worm, as well as traces of lacquer resin on wood fragments.

In the late Neolithic innovations emerged. In some areas people started to experiment with copper metalworking and with sign making. Eventually these new technologies would find fuller expression in the bronze industry and writing of the dynastic period.

RIGHT **This three-legged jug** from a site in Weifang, Shandong, is an example of the sophisticated ceramics of the late-Neolithic Longshan culture.

Homo erectus: Peking Man

The discovery of Peking Man (*Homo erectus*) is the most famous moment in Chinese Paleolithic archaeology. However, since the excavation of the Peking Man site at Zhoukoudian in the 1920s, Paleolithic research in China has made countless new discoveries, contributing to an ever-increasing understanding of human evolution.

ABOVE **This is a recon-struction of the skull of** *Sinanthropus pekinensis,* also known as *Homo erectus pekinensis* or Peking Man. The fossil remains of Peking Man were first found in the 1920s, near Beijing.

The earliest evidence that confirms the presence of humans in East Asia comes from northern China, specifically from a cluster of sites discovered in the Nihewan basin (Hebei), where occupation dates range from *c.* 1.7 million–10,000 BP. Stone artifacts and faunal remains from Goudi (or Majuangou III), a site dated *c.* 1.66 million BP, are the earliest, with lower strata still awaiting excavation. Though no human fossils have been retrieved in the early Pleistocene strata, it is assumed that the occupants of Nihewan belonged to the species *Homo erectus.*

Early Pleistocene Evidence

Artifacts found at Nihewan indicate that humans were already established in East Asia by the early Pleistocene era. This helps explain the early dates of the Yuanmou fossils, which have been considered controversial. If the early dates are accurate, then the two human upper incisors discovered in 1965 at Yuanmou, a fossiliferous basin in southwestern Yunnan Province, may be the earliest human remains from China. The fossil teeth bear some similarity to those of the subsequent *H. erectus* of Zhoukoudian (Beijing), however some scholars maintain that there is a difference between northern and southern Chinese *H. erectus.*

While there were no stone tools directly associated with the fossils, some were found in later investigations. Paleomagnetic dating placed the stratum at *c.* 1.7 million BP, consistent with the associated early

Pleistocene fauna, however other interpretations of the paleomagnetic data suggest a date of *c.* 600,000–500,000 BP, and electron spin resonance of the mammalian fossils gives a date of *c.* 1.6–1.1 million BP. Whatever the actual date of the Yuanmou remains, other fossil evidence confirming the presence of *H. erectus* in East Asia during the early Pleistocene is present. A fragmentary *H. erectus* skull found in 1964 at Gongwangling (Lantian, Shaanxi) has been variously dated to 1.15 million BP or 850,000–750,000 BP. Stone tools and faunal remains from Xihoudu (Ruicheng, Shaanxi) may also date to the early Pleistocene at *c.* 1.8 million BP.

Middle Pleistocene Evidence

Evidence relating to middle Pleistocene hominids centers around the fossil remains and stone tools from several sites, including the Peking Man site. The Zhoukoudian *H. erectus* site was discovered in 1921 by the Swedish geologist Johan Gunnar Andersson. While working for the Geological Survey of China, Andersson was shown some fossils from a nearby quarry by local villagers. Following the discovery and initial investigation, Zhoukoudian Locality 1 (which is also known as Longgushan) was scientifically excavated from

RIGHT **Anthropologists and local workmen** are seen here excavating at Zhoukoudian in the 1970s. The exposed sedimentary layers of the site have been divided into numbered stratigraphic sections.

HOMO ERECTUS IN SOUTHEAST ASIA

The species *Homo erectus* was first identified in China in the 1920s at the Zhoukoudian site near Beijing, though originally this hominid was referred to as *Sinanthropus pekinensis* (Chinese Peking Man). In subsequent years a number of early *H. erectus* fossils were also discovered in Southeast Asia, in particular on the island of Java (Indonesia). The Indonesian evidence from such sites as Trinil, Mojokerto, and Sangiran—along with the new and old Chinese fossils—helped define the characteristics and distribution of *H. erectus,* a species that is now seen as endemic to East and South Asia and possibly ancestor to Asians and native Australians.

1928 to 1937 by a joint team of Chinese and foreign experts.

The pre-war investigations brought to light five skullcaps, portions of seven crania, hundreds of teeth, as well as mandible, femur and other bone fragments of over 20 individuals. These fossils were lost during World War II while being shipped to the United States for safekeeping. Fortunately, casts made before shipping and original notes have allowed researchers to continue the study of these early specimens.

Further excavation was carried out between 1949 and the 1980s by Chinese paleoanthropologists, directed by Jia Lanpo. The excavations showed that Locality 1, a cave approximately 460 ft (140 m) long and 70 ft (20 m) wide, was filled with 130–165 ft (40–50 m) of Pleistocene sediments. Thirteen layers (numbered 1–13) attributable to the middle Pleistocene (*c.* 500,000–400,000 BP) were excavated. Of these, layers 3 through 10 (dated to *c.* 500,000–250,000 BP) yielded human fossils. More recent test probes below layer 13 have revealed the presence of deposits (layers 14–17) dating to the early Pleistocene at *c.* 730,000 BP, though no hominid fossils have been retrieved.

Assessing the Evidence

Post-war excavations between 1949 and the 1980s brought to light dental, mandibular, and post-cranial remains attributable to seven individuals. A recent study of all the fossils places the total count of individuals excavated from Zhoukoudian at 51. These hominids were bipedal, with heavy brow ridges, a brain two-thirds the size of modern humans, and a height of 56–60 in (144–156 cm). The circumstances of their discovery, the type of remains, and the marks on the fossils indicate that the bones had been chewed and probably transported there by carnivores. However, the presence at Locality 1 of thousands of stone artifacts and faunal remains modified by tools and fire indicates that hominids used the caves, and remains were not just brought there by animals. The use of fire at the site has been confirmed by a recent re-analysis of evidence.

ABOVE **This statue depicts Peking Man** using a tool fashioned from rock. Peking Man used rocks such as quartz and flint to fashion tools for hunting and food preparation.

Early *Homo sapiens*

Between 500,000–200,000 BP, archaic modern humans began to appear in Africa, Europe, and Asia. Though separated geographically, archaic modern humans shared traits that place them midway between modern humans and the earlier hominids. The best-known pre-modern humans are the European Neanderthals, but others from Africa and Asia are known.

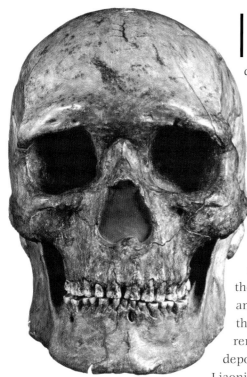

ABOVE **This *Homo sapiens* skull** is from the Upper Cave at Zhoukoudian. The Upper Cave, excavated in 1933–1934, yielded the remains of up to ten individuals along with many artifacts and animal fossils.

In China there are about 30 late middle Pleistocene or early late Pleistocene sites dating from *c.* 280,000/250,000–100,000 BP where remains of archaic modern humans and evidence of their living activities have been found.

Archaic Modern Humans: The Fossil Evidence

The three most significant fossil remains of archaic modern humans come from the sites of Jinniushan, Maba, and Dali. The earliest among the three are the hominid remains from a limestone cave deposit at Jinniushan (Yinkou, Liaoning) in northeastern China, found with chipped stone tools, modified faunal remains, and ash features, and dated to *c.* 260,000 BP. The fossils, which belonged to one individual, consist of an almost complete skull (the lower jaw is missing) and a partial skeleton of about 50 bones. The skull is rather robust and its brain capacity is estimated at 77 cu in (1,260 cc). Initially interpreted as a male aged 20–30, after further analysis in the 1990s, the skeleton has been reclassified as a female aged 20–22. The morphological features—which, though modern, retain elements found also in Zhoukoudian Locality 1 *Homo erectus*—indicate that this was a transitional hominid falling between the late *erectus* and the archaic *sapiens*.

In northern China, an almost complete—though partially damaged—skull was found in a late middle Pleistocene stratum of the Tianshuigou loess terrace in Dali county (Shaanxi). Dali Man appears to have been a transitional *H. erectus* and *H. sapiens* hominid who, though retaining evident links with the Zhoukoudian *H. erectus*, shows more archaic

modern traits. The remains, dated to *c.* 230,000–180,000 BP, were found in a layer that also contained vertebrate fossils, mollusks, carbon particles, and stone tools. The latter are small and simple, consisting mostly of hammered scrapers. In 1958, several fragments of a fossil cranium were found by peasants in a cave near the southern Chinese village of Maba (Qujiang, Guangdong). Dated *c.* 140,000–119,000 BP, the fossils form a skullcap and part of the face of an archaic modern middle-aged male. Though some animal bones were found in association with the human fossils, no stone tools were discovered.

Archaic to Modern: Models for the Emergence of *Homo sapiens*

There are different opinions about the role the archaic modern humans from China played in the overall origin of modern humanity. According to some hypotheses, only African archaic modern humans would eventually develop into anatomically modern humans (*H. sapiens*), while their East Asian and European Neanderthal counterparts would not, having been replaced in their home territories by the spread of the more sophisticated Africans. Others reject this, and argue that European and Asian archaic modern humans also contributed, to different degrees, to the eventual rise of modern humans—this is the theory supported by most specialists in the field.

The dynamics of the appearance of modern humans in East Asia are part of the larger and often contentious debate on human origins. In the recent past, paleoanthropologists have proposed different theories to explain the origins of modern humans. Two of the hypotheses proposed, "total replacement" (also known as the "recent out of Africa" theory) and "multiregional evolution," represent the opposite extremes of the debate. Beyond these two opposing positions, paleoanthropologists have put forward theoretical compromises such as the "African hybridization and replacement" model and the "assimilation model." These are soft versions of the two

(*H. sapiens*) that appeared in Africa between *c.* 200,000–100,000 BP, and spread first to western Asia and by 50,000–40,000 BP to the rest of the Old World, replacing local archaic modern humans without interbreeding with them. The new species that emerged out of Africa is supposed to have obliterated European and Asian archaic modern humans by means of the development of superior technology. Genetic similarities at the mitochondrial DNA and Y-chromosome level in modern humans are explained by population replacement as opposed to interbreeding.

One of the main points of contention is the question of whether the fossils from Africa and western Asia are

LEFT **This is the skull of a European Neanderthal.** Experts disagree about the extent to which modern humans are related to European Neanderthals and Asian archaic modern humans such as those from Jinniushan, Maba, and Dali.

positions and posit different degrees of interbreeding and/or replacement between the newly emerged *H. sapiens* from Africa and pre-existing archaic hominids.

The "Total Replacement" Hypothesis

The "total replacement" hypothesis posits that early modern humans were a new species

indeed fully modern and, if so, whether they indicate that modern humans first evolved in this region and then spread out, displacing the premodern populations in Europe and eastern Asia. Supporters of "total replacement" argue that the fossils from Africa and western Asia are fully modern and significantly predate other modern populations elsewhere in the world, even though

METHODS OF DATING

Archaeologists and paleoanthropologists use different terminologies to place their finds within a chronological framework. They also use a variety of techniques to date them. For the earliest evidence, the most widely used chronology is borrowed from geology and includes such terms as Pleistocene (also known as the Ice Ages, 1.8 million–10,000 BP) and Holocene (the recent age, from 10,000 BP to the present). If stone tools or other crafted objects are present researchers may choose the term Paleolithic (*c.* 2.5 milion–10,000 BP), and divide it into early, middle, and late or upper phases based on the technological and cultural characteristics of the remains. This latter method can be subjective; however, archaeologists use scientific techniques, such as radiocarbon and uranium series dating, to anchor their finds to absolute dates.

LEFT **When determining the age of organic material** using radiocarbon dating, the accepted convention is to report the age in radiocarbon years "before present" (BP).

SKULLS OF EARLY HOMINIDS

A comparison of early hominid skulls shows *Homo sapiens* to have a shorter braincase and higher forehead, with the brain housed higher up and further forward. While some claim *Homo sapiens* to be a new species, others argue that *Homo erectus* was the last new species.

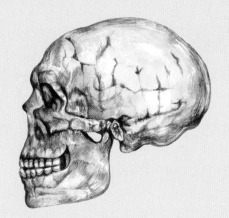

Homo neanderthalensis

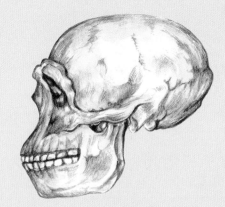

Homo erectus

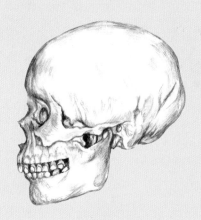

Homo sapiens

they retain some primitive features. The main support for the hypotheses comes from genetics, since both nuclear DNA and mitochondrial DNA show a greater diversity among living African populations than among human populations worldwide. If diversity can be equated with antiquity, it would suggest that humans have been evolving longer on the African continent than anywhere else. More recently, however, the interpretations of genetic evidence have come under criticism.

Another Theory: The "Multiregional Evolution" Hypothesis

An antithetical position known as the "multiregional evolution" hypothesis originally held that pre-modern populations in Africa, Europe, and Asia evolved independently into modern humans in their respective regions without contact with each other. Today the "multiregional evolution" hypothesis has evolved into a softer form than its ancestor (which was called the "trellis model") and while it denies that African *H. sapiens* completely replaced archaic populations in other areas and argues that human evolution happened independently in various locations, it suggests that there was gene flow between the populations of Asia, Africa, and Europe, a fact that would account for genetic and other similarities among modern humans. This is supported by the recognition of anatomical traits in the skulls of modern East Asians that are also found in the

H. erectus populations of China and Java. These features, such as the cheekbones, maxillary incisor shoveling, or the bridge of the nose, are interpreted to represent direct links between the fossil and modern populations.

Another key concept of the theory of multiregional evolution is that modern humans did not have a single origin, or a number of independent origins. It holds that modern human features originated at different times and places, but that there has been no new species since the inception of *H. erectus*. A corollary of this hypothesis is that hominids cannot be considered fully modern unless they are accompanied by a fully modern behavior documented in archaeological remains.

Modern Humans in China

In China there are about 100 late Paleolithic sites with evidence of the presence of *H. sapiens*. The finds fall mainly in the period between 40,000–30,000 and 10,000 BP, with a gap between 100,000–40,000 BP, the period of the transition from archaic modern humans to early *sapiens*.

Two fossil finds that were excavated in the 1950s, but that have recently been redated, could fill the crucial period between 100,000–40,000 BP and thus clarify the origin of modern East Asians. The earlier of the two fossils comprise the skull and partial skeleton of a *H. sapiens* discovered by peasants at the Tongtianyuan cave in Liujiang (Guangxi). Though the fossils have not been directly dated, they and the site have been restudied and have been assigned a minimal age of 68,000 BP, possibly as old as 139,000–111,000 BP. However, given the stratigraphic uncertainties associated with the original discovery, this date has been disputed. Some place the fossils at 30,000–10,000 BP.

The second piece of early evidence concerning the emergence of early modern Asians is a fragmentary *H. sapiens* skull, which was found along with animal bones, shells, and a few stone artifacts at Gaitou cave in Laibin (Guangxi). The skull lacks archaic features, indicating that the Laibin hominid was a modern *H. sapiens*. The recent reexamination of the site enables the find to be dated at *c.* 44,000–39,000 BP.

There is a caveat, however: since the stratigraphic circumstances are not completely clear and the dating was not performed directly on the fossils, the dates are not completely reliable. This has become clear with the recent direct dating of a femur collected in the 1920s at Sulawasu or Sjara-osso-gol (Ordos, Inner Mongolia). Once thought to be of Pleistocene age (*c.* 37,000–33,000 BP), direct dating of the femur proved it to be no more than 200 years old. Other Sulawasu fossils are still undated and may be of Pleistocene age as originally claimed.

More securely dated are the mandible and skeleton fragments of an early modern human that were recently discovered in the Tianyuan cave at Zhoukoudian. These remains have been placed at 42,000–39,000 BP by carbon dating,

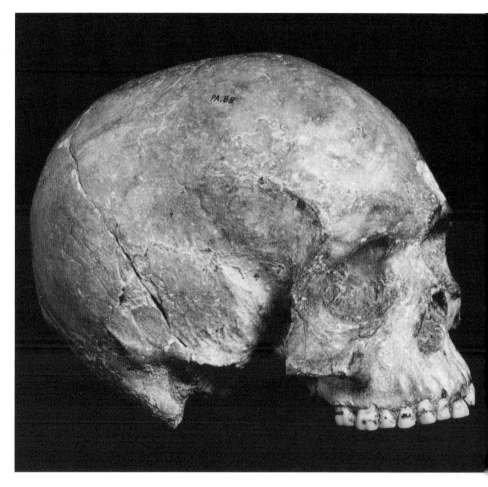

ABOVE **This is a profile view of the skull of Liujiang man,** a *Homo sapiens* found at the Tongtianyuan cave in Liujiang (Guangxi). Accurate dating of this skull may help clarify the origin of modern East Asians.

a finding that makes the Tianyuan remains the earliest dated modern human in Eurasia. Slightly later are the *H. sapiens* fossils from the Upper Cave at Zhoukoudian (Fangshan, Beijing), a site situated on top of Locality 1, Longgushan. The five layers excavated in 1933, and recently dated to *c.* 34,000–29,000 BP, yielded three skulls and other fragments assigned to a male and two females (these fossils, like the other remains from Zhoukoudian, are now lost).

Upper Paleolithic Artistic Artifacts

The Upper Cave served primarily as a burial chamber and, in addition to the human remains, it held such ornaments as perforated animal teeth, stone beads and shells sewn or strung into headbands, necklaces or armlets, as well as flaked flints, a bone needle, and a polished stone artifact. These are some of the earliest artistic artifacts documented for upper Paleolithic China, where there is little portable art, and no painted caves have been discovered. Other evidence of art-making comes from Shiyu (Shuoyan, Shaanxi), a site placed at 30,000–27,000 BP, where a possible ornament was discovered along with a small skull fragment and 15,000 stone tools.

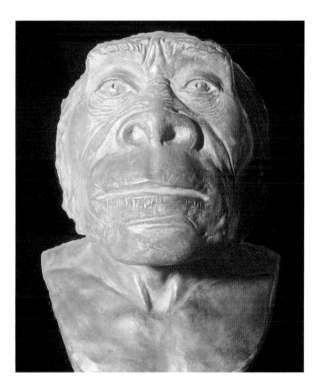

LEFT **A model of the head of Java man,** classified as *Homo erectus*. Anatomical traits in the skulls of modern East Asians are also found in the *H. erectus* populations of China and Java.

Paleolithic Stone Artifacts

During the long span of the Paleolithic period, humans made stone, bone, and other tools to process their food resources. Stone tools were of particular importance because their sharp edges allowed people to cut animal hides and slice meat.

Early humans in China also relied on stone tools to carry out many day-to-day activities. These stone tools appear to have differed from those used in Africa and Europe at the same time, suggesting that early East Asians may have evolved with a degree of independence from their western neighbors.

Archaeologists have identified at least four modes to classify Paleolithic stone technology in Africa, Europe, and West Asia and have associated it with significant changes in hominid population and human behavior. However, except for Mode I tools that are documented with scrapers, choppers, points, and burins at several *Homo erectus* sites—such as Nihewan and Zhoukoudian, Locality 1—Mode II, III, and IV tools are not present in the Paleolithic in China. The Chinese archaeological record does not show any change in technology at the appearance of new human species. It appears that the Mode I core-and-flake technology of the oldest periods continued all the way to the late Pleistocene. This was typical not only of China, but of much of central and eastern Asia beyond the so-called "Movius" line, a virtual boundary passing just north of India that separates the technological traditions of western and eastern Eurasia.

Tools at Zhoukoudian

This is the Upper Cave, Zhoukoudian, where upper Paleolithic stone and bone tools (c. 18,000 BP) have been found, along with the remains of *Homo sapiens*. Mode I flake tools used by Peking Man have also been found at the Zhoukoudian site. They include scrapers and flakes used for defleshing animals, and core choppers used for pounding bones to extract bone marrow.

This is not to say that the Chinese lithic industry underwent no changes through the years, but it appears to have followed a different trajectory from the West, and one that is still little understood. Some scholars have suggested that given the ample supplies of bamboo available in the East, it is possible that early East Asian humans may have used this versatile and sharp material to make tools rather than using stone.

While it is generally true that in China Paleolithic stone tools are confined to Mode I industry, a few sites at the northern or southern edge of the country appear to have hand axes similar to those of Mode II or III industry. The earliest have been collected as surface finds at a number of sites in the Bose Basin (also known as Baise) of the southern province of Guangxi, where there are tools dating to *c.* 800,000–700,000 BP that have been interpreted as Acheulean-like hand axes. Later Shuidonggou, a site in northwest China's Ningxia Province, shows the presence of Levallois core technologies and blade production at around 25,000 BP. These features—also found at other sites in northeast Asia—are a mark of the spread of Initial Upper Paleolithic behavior from western Eurasia. A biface from Lantian Gongwangling and a hand axe from Dingcun may also have been produced with techniques different from Mode I, but their dates are not clearly established because the objects were the result of surface collection.

Paleolithic Stone Scraper
This two-edged flint scraper was used by Peking Man to cut vegetation and scrape flesh from animal skins. Dating to the early Paleolithic period (500,000 BP), it was excavated at Zhoukoudian, Beijing, in 1966.

Ceremonial Jade Reaping Blade
While the simplest of stone tools were used in China during the Paleolithic period, in the Neolithic, the creation of stone blades became an art. Ceremonial blades, such as this late-Neolithic example, were made from jade in the shape of simple implements such as knives used for harvesting grain.

Stone Tool Modes

The Mode I tools of the Olduvan industry, dated at *c.* 2.5–1.6 million years ago, are the earliest. These tools are very simple and include only flakes, cores from which the flakes have been detached, and the hammer-stones that delivered the blow. Mode II, equivalent to the Acheulean lithic industry, is characterized by the presence of bifacial hand axes, a technology used by *Homo erectus* populations starting from 1.6 million years ago in Africa and later in west Asia and Europe. Mode III tools of the African Middle Stone Age and the European Mousterian are characterized by the Levallois technique of core preparation and were in use with the appearance of archaic modern humans around 300,000–200,000 years ago. Finally, Mode IV tools, which appeared in the west with the modern human behavior of the Upper Paleolithic around 40,000 years ago, display a widespread use of blade-making technology.

The Neolithic Revolution

Archaeologist Gordon Childe defined the occurrence of agriculture as "the Neolithic revolution." It marks the moment that humans began producing food rather than just collecting it from nature, a moment that heralded revolutionary social and cultural changes. China experienced this moment at around 8500–8000 BP.

ABOVE **Plant cultivation and the domestication of grains** such as rice were central to the economic foundation of Chinese civilization. This painting depicts rice harvesting in the thirteenth–fourteenth century CE.

Agriculture first appeared in China around 8500–8000 BP, and was characterized by the domestication of foxtail and broomcorn millet and rice in the Yellow and the Yangzi River valleys respectively, and the husbandry of dogs, pigs, and chickens. The advent of agriculture fundamentally changed the trajectory of cultural development in prehistoric China, and laid the foundation for Chinese civilization.

The Neolithic Revolution in China

Before the emergence of agriculture, human beings in China moved about continuously, living mainly in small groups in caves. Once agriculture was established, human beings began to settle permanently in villages. Some of the villages gradually developed into towns, and some of the towns eventually became cities. The earliest walled city in China to date is located in Chengtoushan, Hunan Province, dated to about 6000 BP. It was supported by rice farming.

Agriculture produced more food and facilitated a more stable life in prehistoric China, leading to a significant population increase, which in turn provided the much-needed labor force for farming. A small number of Neolithic village remains dated to 9000–8000 BP have been found in the Yellow and the Yangzi River valleys. However, hundreds of village sites dated to 7500–7000 BP have been found—complete with house remains and kilns—and thousands of them dated to about 6000 BP have been found in the same areas, as well as in northeast China. Meanwhile, in other areas of China where agriculture did not occur before 7000 BP, remains of permanent human settlement are seldom discovered.

Characteristics of China's Neolithic Revolution

There are several places in the world where agriculture occurred indigenously, with the Middle East being the earliest center of agriculture, characterized by the domestication of wheat and barley by 10,000–9000 BP. China is another center where the process by which agriculture was established has some unique characteristics. In the Middle East, people settled down before cultivating plants; in China, it seems that sedentism occurred after cereal cultivation. In the Middle East, pottery occurred long after the advent of agriculture; whereas in China it was the other way round, and pottery was invented simultaneously in several places by hunter–gatherers.

At present, scholars from different disciplines are working on the natural contexts and the questions of where, when, how, and why agriculture occurred in China, as well as the consequences of this "Neolithic revolution." We now know that before the advent of agriculture, the climate had already warmed up after the Last Glacial Maximum, with the Yellow and the Yangzi River valleys becoming temperate

and other biological characteristics of these grasses to ensure the success of plant cultivation and domestication.

Agriculture and Chinese Civilization

Agriculture brought many cultural changes to prehistoric China. As farmers began to produce more food than their families needed, some members of the society were able to work in different fields and make a living by exchanging their goods and services with the farmers. Thus, labor division intensified and artisanship professionalized, eventually leading to state-owned manufacturing workshops, kilns, and other facilities for large-scale production.

The technologies of jade, ceramic, and textile manufacturing developed further after the advent of farming. Although pottery was invented by hunters and gatherers in China, it was the settled farmers who produced very delicately made ceramics, requiring the use of the potter's wheel and kiln. This definitely was not the work of nomadic hunters and gatherers. Farming and other Neolithic technologies provided the economic foundation of Chinese civilization.

The second millennium BCE saw a further widening of the gap between the rich and the poor in farming societies in the Yellow and Yangzi River valleys. Although most tombs were furnished with only a few items, there are small numbers of graves furnished with tens, even hundreds of items. Many of these are labor-intensive items such as jade and/or delicately made ceramics. Social stratification eventually led to the advent of the state.

to warm-temperate zones. In theory, this would mean more edible fruits and animals for human beings to exploit. For whatever reason, some hunter-gatherers in China began to collect grass seeds. A microscopic analysis of stone tools found in Xiachuan, in the middle Yellow River valley, and dated to approximately 13,000 BP indicates that wild grasses were harvested, although the purpose of this harvesting is not yet clear. Phytolith analysis, which is the study of tiny particles that are the detectable parts of plants once growing in the field, also indicates that wild rice, the ancestor of the domesticated rice we eat today, was harvested by hunters and gatherers in the Xianrendong and Diaotonghuan caves in the Yangzi River valley at approximately the same time. The harvesting of wild grasses is a necessary prelude to agriculture, enabling people to gain knowledge of the growth cycle, the habitat,

LUXURY EVER AFTER

As agriculture developed further in prehistoric China it became associated with the production of jade, ceramics, and other items, enabling some members of society to accumulate more wealth than the others. Burial analysis illustrates that there were limited differences in terms of the quantity and quality of grave goods in tombs dated to around 8000 BP in China; however, burials dated to approximately 7000–6000 BP illustrate greater qualitative and quantitative variations in grave goods. In the second millennium BCE, the gap between the rich and the poor in farming societies widened further. Some tombs were furnished with a large number of elaborate items such as carved jade and sophisticated ceramics. This social differentiation was apparent in the graves of the Longshan culture, c. 5000–4000 BCE, renowned for the abundance of its jade items.

RIGHT **Luxury goods found in Longshan graves** include carved jade objects such as this white jade plaque depicting a crested bird.

Native Crops

Domestication of plants requires not only suitable plants and animals, but also suitable habitats and climatic conditions. Parts of China had all of the conditions necessary to begin the process of plant domestication.

ABOVE **The region below the southern bend of the Yellow River** in the Ordos Plateau region featured the largest concentration of agriculture in China during the Neolithic period.

China is a land mass of various ecozones, where hundreds of thousands of native plants grow, under the influences of the winter monsoon from the Eurasian continent and the summer monsoon from the Pacific Ocean.

The Climatic Pattern in China

Generally speaking, the summer in China is relatively warm and wet, and the winter is relatively cold and dry, with temperatures gradually increasing and humidity decreasing from the north to the south. Northeast China is a cool-temperate zone with an average annual temperature of about 42–46°F (6–8°C), and approximately 12–42 cu in (200–700 cc) precipitation. The Yellow River valley is a temperate zone with an annual average temperature of about 53–57°F (12–14°C), and average precipitation of about 18–42 cu in (300–700 cc), while the average annual temperature and precipitation in the Yangzi River valley are approximately 57–60°F (14–16°C) and 73–110 cu in (1200–1800 cc) respectively.

Winter in areas north of the Yangzi River valley is usually very cold, and the variety and quantity of foodstuffs found in nature significantly decreases. Some archaeologists argue that it was the resource-poor winter that forced prehistoric peoples living in these areas to collect the seeds of wild millet and rice, a process that eventually led to the domestication and cultivation of these plants.

Native Cereals and Their Ancestors

The most important native crops in China are foxtail millet, broomcorn millet, rice, and soybean. Genetic studies suggests that the progenitor of foxtail millet is green foxtail, which is an annual plant of the grass family adaptable to various climatic zones and still widely found in China today. The progenitor of broomcorn millet remains unclear, although a wild species of the *Panicum* genus has been proposed as its ancestor. Both millets are particularly adaptable to the cool and dry climate in the Yellow River valley and northeast China, with the fertile loess being an ideal cultivation field.

Soybean is another important native crop in ancient and contemporary China, used for both food and oil. Archaeologists discovered seeds of wild soybean in Bashidang in the middle Yangzi River valley, and Jiahu in the southern middle Yellow River valley: both are dated to about 8500–8000 BP. Wild soybean seems to have been collected by peoples in different areas of prehistoric China. The earliest domesticated soybean to date comes from Zaojiaoshu in the middle Yellow River valley, dated to *c.* 3700 BP.

Other Native Plants

Taro is also a native plant growing in the Yangzi River valley and south China. Neumann has reported that taro was cultivated and domesticated in prehistoric Papua New Guinea, but Lebot points out that there might have been two centers for the origin of domesticated taro, one in the Pacific and another in continental Southeast Asia. In 2003, archaeologists working in south China discovered remains of tuber plants in the Zengpiyan Cave, Guangxi, dated from 12,000–7000 BP, and associated with taro starch residues on a tool surface. Although it is not yet clear whether they are remains of wild or domesticated taro, apparently this plant was continuously collected and exploited in south China. Geographically, Zengpiyan is located at the northern border of the Southeast Asia continent. Further, taro has been one of the cultivated crops in this area for more than 2,000 years according to Chinese historic records, with its root used as a staple food, and its leaves used for feeding pigs.

It is also believed that taro was cultivated and domesticated in south China and adjacent areas.

Finally, there are other native plants that have been domesticated for horticulture in China. Remains of Asian plum, wild vine, and walnut dated to between 12,000 and 10,000 BP have been found at the site of Zengpiyan, south China. Remains of water caltrop, Chinese water chestnut, Asian plum, date-plum, peach, Chinese gooseberry, prickly water lily, pigweed as a leaf vegetable, and wild vine dated to 8500 BP have been found in the Yellow and the Yangzi River valleys. Remains of bottle gourd, the sacred lotus (*Nelumbo nucifera*), acorns, and beans dated to 7000 BP have been discovered in the lower Yangzi River valley. All of the above plants have been continuously cultivated and eventually domesticated in China. Chinese cabbage was cultivated in the Yellow River valley by 7000 BP. Other native crops cultivated in China include the Chinese jujube and the tea plant.

ABOVE **Chinese water chestnuts** are the edible corms of a grass-like sedge found in water margins and bogs. They were cultivated in the Yellow and Yangzi River valleys from 8500 BP.

DOMESTICATED RICE AND ITS ANCESTORS

Rice is one of the five staple crops in the world today. The "ancestor" of domesticated rice is still under debate, with the perennial wild rice being the most likely candidate. Rice is native to the Yangzi River valley and south China, with their high precipitation and mild winter; it usually grows in shallow water. As wild rice reproduces itself by both vegetable and sexual reproduction, each plant generates only a small quantity of seeds, and the ripened seeds quickly shatter. Harvesting experiments confirm that collecting wild rice grains is a laborious process. Nonetheless, it was collected in the prehistoric Yangzi River valley from approximately 13,000 BP onward. Thousands of rice grains have been found in Bashidang, the middle Yangzi River valley, and have been identified as domesticated species dated to about 8500 BP.

LEFT **Wild and domesticated rices** differ in many ways, such as color, number and size of seeds, and length of dormancy.

Neolithic Technology

With agriculture and sedentism, technologies in Neolithic China developed rapidly. While continuously improving farming techniques facilitated an increased food production, the artisanship of the manufacturing of jade, ceramics, and textiles also underwent constant evolution.

The emergence of new technologies in China had very real advantages for survival and the growth of populations. Ceramic vessels enabled the transportation of water and the storage of grain. Textiles for clothing and bedding gave protection from the cold. As villages formed and skills were perfected, new forms of social organization also emerged.

The Development of Neolithic Farming Techniques

In the 1990s, a team of Chinese and Japanese scholars discovered the remains of dug shallow squares connected by small ditches, the latter connecting to a well or a water pond, at an archaeological site called Caoxieshan in Jiangsu Province in the Yangzi River valley. They also discovered carbonized rice grains and large quantities of rice phytolith (opal cells of plants) in the soil of the squares, and concluded that all

were remains of an irrigated paddy field for rice cultivation from around 6000 BP. It was also in the late 1990s that another team of Chinese archaeologists discovered the remains of a rice paddy field dated to at least 6600 BP at another site, Chengtoushan, in the middle Yangzi River valley. These are the remains of the earliest rice paddy field found in the world to date, illustrating the establishment of pre-historic irrigation as a rice farming technique in the Yangzi River valley.

The prehistoric farmers in the Yangzi River valley also learned to select better and larger seeds for cultivation. Another archaeological team in the 1990s discovered layers of rice grains at the Longqiuzhuang archaeological site in Jiangsu Province in the lower Yangzi River valley, dating from approximately 7000–5500 BP. The team reported that the size of the rice grains gradually increased from the early to the later periods, which must have been the result of a purposeful and continuous selection of large grains for cultivation.

Irrigation and grain selection are farming techniques capable of increasing production output, and mechanisms of human interference for the evolution of domesticated cereals.

The Refinement of Pottery

In China, pottery was invented before the advent of agriculture. Potsherds dated to more than 10,000 BP have been found in Nihewan in the Yellow River valley, in Xianrendong and Yuchanyan caves in the Yangzi River valley, and in Dayan and Zengpiyan in south China. These potsherds were made by mobile hunters and gatherers. The walls of the pots are very thick, ranging between $1/2$–$1 1/4$ in (1–3.6 cm), are without decoration or with a simple cord-mark, and are quite fragile due to the structure of the clay and their low firing temperatures.

After the appearance of agriculture, pottery manufacturing skills rapidly improved. White

BELOW **These carbonized rice grains** are from the site of Hemudu, in the Yangzi River valley. Hemudu is one of several sites yielding evidence of early rice cultivation taking place in flooded fields.

chalky ware bowls, pots, and plates with a high foot were fired in much higher temperatures in the middle Yangzi River valley by 7800–7500 BP, with beautiful incisions as decorative motifs. Painted ceramic bowls, vases, and dishes were produced in the Yellow River valley by 7800 BP by the early farmers. Kilns had appeared by 8000 BP in the Yellow River valley and facilitated the manufacturing of white chalky ware. The potter's wheel was used by approximately 7000 BP in both the Yellow and the Yangzi River valleys. By 5000 BP, fast potter's wheels were in use in the lower Yellow River valley to produce "eggshell" black pottery, so named because of its extremely thin walls between $^1/_{32}$–$^1/_{16}$ in (0.5–1.5 mm). Clearly, the technological foundation of ceramic production was well established in China in the Neolithic period.

Manufacturing Jade Implements

Jade implements are among the most important and commonly found artifacts in ancient and contemporary China. The manufacture of jade items can be traced back to at least 8000 BP in northeast China, where adzes, daggers, slotted earrings, and beads made of jade have been found at five archaeological sites. These items were produced by flaking, pecking, sawing, and polishing, and the shapes are quite standardized, illustrating the developing sophistication of the Neolithic artisans.

In the following two to three thousand years, jade implements were continuously manufactured in northeast China, with new and more delicately made items in such shapes as dragons, eagles, and twinned circles. Many of these items are found as grave goods in a small number of burials, indicating that they were mainly for the wealthy and powerful.

Similar discoveries have also been made in the Yellow and Yangzi River valleys from 7000 years onward. By 5000–4500 BP, the techniques of jade manufacturing reached another high level in the two river valleys. Large quantities of well polished and delicately decorated combs, disks, rings, and tubes made from tremolite, actinolite, chrysotile, and agate have been discovered. These items, again, are found mainly in large burial sites, apparently belonging to the very wealthy and powerful of the society at that time.

ABOVE **Jade items, such as these ornamental tortoises,** from Liaoning (*c.* 5000 BP), were used as luxury grave goods in many burials during the Neolithic period.

THE TEXTILE INDUSTRY IN NEOLITHIC CHINA

The technique of manufacturing textiles also developed in Neolithic China. Archaeologists have found spindle whorls made of fired clay in both the Yellow and Yangzi River valleys dated from 8000 BP onward. Apparently fiber yarn was manufactured at that time, which would have been a precursor to cloth weaving and/or knitting. Remains of wooden components of a loom (probably a back-strapped one) dated to 7000 BP have been found in Hemudu, in the lower Yangzi River valley, demonstrating the existence of a weaving industry.

China is well-known for the production of silk. An ivory implement with four silkworms was found in Hemudu, dated to about 6300–6000 BP, suggesting the exploitation of silkworms and most likely the production of silk. Chinese archaeologists have discovered remains of silk threads and tapes dated to 5000–4700 BP in both the Yellow and the Yangzi River valleys. It seems that sericulture and silk production began at least 5000 years ago in China.

RIGHT **Spindle whorls** were used to twist yarn, strengthening it before it was woven. They were made of ceramic or wood.

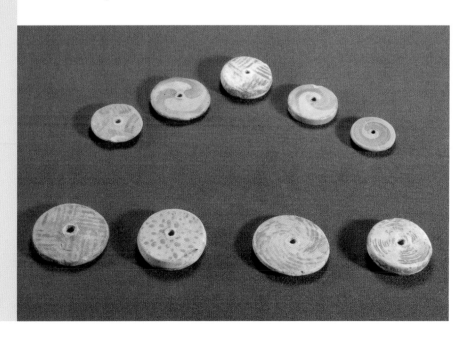

Neolithic Archaeological Sites

To date, thousands of Neolithic archaeological sites have been found in China; some of them are particularly important because they illustrate the origins of agriculture and pottery, as well as other technological developments.

ABOVE **Simple linear designs** are typical of ceramics from early Yangshao sites. This painted Yangshao vase, dated c. 4800–3600 BCE, features a net-mesh motif on a red background.

In China, the term "Neolithic sites" usually refers to archaeological remains with pottery, with or without evidence of agriculture, whereas the term is understood slightly differently in the Middle East and Europe. In other words, Neolithic cultures in China can be created either by farmers or by hunter–gatherers.

Archaeological sites of the Chinese Neolithic are found from the very cold northeast to the tropical south of China. The tools, house remains, ceramics, and burials, as well as other material remains found in these areas, are highly diversified, representing different cultural developments and human adaptations in various natural settings.

Important Neolithic Sites in Northeast China

Among all of the archaeological sites of the Neolithic, the Xinglonggou site in northeast China is particularly important for the origin of agriculture and the early manufacturing of jade implements.

Xinglonggou, which is located on a riverbank in Inner Mongolia, was excavated from between 2001 and 2003 in several stages by the Institute of Archaeology, Chinese Academy of Social Sciences. Here, archaeologists have identified the remains of more than 100 subterranean houses. The sizes of the houses vary, but burials are found in many of them. This burial custom is seldom found in other archaeological sites.

In Xinglonggou, archaeologists also discovered large quantities of ground stone implements and pottery, as well as ornaments and implements made of bone, jade, and shell. These items are found either in burials or on the house floor, and are dated to approximately 8000 BP. The jade items are the earliest found in China to date. In addition, grains of both foxtail and broomcorn millet have been discovered, which are among the earliest cultivated millets found in China, dated to approximately the same time as those found in the middle Yellow River valley.

There are another four sites dated to approximately the same age and with similar artifacts, houses, and burials in northeast China. Some

RIGHT **This sandstone grindstone with roller** (Peiligang, Hebei) was found with grains of millet and tools such as sickles. It is 4 ft (1.2 m) long.

archaeologists have proposed that this area in Inner Mongolia could be a center for the origin of millet cultivation and domestication in China. If true, this may mean that the Yellow River valley will no longer be considered the center of millet agriculture in China.

Important Neolithic Sites in the Yellow River Valley

There are many important archaeological sites in the Yellow River valley, one of which is Cishan, a Neolithic site well known for the quantity of millet discovered there. Located at a loess platform in the middle Yellow River valley, the Cishan site was discovered in 1972 and excavated between 1976 and 1978. It has a total area of about 95,000 sq yd (80,000 sq m).

Archaeologists have found more than 590 pits, two house floors, and more than 640 artifacts at the Cishan site, plus carbonized and decomposed seeds of foxtail millet in 62 pits, all dated to approximately 8000–7700 BP. The depth of these carbonized seeds in different pits varied from 1–7 ft (0.3–2 m). According to archaeologists' calculations, the total weight of the fresh millet seeds, when placed into the storage pits, might have been as much as 50 tonnes (50,000 kg). This discovery shows that millet agriculture must have been quite successful in order for such a large quantity of crop grains to have accumulated. As to the fate of the prehistoric farmers who stored the grain, this remains a question for archaeologists to answer.

There is another archaeological site, Peiligang, dated to approximately the same age as Cishan, but with different ceramics and tools. Peiligang is located at a small hill in the fertile loess plain in central China. It was discovered in 1977 and excavated four times in the 1970s. Archaeologists discovered remains of 22 pits, a kiln, at least one house, and 114 burials. Pottery, ground stone adzes, axes, sickles, chisels, spades, grinding slabs and rollers, stone spearheads, bone arrowheads and drills, as well as animal and plant remains, were also discovered. Although remains of cultivated cereals were not found in Peiligang, grains of foxtail millet have been found in other contemporaneous sites with identical stone and ceramics nearby.

Archaeologists usually interpret different assemblages of ceramics and tools as material remains of different cultures created by separate groups. Thus, the coexistence of the Cishan and Peiligang cultures in the middle Yellow River valley seems to suggest that there were different farming groups living in this area by *c.* 8000 BP.

The Rice Farming Village of Jiahu

Jiahu is an archaeological site located on a small hill between the Yellow River and the Yangzi River valleys. Although the pottery and tools found in Jiahu are identical to those found in Peiligang, the earliest archaeological remains in Jiahu are dated to about 8500 BP. Interestingly, cultivated rice rather than millet was discovered in Jiahu. The remains of more than 30 houses,

300 pits, at least 10 kilns, and more than 300 burials, as well as tortoise shells and flutes made of bone, were also discovered. All of these items tell us that Jiahu was a sedentary and prosperous society with well developed technical knowledge and techniques, as well as music.

Important Neolithic Sites in the Yangzi River Valley

The most important archaeological sites in the middle Yangzi River valley are Pengtoushan and Bashidang sites. Both are located in terraces of the Dongting Lake district. Archaeologists of Hunan Province have discovered one subterranean and five above-ground houses, 15 pits, 21

A LOWER YANGZI VALLEY SITE

The Pengtoushan and Bashidang sites date to 8000 BP or earlier and represent the early farming societies. The Hemudu site in the present Yuyiao County, Zhejiang Province, is an example of a well-developed farming society in the lower Yangzi River valley. Discovered and excavated in the 1970s, the waterlogged deposits of Hemudu yielded well-preserved remains of pile-dwellings constructed using various types of joinery. They also found storage pits, burials, thousands of stone and bone tools and ceramics, hundreds of fired clay spindle whorls, as well as the wooden remains of a loom, the earliest lacquered bowl in China, plus large quantities of domesticated rice leaves and grains, a few grains of wild rice, many wild fruits and nuts, and more than 50 species of animal, fish, shell, and birds. The earliest archaeological remains of Hemudu are dated to approximately 7000 BP, indicating a sedentary society that lived on rice cultivation and extensive hunting and gathering of plant and animal species. The pile-dwelling remains found in Hemudu are also the best preserved prehistoric pile-dwellings found in China to date. An archaeological museum has been established at this site.

ABOVE **The wooden houses of Hemudu,** represented here by the remains of wooden house piles, were very different from the earth houses from northern China dated to a similar era.

burials, and one ditch in Pengtoushan. The majority of the ceramics are a type of round-bottom cooking pot, along with small quantities of bowls, plates, cups, and stands, some of them using rice husks as the tempering agent. Stone tools made of river pebbles, hammers, pestles, choppers, chopping tools, and scrapers, 25 pieces of ground axes and adzes, some ground spades and chisels—along with some stone beads that were possibly used as body ornaments—have all been found in Pengtoushan, and were clearly tools for hunting and other economic activities. It seems that the technique of grinding stone tools had already been developed, along with a desire to decorate the body.

Impressions of rice leaves and straw have been found on fired clay used for house construction in Pengtoushan. Although it is not technically feasible to identify whether the rice husks are the remains of wild or domesticated rice, the discovery of rice husks, straw, and leaves proves at the very least that rice was extensively collected and used by the Pengtoushan residents at around 9000–8500 BP.

The Bashidang site is approximately 10 miles (16 km) southwest to Pengtoushan, about 515,000 sq ft (48,000 sq m), and is particularly important for the occurrence of rice farming in the Yangzi River valley. The site sits on top of a small terrace in the Dongting Lake district, with a river running at its southern border. Archaeologists conducted excavations over five seasons in the 1990s, and discovered the remains of five houses, 31 pile-holes, two hearths, nine pits, five burials, as well as three protective ditches and a protective wall surrounding these remains. Flaked stone choppers and chopping tools, scrapers and burins, a small number of ground stone adzes and chisels, wooden sticks and drills, and bone spades have been discovered here. Because the lower deposits of the site were waterlogged, knitted bamboo mats and large quantities of animal and plant remains were also discovered, including the remains of boar, rodents, three species of deer, four species of fish, tortoise, birds, 67 species of plants, including Asian plum, peach, date-plum, prickly water lily, Chinese gooseberry, pigweed and wild vine, wild soybean, and more than 9,000 rice grains, which have been identified as a cultivated species.

The archaeological discovery made in Bashidang tells us several important things. Firstly, rice was cultivated in the middle Yangzi

One of the most important discoveries in Zengpiyan was several very fragile potsherds found within the earliest deposit. The wall of these potsherds measures to up to 1½ in (3.6 cm), and the firing temperature is too low to be testable by today's ceramic-testing techniques. This technical "primitiveness" suggests that the potsherds may represent one of the earlier attempts at pottery manufacture in China, and perhaps in Asia as well.

Another important discovery in Zengpiyan were the tuber remains and taro residues. After analyzing residues found on the surface of tools, archaeologists suggest that taro was collected in Zengpiyan from 12,000–7000 BP. These are the earliest taro remains found in prehistoric China, suggesting that taro was collected a long time ago in South China, and this may be related to its cultivation in the same region.

Agriculture produced fundamental changes in prehistoric China, and laid the foundation for the development of ancient Chinese civilization.

LEFT **The remains of various plants**, including water caltrop, acorns, beans, and bottle gourd, were found at Hemudu.

River valley by no later than 8500 BP. Secondly, the very rich plant remains illustrate that the Bashidang people exploited many different fruits and vegetables, including the earliest wild soybean found in archaeological sites in China to date. This is crucial data for understanding the occurrence of soybean collection, which eventually led to its domestication. Bashidang is also one of the earliest prehistoric villages with clear evidence of human sedentism and protective facilities (ditches and a wall) to date, proving that sedentism was associated with the development of agriculture in China.

Important Neolithic Sites in South China

All of the above mentioned sites provide data for us to understand the origin of agriculture in China. There are other sites in South China that provide information about the origin of pottery and probably the advent of tuber collection and exploitation. One of these sites is the Zengpiyan Cave in Guilin, Guangxi Zhuang Autonomous Region. The cave was discovered and excavated in the 1970s, then excavated again in 2002. Archaeological remains dated from 12,000–7000 BP have been discovered in the Zengpiyan Cave.

BELOW **Chinese Neolithic burial sites** reveal regional variations in culture. This unusual burial at Xishuipo, Henan Province, features the skeleton of an adult male flanked by white clam shell mosaics.

Agricultural Development

The development of agriculture—and the sedentary ways of life that followed—altered subsistence strategies and dietary habits in China. Agriculture also transformed social relations, served as a catalyst for technological innovation, and gave rise to new religious beliefs.

ABOVE **The cultivation of rice in the middle Yangzi River valley,** as seen here in Yunnan Province, led to the development of permanent villages.

China was one of a handful of centers where agricultural processes and sedentary ways of life first emerged, and agriculture's importance to China can be seen by the high social and cultural status awarded to it. Chinese legends attribute the invention of agriculture to Shen Nong (literally, "God of agriculture"). Like other legendary figures, Shen Nong is an anthropomorphic representation of the essential characteristics of Chinese culture. The results of recent archaeological research, however, demonstrate that agriculture developed in China much earlier than the era identified with Shen Nong in the classical writings. It also shows that agriculture was not introduced to China from outside as some European scholars previously claimed.

The First Agricultural Centers

It is now possible to identify at least two incipient agricultural centers: one in the Yellow River basin and areas to its north in which dry-land agriculture emerged, and one around the Yangzi basin in central China where paddy-field agriculture was developed. These two broad regions were divided into much smaller subregions, each with its own specific ecological conditions and cultural tradition. The rise of agriculture must have been a complex story of interaction and exchange of materials and ideas among these subregions.

The question of why, and under what conditions, people began cultivating the land, domesticating plants and animals, and living in permanent habitations—thereby abandoning the successful adaptation as mobile hunter-gatherers that had sustained human societies for most of their existence—is greatly debated by archaeologists. In China, this was a slow process. Already by the eleventh to tenth millennium BCE there is some evidence of social and technological changes that may have come before the full transition to agriculture.

The Development of Agriculture in Northern China

It is only from the seventh millennium BCE that the data become more complete and by this time it seems that the transition to agriculture and sedentism was already well underway.

From the Yellow River basin there is evidence of relatively large-scale settlements of the so-called Cishan and Peiligang cultures dated to *c.* 6500–5000 BCE. Excavations at sites of this period exposed remains of semisubterranean houses and storage pits that suggest a year round residency of people in what may be called the earliest Chinese villages. Similar evidence is found in the contemporaneous cultures of Houli from the lower Yellow River basin to the east and from the Xinglongwa culture of northeast China.

The earliest evidence of domesticated millet, the staple grain of northern China, was found at the excavations of a Xinglongwa village, some 600 miles (900 km) to the northeast of the Yellow River basin, a discovery that rekindled debate about the origins of agriculture in China. Regardless of the exact location in which grains were first domesticated in northern China, it is clear that by the sixth millennium BCE much of the diet of the population in these early villages was derived from domesticated plants and animals. In the Cishan village, for example, archaeologists

estimate that the storage capacity of the pits excavated was approximately 5.5 tons (5 metric tons) of grains. Bones of domesticated animals such as pigs and dogs have also been found at sites of this period.

ABOVE **Wild millet became the primary domesticated grain** in the Yellow River valley and is still a vital crop today.

The Development of Agriculture in Central and Southern China

Although much recent work has been focused on the early domestication of rice in the Yangzi River basin and areas to its south, little is known regarding the life of the early human communities responsible for this development. It seems that these communities were well adapted to the aquatic landscape of the south, exploiting a variety of plant and animal resources by fishing and bird hunting, before rice became the staple food in this region.

Among sites of the Pengtoushan culture, dated *c.* 7000–5200 BCE, pile dwellings (raised houses on wooden posts) have been found. Pile dwellings were especially suitable for the semitropical environment of central and south China, and are prevalent among the remains of the Hemudu culture (fifth millennium BCE) in the lower Yangzi basin. Other evidence found at the waterlogged site of Hemudu includes over 11 tons (10 metric tons) of rice, as well as other types of aquatic domesticated plants such as water caltrop and lotus root. This constitutes impressive evidence for the growth of southern rice-based agriculture.

BELOW **This ceramic vessel of the Liangzhu culture,** Jiangsu, is slip-painted with black, red, and white designs. It dates from *c.* 3000–2000 BCE.

THE EARLIEST CERAMIC IN THE WORLD

In contrast to the Near East, where ceramic production appeared long after the beginning of agriculture, in East Asia ceramic production preceded agriculture. Potsherds discovered at Nanzhuangtou, north of the Yellow River basin in north China, are dated to around 10,000 BCE. Even earlier dates for the beginning of pottery production are indicated by cave sites in south China such as Xianrendong, Miaoyan, and Yuchanyuan. Pottery found here may be the oldest ceramics so far to have been discovered in the world, although similar claims are made for Jomon ceramics from Japan and potsherds found in the Amur region of south Siberia. While this early pottery is coarse and crumbly, as it was not fired at a high temperature, it marks an important technological revolution. Ceramic vessels enabled humans to store liquids and dry food and to better cook grains and other resources that otherwise may not have been edible.

Neolithic Art

The Neolithic period witnessed a dramatic increase in the amount and variety of artistic production in China. Neolithic art provides us with a rare glimpse into the spiritual world of the prehistoric population.

Compared to the handful of art objects—most of them small beads and ornaments—that are known from the Paleolithic period, thousands of pieces of Neolithic art have been discovered. These include objects made from ceramic, stone, and bone as well as more exotic materials such as semiprecious stones, seashells, and lacquer. Although it is clear that a substantial portion of the art was produced from perishable materials and must have decayed, the surviving artifacts represent a wide spectrum, from small ornaments to monumental art and from simple decorations to complex compositions and three-dimensional statues.

Funerary Urn, Banshan Type, Gansu

This pot is from a site at Banshan, a western settlement. The swirling geometric designs on this pot were probably painted on with sticks of wood with frayed edges that were used like bristles.

Decorated pottery is the most common art of the Chinese Neolithic period. Painted pottery reached its peak with the Yangshao (*c.* 5000–2700 BCE) and related cultures of north China. Vessels from early Yangshao sites at the Wei River basin, such as Banpo and Jiangzhai, have black motifs on red backgrounds. The decorations vary from simple linear motifs to more complex compositions featuring identifiable forms such as fish and plants. The most complex motif depicts a human head (or a mask) in frontal view, flanked on three sides by fish that may be biting it. Although the specific meaning of this motif is unclear, most scholars agree that it has a religious connotation, perhaps relating to beliefs about the afterlife.

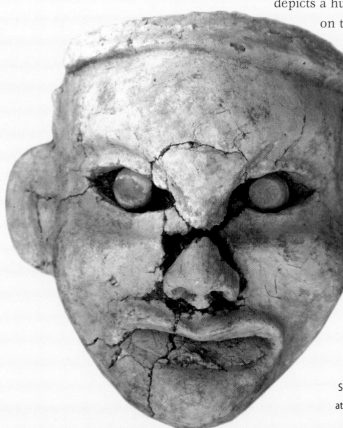

The modeling of three-dimensional figures in clay is as old as ceramic production in China. Small clay figurines of animals are known from early Neolithic sites in north and south China, and some of the pots of the Majiayao culture were shaped to resemble human or animal figures. A number of small human clay figurines as well as stone statues of humans

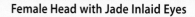

Female Head with Jade Inlaid Eyes

Some archaeologists believe that this clay face found at Niuheliang, Liaoning, is a representation of a female deity to whom the temple is dedicated.

and beasts are known from the Hongshan (*c.* 4500–3000 BCE) and Zhaobaogou (*c.* 5000–4500 BCE) cultures of northeast China.

An example of monumental Neolithic art was found on the floor of a Yangshao period grave at Xishuipo, in Henan Province. Flanking the main occupant of this grave are two figures—of a tiger and a dragon—each almost 7 ft (2 m) long and made up of hundreds of clam shells.

From the Hongshan site of Niuheliang, in Liaoning Province, emerged one of the most impressive discoveries of Neolithic art: a life-size statue of a woman made of clay with jade inlaid eyes. It was found, together with broken parts of other statues depicting humans and animals, inside a uniquely shaped building made of unfired brick. All of the statues were attached to the walls of this "Goddess Temple." Along with jade figurines of animals commonly found at Hongshan graves, these statues represent the unique artistic and ritualistic tradition of northeast China.

The flowering of art during the Neolithic period can be partly attributed to technological developments. Ceramic, for example, was a new medium that lent itself very easily to artistic production. The variety of artistic expression may be even more related to the emergence of social complexity. Much Neolithic art seems to decorate prestige objects that symbolized the position of their owner in the social or economic hierarchy. Other art of this period is associated with religious beliefs and with the development of notions regarding death and the afterlife.

White Pottery Jug, Longshan Culture

This tripod jug, called a *gui*, has hollow legs. This was a popular shape for a ceremonial vessel, and the idea of a tripod with hollow legs was taken up and rendered in bronze by people such as the Shang.

Majiayao Pots

Between the fifth and the third millennia BCE, large quantities of painted pottery were produced by societies from northwest China. At the upper Yellow River basin, graves of the Majiayao culture (*c.* 3100–2700 BCE) contain up to 90 painted pots. These large vases, probably made specifically as burial offerings, were decorated on their upper part so that mourners looking down at the grave could appreciate them. Most of the decorations are complex geometrical motifs but in some, human figures have been identified, perhaps holding hands or even dancing.

Neolithic Ways of Life

By the fifth millennium BCE, Neolithic ways of life that included grain growing
and animal domestication were firmly established in China. Thousands of middle
and late Neolithic sites have been discovered throughout China containing evidence
of these activities.

Hunting and gathering continued, but it was agriculture, including animal husbandry, that became the main economic basis of the Neolithic villages. At the same time, the culture and social makeup of these communities was dramatically transformed.

The Economy of Neolithic Villages

Storage pits, found at almost all sites, suggest that a substantial amount of grain was produced and stored. At Jiangzhai, a site from the Wei River valley, 297 storage pits are dated to 5000–4000 BCE. Even at a conservative estimate that counts only 121 of these pits as contemporaneous, they have a combined storage capacity of 82,749 bushels (2,916,000 liters), enough millet to feed more than 10,000 people for one year.

Remains of houses excavated at the Neolithic villages, however, suggest that their population was much smaller. At Phase I of Jiangzhai, 90 contemporaneous dwellings are estimated to have housed around 300–400 people. An increase in the size of individual villages during the following periods suggests that local communities grew larger. Although Jiangzhai covers only

.019 sq miles (5 ha), large sites of the late Yangshao period, such as Dadiwan, are almost 0.38 sq miles (100 ha) in size and during the late Neolithic Longshan period sites such as Taosi cover as much as 1.15 sq miles (300 ha). Similar trends, visible on the regional level, indicate a dramatic increase in population densities.

Alongside the staple grains of rice and millet, many other types of plants and animals were locally domesticated. Soybean was domesticated in the north and became an important source of protein. Roots and tubers such as yam and lotus were also important food sources, mainly in the south, as were most of the Chinese fruits such as litchi and orange. Among the animals domesticated in China we find pigs, dogs, and chickens.

Plants and animals were not merely prized for their nutritional value, however. Ginseng was domesticated because of its medicinal qualities. Tea was cultivated to produce the beverage we today identify with China. Hemp was used to produce fabrics, and even more famous, the domestication of the silkworm, and its necessary companion, the mulberry tree, was the basis for the flourishing silk industry of China. The earliest

RIGHT **The Neolithic village of Banpo** (4800–3600 BCE) in Xi'an, Shaanxi, had about 100 houses made of timber beams resting on stone bases and supporting thatched roofs. There were fire pits at the center of the dwellings.

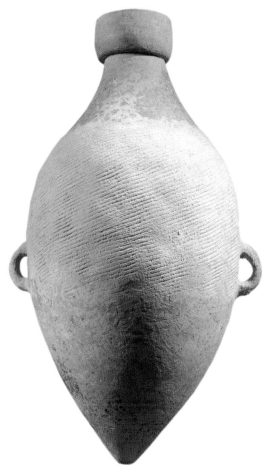

LEFT **This red earthenware amphora,** a water container, dates to *c.* 4800 BCE. It is attributed to the Neolithic Yangshao culture, and was found at the Banpo site.

NEOLITHIC BURIALS

Demarcating a communal area for the dead was a typical feature of the Neolithic way of life in China. Most Neolithic sites include cemeteries that are located outside the residential area, but in close proximity to it. Cemeteries could be small, but at the Taosi cemetery over 1,000 graves have been excavated. The graves in these cemeteries are carefully laid out so as not to intrude into one another. The clear separation of the dead from the living, the above-ground marking of graves, and the artifacts placed in the graves all suggest the development of formal ideas about death and the afterlife, regulation of funeral ceremonies, and perhaps the development of rites to the dead and the ancestors.

evidence for silkworm domestication is a cocoon found at a Yangshao site and dated to the fourth millennium BCE.

Village Life During the Middle and Late Neolithic Period

During the sixth to fifth millennium BCE, houses were round or square in shape and many were semisubterranean. These houses had timber frames, thatch roofs, and wattle and daub walls. Though simple, they represent an investment in permanent structures that is associated with permanent occupation. In many villages, the houses were arranged around an open courtyard where common activities took place. Many of the villages, in north as well as in central China, are surrounded by artificial ditches representing a substantial labor investment and a clear delineation of the community boundaries.

As communities grew larger during the late Neolithic period, community layout was affected. Although most sites were small villages, some of the larger communities were now enclosed by pounded earth walls, a precursor of the city walls of the Bronze Age. In Xishan, a 0.09 sq mile (25 ha) late Yangshao site, the fortifications have walls that are 17 ft (5 m) wide and moats that are 15–40 ft (4.5–12 m) wide and 13 ft (4 m) deep. Some fortifications of the Longshan culture are even more impressive. At Guchengzhai the walls

are up to 130 ft (40 m) wide and are still standing to a height of 50 ft (15 m). At the Yangzi basin and south of it some sites, such as Shijiahe, have similarly impressive fortifications, suggesting that this phenomenon was shared by societies over a very large territory.

Changes are also evident in the internal organization of sites. The central plazas of the early Neolithic period all but disappeared. Dwellings were sometimes constructed in rows of adjoining rooms. For example, at the site of Xiawanggang, a single row house measuring 150 ft (45 m) long contained 30 individual units. Each unit had its own entrance, hearth and sets of domestic artifacts, suggesting that it sheltered a single nuclear family. This crowding of many families together may have been a response to the greater density of the settlement and to the increase of social and economic complexity.

Art, Craft, and Industry

Technological and productivity skills markedly improved during the late Neolithic period. Ceramics were produced on a fast pottery wheel and fired at higher temperatures. Chinese potters produced ceremonial and luxury items that were valued for their superior quality. Nascent bronze casting is further evidence of increasing craft, sophistication, and technological comprehension.

BELOW **Jade pieces such as this *bi* disc** with notches and teeth, were often found in Neolithic tombs, although their function is unclear. Jade was valued for its indestructibility and magical properties.

Social Organization

During the fourth and third millennia BCE, societies throughout China became much more stratified. A new form of social and political organization, which many label "chiefdom," set the foundation for the emergence of state-level society in China.

In contrast to the early Neolithic villages, which seem to have been independent social units, late Neolithic chiefdoms transgressed the boundaries of individual settlements and created regional entities for the first time in Chinese history. Territorially, these chiefdoms were relatively small, each controlling an area of no more than 30–60 miles (50–100 km) in breadth.

Regional Political Units

In places where systematic archaeological surveys have been carried out, such as the Yellow River basin, the east coast, and the northeast, boundaries of such chiefdoms and their social and political hierarchy are evidenced by the clustering of sites and other patterns of settlement distribution. One large site, or a dense cluster of small sites, is usually located at the center of each political entity and the hierarchical scaling of site sizes around it reflects the political hierarchy. The function of sites within this hierarchy is also determined by the structures and artifacts found in them.

The most extensive remains of public work, such as fortifications and large ceremonial and public structures, are usually found in the central site. Huge earthworks, such as the 130 ft (40 m) wide wall at Guchengzhai, not only fortified these locations and made them strongholds of the local elite, but also served as visible symbols of the power of the newly emerged leaders. The ability to recruit, maintain, and manage the large labor force needed for the construction of such monuments is clear evidence of the power that these leaders possessed.

Medium-sized sites—perhaps the loci of secondary elites—were sometimes fortified, but most of the sites within the boundary of each chiefdom were small villages with no walls surrounding them, resembling those of the early Neolithic period in size and complexity.

Centers of Chiefly Authority

Internally, the larger sites—or central nodes of the political hierarchy—are also more complex than other sites in their vicinity. In Taosi, the largest Neolithic site so far discovered in north China, a portion of the site was partitioned off for elite residency and activity. The association of this area with a large granary suggests an elite control over basic resources. In Guchengzhai as well, a monumental elite structure was found. Enclosed by large pounded-earth and wattle-and-daub walls which separated it from the rest of the site, this compound includes a large courtyard possibly used for public gatherings. At the eastern side of the courtyard stood the main building: a large pillared structure constructed on a high pounded-earth foundation and surrounded on three sides by porches.

ABOVE **This clay figure is from the Goddess Temple complex** at Niuheliang. The complex yielded many ritual human figurines, some up to three times life size.

RIGHT **The late-phase Longshan site of Taosi** (c. 2300 BCE–1900 BCE) in Shanxi Province was surrounded by a rammed earth wall, which the settlement outgrew.

Elite enclosures and the elevation of significant buildings on tall platforms were prominent prestige symbols which continued to resonate in Chinese culture until the end of the imperial era.

Ceremonial and Mortuary Practices

In some areas of China, such as the northeast, the power and prestige of the newly emerged elite may have been associated with religious activity rather than with a direct control over resources. An impressive concentration of Hongshan ritualistic monuments is found in the area of Niuheliang, in Liaoning Province, which may have been the center of a local polity. Among these monuments, no less than 25 stone platforms, as long as 90 ft (26 m) each, have been found, some of them surrounded by rings of more than 1,000 large painted pottery cylinders. Other monuments in this area include the "Goddess Temple," where remains of life-size clay statues were found, and a rammed-earth mound 130 ft (40 m) in diameter and 25 ft (8 m) high enclosed by a three-tiered stone-faced platform 10 ft (3 m) high and 200 ft (60 m) in diameter.

The large investment of labor that went into the construction of these monuments and the ceremonial activity that probably took place in and around them would have served to legitimize the position of the elite. In contrast to the Yellow and Yangzi River basins, no Neolithic site walls have so far been discovered in northeast China. This may suggest that although social and political stratification developed in both regions, the forces that shaped them and the justifications for their existence were different.

Ranking of Graves

Evidence of the development of social and economic stratification is found in Neolithic graves. While early Neolithic graves did not differ much in their size and content, by the late Neolithic period there are apparent differences in the sizes of graves, their structure, and the quantity and quality of the artifacts placed in them. In Taosi, a small walled enclosure was set apart as an exclusive elite cemetery that symbolized the growing separation, not only in life but also after death, between the elite and the people they controlled.

At another, much larger cemetery, only less than four percent are considered elite graves, some 11 percent are medium level graves and the rest are commoner graves. Elite graves are 10 ft (3 m) long and 8 ft (2.4 m) wide, contain wooden coffins and as many as 200 grave goods. Commoner graves are, in contrast, barely large enough to contain a body. They include no coffin and only a small number of grave goods, or even none at all.

The grave goods found in elite graves include rare and prestigious objects such as drums covered with alligator skins, jade ritual objects and delicate ceramics, all of which are absent from graves of low-ranking people. It is interesting to note that all the occupants of the elite graves were males, suggesting perhaps the development of a patriarchal society. This, however, may have not been the case in other parts of China, where rich female graves have been excavated.

Among graves of the Dawenkou and Longshan cultures of the eastern coast area, grave size and coffin construction are clear indications of wealth and prestige. Among the artifacts placed in graves, exquisite eggshell pottery goblets and jade artifacts seem to carry high prestige value. In contrast, among the late Neolithic cultures of northwest China, it seems that the sheer number of ceramic vessels placed in the graves, rather than their quality, was the main factor associated with the social position of the deceased.

While the specific funerary attributes are different from area to area, the overall trends are similar. Funerary elaboration and the differentiation of graves served to symbolize and legitimize sociopolitical and economic differences prevalent among late Neolithic societies. It is possible that ancestor worship conducted in cemeteries was used to the same end.

Social and Economic Interdependency

Social complexity developed not only in the form of social, political or economic hierarchies, but also in the form of greater specialization and division of labor. Once people began to devote all or most of their time to one type of activity, such as a specific form of food production, craft, or service, a more complex pattern of interdependency emerges. Such "horizontal" forms of complexity create the need for mechanisms of coordination, exchange, and supply among specialists. They also entail a much more diversified economic system.

Craft Specialization

Evidence of craft specialization is abundant among late Neolithic societies in China. For example, the exquisite ceramic goblets of the Longshan period demanded a superior control of the pottery wheel of which only professionals who devoted most of their time to ceramic production would have been capable. In the same vein, firing such artifacts in a way that would not damage their delicate sides demanded a superior control of the potter's kiln. Such control could only be achieved by specialists, probably different artisans from those that produced the pot in the first place. As the production process itself became more complex, different stages were executed by different individuals, perhaps even at different locations.

Carving complex artifacts from extremely hard stones such as jade is yet another craft that demanded a high level of specialization. For example, drilling the round shaft inside a jade *cong* is a skillful task that is difficult to perform even with modern technology, let alone with the stone tools available to the carvers of the Liangzhu culture. Specialization is also suggested by crafts which were only in their incipient stages, such as bronze and lacquer.

The standard shapes and sizes of ceramic goblets or of jade artifacts found in different sites suggest that each artifact type was produced by only a few workshops and then distributed by merchants—another specialized occupation— to distant locations. We can only hypothesize about other types of Neolithic specialized occupations such as priests and religious specialists. Even among agriculturalists it is quite possible that more intensive production involved the development of specialization and exchange.

Burials and Funerary Practices

Except for children, sometimes buried in urns under house floors, interment inside a vertical earth pit was the norm among Neolithic societies. Larger and more elaborate tombs were furnished with a wooden coffin and provided with a dug-in ledge on which offerings were placed. Offerings consisted of two types: artifacts and food. It is impossible to determine the beliefs that motivated the placement of offerings in graves. They may have been viewed as equipment the deceased would need in the afterworld. Some artifacts, such as jade pendants, could serve as amulets to protect the deceased on the journey to the netherworld, a concept that was common during later periods. Other artifacts were used as part of the funeral ceremony and were not intended to be given to the dead. Large numbers of animal bones could be the remains of funeral feasting and it has been suggested that the tall goblets found in Longshan graves were left by mourners after drinking alcohol from them.

JADE: THE STONE OF IMMORTALITY

During the imperial era, jade was considered the stone of immortality. Jade amulets protected the living and were to help during the precarious journey to the netherworld, or the realm of the Jade Emperor. The fact that many jade artifacts are found in Neolithic graves suggests that the stone already had symbolic value. Interestingly, such a "Chinese" tradition started outside the Yellow River basin. Hongshan jades from the northeast and Liangzhu jades from south China (c. 3300–2100 BCE) are prime examples of early jade artifacts.

Over 100 jade artifacts have been found inside rich Liangzhu graves and many of these artifacts were very complex. Most spectacular are the *cong*, jade tubes that are square on the outside and round on the inside. Although the meaning and function of such artifacts remains unclear, this combination of round and square shapes retained ritual significance in Chinese culture throughout the Imperial era. The circles were thought to represent heaven, the squares to represent earth.

ABOVE **The highly regular design of this ritual jade cylinder or *cong*** would have been achieved using stone tools and abrasive sand, requiring a high degree of skill and precision.

Origins of Writing

Archaeological excavations across China indicate that sign-making began in the early Neolithic period. Signs ancestral to Chinese writing developed in the middle-to-late Neolithic period among central plain and eastern coastal cultures that were transitioning toward increased social and political complexity.

ABOVE **The composite sign on this ritual jade** of the Liangzhu culture (*c.* 3000–2000 BCE) shares some common elements with signs from the Dawenkou culture.

RIGHT **The incised glyph on this pottery urn (*zun*)** of the Dawenkou culture (*c.* 4300–2500 BCE) appears to be a composite of the sun, fire, and a mountain.

The oldest signs proposed as ancestors of Chinese writing come from the early Neolithic site of Jiahu in Henan Province.

The Earliest Chinese Signing Systems

The earliest signs from Jiahu, three graphs carved on what may have been archaic oracle bones, have been dated to *c.* 5500 BCE. The Jiahu evidence has been received with some skepticism given both the early date proposed for the origins of writing and the shape of two of the three graphs that look too similar to either oracle bone forms or modern characters. Other signs have come to light at the site, however, that indicate continued marking activities.

Signs later than Jiahu, dating to the middle Neolithic, have been unearthed at several Yangshao sites in the Wei River valley. The highest concentrations of such signs are from Banpo and Jiangzhai, two early villages in Shaanxi Province. Yangshao signs appear on pottery and are almost always carved on the black band running around the outer rim of select types of red painted vessels, such as *bo* bowls. These containers seem to be of a higher quality than other ceramics and were also used as grave goods. Most signs appear as single graphs, are stylistically similar, recur on multiple vessels and in different villages, and were incised on the vessels before firing. These patterns suggest that mark-making on valuable pottery was an established intra-village convention, even though these signs, like those from Jiahu, may not have any direct relationship with the origins of Chinese writing.

Middle to Late Neolithic: Liangzhu, Dawenkou and Shijiahe Glyphs

Of more significance for the origins of Chinese writing is the graphic production of three middle to late Neolithic cultures: Dawenkou in the lower Yellow River valley, and Shijiahe and Liangzhu in the middle and lower Yangzi River valley respectively. Unlike those of earlier cultures, Shijiahe, Dawenkou, and Liangzhu signs are complex pictographs that are conceptually similar to Shang period Chinese writing.

Carved on large pottery urns possibly used in rituals, Dawenkou graphs consist of composite sun-fire or sun-fire-mountain glyphs, pictographs

representing axes and other objects, as well as abstract signs. Shijiahe signs are structurally very similar to those from Dawenkou and are also carved on pottery urns. Liangzhu graphs, which appear mainly on ritual jades like *bi* disks and *cong* tubes, are composite signs conceptually similar to those of Dawenkou and Shijiahe, but somewhat different in structure as they include birds, stepped platforms, and what may be sun signs. Liangzhu signs also include a few indecipherable inscriptions on pottery.

The similarities between these three sign systems suggests that a regional semiotic system may have developed in China by the late Neolithic. This is not surprising, as archaeological evidence shows that the Dawenkou, Liangzhu, and Shijiahe cultures, which were located in relative proximity, were in frequent contact with each other. Since most of the graphs appear to have been associated with ritual objects, it is possible that this regional semiotic system emerged in response to increased ritual-political needs.

Late Neolithic: Longshan Era Inscribed Potsherds

Inscriptions and graphs dating to the Longshan era, which precedes the Bronze Age dynastic period, are also known. A sizable number of single graphs inscribed on potsherds were recovered in the 1930s at the site of Chengziyai (Shandong), a walled city of the Longshan era. All graphs were engraved, mostly after firing, on frequently used vessels like cups or jars and were highly visible. Eighteen different graphs have been identified: the simplest and most common are straight lines and crosses. Others include multiple lines and what may be numerals. More complex graphs (representing a "leaf" and a "wing") may be nouns.

More recently, three inscribed Longshan era potsherds have been excavated in the eastern coastal area. Two come from urban sites in Shandong Province (Dinggong and Jingyanggang), while another is from the contemporaneous site of Longqiu in Jiangsu Province. Although these inscribed potsherds are somewhat controversial—because the graphs are indecipherable and do not seem to have a logical relationship with later writing—the combined evidence suggests that Chinese writing took shape during the late Neolithic period and became widely used in the early Bronze Age.

THE USE OF PERMANENT VS PERISHABLE WRITING MATERIALS

The earliest deciphered and widely accepted form of writing from China belongs to the Bronze Age inscriptions on oracle bones of the late Shang period (*c.* 1300–1200 BCE) and a few inscriptions on ritual bronze vessels, pottery, or jade that may date to the middle Shang period (*c.* 1500 BCE). Based on this evidence, some scholars have argued that Chinese writing suddenly began during the Shang dynasty (*c.* sixteenth to eleventh century BCE). Other scholars, however, point out that literary sources from the Zhou and Han dynasties, which followed the Shang, imply the existence of Xia documents, and state that writing occurred on bamboo, wood, and silk. The use of perishable materials for writing—which they speculate may explain its absence in the archaeological record—is confirmed by the presence in Shang oracle bone inscriptions of the character *ce* (volume), a pictographic representation of a bundle of bamboo strips, and by *shu* (writing) a pictograph depicting a hand holding a brush.

ABOVE The script used on oracle bones, such as this example from the Shang period, contains glyphs that subsequently evolved into characters used in the modern Chinese writing system.

The "Three Dynasties": The Ancient Kingdoms

Introduction

As in any other major culture, the earliest stages of Chinese history belong to the realm of legend. The beginnings of the "Three Dynasties" remain in this legendary realm, at the same time heralding the beginning of the formative age of Chinese civilization.

Surprisingly, Chinese mythology is relatively minimal: the earliest surviving texts contain only scattered references to cultural and political heroes of the past, and many of these heroes were introduced only at a relatively late stage in the development of the written tradition.

Records of the Grand Historian

By the fourth century BCE, and with greater intensity after the creation of the Chinese empire in 221 BCE, attempts were made to systematize earlier stories. The *Records of the Grand Historian* by Sima Qian (written *c.* 145–86 BCE) is the most influential of these attempts. Sima Qian presented China's history as a sequence of legitimate sovereigns who supposedly ruled "All under Heaven" (the entire known world) from the capitals in the Yellow River basin. The sequence starts with the so-called "Five Emperors," among whom the Yellow Emperor is the most celebrated. The next epoch is known as the "Three Dynasties": Xia, Shang, and Zhou. These two millennia prior to the imperial unification are regarded as a classical age of Chinese history. Traditions ascribe to the rulers and ministers of that age the invention of the entire repertoire of social, political, and cultural institutions characteristic of the Chinese civilization, and also the laying down of its ideological and moral foundations.

Debates about the Past

From the late nineteenth century, many Western, Japanese, and later Chinese scholars began questioning Sima Qian's narrative. They argued that ancient heroes are mythical figures and not historical personalities, and that it is possible to discern long suppressed orally transmitted myths concealed behind the rationalized historical accounts. Other scholars, mostly in China, felt that this assault on the revered past was unacceptable: for them it meant robbing China of its history. In the new, nation-conscious world, the Yellow Emperor, first of the "Five Emperors," was interpreted as a progenitor

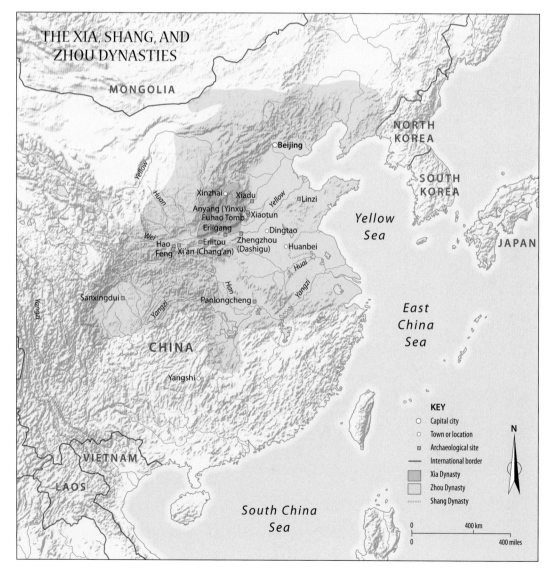

THE XIA, SHANG, AND ZHOU DYNASTIES

MONGOLIA

Yellow

Huan

Xinzhai   Xiadu
Anyang (Yinxu)   Yellow   Linzi
Fuhao Tomb   Xiaotun
Erligang   Dingtao
Wei   Zhengzhou   Huanbei
Hao   Erlitou   (Dashigu)
Feng   Xi'an (Chang'an)
Han
Sanxingdui   Panlongcheng   Yangzi

CHINA

Yangshi

Yangzi

Beijing

NORTH
KOREA

SOUTH
KOREA

Yellow
Sea

JAPAN

Huai

East
China
Sea

VIETNAM

LAOS

South China
Sea

KEY
○ Capital city
○ Town or location
▫ Archaeological site
— International border
▨ Xia Dynasty
▫ Zhou Dynasty
⋯ Shang Dynasty

N

0   400 km
0   400 miles

LEFT **Excavations of the Erlitou site,** discovered in 1959, revealed rammed-earth foundations, paved roads, and bronze and pottery workshops.

doubt, most Chinese scholars identify it with a polity dated to the first half of the second millennium BCE, centered around the Erlitou site in western Henan. Moreover, for most scholars the Chinese Bronze Age, namely the development of large-scale bronze production and parallel increase in sociopolitical complexity, is synonymous with the "Three Dynasties" period.

A Current Perspective

Today, scholarly debate has shifted from the question of the historicity of the "Three Dynasties" to that of their nature. It is clear that—Sima Qian's narrative notwithstanding—even the Shang, let alone the Xia, did not exercise much territorial control beyond the immediate vicinity of their capitals; and that they should be considered powerful regional polities rather than nationwide "Chinese" dynasties. As in the preceding Neolithic period, throughout the Bronze Age there were multiple centers of civilization in different parts of the Chinese world, many of which were not ruled from the Yellow River basin.

We should therefore view the "Three Dynasties" not as a succession of quasi-imperial regimes, but as partly coexisting centers of civilization in the Yellow River basin, parallel with other complex—though not necessarily equally developed or equally persistent—societies in other parts of the would-be China.

This understanding aside, the semilegendary record has became a part of the national history. The "Three Dynasties" are described as such in textbooks and glorified in public monuments.

of the Chinese nation. Some even suggested adopting a new calendar, beginning with the year of his putative birth, *c.* 2700 BCE. This date eventually gave rise to the still popular claim of the "five-thousand-year-old" Chinese civilization.

National sensitivities aside, few critical scholars—in China or elsewhere—today accept the historicity of the "Five Emperors," although occasional attempts are made to identify their domains with one of the Neolithic cultures of the third millennium BCE. In the case of the "Three Dynasties," however, the situation is different. The historicity of two of them (Shang and Zhou) is indisputable and while the existence of the Xia dynasty cannot be proven beyond reasonable

LEFT **The Yellow Emperor, Huangdi,** is popularly celebrated as the founder of Chinese civilization, responsible for the invention of writing, silk, boats, ceramics, and coins.

THE "THREE DYNASTIES" PROJECT

In 1996, an attempt was made to resolve doubts concerning the "Three Dynasties." Under the direct encouragement of the leading Communist Party officials, teams of Chinese scholars collaborated to determine the exact dates of the "Three Dynasties" from the dawn of the Xia up to 841 BCE (from which year an exact chronology exists in Sima Qian's *Records of the Grand Historian*). This multidisciplinary project, which analyzed a great variety of textual, epigraphic and material data, yielded only tentative results: it fixed the beginning of the Zhou dynasty to *c.* 1046 BCE, but provided only approximate dates for the beginnings of the Xia and the Shang (*c.* 2100 and 1600 BCE respectively). The riddle of precise chronology—like many other riddles of the "Three Dynasties"—had not been resolved.

The Legend of the Xia

The legend of the Xia dynasty (*c*. 2100–1600 BCE) illustrates the advantages and disadvantages of the dynastic principle of hereditary rule. While the Xia founder, Yu, is a heroic figure, the Xia's last ruler was a reviled tyrant who was justly overthrown.

The Xia dynasty is located at the nexus of legend and history. Its founder, the Sage King Yu, is a celebrated cultural hero. However, its last ruler, Jie, was so blackened by historians eager to present him as a paradigmatic villain that it is all but impossible to ascertain reliable features of his rule. The sketchy accounts of other Xia kings appear much less biased and are unlikely to be pure fantasy, but their brevity diminishes their historical value. Nevertheless, the legend of the Xia is important not only because it contains a kernel of historical truth, but also because of its political meaning: it clarified the advantages and disadvantages of the principle of dynastic rule.

The Tradition of Selflessness

The tradition holds that prior to the Xia there were no established rules of succession from one ruler to another. The two last of the mythical "Five Emperors," Yao and Shun, were particularly noteworthy for their willingness to yield the throne to a more able candidate. Yao elevated his minister, Shun, and abdicated in his favor, while Shun similarly abdicated to his worthy minister, Yu. Many thinkers lauded these acts of abdication as examples of absolute selflessness, implicitly questioning the desirability of hereditary rule. The exceptional achievements of Yu, however, marked the end of the era of righteous abdication and afforded the principle of dynastic rule some moral justification.

Yu and the Rule of Succession

Of all China's cultural heroes, Yu appears as the most attractive personage. His primary merit—one that puts him on a par with other mythical figures worldwide—was his ability to overcome a devastating flood. Unlike Greek Deucalion and biblical Noah, Yu did not go to sea to escape the flooding waters, rather he went into combat against them. Yu's father, Gun, tried to block the rising waters using dykes constructed with miraculous "swelling soil," but failed and was summarily executed. Yu took on his father's assignment and his solution, based on channeling and dredging the waters to the sea, relieved the threat. Legends laud Yu as a selfless hero who

BELOW **This illustration depicts King Yu controlling the flood** by directing the people to dig trenches that will channel the threatening floodwaters toward the sea.

even that Yu prearranged the ascendancy of his son, making only an empty gesture of abdication. Whatever legend we accept, the results were unequivocal: Yu's descendants prevailed, establishing both the Xia dynasty and the rise of inheritable power.

The Dynastic Cycle

In sharp distinction to the inflated image of Yu, neither his son, Qi, nor any of the subsequent Xia rulers are credited with substantial achievements; almost the only information about their rule, preserved in early sources, refers to succession struggles, rebellions, occasional expulsion of the rulers, and even cases of regicide. Nonetheless, Yu's merits sufficed to legitimize the Xia dynasty in the eyes of posterity and even to raise its prestige beyond that of later dynasties; hence, the term "Yu's traces" became a designation of the entire known world, while "Xia" became the earliest self-appellation of the Chinese. Conveniently, a few important ethnic groups in southern parts of China traced their ancestry to Yu, which facilitated their eventual incorporation into the expanding "Chinese nation."

The end of the Xia was inglorious. Sima Qian's *Records of the Grand Historian* briefly narrate the gradual deterioration that peaked under the last ruler, Jie, one of the paradigmatic "last evil rulers" in Chinese history. His putative atrocities, negligence, and ineptitude caused widespread resentment, and he was eventually overthrown by Tang, the founder of the Shang dynasty. It is likely that the story of this violent replacement of the ruling monarch was a retrospective construction by Zhou historians that served to justify the similarly violent overthrow of the Shang by the Zhou. The imagined life span of the Xia dynasty—from a meritorious founder through the generally unimpressive chain of mediocre rulers down to the vicious tyrant—became a classical example of the dynastic cycle "from growth to decline." This narrative was employed thereafter to depict the history of all major dynasties.

"racked his body and wearied his mind, living outside his home for 13 years, not daring to enter his house even when he passed its gate."

Having tamed the flood, Yu began creating order out of the existent chaos. He channeled the rivers eastward, "laid down" the land, and allowed agriculture to prosper. After ordering the natural world, Yu brought order to society. He divided China into "nine provinces" and "five zones of submission" that ran concentrically from the capital; he also established special tribute quotas for each zone, emphasizing the superiority of the capital and of the monarch over the rest of humankind. These deeds marked Yu as a true creator of Chinese civilization.

Yu's superhuman merits made him singularly deserving of the throne, which he indeed secured with Shun's abdication. Yet here, however, the chain of abdications abruptly ended. Various texts assert that Yu intended to yield the throne to one of his ministers, but the first incumbent died prematurely, while the second, Yi, failed to attract popular support and yielded the power to Yu's son, Qi. Other texts propose a less amicable pattern of power transfer, suggesting that either Qi attacked Yi and seized the throne by force, or

The Search for the Xia

The search for the Xia started at the beginning of the twentieth century, as part
of the debate on the veracity of the traditional history of China, and evolved,
50 years later, into a large-scale archaeological endeavor. It is closely linked to
China's search for national identity.

ABOVE **The walled complex
excavated at Erlitou,**
western Henan, contained
the remains of workshops
that included kilns, bronze-
casting molds, the remains
of stone and bone artifacts
and fragments of crucibles.

In the early twentieth century the discovery
of the oracle-bone inscriptions proved the
historicity of the Shang dynasty, inspiring the
search for similar proofs for the Xia. However,
after more than a century of intensive research,
no epigraphic evidence for the Xia's existence
had been found. The focus shifted to archaeology.
How should the remains of the Xia be identified
in the mute archaeological record? Many archaeologists overcame this methodological hurdle by
accepting the geographical and chronological
information provided by the *Records of the Grand
Historian* and setting out to find the archaeological culture that best fit those definitions.

Surveying the Ground
During the 1950s and 1960s, large-scale archaeological surveys were designed to study the area
that the *Records of the Grand Historian* designated
as the core of the Xia polity, and discover sites
that could be accepted, chronologically and culturally, as the Xia "capitals." It was during those

surveys that the Erlitou site, in western Henan,
was discovered. Mainstream scholars identified it
as the center of the Xia dynasty and the focal
point for the development of state-level society in
China. Skeptics argue, however, that such "discovery" is based on a circular logic that first assumes
the existence of the Xia and then identifies it
with whatever site best fits the predetermined
parameters. Currently, this debate is uresolved.
We can only examine the Erlitou discoveries and
evaluate their social and historical significance.

Erlitou
The Erlitou site covers a huge area of over
1.15 sq miles (3 sq km). Although only a small
portion of it was excavated and the results of
collections made on the surface of the site have
not been systematically published, it seems that
this area was intensively occupied from the
nineteenth to the sixteenth centuries BCE. Some
scholars estimate that during that period between
18,000 to 30,000 people lived on the site. This site

XIA BRONZES

Among the artifacts found in Erlitou, bronze vessels received the highest scholarly and public attention. Though only some 20 vessels have so far been discovered, they are much more complex than any bronze artifact known from the Neolithic period and represent a dramatic increase in the quality and quantity of bronze production in China. Even more importantly, those vessels are seen as marking the beginning of the lengthy Chinese tradition of casting ceremonial bronze vessels. If this identification is correct, then, although the Erlitou vessels are very modest in size and decoration in comparison to ceremonial bronze vessels of the Shang and Zhou periods, they are indeed very significant. They may be considered the beginning of an important tradition that attained particularly high symbolic value not only in Bronze Age China, but even in the imperial era and beyond.

RIGHT **Vessels such as this bronze *jue* or tripod cup** were used for warming cereal wine. The tripod vessels found at Erlitou are perhaps the earliest bronze vessels and were produced in segmented clay molds.

forms the nucleus of a settlement hierarchy that includes two secondary centers of between 0.15–0.23 sq miles (0.4–0.6 sq km) each, several large settlements of about 0.07 sq miles (0.2 sq km), and many small villages. In contrast to large sites and central nodes of the political hierarchy during the Neolithic period, Erlitou is not a fortified site, a fact that bothered Chinese archaeologists who would like to call it a city.

Territorial Influence

The size of the territory controlled by Erlitou is unclear. Most of the known Erlitou sites are concentrated in a radius of 60 miles (100 km) around the main Erlitou site and the secondary centers are even closer to it. This scale is more in line with a chiefdom than with a state-level society. However, some archaeologists argue that the Erlitou polity expanded dramatically beyond that core area to exploit resources and perhaps even colonize locations at a distance of up to 300 miles (500 km) from the center. Such claims are yet to be conclusively proven and they lie at the heart of the debate on the sociopolitical nature of the Erlitou (or "Xia") polity.

The internal organization of the Erlitou site also suggests social complexity and hierarchical political organization. An area at the center of the site is dubbed the "palatial area" after the many large buildings erected on rammed-earth platforms found in it. Among those buildings two complexes, named "Palace 1" and "Palace 2", are the best known. "Palace 1", the larger of the two, covers an area of over 100,000 sq ft (9,600 sq m). It is a compound enclosed by a wall and roofed corridors, with a large gate in the southern wall leading into a wide courtyard. Facing this gate on the northern side of the courtyard is a sizable rectangular building, some 3,300 sq ft (300 sq m) in area. The entire complex stands on a platform that is 32 in (80 cm) above the ground and the main interior building was placed on even taller foundations. Erlitou was clearly an impressive public building, but if by a "palace" we designate the residency and offices of a king, then the actual roofed area of this complex is quite small and perhaps insufficient. It could have been used, instead, for public gatherings—in the large courtyard—and for ceremonies.

LEFT **An aerial view of Erlitou** shows the palatial compound on the site. Within the city, different functions were separated and subdivided.

The Rise of the Shang

The origins of the Shang, like those of the Xia, are obscured by myths and legends. While archaeology has revealed the broad processes that built this dynasty, many riddles—such as the geographical extent of the early Shang state—are unresolved.

Sima Qian tells that the Shang progenitor, Xie, was miraculously conceived after his mother swallowed an egg laid by a black bird. Xie assisted Yu in taming the floods, and was invested with a feudal estate by Emperor Shun at a place called Shang, which gave the dynasty its name. A similar legend is told of the ancestor of the Zhou, Hou Ji, unifying the forefathers of the "Three Dynasties" and connecting them to the same legitimizing thread.

Beginnings of the Shang

BELOW **These remains are from a Shang sacrificial site,** Henan. **Shang cult centers show evidence of human sacrifice with victims sometimes beheaded.**

King Tang, the first ruler of the Shang dynasty, is described in more realistic terms. His supposed moral superiority allowed him to overwhelm the vicious tyrant, Jie of the Xia, and found a new dynasty. Tang was able to restore harmony not only to the human realm but to the cosmic order as well; a touching legend tells that he even volunteered to sacrifice himself to release the people from devastating drought.

The traditional sources reveal little about Tang's descendants, 30 of whom ruled the Shang. While the oracle-bone inscriptions provide rich information about the later period of Shang history, neither they nor the textual sources clarify fundamental questions about the origins of the Shang and the development of the early Shang state. It is here that archaeology becomes particularly helpful.

The Search for the Early Shang

According to a model developed by the eminent archaeologist of the Shang, Chang Kwang-chih, the "Three Dynasties" were polities that coexisted in north China, reaching prominence at different

times. According to this model, the Zhou rose in the Wei River valley in the west, while the Xia developed in the central Yellow River basin; but where did the Shang come from? Chang proposed an eastern location. Based on Chinese historical geography, he identified Shangqiu (literally "the Shang ruins") in eastern Henan as the location of the dynasty's ancient capital, the "Great City Shang." According to this model, which is supported by some of the inscriptions, while the political center moved westward, the "Great City Shang" remained the center of ancestral worship.

Chang and his students, in collaboration with Chinese colleagues, started large-scale field research aimed at locating the remains of the "Great City Shang." However, as Chang himself predicted, this effort was hampered by approximately 35 ft (10 m) thick layers of loess deposited by the Yellow River and its tributaries. The Shang capital, if it ever existed in this region, was completely covered by the alluvial layers.

Archaeology of the Early Shang State

In contrast to the pre-state phase of the Shang, which remains obscure, archaeological research has revealed much about the early phases of the Shang state. Excavations at sites of the Erligang (*c.* 1600–1300 BCE) and Huanbei (*c.* 1300–1250 BCE) phases suggest that during the period predating the epigraphic evidence of the oracle bones, the Shang was already a very powerful state with a developed political hierarchy and a complex economic and social system.

Some of the more impressive findings of these periods provide evidence for a qualitative leap in the scale and complexity of bronze production. Erligang bronzes are not only more numerous, but their shapes and decorations are immensely more complex than anything seen before. Some of those vessels are 3 ft (0.9 m) tall and show great technical sophistication.

No less impressive are the scale of early Shang cities and the massive size of the walls that enclosed some of them. At Zhengzhou, the total area of the Shang city is estimated at 5 sq miles (13 sq km). The huge walls of up to 100 ft (30 m) wide at the bottom, still stand to the height of 17–35 ft (5–10 m).

Excavations at Panlongcheng, a middle Yangzi River site, revealed not only a small pounded-earth enclosure, but also bronze vessels and other artifacts identical to those found at Zhengzhou. Some see this as evidence that the Shang controlled a huge territory in the middle and lower reaches of China's two largest rivers. Others see Panlongcheng as a remote outpost and argue that while the cultural sphere of the Shang may have been large, the area directly controlled by the state was much more limited.

ABOVE **Shang ritual food vessels** took many forms. The importance of ritual to the Shang meant the emergence of new types of ritual vessels, along with new techniques such as casting vessels in two stages.

SANXINGDUI

Findings at Sanxingdui, in the Chengdu plain of Sichuan, are the most astonishing discovery made outside the core area of the Shang, and actually among the greatest discoveries ever made in China. Inside two pits, alongside animal bones, elephant tusks, and cowry shells, archaeologists found more than 700 artifacts, among them large bronze heads, masks and statues of a type never before seen in China. Those artifacts may have once furnished the temples of the nearby city whose earthen walls are still visible. The scale of bronze production and the unique style of the artifacts indicate the presence of an independent local center during the late Shang period.

RIGHT **A Sanxingdui figure on display at the Sanxingdui Museum,** Sichuan. Sanxingdui artifacts may have had a sacrificial function.

Bronze Casting

The Neolithic period witnessed a dramatic increase in the amount and variety of artistic production in China. Neolithic art provides us with a rare glimpse into the spiritual world of the prehistoric population.

Metallurgical knowledge developed gradually in China. During the Neolithic period, people began constructing crucibles that could reach and sustain the high temperature needed to melt metal ores. They learned that by alloying copper ores with the much rarer tin ores, the durable metal we call bronze is created. By the early second millennium BCE, some societies, most notably the one centered on the Erlitou site, reached a high level of sophistication and were able to produce complex bronze vessels. However, it was not until the early Shang period—around 1500 BCE—that bronze vessels began to be produced in substantial quantities and acquired their high status in Chinese culture.

Bronze Spear, Anyang

This spear was found in the tomb of a Shang military officer. Shang weapons also included the *ge*, a halberd or dagger axe, with a bronze blade mounted at right-angles to a wooden shaft.

Although metal production developed late in China in comparison to civilizations such as Egypt, Mesopotamia, and the Indus valley, once it took off, it exceeded in scale anything known from Bronze Age societies worldwide. The total weight of bronze artifacts inside the tomb of Fu Hao (Lady Hao), *c.* 1200 BCE, is more than 3,307 lb (1,500 kg). A single square cauldron, known as Simuwu, found elsewhere in Anyang, weighs 1,929 lb (875 kg). This gives an indication of the immense amount of bronze that once furnished the much larger royal tombs.

Producing vessels on such a scale and of such complexity required a very high level of technology and specialization. It also required an extensive system that involved quarrying the ores, casting them into ingots and transporting them to the production centers where craftsmen produced molds and cast the vessels. Building the large furnaces needed for the casting of such large vessels and providing their fuel were other features of this complex system.

The location of bronze foundries and the type of artifacts produced in them suggest that this was a state-level industry controlled directly or indirectly by the Shang court. In both Zhengzhou and Anyang, foundries were associated with royal and elite buildings.

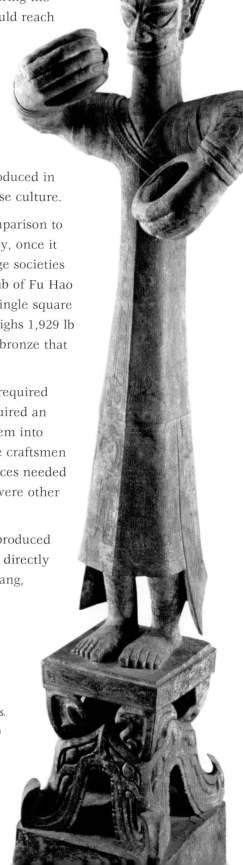

Bronze Statue, Sanxingdui

This statue, found among a haul of bronze masks and heads, is very different in style from any Shang bronzes. It is a male figure more than 7 ft (2 m) tall, standing on a pedestal decorated with an upside-down mask.

Bronze Amulet or Plaque in
***Taotie* Style, Inlaid with Turquoise**
Bronze objects were sacred, often used as instruments of worship and communion with the dead. A plaque such as this might be placed on the chest of a body before burial.

Bronze Casting Technology

Casting complex three-dimensional objects is technologically challenging. Problems to be solved include maintaining even distance between mold parts and preventing air pockets from blocking metal flow. Elsewhere, many of these problems were solved by the lost wax technique, which was unknown in China until around 400 BCE. However, Shang casters used the piece-mold technique, which, despite being more cumbersome, allowed them to produce very complex artifacts.

A piece-mold is built around a solid core in the shape of the internal volume of the vessel. When the pieces of the outer mold are assembled, metal spacers are used to preserve a narrow gap between them and the core, into which the melted metal is poured. Decorations inside the outer mold will appear on the outer walls of the finished vessels. Complicated vessels were cast in several steps, with each part cast on the top of a previous one, to prevent blockage by air pockets.

During the early Shang period, the production of the prestigious bronze vessels was evidently carried out only at the Shang capitals; yet by the end of this period other polities, such as the Zhou, were also producing them.

Bronze foundries during the Shang and the Western Zhou produced two types of artifacts: weapons and ritual vessels. Few if any bronze tools have been found, further suggesting that this industry was catering to the needs and priorities of the royal clan and the elite.

Many types of bronze vessels are known from the Shang; yet their decorations are quite homogenous. Those decorations, and in fact all known Shang art, combine a limited number of motifs, such as spirals and meanders, resulting in geometric designs. The results sometimes resemble mythological creatures, a good example being the *taotie*, a mask or the upper part of the head of a monster. The meaning of such motifs is not clear, but the large region throughout which they are distributed suggests the creation of a common artistic vocabulary, which may be an initial step in the formation of shared identity.

The Shang State Structure

The Shang was a theocratic and kin-based state centered on the king. It operated within a network of smaller, partly dependent, polities. Skilful diplomacy, efficient maintenance of human resources, and military prowess preserved the Shang's hegemony for centuries.

The Shang is the first polity on Chinese soil that can be analyzed not only from legends and archaeological remains, but also from contemporaneous sources: the inscriptions on oracle bones, which record divinations by the Shang kings. Although the inscriptions cover only the last two centuries of Shang history and focus almost exclusively on the royal court, they supplement the scanty information from later textual sources and provide insights into issues that are not preserved in the archaeological record.

The King and the State

The Shang state was a king-centered polity. The monarch's power derived primarily from his exclusive access to the deified ancestors, whose multifaceted support was crucial for the state's survival. Ancestral spirits helped the king to solicit the support of other divine powers, including the Supreme God, Di. Yet the king, who named himself "I, the one man," was not only the supreme priest but also an active political actor: he appointed high officials, occasionally led the armies and actively toured his land, taming it through regular hunting expeditions and displaying his awesome majesty to allies and to potential adversaries. The king and his court also controlled key industries, such as bronze, and were involved in the procurement of natural resources in regional trade.

In light of this complex role, it may have been important to the Shang to have a mature person occupying the throne, perhaps explaining the Shang system of succession in which the throne frequently passed from elder to younger brother, before being restored to descendants of the main line. While the emphasis on the need for a mature ruler was discontinued in later dynasties, other aspects of the Shang legacy, especially the notion of the monarch as possessor of absolute pontifical and mundane power, became a major characteristic of Chinese political culture.

Kinship and Power

The Shang conceived of a square world, with themselves occupying the core area, while the lands of allies and of potential enemies lay outside. Even the core area was not territorially integrated, but rather resembled a hierarchically organized network of towns and villages ruled by the king's relatives. Territories close to the Shang core area were generally placed under the control of the king's immediate kin; further areas were controlled by descendants of former kings, and by allies of the royal lineage, with whom marital ties were maintained. The entire state may well be defined as a confederation of descent groups, with individual lineage serving as a building block of the state.

A lineage maintained a common dwelling and a common cemetery, and it was subordinate to

BELOW **The divinatory inscriptions on oracle bones and turtle shells** were the precursors to list making and other types of record keeping that were required to administer an expanding state efficiently.

the head of the lineage who might have acted as a "mini-king" in his locality. Each lineage had its own deified ancestors, with whom the head of the lineage communicated, and who were supposed to protect their kin in the same way that the royal ancestors granted protection to the Shang community as a whole. Lineage members supplied military and work forces to the head of the lineage, and through him, to the king. Territorial control, one's position within the state's hierarchy, and one's kinship relations with the king were closely related, reflecting the ongoing "tribal" nature of the Shang polity.

Administration of Resources

The Shang was not, as is sometimes erroneously assumed, a fully developed bureaucratic state, akin to later Chinese polities; but its success would be unimaginable without nascent bureaucratization. Military and civilian projects demanded increasing administrative sophistication and specialization. The Shang seems to have been able to mobilize thousands of conscripts for multiple projects: from military campaigns to construction of huge tombs for the deceased kings, clearing new lands and the like. It is estimated, for example, that the construction of the pounded earth wall of what may have been the early Shang capital in Zhengzhou, required the investment of 13 million labor days. This mass mobilization surely benefited from the widespread use of writing. Although currently only religious texts of the Shang survive, being inscribed on bones and bronzes, there is little doubt that much more was written on perishable materials (bamboo and wood), and that those documents served Shang administrators and officers.

Aside from ad hoc mobilization, performed primarily through the heads of subordinate and allied lineages, the Shang

kings had at their disposal permanent military and civilian employees. Of these, craftsmen appear as particularly important. Shang bronze manufacture demanded remarkable professional skills, and similar refinement might have been attained in other fields of craftsmanship, most notably preparing bone artifacts. Remnants of Shang workshops reveal a considerable degree of specialization: some bronze casters prepared primarily sacrificial vessels, while others focused on tools and weapon production. The location of those workshops only in the central nodes of the political system and in association with elite dwellings suggests that they were directly controlled by the court, which was probably responsible not only for coordination among different production units, but also for the supply of raw materials and the distribution of the finished objects. Such multiple tasks necessitate the existence of a relatively sophisticated administration.

Efficient maintenance of human resources might have considerably benefited the Shang economy. This was specifically true in agriculture. While Shang peasants continued to use

LEFT **This bronze axe blade** was found in a Shang tomb at Sufutun, Shandong. It may have been used for executions as the site yielded 48 sacrificial victims.

BELOW **Burial pits with chariots and horses** were found at the Shang site of Anyang, Henan. They were arranged in a line, with chariots and horses facing eastward.

ABOVE **This container for cowries,** from Shijiazhuang, second century BCE, depicts kneeling women making offerings on the lid. The practice of exchanging cowries for tribute began with the Shang.

bone and wooden tools which were employed by their Neolithic forefathers, overall agricultural production might have increased due to the state-organized efforts to clear new lands and to improve work organization. Shang oracle-bone inscriptions suggest a great degree of royal attention to the development of new and better fields, including such issues as drainage, clearing and fertilizing the land, and raising field boundaries. A well-organized system of royal farms supported an expanding ruling elite, an impressive handicraft industry, and a formidable army. Eventually, efficient organization of labor became one of the hallmarks of Chinese regimes from the Shang period onward.

Shang Diplomacy

The Shang was neither an empire nor even a territorially integrated state, but rather a confederation of lineages and small polities, which were part of a complex network of shifting alliances. Some of the neighboring polities were independent of and occasionally hostile toward the Shang; others were culturally related but politically autonomous; still others were Shang allies and dependencies. The Shang might have been more powerful economically and militarily than any of its neighbors; but to maintain its hegemony it employed a variety of additional means aside from outright coercion and intimidation. These included establishing marital ties with leaders of other polities, occasional mutual visits, the Shang king's sacrifice to local deities and to ancestors of other lineages, who were thereby incorporated into the Shang pantheon, and the employment of alien dignitaries in the Shang court, including in an important capacity as assistant diviners. In all likelihood, leaders of neighboring polities generally recognized the religious superiority of the Shang king and his preferential access to divine powers; this may explain their inferior position vis-à-vis the Shang.

The Shang dependents and allies were supposed to provide the king with laborers and soldiers from among their kin and subordinates, but this was not a trivial matter; to receive this support the Shang kings had to exercise considerable diplomatic skills. Allies of the Shang also sent tribute offerings to the court. Those included animals and prisoners of war, to be sacrificed in the ancestral cult. Tribute offerings of turtle shells and cattle scapulas used by the kings for divination were particularly important. In exchange, the tributaries were granted gifts by the Shang kings, such as cowries (perhaps used as a money equivalent), weapons, and cattle. This exchange was probably less important economically, but of much symbolic value. It anticipated the tribute system which emerged much later, in the imperial period, to maintain China's relations with the outside world.

Shang Military Might

Aside from a variety of diplomatic, cultural and religious means, the Shang kings maintained their hegemony through occasional resort to arms. The Shang might have enjoyed relative military superiority over its neighbors, most specifically due to its ability to mobilize con-siderable numbers of conscripts. Shang armies routinely reached the size of several thousand soldiers, and occasionally they could be as large as 10,000 combatants and more. Their weapons, produced in the Shang royal workshops, may have been superior to those of the Shang foes. The Shang may have been the first to employ chariots, which were apparently introduced into China from the West around 1300 BCE. Remains of about 20 chariots, each drawn by two horses, have been discovered inside ritual pits around

modern Anyang, near the late Shang capital at Yinxu. There is, however, some question about the extent to which chariots were actually deployed in warfare during the Shang period. In the oracle bone inscriptions, chariots are mentioned in relation to royal hunts but not in combat, and the archaeological data suggest that the vehicles were adorned, perhaps for public display. On the other hand, it is conceivable that the high-wheeled platforms were used for archery and observation and might have been impressive enough to overawe some of the Shang's enemies. By the end of the Shang period, chariot warfare, undertaken with weapons such as axes and halberds, had become more common.

Shang Conflicts

Wars must have been challenging. In the late Shang period, a single expedition required the king to leave his capital for seven months; other military undertakings demanded repeated mobilization of conscripts and caused the kings to make anxious queries to the ancestors about the outcome of the campaign. Occasional setbacks aside, however, the Shang remained the most formidable military power in the Chinese world until the Zhou challenge around 1046 BCE.

ABOVE **This dagger-axe** from Anyang has a jade blade and a bronze handle that is incised with designs including an animal mask.

HUMAN SACRIFICE AND ROYAL POWER

The Shang are notorious for their widespread predilection for human sacrifice. According to some calculations, oracle-bone inscriptions mention over 14,000 human victims; and among sacrificial pits excavated at the late Shang capital at Yinxu, near modern Anyang, over 1,000 contained human skeletons, sometimes up to 12 in a single pit. Other victims have been found inside the Shang's royal and elite tombs and inside the foundations of houses and walls. The inscriptions identify most of the victims as Qiang tribesmen; most of these were young males, probably captured specifically to be offered sacrificially.

Among the many explanations for this habit, the most compelling is that human sacrifice increased the king's awesome majesty. The Qiang were singled out as "the Other"—the inhuman enemy who did not deserve enslavement but only decapitation. Their sacrifice defined the limits of the Shang collective and frightened potential enemies. Shang successors, the Zhou, eventually discontinued the custom. Scattered instances of human sacrifice continued in later Chinese history, but never again equaled the scale of the Shang period.

RIGHT **These human skulls** are from Tomb M1001, Anyang. Skulls of victims were buried separately from decapitated torsos. The remains were found in small pits or near the tomb's access ramps.

The Shang City of Anyang

The archaeological exploration of the Shang began at Anyang, the location of the last Shang center. Although many additional Shang sites have since been discovered and excavated, some with quite impressive results, much of our knowledge of the Shang is still derived from Anyang.

Yinxu, "The Ruins of Yin"—Yin being another name by which the Shang were known—is the traditional name of an area near modern Anyang. It was here, on the banks of the Huan, a tributary of the Yellow River, that the first oracle bones were found. Following this astounding discovery, the first large-scale Chinese archaeological expedition set out to scientifically excavate the site in 1928 and clarify the history of the Shang. This project became the most prestigious endeavor of modern Chinese archaeology.

BELOW **Teams continue to survey Anyang,** one of the largest Bronze Age sites in the world. Methods used include excavation, core drilling, DNA testing, and geoarchaeology.

The Yinxu site covers a huge area of approximately 14 sq miles (36 sq km) on both sides of the Huan River. This should not be seen, however, as a continuous and densely occupied "city" but rather as an aggregation of loci of royal and elite activity and the dwellings of a subservient population. The fact that so far no defense walls have been found here supports the view that Yinxu was more diffuse in comparison to previous centers of the Shang. During the initial Yinxu project, which lasted from 1928 until the Japanese occupation in 1937, an area of 55,000 sq yd (46,000 sq m) was excavated in 11 places; and since than many more locations have been explored, each known by the name of the closest village.

The Ceremonial Center

The high ground at the bend of the Huan River, known as Xiaotun, is identified as the ceremonial, and perhaps palatial, center of Yinxu. The entire area is bound from west and south by an artificial ditch that together with the band of the Huan River separates it from the rest of the site. Eighty years of archaeological explorations inside this enclosure revealed remains of more than 50 pounded-earth platforms and accompanying sacrificial pits, caches of oracle bones, and remains of bronze and stone workshops, in addition to the elite burials, such as the Fu Hao tomb.

The earth platforms were foundations for a series of rectangular buildings with long corridors. Based on other examples from earlier Shang sites and on the artifacts found in and around those buildings, they are identified as the remains of a large palace or temple complex. It is unclear whether this was indeed the residency of the Shang kings, but the many pits containing bones of sacrificial animals and humans, associated with many of the buildings, suggest it was here that many of the royal ceremonies mentioned in the oracle-bone inscriptions took place. Indeed, as most of the known inscriptions were found at Xiaotun, it is reasonable to assume that this was the main location for the divination of the Shang kings.

The Royal Cemetery

Across the river from Xiaotun, at a place called Xibeigang, 14 large tombs were located. Among them, the eight tombs with four ramps each are identified as graves of Shang kings, while an additional unfinished shaft may represent the purported grave site of the last king, Di Xin, who was deposed by the Zhou. By any standard, the royal tombs are huge and they are the best evidence for the power and prestige of the Shang royalty. For example, the size of the main shaft of tomb M1001 is 50 x 60 ft (14 x 19 m) and it is 35 ft (10 m) deep. Inside this shaft, the archaeologists found remains of pounded earth and wooden structures and the ramps that lead to it from the four cardinal directions are up to 100 ft (30 m) long. Although almost all of the graves were thoroughly looted in antiquity, the few remains found in them and the comparison with much smaller Shang burials, which remained intact, make it clear that they were lavishly furnished.

Some people believe that the shape of the royal tombs—a square from which arms radiate to the four cardinal directions—represents the shape of the universe according to the Shang world view. This observation remains debatable; but it is clear that Yinxu was the focal center of the concentric Shang polity. Xibeigang appears to have been a center of vibrant ritual activity associated with royal funerals. It was probably also a center for worshipping and communicating with the ancestors. Scattered among the royal tombs are sacrificial pits, each of which apparently served one such ceremonial activity. Many of those pits contain human skeletons or skulls, evidence of the human sacrifices that are so often mentioned in the inscriptions.

ABOVE **The tomb of Fu Hao** (Lady Hao) was found intact. Among its dazzling array of grave goods were more than 200 bronze vessels, along with jade, ivory, stone, and bone objects.

YINXU: BIRTHPLACE OF CHINESE ARCHAEOLOGY

Research at Yinxu began as a search for more epigraphic sources on the Shang and evolved to become the training ground for the first generation of Chinese archaeologists. Directed by the newly founded Academia Sinica, the Yinxu project determined the peculiar course of Chinese archaeology. Although much has changed in recent generations, the Yinxu synthesis—blending Western-derived techniques adapted to the conditions of north China with historical orientation and sensitivity to the "Chinese" attributes of the discoveries—still characterizes archaeological work in China. Among the participants of this project was Li Ji (1896–1979), the Harvard graduate who was the first Chinese researcher to undertake an archaeological investigation. Another participant, Xia Nai (1910–1985), became the most prominent figure of Chinese archaeology on the mainland. Since the 1950s, he directed many important excavations, later serving as the head of the Institute for Archaeology and Vice President of the Chinese Academy of Social Sciences.

RIGHT **These archaeological tools and mementos** belonged to one of the many Chinese archaeologists who participated in excavations at the Anyang site from 1928 onward, uncovering evidence of Shang civilization.

Shang Religion

Shang rulers and elites were extremely pious, soliciting divine support for their actions and diverting considerable resources to burial and sacrifice. Gradually, interaction with the divine sphere became ritualized, a trend that continued under subsequent dynasties.

Scholars disagree on the subject of religion in early China: some assume that it was an essentially "secular" civilization, while others point to a variety of religious phenomena that permeated the lives of commoners and elites. This debate is irrelevant, however, to our understanding of the Shang. From all points of view, this dynasty seems to have been the most pious in China's known history. Its rulers associated a great variety of natural and political phenomena—from drought to foreign invasions—with the malevolent or benevolent activities of divine powers; they earnestly tried to understand the deities' intentions; and they invested a significant portion of their scarce resources in ancestral cults and sacrifices. Interactions with the super-human sphere occupied much of the Shang king's time.

The Influence of Divination

What distinguishes the Shang from later dynasties is neither the richness of its pantheon nor the importance of ancestral worship—for those are persistent features of Chinese culture—but, rather, the degree of the deities' perceived impact on the management of the state. Divination questions, recorded in the oracle-bone inscriptions, show the Shang kings anxious to solicit divine support for any major (and often even minor) undertaking: from opening up new fields to repulsing foreign invaders. Gradually, however, the scope of questions addressed to the ancestors decreased, perhaps indicating the growing self-confidence of the Shang royalty. This development anticipated the later tendency to treat divination as a means to "resolve doubts" and not as an everyday mechanism of seeking divine approval for a variety of political activities.

Shang Religious Assumptions

The Shang religion was based on several basic premises, most of which are traceable to Neolithic beliefs, and many of which continued to influence Chinese religious experience for centuries to come. First, the Shang people presumed continuity and interrelation between the world of the living and the world of the dead. The ancestors did not disappear after their death, but just relocated to a new residence, from which they continued to interfere in the affairs of their kin. Second, the deceased continued to share to a considerable extent the desires and expectations of the living; hence the living could communicate with and influence them. Third, the relations between the living and the dead were reciprocal: deities would grant their blessing and protection conditionally, in exchange for appropriate offerings of food and drink. Ancestral spirits were particularly dependent on ongoing sacrifices by their descendants and they were

BELOW **The Yellow River,** seen here in Qinghai Province, was one of the many natural powers deified by the Shang, under the overall control of the supreme god Shang Di.

with a "shaman," a person who mysteriously communicates with the spirits, gave way to a more sober perception of a king as a chief priest, in whose activities the realm of the mystical is subdued by ritual intercourse with the divine sphere.

The Shang Pantheon

The Shang pantheon was very diverse, consisting of multiple deified humans in addition to a variety of natural powers. Human deities included spirits of former kings, predynastic rulers of the Shang, royal consorts, and "former lords": a category of non-ancestral spirits that included high-ranking officials of the early Shang period and, possibly, deified ancestors of other lineages who may have been incorporated into the Shang pantheon. The preponderance of former humans in the pantheon illustrates a blurring of the dividing line between the mundane and the divine realms. This link was further manifest in the person of the king, a leader of the living community who, with his death, would inevitably join the royal pantheon. Death was a sort of "promotion" for the king.

Ancestral spirits were by far the most important divine protectors of the Shang. They were essential in intervening on behalf of the Shang in front of other powers; and they were generally benevolent gods. If angry, ancestral spirits could harm a king—for example, by sending illness—but they would not destroy the Shang community as a whole. Malevolent deities might send drought, locusts and marauding invaders; and it was with the help of the ancestral spirits that such a deity could be identified and appeased. Ancestors differed in their potency. Younger spirits were less powerful than older ones, but they were more active on a personal level, communicating with the king through dreams and illnesses, among other things. The more removed the spirit was by the passage of generations, the more

expected to act in favor of their living progeny and not harm the Shang collective. Being particularly close to the Shang royalty, ancestral spirits were also more predictable than other powers, and relations with them could be managed with relative ease.

Optimism is perhaps the most remarkable feature of the Shang religion. Despite their overall dependence on the divine powers and fear of the deities' wrath, the Shang kings and other elite members believed their relations with the supernatural sphere to be manageable, and that proper handling of sacrificial activities would avert potential harm to the living. Shang divination in particular reveals this optimistic belief in the predictability of the deities' actions and in the ability of the king to comprehend their intentions. Unlike oracles elsewhere, Shang diviners tried to be as clear and specific as possible regarding the deities' will. Plain questions of "yes" and "no" (or "auspicious"/ "inauspicious") were posed to the deities, leaving them with no choice but to give unequivocal answers. The highly regularized divination process left little if any room for mysticism or ecstatic revelations. It is for these reasons that the formerly popular equation of the Shang king

ABOVE **Fu Hao's tomb,** seen here being excavated in 1976, was at the bottom of a deep pit and was lined with timber. The area around the tomb was used for funerary ceremonies.

impersonal it became, and the more important for the community's (rather than an individual king's) well-being.

Natural Powers

Aside from ancestral and other human spirits, the Shang pantheon comprised many deified natural powers, including deities of the sun, the earth, thunder, winds, and the Yellow River. Of those powers, the single most important was Di or Shang Di (the "Supreme God"). Rather than being directly related to the Shang, Di seems to have been an impartial supreme deity with exclusive ability to issue orders to other powers, specifically those in charge of natural phenomena.

His importance notwithstanding, Di received less attention in the Shang divination records with the passage of time. Perhaps his impartiality and exaltedness turned him into an inscrutable deity, whose will—unlike that of other powers—could not be fully comprehended. The exceptional position of Di anticipated his fusion with the supreme and impartial deity of the subsequent Zhou dynasty—Heaven.

Burials and Sacrifice

To ensure ancestral support, the living had to provide for the dead; this was done through

properly arranged burial and sacrifice. The elite of the Shang invested heavily in burials, turning the tomb into a lavish display of conspicuous consumption. Although most royal tombs were looted, both in antiquity and in modern times, their remnants still bear witness to an extraordinary investment of labor and resources. The opulence of the single tomb preserved intact, that of a royal consort, Fu Hao, suggests that the royal tombs originally held incredible riches. The tomb is comprised of a 35-ft (10-m) deep vertical shaft with four lengthy ramps leading to it; a wooden chamber was placed inside the shaft, and although the timber decayed long ago there is evidence that it was carved, painted, and sometimes covered with lacquer. The deceased were provided with a great variety of sacrificial goods ranging from human and animal victims to bronzes, jades, marble and stone sculptures, shells, wooden, bone, and other artifacts, each displaying the best of Shang artisanship.

After the burial, communication with the deceased was through regular sacrifices. Deities were offered the meat of domestic animals, millet brew (frequently mistranslated as "wine"), and human victims. The aroma of brew and blood, and the smoke of roasted meat—signaling consumption of these offerings—were essential to the ritual, in which a deity was occasionally "hosted" or "feasted" by the king. In exchange for these offerings the deity was willing to bless the king and his entourage and to interfere on their behalf. Kings were anxious to please their guest deities, and repeatedly attempted to divine the proper number of animals and humans to be slaughtered, with the numbers fluctuating between a few items and several hundreds.

The Bureaucratization of Religion

David Keightley, the leading scholar of Shang society and religion, noticed the surprisingly "rational" and regularized nature of the Shang religion, which he dubbed its "bureaucratic features." These features are somewhat surprising in light of the overt religiosity of the Shang elite. It seems that the Shang people tried to subject their relations with the deities to a more or less strict set of rules. Thus, they established a five-ritual cycle, meaning that five standard rites were to be performed in a given sequence for each of the major ancestors. Communication with the ancestors was not random, but took place on a specific day of the Shang ten day "week,"

according to their temple name (which invariably contained one day's number). The size, shape, and furnishing of a tomb reflected the deceased's position within the Shang hierarchy. Similar "bureaucratic" logic determined Shang divination with its highly regularized questions to the deities, meticulous recording of queries and answers, and preservation of the record on the oracle bone. The tendency toward regularization became increasingly pronounced with the passage of generations; hence, by the end of the dynasty certain divinations were performed only on specific days of the week (for example, divination concerning hunting took place on the fourth, fifth, eighth, and ninth day). These features doubtless contributed to the sense that human interaction with the divine sphere was manageable. This tendency toward ritualization of religious activities became even more pronounced under the subsequent Zhou dynasty.

ABOVE **This wine vessel from Fu Hao's tomb,** which is heavy and monumental in style, is typical of the bronzes of the Shang elite.

FU HAO'S TOMB

The tomb of Fu Hao, a royal consort who lived in the early thirteenth century BCE, is the only excavated tomb of a high-ranking member of the Shang elite to have escaped devastation by ancient and modern looters. Its discovery in 1976 is one of the most important events in Shang archaeology. While the tomb is much smaller than that of the Shang royal tombs, its assemblage of mortuary goods is amazingly rich. The tomb contained about 1,600 mortuary artifacts, 7,000 seashells, and bones of 15 human and five dog victims. Most noticeable among the artifacts are more than 200 bronze vessels, many of them inscribed with the lady's name, 130 bronze weapons, and 590 jade artifacts. The large number of weapons in a female tomb, including 89 blades—which had possibly served to behead sacrificial victims at the funeral—is not incidental: epigraphic evidence confirms that Fu Hao occasionally led Shang armies into the battle. Apparently, in the Shang dynasty, women's political status was higher than in later periods of Chinese history.

RIGHT **This ivory beaker inlaid with turquoise** was found in a box on top of Fu Hao's coffin, and may have been for personal use.

Oracle Bones

Around 1899, bones and turtle shells with ancient characters incised on them were first discovered, causing a stir among those working in the fields of Chinese archaeology and paleography. The inscriptions were identified as records of divinations performed by the Shang kings, and their discovery provided proof for the historicity of the Shang dynasty—disputed at the time. It encouraged scientific exploration of the Shang capital and its vicinity, which, in turn, yielded hundreds of thousands of additional bone inscriptions.

Divination by heating animal bones and observing the shape of the resultant cracks began in China in the Neolithic period. The Shang used only large flat bones, mostly the undersides of turtle shells and cattle scapulae; from about 1250 BCE, the content of the divination was incised on the same bones. The ritual specialist carefully prepared the bone, cleaning it and making hollows into which heat was applied. The shape of the ensuing cracks and, possibly, their sound served as an indication of a deity's reply to the query. The diviner then suggested his interpretation, and the king made the final prognostication. The inscription on the bone recorded this process, and in many cases added a verification, which usually proved the king's perspicacity. In cases when the divination was performed outside of the Shang capital the inscribed bones were brought back to the center and were kept there, perhaps for future reference.

Most of the 48,000 inscriptions that have been published deal with sacrificial rites, but there are a great variety of other topics, such as weather conditions, astronomic phenomena, military

Anyang, a Rich Source for Oracle Bones
Oracle bones were first discovered in 1899. They were identified when a scholar was prescribed "dragon bones" as a remedy. Before grinding the bones to administer the remedy, he noticed glyphs on them. He then traced them to their point of origin: the site of Anyang.

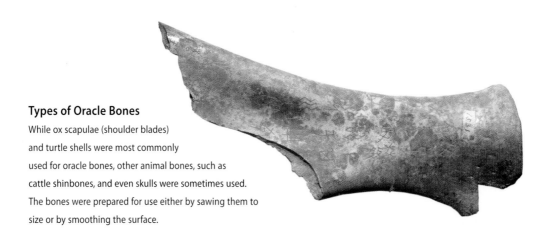

Types of Oracle Bones
While ox scapulae (shoulder blades) and turtle shells were most commonly used for oracle bones, other animal bones, such as cattle shinbones, and even skulls were sometimes used. The bones were prepared for use either by sawing them to size or by smoothing the surface.

campaigns, political alliances, the king's illnesses, the consort's childbirth, establishment of new settlements, and prospects of hunting expeditions. The meticulous work of Chinese researchers has enabled isolated inscriptions to be combined into chains of divinations about the same or related events, providing us with an invaluable source of knowledge about the Shang and about the formation of Chinese culture in general.

A few important changes occurred in the nature of the inscriptions over time. One concerns the form of the queries. In earlier inscriptions, the query was frequently made as two complementary charges: a positive and a negative one (i.e., "during the next week there will be disaster/there will be no disaster"). Later, only "positive" questions remained: the kings evidently disliked mentioning the potentially negative outcome of the divined event. Parallel to this, the scope of divination narrowed. By the late Shang period, sacrifice, hunting, and military campaigns were subject to divination, but topics such as agricultural activities, the opening up of new fields, and establishment of new settlements were not. This may indicate that the kings had self-confidence to act without consulting the deities. The shrinking sphere of the inscriptions anticipated the decline of this medium. Soon after their ascendancy, the Zhou leaders abandoned the practice of scapulae divination, so that the very existence of the Shang oracle bones had been completely unknown for three millennia before a chance discovery brought them to light.

Inscriptions and Chinese Writing

Despite rudimentary evidence for earlier forms of writing, the oracle-bone inscriptions are still the earliest deciphered inscriptions known from China and are the most important source for studying the development of the Chinese writing system. That all known Chinese scripts derive directly from the oracle-bone writing is clear from the fact that the deciphering of this previously unknown ancient script was easier than understanding ancient scripts from other civilizations. Moreover, the script on the bones reflects an already developed writing system: while many characters are pictographic, others are "loangraphs," i.e., they borrow a graph with similar phonetics to depict a more abstract notion.

Reading an inscription is still a challenging task. Even when individual graphs are recognizable, their precise meaning may be debatable. Thus, some scholars interpret the phrase *da shi ri* as referring to the solar eclipse, while others argue that it refers to the meal time. Only by comparing a large number of similar inscriptions is it possible to arrive at scholarly consensus.

The Fall of the Shang

Details of the Shang demise are obscure, perhaps because the story was told by
the victors as the moral tale of a monstrous tyrant who lost divine support and
was overthrown. The tyrant's foes then established the illustrious Zhou dynasty.

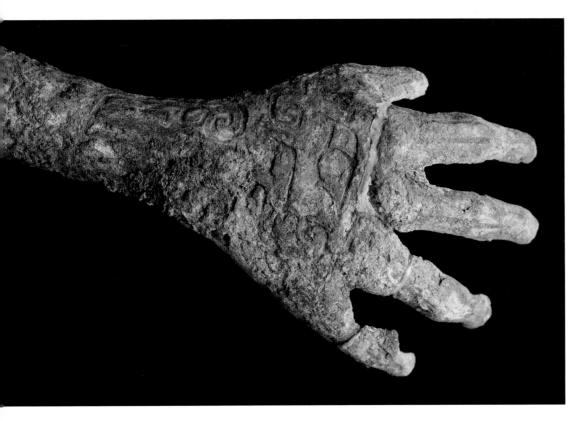

ABOVE **This mysterious
bronze hand** was found in
the tomb of a Shang officer.
Shang power and prestige,
which relied on displays of
awesome power from its
kings, diminished during the
eleventh century BCE.

The royal hunting expeditions, being conducted mostly in the vicinity of the capital, also reflect the shrinking state. Although there are no records of military debacles or major foreign incursions during this period, the overall power of the dynasty seems to have decreased considerably. As the Shang territories shrank, so did its prestige, allowing the formation of the Zhou-led anti-Shang coalition.

Zhouxin: The Paradigmatic Tyrant

Most textual sources that deal with the fall of the Shang depict its last ruler, Zhouxin, as the worst tyrant in human history. The blackening of his image may have begun during his lifetime as part of the Zhou attempt to build an anti-Shang coalition. Interestingly, however, the true proliferation of anti-Zhouxin stories occurred much later, many centuries after he was overthrown.

Our view of the last generations of the Shang is opaque. The diminishing scope of divination makes the oracle-bone inscriptions less informative. Sima Qian's *Records of the Grand Historian*, the primary textual source, was written a millennium after the events and supplies little detail about the rulers prior to Zhouxin, the final Shang ruler. Zhouxin is presented as an ultimate monster whose acts led to the downfall of the Shang; but few reliable details of his rule can be reconstructed from within the legend.

From the scanty information at hand, we can distinguish a process of gradual reduction in size of the Shang state in the eleventh century BCE. Many former allies and dependencies of the Shang whose names appear often in early inscriptions disappear from those of the last 50 years of Shang rule. Only seven inscriptions from that period mention the king's alliances, a drastic decline in comparison with over 600 alliances recorded during the previous century and a half.

Demonization of Zhouxin progressed gradually. In the earliest Zhou documents he is depicted as an arrogant and negligent ruler and is accused of heavy drinking, but there is nothing exceptionally evil in his image. Over time, however, a variety of heinous crimes were attributed to Zhouxin: he reportedly dismembered one of his aides and pickled another; dissected his uncle, Bigan, to check the number of openings in his heart; and scared to death other critics of his regime. He is blamed for inventing particularly cruel tortures and amusing himself by, among other things, causing his subjects to tread on a wooden beam above burning charcoal: "those who failed—fell down and died; those who refused—were fettered in shackles." He also "built ponds of ale and forests of [roast] meat," arranged all-night orgies, and refused to attend affairs of state." Later traditions introduce a femme fatale personage behind Zhouxin's cruelty and debauchery: his concubine, Daji, supposedly an evil fox spirit, whose sadism hastened the demise of the Shang.

The inflation of Zhouxin's crimes in later texts discloses not only historians' predilection toward sensationalism, but more importantly reveals a significant political motive. The overthrow of Zhouxin became the first instance in Chinese history of replacing a legitimate monarch by his nominal subject (a similar "overthrow" of the Xia by the Shang was in all likelihood a later invention). By dehumanizing Zhouxin, preimperial and imperial historians attempted to set limits on the right to replace the reigning monarch. Only a demonically wicked ruler should be overthrown; an average one, even if inept and immoral, would always seem preferable when compared with the Shang tyrant. By intensively blackening Zhouxin's reputation, some historians actually managed to whitewash their contemporary rulers.

The End of the Shang

Whatever Zhouxin's real or imagined crimes were, his age witnessed growing dissent among the erstwhile allies of the Shang. As Zhouxin was busy quelling unrest in the east, real troubles began in the west. One of Zhouxin's formal nominees, King Wen of Zhou, organized a broad coalition and began expanding eastward, approaching the core area of the Shang.

King Wen did not complete his mission; but soon after his death, his son, King Wu, led the

assault on the Shang. In the decisive battle in early 1046 BCE, Zhouxin was utterly defeated, committed suicide, and was mutilated by the victors after his death. The centuries-old Shang rule came to an inglorious end. Despite this, the Shang polity did not vanish. Its remnants survived, as a vassal state of the Zhou, named Song, for another nine centuries.

The Shang Legacy

The Shang dynasty can be seen as a turning point in the history of China. Although the Zhou are usually credited with bringing about the "golden age" of Chinese history, many of the cultural and social characteristics of Chinese civilization are traceable to the Shang period. Of those, the Chinese writing system is perhaps the most notable. Even if it existed in rudimentary form prior to the Shang, it was only with this dynasty that writing began to reach its pivotal position in defining Chinese civilization. Other features of the Shang—such as ancestor worship, bronze casting, and calendar keeping— all form part of the lasting contribution of this dynasty to later generations. Moreover, the Shang marks the beginning of a particular combination of social, political, and religious power systems, which remained, albeit with considerable modifications, to characterize Chinese civilization.

ABOVE **Daji, consort of Zhouxin**, was said to be possessed by an evil fox spirit. Legend has it that after the defeat of Zhouxin by the Zhou, the spirit was driven out by a Zhou official.

LEFT **The crimes of Zhouxin**, last emperor of the Shang, were depicted in gruesome detail by later generations, providing justification for his overthrow by the Zhou.

The Rise of the Zhou

The shock of the Zhou conquest of the Shang was mitigated by the cultural proximity of the two polities; yet soon after stabilizing its rule, the Zhou began to implement novel administrative and ideological departures.

The dynastic legend of the Zhou conspicuously resembles those of the Xia and the Shang. All three dynastic legends may have been modified to emphasize cultural unity between the "Three Dynasties." Like Yu of the Xia and Xie of the Shang, the Zhou dynastic progenitor, Hou Ji ("Lord Millet"), was miraculously conceived; like them, he served as a minister in the courts of the legendary emperors, Yao and Shun. Moving from legend to history, we find the Zhou as a polity on the fringes of the Shang-centered political order. Its original location is hotly disputed; but in the twelfth century BCE, the Zhou were firmly established in the Wei River valley (central Shaanxi), an area that became the birthplace of some of the most illustrious dynasties in China's history. There, the nascent Zhou polity closely followed Shang cultural patterns. Archaeological discoveries from the Zhou heartland show that the Zhou adopted, with some modifications, Shang ritual architecture, bronze-casting techniques and oracle-bone divination. The two polities may even have tried to establish a marital alliance. Nonetheless, their relations were soon marked by competition rather than cooperation.

ABOVE **Hou Ji, also known as "Lord Millet,"** was the dynastic progenitor of the Zhou dynasty. He was deified as Shen Nong, Lord of Agriculture.

The Conquest of the Shang

In the middle eleventh century BCE, under the assertive leadership of King Wen, the Zhou began expanding eastward, threatening the Shang. The legend tells that the Shang "tyrant," Zhouxin, once imprisoned King Wen but later allowed him to be ransomed. Zhouxin later tried to accommodate King Wen by proclaiming him a "Western Overlord." King Wen, however, refused to accept the role of Zhouxin's nominee.

In 1059 BCE, a rare astronomical event occurred: a momentous conjunction of the five visible planets. Similar occurrences in 1953 BCE and 1576 BCE had coincided with the supposed

rise of the Shang and the Xia, so that King Wen may have believed that Heaven favored him. This may be the origin of the Zhou doctrine of "Heaven's Decree." King Wen rebelled against the Shang; and although he died before the decisive encounter, his son, King Wu, continued the rebellion. In 1046 BCE, King Wu and his allies wiped out Zhouxin's army, and entered the Shang capital. The victorious king behaved prudently: he performed sacrifices in the Shang temples and refrained from intimidating the conquered population (although after returning home he reportedly sacrificed the captured Shang officers, in accordance with Shang customs). King Wu even allowed Wugeng, the son of the last Shang king, Zhouxin, to assume leadership over the Shang populace and continue sacrifices to the Shang ancestors. King Wu did, however, place him under the control of two of Wu's brothers. This policy of accommodating the defeated enemy was frequently emulated by subsequent dynasties.

The Duke of Zhou's Reforms

King Wu died two years after the conquest of the Shang, leaving a young heir, King Cheng, and selecting one of his brothers, the Duke of Zhou, to serve as regent. This arrangement immediately backfired, as the two other brothers, left to supervise the subjugated Shang populace, joined hands with the nominal Shang leader, Wugeng, and challenged the Duke of Zhou, whom they may have suspected of plans to usurp the throne. Once again the Zhou armies had to march eastward; the "second conquest" of the Shang took almost two years to finalize. This victory became the true watershed: a series of new administrative measures and religious developments marked the maturation of the Zhou rule.

One of the first steps taken by the Duke of Zhou was to weaken decisively the remnants of the Shang to prevent a new rebellion. The Shang elite were relocated eastward, to a new state named Song; a few of the elite Shang lineages were resettled elsewhere; and a Zhou settlement was established in the Shang heartland. Then the

Duke of Zhou consolidated the Zhou control of the newly conquered eastern territories. He established a secondary capital, Chengzhou, near modern Luoyang, in an area that was roughly in the center of the newly formed realm; in addition, he ordered the establishment of a few dozen settlements in strategic locations in the east. These settlements were ruled by members of the Zhou royal family, or close allies, to create a security network and help integrate the newly conquered realm into a coherent whole. This system differed considerably from the concentric rule of the late Shang kings and symbolized Zhou willingness to discard the Shang models.

Zhou Innovations

The "second conquest" marked a further series of innovations. The Zhou dispensed with the Shang system of a single capital, establishing instead two centers: the double cities of Feng and Hao in the Wei River valley in the west (hence "Western" Zhou), and Chengzhou in the east. They abandoned the Shang custom of large-scale human sacrifice and stopped using oracle bones for divination. The Duke of Zhou is also credited with a series of novel ideological departures, particularly the doctrine of "Heaven's Decree"

that became the cornerstone of the Zhou dynastic ideology. Later Confucian tradition lionized him as the embodiment of a "worthy minister"; and even if the plaudits were exaggerated, the success of his regency is undeniable. When King Cheng finally assumed power in 1035 BCE, the Zhou were incomparably stronger and more mature than a decade previously. The golden age of the Zhou had begun.

Age of the Western Zhou

The Western Zhou began with a period of relative stability. Religious, ideological, and administrative factors—particularly their role as intermediaries between the divine and the mundane worlds—enabled the kings to successfully perpetuate their authority.

The territory under Zhou control was considerably larger than that ruled by the Shang. It comprised most of northern China in addition to parts of the Huai and Han River basins to the south.

Territorial Expansion and Dual Political Structure

Zhou expansion, which was achieved primarily in the immediate aftermath of the conquest of the Shang, required considerable administrative modifications. The Zhou adopted a system of dual governance: namely, direct royal rule in the west, and decentralized control in the east.

The Wei River basin and the area around the secondary capital, Chengzhou, comprised the royal domain. These territories supported the Zhou king economically and militarily; the western capitals of Feng and Hao hosted six royal armies, while the strategically positioned town of Chengzhou hosted eight. Within the royal domain the lands were considered the absolute possession of the king: he allocated fields to meritorious servants, but was theoretically able to confiscate

and reallocate lands whenever necessary. This direct rule required an increasing number of officials and allowed gradual bureaucratic sophistication. In the east, in contrast, royal authority was indirect. Settlements established at the beginning of Zhou rule turned into the nuclei of autonomous polities, possessing separate administrative and military systems, patterned after that of the Zhou royal domain. Insofar as these and other indigenous polities remained subordinate to the Zhou kings, the Zhou prospered; yet in the long term they became a source of potential challenge to the royal authority.

Heaven and Men

The ability of the Zhou kings to maintain their authority derived not only from the military and economic power of the royal domain, but also from their religious legitimacy. In this, as in many other aspects, the Zhou resembled the Shang. Like the Shang monarchs, the Zhou kings acted as intermediaries between the divine and the mundane spheres, presenting themselves as the exclusive representatives of the supreme deity, Heaven. This deity ostensibly resembled Di, the supreme God of the Shang. Yet unlike Di, whose support to the Shang derived primarily from the presence of the Shang ancestral spirits in his vicinity, Heaven was an impartial deity, preoccupied with the ruler's performance rather than with his pedigree.

Heaven actively supervised the monarchs, rewarding the good and punishing the evildoers. It supported only virtuous rulers who possessed the sacred substance of *de* (virtue, charisma, inner power). Possession of *de* was manifested in moral behavior and proper handling of the ruler's tasks, specifically, caring for "the people." A licentious, negligent, or oppressive monarch, like Zhouxin of the Shang, would provoke the people's resentment and lose Heaven's support. He could then be legitimately overthrown. A new incumbent, King Wen of Zhou, gained Heaven's support thanks to being able to manifest his *de* and gaining support from the people below;

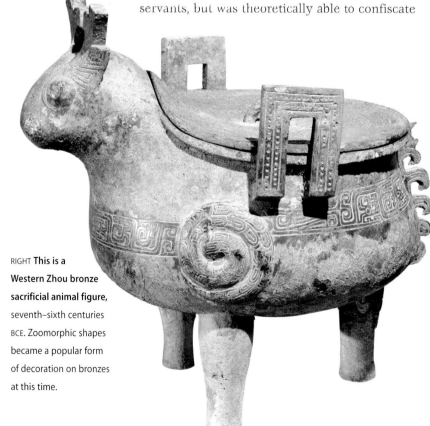

RIGHT **This is a Western Zhou bronze sacrificial animal figure,** seventh–sixth centuries BCE. Zoomorphic shapes became a popular form of decoration on bronzes at this time.

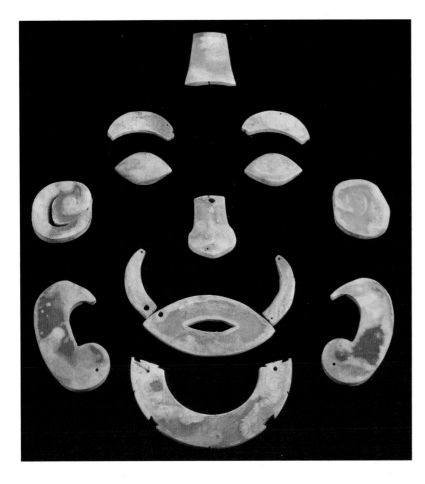

Despite being effective for justifying the overthrow of the Shang, the concept of "Heaven's Decree" proved to be a double-edged sword—it was used in the future against the Zhou itself.

To prevent another contender from claiming the Decree, the Zhou kings limited interactions with the supreme deity to monarchs. The title of "Son of Heaven," appropriated by the kings in the early generations of the Zhou rule, symbolized their quasi-kinship relations with the deity. These relations were further buttressed by claims that the Zhou dynastic ancestors were present in the Heavenly abode of Di. Exclusive access to Heaven became a powerful source of royal legitimacy, but it also imposed heavy responsibility. The Zhou king was repeatedly reminded that "the Decree is not constant."

LEFT **These Zhou-dynasty jade funerary items** are from the tomb of Lord Guo, Henan. The perforated jade pieces would have been sewn onto cloth to form a mask.

thus he established a new dynasty. Insofar as his descendants possessed sufficient *de* they would enjoy Heaven's blessings and ensure the well-being of their subjects. The king acted as a link between Heaven and men, but only insofar as his morality and political performance satisfied Heaven's (and his subjects') demands.

To preserve the dynasty, it was necessary for a Zhou king to behave morally and prudently, and care for the people's needs. The doctrine of "Heaven's Decree" promulgated a notion of the king's responsibility and served not only to bolster the ruler's authority but also to restrain his abuses.

BELOW **Coiled dragons and other undulating designs** were an innovation of the Western Zhou period, as seen on this jade ritual disk decorated with dragon and phoenix motifs.

THE DOCUMENTS AND THE POEMS

The Western Zhou was the formative age of so-called canonical literature. Two major texts, the earliest layers of which date from that period, are the *Book of Documents* and the *Book of Odes*. The first comprises declarations by the earliest Zhou leaders, and was considered to contain the quintessence of their political wisdom. Eventually, numerous spurious documents were added in the centuries after the fall of the Western Zhou, some of which were attributed to Zhou kings, and others to earlier sovereigns. Even the authentic documents were "polished" by later transmitters; but generally, they are considered a reliable repository of Zhou thought. The *Book of Odes* is a more heterogeneous collection, comprising sacrificial hymns and odes to the Zhou nobility in addition to later, more diverse pieces. Some odes contain criticism of inept kings and courtiers, complaints against injustice and oppression, and even provide a glimpse of popular customs of the early Chinese polities.

Feudalism and Kinship

The Western Zhou's decentralized mode of rule was based on the intermingling of political and kinship authority. Despite weak political structures, the cultural unity of the aristocratic elite preserved the Zhou world.

The Zhou decision to delegate power to local leaders outside the royal domain created a peculiar decentralized system, which superficially resembles European feudalism. This system was beneficial both economically, as it allowed administrative costs to be cut, and militarily, as armies of regional lords could quell local challenges more efficiently than royal armies dispatched from the capitals. In the long term, however, decentralization was potentially threatening. Regional armies might be used to support anti-Zhou rebellion or local secession. Preserving the obedience of the regional lords was a challenging task.

BELOW **This horse skull with cowry shell tack** was part of the chariot pit burial for a nobleman of the Western Zhou dynasty, most likely from an inspection chariot. Cowry shells were used as money in this period.

Systems of Control

The Zhou kings developed a variety of means to control local potentates. Regional lords were required to travel periodically to the Zhou capital and to receive investiture from the Zhou kings. They sent annual tribute to the Zhou as a token of submission, and had to provide military support to the kings. This, in addition to the considerable military and economic superiority of the royal domain, sufficed to quell any potential unrest by the regional lords during the first generations of the Zhou rule. Moreover, the position of the Zhou king as a head of the royal lineage also helped to stabilize the political system. As most regional lords were either descendants of the former kings or connected to royalty through marriage, they were subordinate to the kings in kinship terms. This preponderance of kinship hierarchy as the central component of political structure distinguishes the Zhou model from European feudalism, with its quasi-legal ties between the lord and his vassals.

Kinship, Power, and Ancestral Cult

The political structure of the Zhou can be seen as a system of graded lineages, in which kinship relations determined political hierarchy. Each lineage, which remained a primary building block of the political order, was hierarchically organized. Usually, the elder son of the primary wife inherited the head position, while other siblings received lesser aristocratic ranks. If granted a land allotment, they established a new branch lineage that remained subordinate to the major branch. Thus, the Zhou king headed the major branch of the royal lineage; regional lords who descended from sons and brothers of earlier kings headed minor branches and hence were subordinate to the reigning monarch. In each of the regional states, the lord headed a local ruling lineage, and his brothers and minor sons established collateral branches that supplied local officials. The kinship hierarchy therefore closely paralleled and buttressed the political one.

BRONZE INSCRIPTIONS

The Shang began the tradition of inscribing ritual bronze vessels, a practice that peaked during the Western Zhou. While most inscriptions are short, some contain lengthy narratives, telling about the circumstances of casting the vessel, and they considerably augment our scanty information on Western Zhou life. Inscriptions were usually incised on the core of the mold and thus cast into the internal side of the vessel. During the ceremony, they could not be seen because they were covered with food or brew. Scholars therefore assert that the addressees of these inscriptions were not the living, but ancestral spirits who "swallowed" the inscription together with the food. Most inscriptions end with a blessing to the owner of the vessel: these blessings were literally "put in the mouth" of the ancestors who were supposed to pronounce them once the offering was consumed. This suggests that the interaction with the spirits was strictly regulated and allowed no uncertainty.

RIGHT **This bronze ritual grain vessel,** or *gui,* features a lengthy inscription on the inside. It is from the Famen Temple at Fufeng in Shaanxi and dates from the Western Zhou period.

Insofar as every leader depended on the ongoing subordination of his kin, preserving the power of kinship structures was in his best interests, and this in turn ensured his ongoing subordination to his lineage superior, such as the regional lord or the king.

The head of the lineage enjoyed absolute economic, political, and religious superiority over his kin. The lineage's land was his possession and it was up to him to redistribute it between the kin (thus, the kings nominally owned all the lands "under Heaven," while regional lords possessed all the lands within their polity). Equally significant was the lineage head's exclusive access to the deified ancestors, whose blessings only he could ensure. The ancestral cult remained exceptionally important for the Zhou, indicated for instance by lavish furnishing of the aristocrats' burials. Of particular importance were annual ancestral sacrifices and the subsequent feast, which gathered lineage members together, strengthening the lineage's internal cohesiveness and buttressing its internal hierarchy. Yet as generations passed and the size of the lineage increased, its cohesiveness inevitably weakened. Kinship-based political hierarchy served only as a temporary curb on forces of disintegration.

Uniformity of Aristocratic Culture

Kinship ties among the ruling elites throughout the Zhou territories allowed for the proliferation of a uniform aristocratic culture. Burial sites of aristocrats, the arrangement and furnishing of tombs, the shapes and functions of bronze vessels, and the inscriptions on these vessels all follow a roughly uniform pattern, reflecting an increasing cultural cohesiveness among the elite. While at the lower social levels the Zhou world remained heterogenic, in terms of the upper strata we can speak of the formation of Chinese culture. Moreover, even when the political and military power of the Zhou kings weakened, their domain remained the cultural hub of the Zhou world, with significant modification in ancestral rites during the latter half of the Western Zhou period. The persistent cultural cohesiveness exhibited by the upper strata may have helped the Chinese world to survive the ensuing centuries of political disintegration.

LEFT **Western Zhou bronze bells,** such as these from the eighth century BCE, were strung together in chimes or groups and suspended with the bell facing down, making them easier to strike.

The Western Zhou Collapses

Structural problems during the rule of the Zhou gradually weakened the kings and generated tensions with regional lords and with aristocrats within the royal domain. Foreign challenges hastened the collapse of the Western Zhou, ending the period of relative political stability.

RIGHT **As well as the traditional** *taotie* **motif** (center), the jades of the Western Zhou feature sinuous animal forms such as coiled dragons and plumed birds.

The decline of the Western Zhou was a result of a series of systemic failures in the Zhou model of governing. As generations passed, it became increasingly difficult to maintain royal control of—and superiority over—regional polities.

Several imprudent attempts by the kings to intervene in succession crises in eastern polities backfired, causing increasing tension between the kings and their nominal underlings. These tensions, along with occasional military clashes, diminished the prestige of the royal house; although its authority was not defied openly, its impact on political dynamics outside the royal domain greatly decreased.

The Weakening Center

The royal domain was increasingly hard to manage. The kings employed a growing number of officials, but rather than being paid on a regular basis, they were granted land allotments from within the domain territories. Although these allotments were theoretically alienable, in reality they frequently became the hereditary possession of local noble lineages. The lords of such lineages, with domains of their own, appointed their own officers and officials with posts and titles that themselves became hereditary. In this way, the number of aristocratic families with patrimonies in offices and associated lands grew. Gradually, land resources under the king's jurisdiction shrank, and it was increasingly difficult to reward meritorious officials.

The result was a progressive weakening of the royal house, which no longer commanded sufficient economic resources to impose its will on the subjects. When King Li tried to reverse the tide and reallocate the land, his actions caused widespread resentment, and the king was overthrown in 841 BCE, later dying in exile. For 14 years the royal domain was ruled not by the king but by one of the nobles. This unprecedented situation indicated the depth of the crisis of authority.

External Challenges

As often happened throughout Chinese history, the internal weakness of the rulers coincided with strong external challenges. The reversal of military fortune of the Zhou kings had already begun in 977 BCE, when the southern expedition of King Zhao against the state of Chu ended with a disastrous defeat during which royal armies were annihilated, and the king drowned in the Han River.

Later, the Zhou faced challenges in the Huai River basin in the southeast, where local Yi tribesmen successfully repulsed the royal armies and eventually threatened the secondary capital, Chengzhou. Even greater trouble emerged there in the mid ninth century BCE, as Marquis E, the border protector, rebelled against the Zhou, defeated the royal armies, and was quelled only by private forces of one of the powerful nobles. The Zhou subsequently lost control of parts of their southern periphery.

The Xianyun: Trouble from the Northwest

The most serious troubles came from the areas to the northwest. These arid northern territories were inhabited by a variety of tribesmen who practiced a mixed agricultural and pastoral economy. Among those ethnic groups, the inhabitants of the areas in the northern and western vicinity of the Wei River valley initially were amicable or submissive to the Zhou; but by the ninth century BCE the situation had changed, possibly due to Zhou attempts to expand northward and westward.

The Xianyun, a chariot-fighting polity that occupied areas within striking distance of the Zhou capitals, became a major menace. The Xianyun were not powerful enough to conquer the royal domain, but Xianyun pressure generated lasting tension on the borders, severely depleting Zhou military resources. Late Western Zhou odes from the *Book of Odes* vividly depict the misery of the soldiers who had to campaign repeatedly against the Xianyun. The vulnerability of the royal domain was becoming increasingly evident.

The Collapse in the West

King You (reigned 781–771 BCE) and his consort, Baosi, are traditionally blamed for the collapse of the Zhou. Nevertheless, the king's imprudence and the consort's plots, even if real, only hastened the inevitable crisis.

A combination of succession struggles, partisan conflicts at the court, and worsened relations with regional lords resulted in disaster.

A coalition of disgruntled officials, neighboring lords, and the alien Quanrong tribesmen (possibly related to the Xianyun) overran the capital, killing the king, and putting an end to the Western Zhou. When a new king, Ping, ascended the throne, his advisors preferred to relocate to Chengzhou, abandoning the vulnerable western regions.

Relocating the Zhou court to the east had far-reaching consequences. The eastern royal domain was much smaller and could no longer provide the dynasty with sufficient economic and military resources. It survived only due to the symbolic legitimacy of the royal house.

While the line of the Zhou Sons of Heaven continued for another five centuries, very rarely were they able to impose their will on unruly regional lords. With an increase in the development of regional independence, the longest period of political fragmentation in China's history began. Regional conflict and moral crisis were the order of the day.

BLAMING HEAVEN

Odes from the *Book of Odes* which date from the last years of the Western Zhou abound with explicit resentment directed at the supreme deity, Heaven. They blame Heaven as "a cruel affliction," a merciless deity that "keeps its grace from us" and generates disorder. This "blasphemy" apparently reflects the frustration of Zhou statesmen with Heaven's indifference. According to the theory of Heaven's Decree, as the Zhou lost their virtue, a new, morally upright contender should have restored order; but this did not happen. The Decree was not transferred, it simply disappeared. Did this mean that Heaven was unable or unwilling to arrange human affairs? A poem that says, "the disasters of the people below do not descend from Heaven but arise from men" foreshadowed a shift from the divine to the mundane realm in search of political solutions.

Spring and Autumn Period

During the Spring and Autumn period (770–453 BCE), the Zhou world became a scene of incessant conflict within and between regional powers, and of escalating disintegration of political units. This was one of the gravest systemic crises in China's history.

RIGHT **This bronze wine vessel** is decorated with scenes of aristocratic life, showing pursuits such as hunting, warfare, boating, rituals, and music-making.

BELOW **Items of personal adornment** such as this gold dagger handle with turquoise inlays reflected the increasing status of Zhou nobles. Other high-status items included decorative belt hooks, swords, and scabbards.

The Spring and Autumn period was marked by a progressive crisis of central authority. The Zhou kings were the first to lose their power, being unable to restore their prestige after the disastrous loss of their western domain. Regional polities, nominally subordinate to the Zhou monarchs, soon became engulfed in a bitter internecine struggle, and the statesmen of the age sought in vain to stabilize the newly emerging multi-state system. The first stabilization attempt was the so-called "system of hegemony." The most powerful regional lord acted as a surrogate of the Zhou king, combining the legitimacy of the royal representative with the awesome power of his armies. This system of unilateral hegemony proved unsustainable in the long term. By the late seventh century BCE it was replaced by a dual system of alliances, led by two competing superpowers: Jin in the north and Chu in the south.

The alliance leaders tried to stabilize their coalitions, acting as arbiters in inter- and intra-state conflicts, and pretending to be protectors of the old sociopolitical order. They perpetuated ties with allied states through vibrant diplomatic activities, including periodic meetings of the state leaders and swearing solemn alliance covenants. Yet this system also proved unsustainable. Alliance leaders too frequently valued the narrow interests of their state over that of their allies; treaties and solemn oaths were repeatedly violated, and the effectiveness of the system of covenants was undermined. Incessant incursions by Chu and Jin devastated intermediate states, whose leaders lamented:

"Everything is ravaged and destroyed…All are full of sorrow and sadness and do not know how to protect themselves."

Tired of incessant warfare, the leaders of middle-sized states initiated two "disarmament conferences" in 546 and 541 BCE. The organizers proposed the creation of a mega-alliance, led simultaneously by Jin and Chu, thereby stabilizing the divided world. This initiative, however, failed miserably due to the lack of mutual trust between the major powers. Internal crises in both Chu and Jin and the rise of new "peripheral" powers further jeopardized the fragile inter-state order. By the end of the sixth century BCE, the multi-state system sank into a war of all against all, giving the subsequent period the ominous name of the age of the Warring States.

Domestic Turmoil

The process of fragmentation did not end with the dissolution of the Zhou realm into competing polities. Each polity, in turn, witnessed increasing internal turmoil due to the concentration of power in the hands of a few aristocratic lineages. Heads of those lineages, most of whom were related to the regional lord, monopolized high positions at court, turning offices—and the accompanying territorial allotments—into their hereditary possessions.

In their capacity as hereditary servants of their polity, aristocrats tended to consider themselves as co-masters of the state, treating the local lord as a figurehead. They vehemently protected the interests of their lineage against their lords and against competing ministerial lineages, thus generating endless domestic conflicts.

By the sixth century BCE, most polities became engulfed in a complex web of inter- and intra-lineage struggles, in addition to constant conflicts with neighboring powers. The resultant turmoil may be considered the deepest systemic crisis in Chinese history prior to the first half of the twentieth century.

Ongoing Cultural Unity

Despite the severe political fragmentation and endless wars, the aristocrats of the Spring and Autumn period maintained a remarkable degree of social cohesiveness and cultural uniformity, as reflected specifically in their adherence to Zhou ritual culture. Elaborate rites, developed in the Western Zhou period, permeated all imaginable spheres of the nobles' activities, buttressing the hereditary hierarchic order, and becoming a source of a transregional aristocratic identity. Aristocrats from different polities routinely intermarried, but never married the commoners of their own state. They shared a common textual culture, spoke a mutually intelligible language —which differed from the colloquial language of the commoners—and performed common ceremonies during the inter-state meetings and even on the battlefield.

THE YANGZI DELTA

Since the decline of the late Neolithic Liangzhu culture, the Yangzi delta had not played a significant role in the life of the Chinese world; yet in the sixth century BCE the rapid rise of local polities radically reshaped the balance of power in the Zhou realm. The states of Wu (in southern Jiangsu) and Yue (in northern Zhejiang) were culturally distinct from the Zhou world; but their elites quickly adopted Zhou ways and even forged genealogy that legitimated their participation in the lives of the Zhou states. Both states scored a series of amazing military successes, but their "hegemony" was brief: Yue destroyed Wu in 473 BCE, and soon thereafter disintegrated. It would be many centuries before the Yangzi delta rose again to "national" prominence.

Obvious similarities in the shape and size of the nobles' tombs from different parts of the Zhou world and in the mortuary assemblages within those tombs, indicate the existence of the uniform rank system that transcended the boundaries of individual polities. Even the elites of the neighboring non-Zhou polities were gradually absorbed into this aristocratic ritual culture, which allowed in turn a cultural expansion of the Zhou world despite its political fragmentation. The cultural unity of the elites mitigated the impacts of centrifugal political forces and was arguably instrumental in facilitating future political unification.

BELOW **Bells, such as these two bronze *bo* bells,** were the instruments of the elite within Zhou aristocratic culture. The *bo* was the earliest form of the imperial court bell.

The Warring States Period

The Warring States period (453–221 BCE) was an age of radical reforms and profound social changes. The sociopolitical processes of this age contributed decisively to the regeneration of political unity in the Chinese world.

The disintegration of the powerful state of Jin in 453 BCE under the pressure of three rival ministerial houses became the most vivid example of the deep systemic crisis threatening the aristocratic sociopolitical order. After centuries of incessant inter-state warfare and debilitating domestic struggles in major states, statesmen yearned for restoration of political stability. It was increasingly clear that such stability and peace would never take place unless the entire Zhou world was reunified under an efficient monarch. For this to happen, the proper functioning of an individual state had to be restored.

The fifth century BCE saw the launch of a series of reforms in major states aimed at restoring the ruler's power and curbing the forces of disintegration. Although devastating conflicts continued for another two centuries, China began the process of renewed centralization, which was crowned with imperial unification in 221 BCE.

The Changing Political Map

During the two centuries of the Warring States period, the map of China changed profoundly. Dozens of small and middle-sized polities of the Spring and Autumn period were annexed by stronger neighbors; and only seven large powers remained to dominate the political landscape. Powerful "peripheral" states—Qin in the west, Chu in the south, and Qi in the east—competed with the heir-states of Jin, particularly Wei in the middle of the Yellow River basin, for "universal" supremacy. These Warring States were more populated, more tightly centralized, and better territorially integrated than earlier polities. They expanded aggressively, swallowing weaker neighbors and absorbing minor polities and tribes on the fringes of Chinese civilization. It was during this period that the borders of the Zhou realm expanded to incorporate much of the Yangzi basin in the south and the southern fringes of the steppe belt in the north. Numerous indigenous tribes, which had survived for centuries in territorial pockets between major polities, were now absorbed into new states, and disappeared from historical accounts. Thus, during the Warring States period the contours of what would become China were evident for the first time.

The Bureaucratic State

The Warring States differed markedly from the aristocratic polities of the preceding age. In contrast to the hierarchically organized network of autonomous settlements of major aristocratic lineages, surrounded by rural hinterland, that was characteristic of the Spring and Autumn period, the newly emerging states did not tolerate autonomous units. Instead, they established an effective and all-penetrating bureaucracy that began actively intervening in the economic and social life of the lower strata of the population. The new state was territorially integrated, as is evident from the lengthy protective walls that demarcated its territory and separated it from its neighbors, and the territory within the walls was administratively integrated as well. Individual households became the major tax-paying units and the sources of conscription. This required much tighter

BELOW **This bronze tiger** with gold and silver inlays, dated 310 BCE, is an Eastern Zhou item from Pingshan Xi'an, Hebei Province.

LEFT **These stone figures** of a prostrate woman and a man with a tattooed face are artifacts of Chu, one of the peripheral states of the Warring States period. They were found at Shangsha, Hunan Province.

ties between the state apparatus and the population than had ever existed before.

The rapidly expanding officialdom maintained an increasingly effective census, trying to control the movements of the population and all of its everyday activities. Administrative documents from the Warring States period, unearthed since the 1970s, disclose an unbelievable degree of administrative intervention in everyday life. The state was concerned with everything, from weather conditions and the quality of iron utensils to the fitness of oxen used in agriculture. Oxen, for example, were measured every season, with punishment inflicted on local officials and village heads if their girth decreased. No less amazing is the precision of the census: one of the legal documents tells of punishing officials guilty of incomplete registration of "two youths of noble rank" in one case, and of several other persons in the other.

The degree of bureaucratization of the Warring States surpasses that of any comparable polity elsewhere prior to the emergence of modern European states in the eighteenth to nineteenth centuries CE. The state reached the most remote villages, mobilized their dwellers as tax payers, and military and labor conscripts; and elaborate laws and ordinances regulated the lives of commoners and officials alike. Effective mobilization of the populace allowed the rulers to allocate huge human resources to a variety of military and civilian

projects; but this effectiveness had its price. In many states, frustrated peasants tried to escape the oppressive administrative apparatus, fleeing to neighboring polities. To prevent this waste of human resources the Warring States instituted a system of passports, and tried to regulate population movements. These attempts met with only relative success, however; the idea that peasants may "vote with their feet" against the oppressive regime became deeply ingrained in the texts of preimperial ideologues.

Social Mobility and Changes in the Elite Composition

The formation of the new state was intrinsically linked to deep social changes, the most important of which was the decline of the hereditary aristocracy. In the aristocratic Spring and Autumn period, the noble lineages based their power on the system of hereditary office-holding and of hereditary allotments. In the

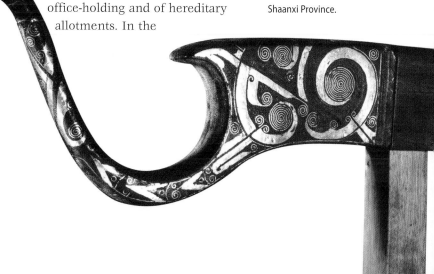

BELOW **This silver-inlaid bronze chariot mount** with a geometric pattern dates from the Warring States period, from Yongji, Shaanxi Province.

BELOW **This bronze short sword,** Eastern Zhou, third century BCE, is from the state of Wu. It is of typical Warring States form with a bronze pommel and two ridges on the handle.

wake of the Warring States reforms, both systems were abolished. Administrators were henceforth selected from a much broader pool of educated elite, and they received annual payments of grain or precious metals rather than being granted a lifelong territorial allotment. These changes deprived the nobility of its major sources of power, leading to its gradual decline and merger into the new elite.

Members of the new, broader, elite were usually designated as *shi*. Originally, the *shi* were of the lowest aristocratic stratum, and made their living as administrative and military retainers of high-ranking nobles. Their military and administrative expertise eventually made them indispensable for rulers of the Warring States. In sharp distinction to the upper segments of nobility, the *shi* generally lacked independent resources and had to seek an official appointment or patronage of a powerful potentate to ensure their livelihood. This made them more prone to identify their interests with those of regional rulers. It was no accident that their rise coincided with reforms aimed at curbing the power of aristocratic lineages and enhancing the ruler's authority.

The *shi* was a dynamic and open stratum that absorbed both nobles and commoners, and comprised both current and aspiring elite members. Its dynamism is most explicit in the intellectual sphere, as it supplied most of the renowned thinkers of that age. These thinkers contributed to the development of a distinct *shi* ethos that emphasized their pride, independence, and moral and intellectual superiority over the rest of society and even over the rulers. This ethos shaped the self-image of the Chinese intellectual elite throughout the subsequent imperial millennia.

Far-reaching changes in the composition of the elite were part of the overall increase in social mobility during the Warring States period. Several states, most notably Qin, adopted a new flexible system of promotion, granting aristocratic rank in exchange for military merit and for high tax yields, thereby allowing commoners to enter the elite ranks. Although we cannot quantify the number of commoners who advanced in this way, it was not negligible. Thus, predictions of a child's future that appear in the

Qin *Almanacs* display the extraordinarily wide range of possibilities awaiting the newborn: from becoming a high-ranking minister, a noble, or an official, to, in the opposite direction, becoming a mere servant or (in the case of females) a concubine. The Warring States period may have witnessed some of the highest rates of social mobility in Chinese history.

Popular Customs and Cultural Diversification

The demise of the hereditary aristocracy and the entrance of members of lower strata into officialdom disrupted the cultural unity of the Zhou world. As newcomers were less versed in the aristocratic culture of the Zhou, they inevitably contributed to an increasing cultural heterogeneity. Cultural changes are particularly explicit in mortuary practices. Instead of uniformly arranged aristocratic tombs with their standardized assemblages of bronze vessels, we find that local customs vary greatly, and that the rigid norms of the past begin to disappear. Similar diversification is observable with regard to the written language, as adoption of "popular" script led to numerous orthographic variations. The same was true of spoken language, where the

incidence of colloquialisms increased. Yet despite the fact that the unity of the elite culture was dissolving, the result was not total chaos because continuous inter-state interactions kept some common cultural norms intact.

Qin and Chu: Asserting Local Identity

Cultural diversification in the Zhou world was most explicit in the "peripheral" states of Qin and Chu. Motivated either by a desire to reassert themselves against the Zhou center, or by a need to incorporate newly conquered peripheral populations, or possibly even by a wish to increase domestic cultural cohesiveness at the expense of external ties, the elites of these states began adopting new forms of cultural expression. Horizontal burial shafts, unknown before and now becoming the predominant form of burials in the Qin, are evidence for the adoption of local practices that reflect perhaps new ideas about the afterlife. In Chu burials, wooden statues of fantastic animals coated with colorful lacquer represent a unique artistic taste and suggest the development of local mythology.

The estrangement of Qin and Chu from the core Zhou states can be seen not only in the

SHANG YANG'S REFORMS

Shang Yang (died 338 BCE) is the most renowned and most controversial of the great statesmen of the Warring States, whose reforms propelled the state of Qin to the position of the major superpower. Having proclaimed that the state's success derived exclusively from agriculture and warfare, Shang Yang developed a series of measures aimed at directing the entire population to these pursuits. He ordered development of fallow lands, promulgated clear, impartial, and infamously harsh laws, and proposed a series of economic and social incentives to turn agriculture into the most advantageous pursuit for the commoners. To encourage conscripts to brave death, Shang Yang granted aristocratic ranks for severing enemies heads, while to prevent their desertion, he divided the population into the groups of mutually responsible five or ten families. Members of the group had to denounce criminals from within their ranks or else face cruel punishment. Controversial as they were, Shang Yang's reforms undeniably facilitated the rise of Qin.

archaeological evidence, but also in contemporaneous texts, which abound with pejorative remarks against the alleged "barbarianism" of Qin and Chu. Yet cultural diversification was ultimately checked. The very fluidity of the *shi* employment patterns, and their routine shifts from one state to another, perpetuated cultural ties throughout the Zhou world. Moreover, as most *shi* promulgated their commitment to the interests of All-under-Heaven rather than to an individual state, they did not endorse the nascent "national" cultural and political identities of the Warring States. Lacking ideological legitimacy, the cultural diversification of the Zhou world did not develop into a meaningful political phenomenon that could threaten future political unification.

LEFT **The tomb of Marquis Yi** (died 433 BCE) was found intact in 1977. Marquis Yi was a nobleman of Zeng, a principality enclosed within the state of Chu. His tomb contained over 10,000 bronze vessels.

LEFT **This bronze jar and matching basin** are from the tomb of Marquis Yi. The intricate decorations of dragons, tigers, and scrolls were created using the lost-wax technique.

Intellectual Life

The three centuries prior to imperial unification were the formative age of Chinese intellectual tradition. Competing thinkers sought remedies to sociopolitical turmoil; their answers laid the ideological foundations for the unified empire.

The severe crisis of the Zhou world spurred an unprecedented upsurge of intellectual activity. It is no coincidence that the era from the fifth to the third centuries BCE is often referred to as the age of the "Hundred Schools" of thought.

The "Hundred Schools"

While the name may be misleading, as most of the so-called "schools" are subsequent classifications of disparate texts rather than cohesive ideological currents, it conveys well the immense pluralism of the contemporary intellectual life. This was an age of bold intellectual departures and remarkable freedom of thought, unhindered by either political or religious orthodoxies. Thinkers competed freely for the rulers'

patronage, moving from one court to another in search of better employment. They proposed widely ranging remedies to social, political, economic, and military maladies, their views moving from harsh authoritarianism to anarchistic individualism, from the support of a laissez-faire economy to the advocacy of state monopolies, from blatant militarism to radical pacifism. Their joint activities shaped China's intellectual tradition for millennia to come.

In this age of deep sociopolitical crisis, Chinese thought was dominated by political and practical concerns. Speculative philosophy and metaphysical or ontological questions remained secondary to the search for stability and orderly rule. Doctrines had to be not only intellectually convincing, but primarily practical. This political focus also explains certain common ideas apparent beneath the pluralism of competing doctrines. Thus, rival thinkers unanimously advocated unification of "All under Heaven" as the only solution to the political turmoil; none promulgated the idea of independence of his natal state.

Most thinkers further agreed that the monarchical system was the only acceptable form of political organization: individual rulers were bitterly criticized, but no systematic alternative to monarchic rule was ever proposed. In addition, thinkers strongly supported the meritocratic principle of rule: the majority agreed that an individual's position should reflect his abilities rather than his pedigree. These ideas became the backbone of traditional Chinese political culture.

Confucius

Confucius (551–479 BCE), the most celebrated thinker of the "Hundred Schools," lived in the late Spring and Autumn period, and witnessed the decline of the aristocratic order. A member of the then lowly *shi* stratum, he tried desperately to find an appropriate position in the service of regional lords, but he was repeatedly frustrated. Yet he educated numerous disciples, who carried on his teaching and recorded his supposed sayings in the so-called *Analects*.

BELOW **This portrait of Confucius from Xi'an is** carved on a stone stele from the Tang dynasty, dating from CE 618–907. The followers of Confucius helped secure his reputation as China's greatest sage.

LEFT **This cave near Qufu,** Shandong Province, is the legendary birthplace of Confucius. Qufu served as the capital of the state of Lu during the Spring and Autumn period.

Confucius posed as a conservative. He proclaimed that he only "transmitted" the ancients' wisdom rather than creating anything new; he repeatedly declared his adoration of the Western Zhou model and of the ritual system, which was the backbone of the aristocratic hierarchic order. Behind this conservative veneer, however, Confucius presented a series of novel departures. The most important of these was reinterpretation of the term *junzi* ("superior man," originally referring to nobles only) from a pedigree-based to a moral designation. Only a morally upright person is a truly "superior man" who deserves elite status. This redefinition eventually opened the way for the social advancement of the *shi*.

The *Analects* contains many discussions about the proper conduct of the superior man. He is supposed to be benevolent, intelligent, and morally courageous. He prefers righteousness to profits, is broad-minded, and is able to yield. He is filially pious and loyal to his lord, although by no means servile. He is engaged in constant self-cultivation: he studies canonical Zhou texts, ancient rites, and music; and thereby cultivates his morality. The ultimate goal of self-cultivation is sociopolitical engagement, "to rectify oneself, thereby bringing peace to the hundred clans." Yet government service, even if highly desirable, should never be performed if it requires compromise of one's moral Way (*Dao*). Confucius is explicit: "Riches and honors are what every man

desires; but if they cannot be attained in accordance with the Way, do not accept them."

The Followers of Confucius

Confucius's moral non-conformism hindered his career; it was up to his more successful disciples and followers to translate his moral imperatives into political life. In a world of cruelty and war they tried to unify morality and politics. This idealism is most explicit in the thought of Mengzi (fourth century BCE), Confucius's most dedicated follower.

Mengzi believed in "moral government": the one that would create appropriate economic and political setting to allow the people to realize fully their intrinsic goodness. If the ruler cultivated his morality and let it emanate to broader spheres, the world would uniformly submit to him, since "the people turn to the benevolent as water flows downward." Alternatively, the immoral tyrant loses his right to rule and may be legitimately overthrown and executed.

Xunzi (*c.* 335–238 BCE), another great follower of Confucius, disagreed with Mengzi's idealism. He argued that morality is an important means of government for superior men; but that "petty men" are intrinsically immoral and avaricious and should be restricted with punitive laws instead. Only "superior men" are able to overcome this through relentless self-cultivation; their lives therefore would be regulated by ritual norms rather than punishments and oppression. Xunzi's synthesis of moral imperatives with

BELOW **This is part of a Tang-dynasty manuscript of** the *Analects* of Confucius, with annotations by Zheng Xuan, unearthed in 1967 at Turfan, Xinjiang.

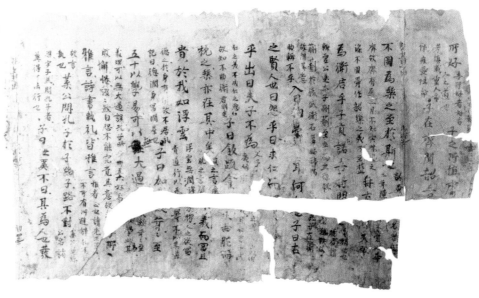

practical considerations was more viable than Mengzi's idealism, although Mengzi became more popular among Confucians of later ages.

Mozi

Mozi (fifth century BCE) promulgated his own peculiar blend of idealism and pragmatism. He radicalized the moral imperatives of Confucius: benevolence should be truly universal and the principle of "universal love" should replace hierarchic ritual order. But how to implement this? Mozi envisioned an ideal world, ruled by the "worthiest and most able man," who would impose uniform values and behavioral norms on his subjects. He would be supervised by Heaven, which Mozi, in marked distinction from contemporaneous thinkers, envisioned as a sentient and extraordinary active deity. Below, the supreme ruler would be assisted by "the most benevolent" men, who would head each administrative unit. The subjects would simply "unanimously approve whatever the superiors approve, and unanimously disprove whatever the superiors disprove"; thereby universal morality would prevail.

Mozi was not a pure idealist, though. Rather, he recommended radical implementation of meritocratic principles of rule; advocated reduction of aristocratic conspicuous consumption as exemplified in lavish burials and expensive ritual music; and supported promulgation of artisanship

to address the people's needs. To prevent aggressive warfare, which Mozi considered to be murderous criminal behavior, he reportedly established a "swift intervention force" to assist small states attacked by their aggressive neighbors. He and his disciples also devoted considerable effort to developing convincing arguments to support their controversial doctrines, and contributed to the marked sophistication of philosophical discourse. For a short while Mozi's hierarchically organized "party" ensured a rapid proliferation of his doctrines and his popularity rivaled that of Confucius. Despite this, Mozi's peculiar mixture of idealism, pacifism, and religiosity, coupled with the ideological inflexibility of his disciples, proved unsustainable, and his teachings disappeared shortly after the imperial unification.

Laozi and the Way

Laozi (often known as Lao Tzu) is a semilegendary figure who is associated with an eponymous short text that was most likely composed in the fourth century BCE. Despite its brevity, the *Laozi* (or *Daodejing*) had a truly revolutionary impact on the philosophical discourse of the Warring States, especially through adding metaphysical dimensions to ethical and political discourse. The text presupposes the existence of a primeval and spontaneous Way *(Dao)*, which influences all levels of existence from the cosmos, down to society and the individual. The Way is ineffable and incomprehensible to the human senses; yet, the text explains some of its functioning principles. Thus, as the Way "moves in the opposite direction," things differ from their external appearance. This explains many of the *Laozi*'s paradoxes, such as: "the supreme virtue is not virtuous," and "correct words appear as their opposite." The author calls himself "muddled and confused," and this implies, perhaps, that the mysterious Way cannot be grasped via conventional learning and cannot be expressed by regular words.

The ideal person, who understands the principles of the Way and implements them in his everyday life, is correlated with the Sage. He is often depicted as a divinized universal ruler who exercises his rule through non-action and tranquility. While remaining a shadowy

BELOW **This statue of Laozi** is at Mt. Qingyuan, Quanzhou. Laozi is the semi-legendary philosopher credited with writing the *Laozi* (also called the *Daodejing*). The name Laozi means "Old Master."

FAR LEFT **Legend has it that Laozi**, saddened by the evil of men, rode a water buffalo into the desert. This statue of Laozi on a water buffalo is from the Song dynasty, CE 960–1279.

LEFT **This third century** BCE **bronze vessel** is reputed to be the earliest surviving piece with Daoist symbols. It depicts the mountain of the immortals.

presence himself, he allows the people to "transform themselves," "rectify themselves," and "enrich themselves." When the Sage exercises his rule, "the myriad creatures will submit of their own accord." He neither enlightens his subjects nor overburdens them with military tasks and taxes, but rather segregates them in small communities, where they enjoy their life and do not "visit each other" until "old days and death." Thereby, perhaps, the ultimate tranquility will be achieved.

Zhuangzi

Among multiple followers of the *Laozi*, Zhuangzi (fourth century BCE) appears as the most original thinker. In his interpretation, the Way is not just ineffable, but, probably, ungraspable. Our words are too detached from reality, our life span is too short, and our vision is too narrow to allow comprehension of cosmic truths; and, therefore, those who proclaim themselves knowledgeable are either fools or impostors. Each creature has its own Way, and imposing one's truth on the rest of the world is stupid and morally deplorable. Zhuangzi boldly attacked society and the state; the rulers are robbers, serving them is immoral; reclusion and disengagement from the world are the only laudable choice. Zhuangzi's "anarchism" remained the single most powerful voice of protest against the hegemonic monarchistic order.

The "Legalists"

Most thinkers of the "Hundred Schools" believed that moral ends require moral means. This view was disputed by the "Legalists," of whom Shang Yang and Han Feizi (died *c.* 233 BCE) are representative. In the changing world, driven by self-interest and deceit, only force and coercion bring order. To eradicate wars, one must wage wars; to eradicate punishments, one must double punishments. The people are stupid; ministers and traveling thinkers are deceitful; the ruler should pursue the goal of a powerful universal state, which is the only way to impose orderly rule. In a paradox worthy of the *Laozi*, only war, coercion, and cruelty will bring tranquility and peace.

A CONVERGENCE OF OPPOSITES

Thinkers of the Warring States bitterly disagreed with each other, and at times proposed to silence their opponents, but the dominant trend was toward mutual influence and intellectual synthesis. Since thinkers extensively borrowed each other's vocabulary and ideas, this eclecticism somewhat invalidates their division into competing "schools." Mutual enrichment was furthered by collaborative projects in which multiple thinkers were engaged in preparing a single multi-authored text. The most famous of these projects is the *Lüshi Chunqiu*, composed in the state of Qin on the eve of the imperial unification with the ultimate goal to synthesize intellectual trends of the "Hundred Schools" into a coherent whole. The tendency to emphasize similarities rather than differences continued well into the imperial period.

Urban Transformation

The Warring States period was an age of rapid urban development. Cities grew in number and size, and their function diversified. They were no longer only political centers but became hubs of commercial activity and cultural and intellectual vigor.

RIGHT **The inscription on this coin** reads *banliang,* which indicates the weight of the coin. These coins circulated in the Qin state during the Warring States period (*c.* 453–221 BCE).

The changing nature of cities reflects the sociopolitical and economic transformations of the Warring States period, but it was also a major catalyst for these changes. From the Shang dynasty to the Spring and Autumn period, cities in China primarily served the elite as political and ritualistic centers. While some of those cities were monumental in the scale of their structures, their populations were not very large and the range of activities conducted in them was limited.

The First Wave of Urbanization

The first real wave of urbanization in Chinese history happened during the Warring States period. Numerous new cities were established and their scale was much larger than before. Cities like Linzi, the capital of Qi, are reported to have housed populations of several hundred thousand people, a tenfold increase from previous periods. Archaeological exploration at some sites has confirmed their huge scale. The walls of Yongcheng, the capital of Qin (*c.* 677–383 BCE), enclose an area of about 7 sq miles (18 sq km), while the size of Xiadu, the capital of the northeastern state of Yan, is more than 11 sq miles (30 sq km), a huge scale even by modern standards.

Urban Culture

The cities of the Warring States differed from those of earlier periods not only in size but also in their very nature. Excavations suggest that their population was much more heterogeneous than before, and they became a true hub of economic, commercial, and cultural activity. Many of the cities were located near major rivers that provided water to the swelling urban population, but could also serve as transportation routes through which commodities traveled to and from the urban markets.

Much less rigid urban planning reflected an emphasis on utility rather than on ritualistic precision. Cities became more clearly divided internally, and the fortified enclosures of elite residences testify to social tensions and widening gaps between various urban strata. New architectural techniques, which allowed construction of tall structures built around a solid earthen core, changed the skyline of the cities. The symbolic effect of the city walls, which were still formidable, was now rivaled by gate towers, towering palaces, and royal burial mounds (the latter constructed outside city walls).

THE IRON REVOLUTION

The development of blast furnaces enabled Chinese metallurgists to cast high-quality iron tools a millennium and a half before the rest of the world. Small-scale iron production started during the Spring and Autumn period, but only during the Warring States did it reach a substantial scale. Iron weapons soon replaced the less durable bronze weapons. More importantly, it is only from this point that traditional agricultural tools, which had been made from stone and wood, were replaced by superior iron implements. For most of the population this was the real beginning of the metal age. Iron plows, drawn for the first time in Chinese history by draft animals, revolutionized agriculture, allowing the opening of new fields and bolstering agricultural productivity. In some states, the government closely supervised and encouraged dissemination of cast iron tools to the peasants; elsewhere the peasants had to buy them from the state or from large private manufacturers. This forced their integration into the market economy.

LEFT **This silver inlaid bronze binding** for a vessel is from the Eastern Zhou dynasty. It has three small feet and would have encircled the lower part of a lacquer vessel, such as a *zun*.

Trade and Commerce

The Warring States period witnessed great economic expansion. This prosperity was partly caused by the revolution of iron casting that greatly increased agricultural productivity. Increased state involvement in agriculture, especially the construction of large irrigation projects and the development of virgin lands, further catalyzed economic growth. In addition, the extensive construction of new roads and canals that were first used to transport troops, but also enabled better transportation of goods, boosted an unprecedented surge in local and inter-state trade.

The most important commodities of inter-state trade were staple foods and basic commodities such as grains, salt, and iron artifacts, suggesting that trade was carried out in large volumes. These commodities were necessary to feed the swelling populations of the cities and to provide for large standing armies. Concomitantly, the ascendancy of new elites created a demand for prestige materials and luxury goods, such as jade, lacquer, and bronzes, which were intensively traded. This change in elite taste is most clearly reflected in bronze vessels. Vessels cast with the lost-wax technique and decorated with inlays of gold and silver were much more ornate and colorful in comparison to the solemn ritual vessels of the past. Many of the new vessels no longer served for religious ceremonies but for lavish court feasting.

In contrast to later periods in Chinese history, the leaders of the Warring States period appreciated the benefits of trade. Major states benefited enormously from transit taxes levied on goods that passed through customs stations on the way to and from the major cities, and from taxing the activities inside the state-controlled urban markets. Even minor polities could reap huge economic benefits from inter-state trade. Thus, Dingtao, the capital of the tiny state of Song, was so rich that all major powers vied to control it.

Private merchants prospered as well, despite oppressive taxation and direct competition from the state apparatus. Some of the merchants attained fabulous wealth; and at least one of them, Lü Buwei, translated his economic success into political power, becoming for a short while the de facto leader of the powerful state of Qin. His example is extreme, but others also used their money to gain power and influence.

BELOW **Jade *bi*-disks** were highly prized during the Zhou dynasty. This one is decorated on both sides with a continuous band of five partially dissolved dragons' heads and bodies.

Currency and Coinage

Shovel Coins

Coins in the shape of shovels (right), called *bu*, were the earliest coins in China. This bronze shovel coin with rounded corners dates from the eighth to the seventh century BCE.

Bronze Blade Coin

Blade coins were the main coins circulated in the Yan state. Additionally, there were also needle-headed sword, pointed-headed sword, and Yan sword coins.

The minting of coins started in China during the second half of the Spring and Autumn period, around 550 BCE. The advent of currency systems envigorated the economy and facilitated tax collection.

The two early centers of coin production were the Zhou royal domain near present-day Luoyang and the state of Jin. These were both bustling commercial centers and benefited greatly from the new monetary system. The new invention spread rapidly, so that by the beginning of the Warring States period every major power minted its own coins.

The earliest coins in China, known as *bu*, were shaped like a shovel. They appeared first in Jin and continued to be produced by Jin's succeeding states: Zhao, Wei, and Han. Knife-shaped coins were typical of the eastern states of Qi and Yan, while round coins started during the Qin dynasty. Most coins had holes to thread them together into strings and these strings of coins were used in regular transactions.

With the exception of Chu, which had a different monetary system and minted golden coins, Eastern Zhou coins were all made of bronze. This material firmly connected the monetary and political systems. Since the time of the Shang, bronze was associated with the most important state affairs, such as ritual and warfare, and it was the most prestigious material. The value of the new bronze coins reflected not just their metal content—as bronze was relatively common—but the backing of the state that minted them.

Although coins were certainly important for private commerce, their value was even greater in state affairs. The decision of several states to begin collecting taxes in cash (rather than just in grain or fabrics as had previously been the case) had far-reaching consequences for the peasant economy. To gain coins, peasants had to enter the market, which tied them to the political economy of their states. Coins were used also to reward meritorious soldiers, and as payments to artisans, to state laborers, and, possibly, to low-level officials. Several states began regulating minting, and also tried to ensure smooth circulation of the state-issued coins:

Coins and Coin Molds

During the Qin and Han dynasties, coins were mainly cast by mold-casting techniques. Many metal models and metal molds of that period have been unearthed. Two types of pottery-mold casting—vertical casting and stack casting—were adopted. The coin shown here is known as the *wu zhu* coin. It was a product of the Western Han dynasty. This type of circular bronze coin with a square central hole was minted from the first century CE.

Qin legal codes prohibited merchants from refusing coins on the grounds of supposedly bad quality. Close links between coins and the state machine continued into the imperial era.

Proliferation of coins occurred during a time of great commercial development in China, and, in turn, greatly accelerated the exchange of material wealth. Both the state and private businessmen benefited from the rapidly expanding commerce. Widespread use of currency allowed easy storage and smooth transportation of resources, and improved the ability to determine and negotiate the value of goods.

Interestingly, although different types of currency coexisted, most states recognized the validity of coins minted by rival states. The fact that the scaling of coins was similar in most states further facilitated inter-state commerce. This commerce was another factor that countered the centrifugal tendencies of the Warring States period. The only clear exception to this was the southern state of Chu, whose different currency system might have been intentionally designed to emphasize local differences and hinder economic contacts with other states.

Cowry Shells as Currency

It is widely assumed that other types of currency preceded the advent of coin minting in China. Western Zhou bronze inscriptions use the word *bei* (cowries) to denominate units of wealth. Cowries were often found buried in large numbers, perhaps as markers for wealth, in special bronze containers. Many argue, based on this and other textual evidence, that cowry shells functioned as coins during the Western Zhou and earlier periods, although this is not supported by archaeological evidence.

The shape of the early coins suggests that certain objects, such as bronze artifacts and bolts of cloth, were used to facilitate exchange and as a universal measure of value. Yet the abstract notion of currency could not develop before the introduction of coins.

Conscription and War

During the Warring States period, technological and administrative developments brought about the appearance of mass conscript armies, changing the nature of warfare in China.

From the Western Zhou into the Spring and Autumn period, Chinese armies were led by aristocrats who fought on chariots. Chariot warfare required lengthy training and the development of unique skills; hence it was predominantly reserved for the nobility. It also facilitated a degree of chivalry, respect, and even collaboration between rival armies: the chariots were effective only in the open field, and to deploy them efficiently, the pitched battle had to be pre-arranged. This turned chariot warfare into a kind of noble game. Infantrymen played a largely subordinate role, acquiring importance only when fighting in mountainous or river-intersected terrain, or on the streets of a capital city during domestic conflicts.

By the Warring States period, the composition of the armies had profoundly changed. New armies comprised primarily of infantrymen, with limited assistance from chariots—and by the end of the period, from cavalrymen as well. The armies were drawn from peasant conscripts, whose training was much simpler than that of chariot fighters. Most conscripts served for a fixed period of time; a few joined professional units, such as elite troops or the navy. The nature of warfare had consequently altered beyond recognition. Previously, in pitched battles, individual courage had determined victory. This gave way to prolonged campaigns, requiring logistical sophistication and the ability to coordinate large units, rather than only individual valor. Armies greatly increased in size (reportedly from dozens to hundreds of thousands of combatants), and the conflicts became much longer. Moreover, the peasant conscripts were not prone to display courtesy on the battlefield; rather, wars became more violent and destructive, and killing prisoners and civilians became an essential part of the new type of warfare.

Military Technology

The Warring States period witnessed revolutionary changes in military technology, which both responded and contributed to the newly developing infantry armies. The invention of the crossbow became the single most important development. A crossbow was more precise and more powerful than the traditional bow, and it was relatively easy to train peasant conscripts to operate it. The state administrators closely supervised production of crossbow triggers in the state-run workshops, where skilled artisans ensured the accuracy and effectiveness of the new weapon. Mass production and technological sophistication characterized other military utensils, such as lances, iron swords, and armor and helmets consisting of leather and iron plates. Impressive developments occurred in the realm of siege warfare: attackers would dam a nearby river to flood the besieged city or would dig tunnels to bring the walls down, while the defenders used large bellows to pump smoke into the tunnels and suffocate the attackers. By the end of the period, several armies began adopting

RIGHT **These bronze swords** are from the Warring States period, 453–221 BCE. Swords of this era typically had solid hilts with two rings on them.

cavalry, especially in skirmish and reconnaissance; yet only in the early imperial period did cavalry begin outweighing infantry as the most important part of the army.

The Logistics of Conscript Armies

Military changes during the Warring States were accompanied by profound administrative readjustment. Effective mobilization of the peasants required the establishment of firm control over their movements, triggering increasing

THE ART OF WAR BY SUNZI

A short text from the fourth century BCE, *The Art of War* —attributed to the semi-legendary general Sunzi (or Sun Tzu)—is one of the most renowned masterpieces of military thought. Sunzi treats war holistically: it is not just a battle, but a competition of efficient administration, good economic infrastructure, and competent rulership. War is predicated on political goals rather than just on military victory, and it is better to attain those goals without actual combat if possible. If war is inevitable, it should be swift and decisive. Deception is the way of warfare: it allows no chivalry. Commanders should lead their soldiers "like a shepherd driving a flock of sheep": they are not supposed to contemplate his plans; but nor should the ruler interfere in his commanders' actions. Remarkably for the military essay, *The Art of War* is not fond of violence: it is a regrettably indispensable part of human experience, but a skillful commander should reduce rather than increase it.

RIGHT *The Art of War* was the first military treatise ever written.

intrusiveness of the government apparatus. To ensure adequate supply for the armies during prolonged campaigns, the state had to prepare sufficient reserves and to improve transportation. In particular, improvement in waterway communications in the Warring States period may have been directly related to military demands. Finally, to increase the number of potential conscripts, the rival states took various measures aimed at attracting foreign immigrants and increasing the native population, even if that meant taxation on unmarried youth to encourage early marriage.

Motivating conscripts to fight was the most challenging task. Some argued that only a benevolent ruler would gain the loyalty of his subjects, who would then defeat the ruler's enemies even when "armed with nothing but staves." Others believed the people could be manipulated to fight only if their individual interests and fears were addressed: high rewards to good soldiers and heavy punishments to deserters would turn cowards into brave fighters. Alternatively, the great military thinker, Sunzi, considered the problem as primarily military and tactical: the soldiers should be placed on the "fatal terrain," "from which there is nowhere to go" and only then will they fight to death. Interestingly, no thinker argued that the soldiers could be motivated to brave death for the sake of the "motherland" or as a manifestation of their manliness. Calculation of individual costs and benefits was the only valid moving force behind the soldiers' behavior.

LEFT **This iron foundry mold for axes,** excavated in 1953 in Xinglong, Hebei, consists of two halves and a core.

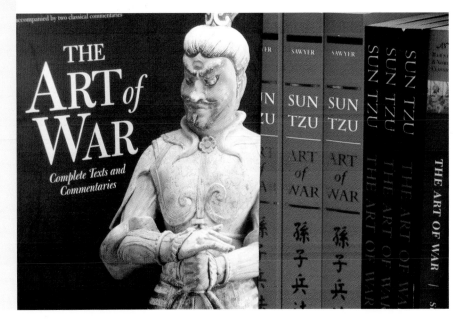

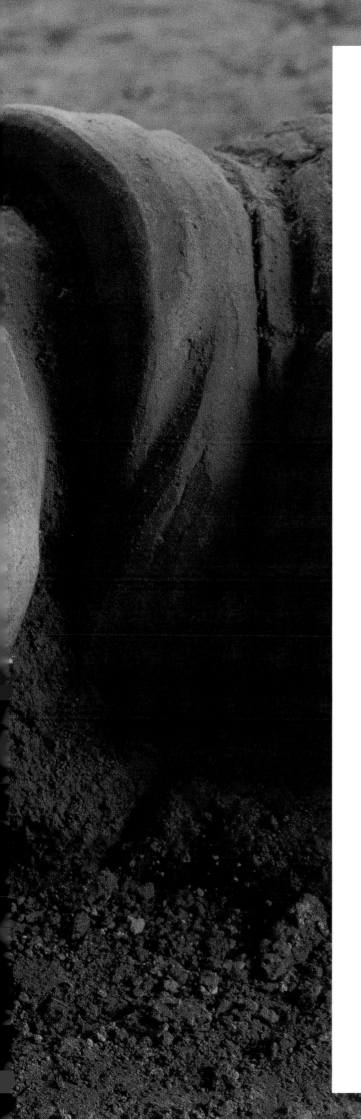

Unification and Expansion: The First Chinese Empires

Introduction

The Warring States era, the last phase of the Eastern Zhou, came to an end in 256 BCE
when Qin, one of the six kingdoms that controlled China, conquered the state of Zhou.

After the fall of Zhou, Qin set out, over the next 36 years, to destroy and annex the remaining states. The state of Han fell to Qin in 230 BCE, Zhao followed in 228 BCE, then Wei in 225 BCE, Chu in 223 BCE, Yan in 222 BCE, and finally the state of Qi surrendered in 221 BCE, leaving Qin to rule "all under Heaven," as China's first centralized empire.

The Qin Dynasty

Since no previous title was sufficient to describe the scope of the ruler's new power, a new title was devised, that of "emperor" (in Chinese *huangdi* meaning "august god"). Under the First Emperor's rule, independent states were replaced

with centrally administered units known as "commanderies." The hereditary aristocracy was dissolved and bureaucrats appointed in their place. These administrative changes were matched by an ideological shift, with the strength of the state now viewed as resting on warfare and agriculture rather than on the virtue and charisma of the ruler. Massive public works projects were undertaken to build up the empire's defenses. Peasants were resettled to work previously uncultivated land and to extend the borders of the empire even farther through military conquest.

To prevent criticism based on historical precedents, the First Emperor proscribed the circulation of the classical texts associated with

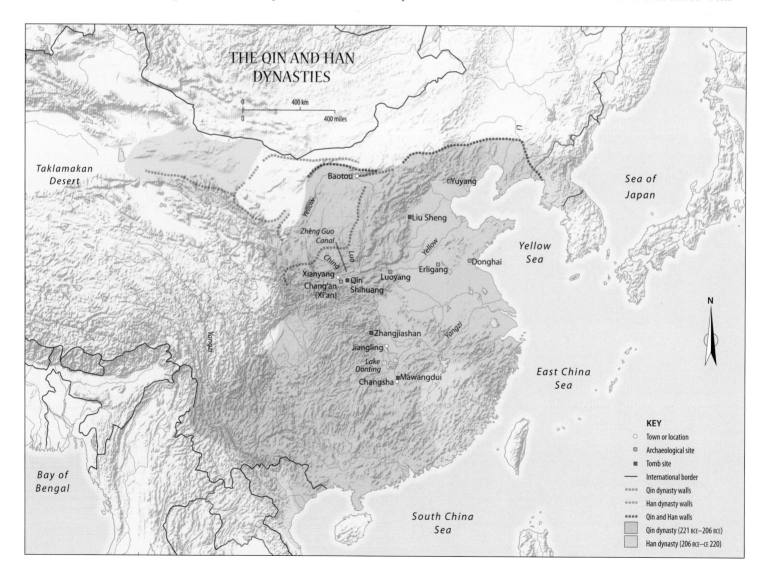

THE QIN AND HAN
DYNASTIES

0   400 km
0   400 miles

Taklamakan
Desert

Baotou

Yuyang

Sea of
Japan

Liu Sheng

Zheng Guo
Canal

Yellow

Yellow

Yellow
Sea

Ching

Luo

Erligang

Donghai

Xianyang
Chang'an
(Xi'an)

Qin
Shihuang

Luoyang

Yangzi

Zhangjiashan

Jiangling

Lake
Donting

East China
Sea

Changsha

Mawangdui

Bay of
Bengal

N

KEY

○   Town or location
▫   Archaeological site
▪   Tomb site
—   International border
••••   Qin dynasty walls
••••   Han dynasty walls
••••   Qin and Han walls
▨   Qin dynasty (221 BCE–206 BCE)
▨   Han dynasty (206 BCE–CE 220)

South China
Sea

Confucianism. Discontent smoldered among a silenced intelligentsia, a disenfranchised aristocracy, and a large mass of ordinary people who suffered under the yoke of warfare and hard labor, as well as increasing misrule after the First Emperor died and his incompetent son, known as the Second Emperor, came to the throne. The first major revolt began in 209 BCE. After a brief 15 years, in 206 BCE, the Qin dynasty ended with the suicide of the Second Emperor and the disintegration of the Qin state.

The Former Han Dynasty

In 206 BCE, Xiang Yu, a general of noble background, led a large and powerful group of rebels and created a confederacy of 19 kingdoms. Xiang's failure to win the loyalty of those who served him, however, prevented him from establishing his own dynasty and ruling all of China. The unlikely beneficiary of this attempt was Liu Bang, a man of peasant background who defeated Xiang Yu in 202 BCE and founded the Han dynasty from which emerged many of the institutions and conventions of all later periods of Imperial China.

During the first 50 years of the Former Han dynasty, the imperial government sought to bring stability to an empire plagued by unrest. The government deliberated over how best to bring the dangerously autonomous kingdoms under the thumb of the central government and at the same time struggled with a way to subdue powerful imperial consort families with dynastic ambitions of their own. It was not until 154 BCE when the imperial government put down a rebellion by seven powerful kingdoms ruled by members of the Liu imperial family, and implemented the policy that all senior officials in the kingdoms be appointed by the central government, that political equilibrium was finally established. On the Han borders, the nomadic Xiongnu tribes, were a continuing threat.

Relative stability during the reign of Emperor Wu brought about far-reaching changes in the development of state ideology. Emperor Wu (reigned 141–87 BCE) decreed that the five Confucian Classics should form the basis of imperially sponsored scholarship. He established an imperial academy that employed specialists in the Five Classics to train students who would later serve as advisors to the emperor. However, in spite of imperial efforts to foster an atmosphere of high morals at court and among the general populace, a series of weak emperors toward the end of the Former Han left the dynasty open to the usurpation of Wang Mang. As regent to the child emperor Ping, Wang Mang was well positioned to seize the reins of government and establish his own short-lived Xin dynasty (CE 9–23).

The Later Han Dynasty

Wang Mang's Xin dynasty began to crumble when the Yellow River changed course and devastating floods caused famine and social unrest. In the ensuing general chaos, a large-scale rebellion erupted and the Xin dynasty collapsed. In CE 25 Liu Xiu ascended the throne as Emperor Guangwu, the first legitimate ruler of the Later Han. The dynasty, though spanning 200 years, was weakened by a series of underaged emperors and ambitious regents, empresses, and eunuchs who contended among themselves for power. The final blow was delivered by another large peasant uprising known as the Yellow Turbans. The last ruler of the Later Han, Emperor Xian, meekly abdicated in CE 220.

In the following four centuries, the Han was upheld as an ideal of unity and good order. Though somewhat romanticized by later historians, it was this order that allowed the development of a dazzling array of cultural achievements and technological advances such as paper, refined agricultural implements and techniques, advances in silk and lacquer production, seismographs, and the prototype of the civil service examination. It is no surprise that the dominant ethnic group in China today refers to itself as "people of the Han."

ABOVE **Great Emperor Wu**, the seventh emperor of the Han dynasty, established a strong centralized government and, through military campaigns, almost doubled China's territory.

BELOW **A statue of the First Emperor** looks out over Chengshan Cape, Shandong. Legend has it that the emperor twice came to the Cape seeking herbs to give him everlasting life.

The Path to Power

The last two or three centuries of the Zhou dynasty witnessed radical changes in the political organization of China and rapid progress in the development of technology. States that made the best use of these new developments grew in strength and annexed their weaker neighbors.

ABOVE **Bronze fittings like these were fixed to various forms of dagger axes**, or halberds, which were used as military weapons from the Shang period (1500 BCE) to the Han and beyond.

In 403 BCE, the beginning of Warring States period, only seven major states survived from the more than 170 states of the earlier Spring and Autumn period (722–256 BCE). The geographical locations of these states played a significant role in their survival.

Six of the surviving states clustered around the Yellow River. Because neither Qin nor Chu were surrounded on all sides by well-established Chinese states, they were able to take advantage of this geographical feature to expand their territories and draw an increasingly large population into their cultural sphere.

The Qin did not enter the feudal domain of the Zhou dynasty as a state until the reign of Duke Xiang (reigned 777–766 BCE), some seven centuries after the more well established states. Qin also carried a reputation among the older Chinese states of being culturally different from the more central states. It was considered less civilized and given to practices that were deemed barbaric, such as human sacrifice. Duke Xiao of Qin (reigned 361–337 BCE) was determined to improve Qin's standing in the world, strengthen his state, and regain territory that had been lost in 385 BCE. In pursuit of these goals, Duke Xiao welcomed advisors from any of the other feudal states who might present a plan to help the Qin. The same year, the Legalist reformer Shang Yang arrived in Qin with ideas that would alter the entire course of Chinese history.

ABOVE **The military skills of the Qin dynasty soldiers** played a large part in the conquest of the surrounding weaker states. After death, life-sized replicas were placed in the First Emperor's tomb at Xi'an to keep the emperor safe in the afterlife.

MAINTAINING ORDER

To maintain order in the Qin state, Shang Yang implemented the practice of "group responsibility." This measure involved dividing the entire population into units of five to ten families in which each member was held responsible and punished for the actions of any other member of the group. He also weakened large clans by decreeing that one family could have no more than two adult males living in the same house, and instituted a system of non-hereditary ranks based on meritorious service to the state, usually military or agricultural in nature. Shang Yang promoted the primary occupations of warfare and agriculture while discouraging trade for profit and the circulation of luxury goods. He also called for the standardization of weights and measures—just one of his many policies that focused on keeping clear accounts of state resources. All of these policies set the stage for Qin's eventual victory over the six remaining states.

The Reforms of Shang Yang

In Duke Xiao of Qin, Shang Yang found a ruler ready to listen to his plans for Qin's supremacy. From 350–338 BCE, Shang Yang initiated a series of radical reforms that changed the administration of the state by emphasizing meritocracy and devolving power from the nobility. He established a new capital at Xianyang, divided part of Qin into counties, appointed non-hereditary magistrates to administer them, and allowed people to buy and sell land. Shang Yang stressed a strict legal code as the best tool for governing a state, and proclaimed that this law should apply equally to all people of Qin.

Seven States and One Victor

In 256 BCE, Qin conquered the state of Zhou, bringing the Zhou dynasty to an end, and from 230–221 BCE, Qin destroyed the six remaining kingdoms. Historians in China have long speculated about the reasons for Qin's triumph. Protected by mountains and girded by the Yellow River, the Qin possessed natural defenses that made it difficult to attack. It created irrigation systems and canals which provided crucial water supplies to support agriculture. In addition, Qin kings were mostly competent and long-lived, thus sparing the state violent shifts in policy and rule by under-aged kings. As a state on the periphery of Chinese civilization, Qin is said to have valued

military skills and ruthlessness in war. Their outsider status also made them more open to social, political and cultural innovations and able to make use of talented men from other states.

Uniform Application of the Law

A year after Shang Yang persuaded Duke Xiao to promulgate a new law code, there were numerous complaints. Shang Yang claimed that their discontent stemmed from the failure to punish members of the elite who violated the laws for which the rest of the population were penalized. In order to assuage their complaints, when the Qin heir apparent committed a crime, Shang Yang punished the boy's tutor who was, after all, responsible for the boy's behavior. This object lesson seems to have been effective. We are told that after this incident, the people accepted and obeyed the laws.

However, historical records suggest that a smoldering resentment lay beneath the veneer of Qin's acceptance of the new system, in spite of its astonishing power and efficiency. When Duke Xiao died and the heir apparent came to the throne, disgruntled court factions accused Shang Yang of treason. He fled back to his native state of Wei. However, the people of Wei, still smarting from Shang Yang's attack on their state, sent him back to Qin. There he was killed by Qin forces and his body was torn asunder by two carriages.

ABOVE **Located at Xi'an near the First Emperor's tomb,** this granite statue, created in 1993, celebrates Emperor Qin's unification of China.

Centralization

The First Emperor's most radical policy was to dissolve the feudal aristocracy and their autonomous states and replace them with commanderies that were administered by non-hereditary, centrally appointed officials.

RIGHT **This bronze war drum from the Eastern Zhou era** was obviously prized by countless generations as it was found among relics of a Qin building in Xianyang.

BELOW **Qin Shihuang (the First Emperor),** seen here with two of his ministers overlooking the Yellow Sea, extended the 10,000 *li* wall right up to the Yellow Sea.

When the Zhou conquered the Shang in 1045 BCE, eight centuries before the establishment of the Qin dynasty, King Wu had been faced with the task of ruling a large and wide-ranging territory. To extend Zhou rule across the land, he divided China into fiefs which he bestowed on close relatives of the Zhou royal house. The men who ruled these fiefs were generally titled "dukes," and though somewhat autonomous, all owed fealty to the king. This system worked successfully, until the relationship between the king and the feudal lords became increasingly distant, and the size of the feudal kingdoms began to dwarf the king's domain.

From Feudal Lord to King

In 344 BCE, Duke Hui of Wei, one of the feudal lords, usurped the title king and it was not long before other feudal lords followed suit. In 325 BCE the ruler of the state of Qin followed their lead and also adopted the title of king.

In 221 BCE, when the First Emperor gained control over all the feudal kingdoms, a number of his ministers urged him to continue as King Wu had done and set up his sons and other relatives as kings of the various territories. Wisely, he resisted this temptation and adopted the policy suggested by his most famous adviser, Li Si.

Li Si, Architect of the Qin State

Li Si, who came from the state of Chu, was a student of Xunzi (*c*. 310–218 BCE), the great Confucian philosopher. In spite of an education that stressed cultivating high ideals and ethical leadership, his political career seems to have been primarily motivated by a fondness for power and profit. He was generally reviled by the Confucians and came to be known as an exponent of Legalism, a philosophy that was diametrically opposed to Confucianism. While he was still a student of Xunzi, it became clear to Li Si that his native state was doomed and that Qin would not cease until it had conquered all the feudal states. He therefore traveled west to seek his fortunes in Qin. After proving his usefulness in a variety of government positions, the First Emperor eventually rewarded Li Si by making him chancellor, one of the top posts in the government.

After the First Emperor's final victory over all the feudal states, the court discussed the best way to rule his vast empire. Li Si strongly disagreed with ministers who urged the emperor to grant feudal kingdoms to his relatives. Li Si pointed out that King Wen and King Wu of Zhou had enfeoffed a large number of their relatives who over time had taken to attacking each other as mortal enemies, and even the Son of Heaven had been powerless to stop them. Furthermore, the reason individual kingdoms had been able to grow to their current size and power was not through the efforts of royal kin, but through the increasing use of military and administrative professionals who had no ties to either the state or the state's ruling family. The emperor agreed, adding that the centuries of warfare waged by the feudal lords had plagued the people for centuries.

The emperor went on to divide the empire into 36 commanderies which were to be administered by centrally appointed officials. Thus, with one decree, the political and social system that had been in place for almost a millennium was swept away, affecting both aristocrats and commoners alike.

The Dissolution of the Feudal Kingdoms

In the process of reorganizing the empire, one of the logistic problems that required delicate handling by the emperor was how to maintain control over rebellious, disenfranchised aristocrats. To alleviate this problem, the emperor therefore confiscated all weapons and had them sent to Xianyang, the Qin capital. There the weapons were melted down and recast into large bells, and twelve enormous statues which each weighed some 29 tons (26 metric tons). These were then placed in the palace grounds. The emperor then selected 120,000 of the most wealthy and powerful families from all over the empire and forced them to move their households to the capital where they were placed under strict surveillance. For each feudal state that he annihilated, he built a replica of their palaces in the capital as a way of humbling the people of the conquered state and of giving palpable form to his dominion over them.

On the other hand, his treatment of ordinary people was somewhat different. As had been the case in the state of Qin since the time of Shang Yang, all people in the empire were now graded in a system of 20 non-hereditary ranks (with a woman generally adopting her husband's rank). Individuals had the opportunity to increase their status—which included rights to land, titles, tax remissions, and slaves—but only through military achievement and agricultural production. It was through this system of ranks that the emperor sought to establish a direct relationship between himself and ordinary people, thus overriding any loyalty the people might have previously felt toward clan or kingdom. Although people now also owed the central government taxes, and military and labor services, land was no longer monopolized by the nobility and ordinary citizens were able to buy and sell land. All of these policies worked to buttress the legitimacy of the new imperial government and to obliterate any family or state ties that might prove a challenge to imperial power and authority.

ABOVE **This sculptured bronze head of a warrior** demonstrates not only the skill of Qin artists but also the regard in which the military was held.

Public Works

The power of the Qin rested on warfare and agriculture. Utilizing the forced labor service required of all adult males, the Qin marshaled workers in unprecedented numbers to construct a sophisticated system of roads, canals, and irrigation projects.

One of the First Emperor's greatest projects was to build a series of roads, called *chidao*, which can be literally translated as "expressways." With a terminus in the capital city of Xianyang, these expressways extended east, southeast, north, and northwest.

Roads

It is estimated that the total length of Qin roads was an astonishing 4,250 miles (6,840 km), which surpasses estimates of the extent of Roman roads. The most impressive of these was the Straight Road of Meng Tian.

Meng Tian was one of the Qin Empire's most illustrious generals. In 212 BCE, he was ordered to construct a north–south road measuring some 500 miles (805 km) in length. The road, which was planted with trees every 30 feet, went from the area of modern-day Xi'an to a point 100 miles (160 km) west of the present-day city of Baotou in Inner Mongolia. In an effort to construct a road that was as straight and uniform as possible, Meng Tian cut through mountains and built up valleys. It is conjectured that the end-point of this road provided the Qin government with a means of keeping an eye on the activities of the Xiongnu and other nomadic peoples in the area.

Another feature of Qin roads that formed an important part of the First Emperor's grand unification and standardization scheme was the decree that all vehicles should be equipped with standard-sized axles. Many roads of ancient China were composed of loess, a silty substance that developed deep cement-like ruts. Before Qin's standardization, travelers going from one state to another were forced to realign their axles when entering a state whose cart ruts could not accommodate them.

Canals

Of equal importance to roads were the Qin's numerous hydraulic projects. Among them the Zheng Guo Canal, named for an engineer from the state of Hann. Before the Qin unification, the Hann ruler secretly sent Zheng to Qin with an impressive irrigation plan intended to bankrupt Qin. The king of Qin soon learned about the scheme, but when confronted, Zheng assured the king that his plan was practicable. He was allowed to continue work, resulting in a canal 75 miles (120 km) long, beginning north of Xianyang and reaching as far as the Luo River in the northeast. The canal was built alongside and just north of the Wei River. It provided irrigation for the area north of the Wei River, opening some 450,000 acres of land for cultivation and played a large part in making Qin one of the richest and most powerful states in its time.

The First Emperor also commissioned the construction of "Magic Transport Canal." This waterway linked two rivers in present-day Guangxi Region—the Xiang flowing north; and the Li, flowing south. The canal was designed primarily for freight transport between the Yangzi River in the north, via Lake Dongting and the West River, to Canton in the south. This canal was crucial for shipping supplies to Qin armies in their conquest of the southern kingdom of Yue in 219 BCE. The waterway, which provides a direct route of 1,250 miles (2,012 km) from the lower Yellow River via other canals and rivers, to Canton, has been in continuous use for more than two millennia.

BELOW **This copper cart with horses** was excavated from the First Emperor's tomb in Xi'an. These figures are approximately life size.

LEFT **The Dujiang Yan prevented floods** when the Min River overflowed in summer. At other times, when the river was low, the dam alleviated drought on the western Sichuan Plain.

The Guanxian Irrigation System

Li Bing, who in 250 BCE became the governor of Shu (an area roughly equivalent to present-day Sichuan), was ordered to head a large irrigation project to control the fury of the Mo river and to open up channels to irrigate the region of Chengdu. Li Bing divided the Min River, which flows from the hills north of the Sichuan basin, into two feeder canals. He accomplished this feat by creating a division-head of piled stones that divided the river into the Inner River and the Outer River. The Inner Canal, which was used for irrigation, was created when Li Bing made a cut of 130 feet (40 m) through surrounding rock. The Outer Canal acted as a flood channel. Today, the whole system of canals and dams is known as Dujiang Yan (Capital River Dam).

What had once deluged the area with floods was now used for agricultural purposes. Further-more, millions of small canals were added to the larger ones, extending the irrigation system far beyond its original scope. It prevented both drought and flood, and it also allowed a relatively small area to feed a large population. The canal is still in use today and tourists who visit the area can pay their respects to Li Bing in a temple dedicated to his memory.

The Cost to the People

With improved agricultural output and more efficient communication with the rest of the empire, ordinary people clearly benefited from these public works projects. However, they were forced to rely on the central government to maintain roads, canals, and irrigation systems. In this way, while their living conditions improved they also had to increasingly depend upon the state. The forced labor service required of all adult males also involved work that did not benefit anyone but the emperor himself. Projects such as the construction of some 700 palaces must have generated great resentment among the people and would surely have contributed to the mass rebellion of 209 BCE.

LEFT **A statue to engineers Li Bing and son**, stands in Chengdu. Li Bing wrote of the dam building: "Dredge the riverbed when the water is deep and build low dykes when the water is low."

The Great Wall

The Great Wall, recently proclaimed as one of the New Seven Wonders of the World, was regarded for millennia by the Chinese not as a great cultural achievement but as a symbol of the First Emperor's cruelty and tyranny.

ABOVE **To build the Qin wall,** huge wooden scaffolds were built and forced labor was used to tamp the earth to form high, thick walls. The tamped-earth method is still used in parts of China today.

Evidence of wall building in China extends back as far as remote antiquity. Archaeologists have discovered village walls, dating from China's Neolithic period, that were built using the tamped-earth or rammed-method. To create walls using the tamped-earth method, workers pour soil between two wooden frames and then pound on it with force to create multiple, compacted layers of earth.

The First Walls and Walled Cities

A wall of tamped earth was discovered in Erligang in Henan that dates from the Shang dynasty (1400 BCE). It is 4.3 miles (7 km) long and in places still more than 10 yd (9 m) high. Archaeologists have suggested that the Shang state was actually a small network of walled cities, presided over by a king who moved from settlement to settlement.

The Western Zhou also organized their state around walled cities inhabited by the king and his royal kinsmen, and functioning as military strongholds. Peasant populations lived in the areas that surrounded the walled cities.

After the collapse of the Western Zhou in 771 BCE, individual city states of the Spring and Autumn period, which had populations ranging from 3,000 to 10,000 people, became independent powers who felt less and less obliged to defer to the Zhou king.

Chinese rulers continued to use tamped-earth walls in the Warring States period (475–221 BCE) to mark state borders, and for use as defense against nomadic incursions along the northern frontier. As well as being used for defense, rulers utilized walls to divide their cities into two halves—one half for public and governmental buildings and the other half for residential, commercial and industrial purposes. As they grew, large Warring States cities constructed outer walls measuring some fifteen miles (24 km) around and had populations of more than 200,000 people.

At the beginning of the Qin dynasty (221 BCE), the First Emperor ordered the demolition of city walls throughout the empire in order to cripple the defenses of these former states. He then began wall construction on his own terms.

The Qin Wall

One of the largest construction projects of the Qin dynasty was a new border defense system referred to as the "ten-thousand *li* long wall" (one *li* was equivalent to 546 yd or 500 m). After conquering his rivals among the Chinese feudal states, the first emperor then set his sights on the nomads in the north. He sent his general Meng Tian with 300,000 men to drive the nomads out of the north and begin work constructing frontier fortifications to guard the territory.

Meng Tian repaired and connected existing Warring States walls rather than building an entirely new wall. The Qin work went on for ten years and the construction was in many respects far more complex than building a stationary monument such as a pyramid, due to the shifting terrain and ever-increasing distance between the source of supplies and the building site.

It has been argued that in Qin times, there was not one "Great Wall," but a system of walls, which served primarily to mark the border and set up a line of defense, and were not intended as an impenetrable barrier. Indeed, close readings of early evidence provide little in the way of proof for the existence of one monumental wall called the Great Wall.

Very little remains of the wall erected by the First Emperor. Archaeologists have identified sections of surviving Qin walls in Shanxi, Gansu, Hebei, and Liaoning provinces. Qin walls were almost certainly constructed primarily of tamped

developed strategies for dealing with the problem, including offensive warfare, diplomatic relations, or intermarriage, but none seemed to present a permanent solution. Wall building was frequently criticized because it was so expensive and required enormous state resources.

The Wall as Security

Defensive walls meant different things to the Chinese people at different periods of their history. We can arrive at a more nuanced understanding of the variety of meanings the Chinese have ascribed to the wall if we examine its changing significance in legend.

One early legend, which is regarded by some as a reliable historical account, illustrates the concept of defensive walls as the foundation of the state's security. The tale relates to the last king of the Western Zhou dynasty, King You (reigned c. 781–771 BCE), who had a concubine named Bao Si. Because she rarely smiled, King You went to great lengths to amuse her. Finally

LEFT **The Qin "ten-thousand *li* long wall"** was built of tamped earth, and only remnants—such as this section near Hengshan, Shaanxi Province—remain.

earth, and occasionally clay, twigs, and gravel. They were built quickly for defense at specific places and eroded easily if not maintained. In contrast, the Ming dynasty wall visitors see today near Beijing was built with stone.

It is clear that the main impetus for wall building along China's northern frontier was the almost continuous threat nomads began to pose to Chinese peace and order from the middle of the first millennium BCE onward. Each dynasty

BELOW **The Jiayuguan Pass** in Gansu Province was the first pass at the west end of the Wall. It was built during the Ming Dynasty.

he discovered he could induce her to smile by lighting the capital's beacon fires—the emergency warning system that brought troops to the rescue in the event of an enemy attack. To use this signaling system, a fire was lit on a watch tower. When the sentry at the next tower saw the flame, he lit his beacon fire, and so on all along the Wall to alert defending soldiers and send for help. In the case of King You, when troops arrived, they found the fires had been lit only to please Bao Si.

Bao Si's entertainment was soon to have fatal consequences for the dynasty. After repeating this trick several times, when Barbarians and rebels actually descended on the capital and You lit the beacon fires, no one came to his rescue. The barbarians murdered the king, captured Bao Si, took up all of the king's ancestral treasures, and fled. This event brought the Western Zhou dynasty to an end. Lines from a poem about these events says: "A clever man builds walls for cities,/A clever woman tears walls down." In this poem, wall building is associated with shoring up one's safety from Barbarian incursion, the health of the dynasty and the forces of civilization. The poem serves as a warning to the ruler who shifts his priorities from maintaining defensive fortifications to indulging his private fancies.

The Wall as Symbol of a Tyrant

One of the earliest accounts in which the Qin Wall is reviled concerns the tragic fate of Meng Tian, the Qin general who oversaw the wall's construction. He was falsely accused of a crime by the First Emperor's son and subsequently sentenced to die. Musing on why Heaven should decree his punishment in spite of his innocence, he surmised that his crime had been to "cut the arteries of the earth" during the construction of the Wall. His own assessment of the Wall seemed to be that it was an arrogant effort to reconfigure nature to conform to the will of Qin.

The same dimwitted son of the First Emperor also proposed the absurd idea of lacquering the city walls. One of his sarcastic courtiers remarked that, "It would be a large expense and a burden on the people, but just think how nice it would look!" The courtier then composed a verse, which went something like: "Lacquered walls—how brilliant!/When rebels come, down they'll slip!" The idea was dropped.

Although the First Emperor had used the Wall to clear the nomads from the whole Ordos area, they reclaimed their territory soon after he died. Thus, in the next dynasty, that of the Han, the Qin Wall becomes a symbol of the worthlessness of the First Emperor's defense system and of his cruelty toward his people. Stressing the experience of those who labored and even died for the First Emperor's Wall, the following poem was written in about 217 CE.

> *I watered my horses at the Long Wall Well,*
> *The cold water stings my horses' bones.*
> *I tell the officer at the Long Wall,*
> *"Don't detain us Taiyuan men forever!*
> *Conscript labor has a limit!*
> *Swing your hammers! Raise your cries!*
> *We would rather die fighting!*
> *Why be bored building the Long Wall?"*

> *The Long Wall twists and turns,*
> *Twists and turns three thousand miles.*
> *Border towns are full of strong young lads,*
> *Villages are full of widowed wives.*

The most famous tale from the tradition of the Wall as the whim of a tyrant is the story of Meng Jiangnü. According to the legend, the husband of Meng Jiangnü had been sent to perform conscript labor on the wall. As winter loomed, Meng set out to take warm clothes to her husband. When she finally arrived at the Wall, she learned that her husband was dead. To make matters worse, his body had been used as fill in the wall. Meng Jiangnü, overcome with grief, knelt down and wept. The intensity of her grief, however, broke open the wall and revealed her husband's bones. She then collected the bones and returned to her native village to give them a proper burial. People in traditional China hearing this story would say that it was Heaven who heard the cries of Meng Jiangnü, and, responding to her sense of sorrow and injustice, made the wall fall down. Thus, the wall in this story symbolizes not only human suffering but divine wrath.

Symbol of Chinese Ingenuity

In the 1970s the Chinese Government sought to present the First Emperor of Qin as a cultural hero; they were fueled, perhaps, by the discovery of the Qin terracotta army in 1974. At the same time, Mao Zedong was compared favorably with the First Emperor. This abrupt about-face, therefore, also required that Meng Jiangnü be painted as a counter-revolutionary. The campaign to impute Meng Jiangnü's character even resulted in school children being asked to write essays denouncing the erstwhile heroine. Nevertheless, from the early twentieth century onward, the Great Wall has lost its bad reputation and come to represent Chinese genius and ingenuity.

ABOVE **Wherever there were large bolders** in the path of the Wall, they were included in the fortifications.

A GREAT WALL BUT NOT THE GREAT WALL

The wall we see today on the outskirts of Beijing is not the Qin Wall, but one built in the Ming dynasty (CE 1368–1644). When the Ming began construction of their defensive wall, they wanted to avoid association with the despised Qin Wall which was regarded as the work of a tyrant and utterly lacking in military utility. So they called their fortifications "border walls" rather than the earlier Qin term "long walls." However, their wall, too, proved a failure when it became clear that it did nothing to stop the people it had been designed to keep out. It was not until after the fall of the Qing dynasty in 1911, that the Wall, as an example of engineering genius, became a symbol of Chinese national identity and pride.

LEFT **The Great Wall at Badaling** is on the highest section of the Jundu mountain and historically protected the Juyongguan Pass. It was the first section to open for tourism in 1957.

Cultural Unification

The Qin achieved political unification of China under one supreme ruler.
This process went far beyond the imposition of a new administrative
structure. Equally important was the unification of culture.

BELOW **While most of the bindings** have not survived, the bamboo strips that made up these ancient books have, and they provide a wealth of information.

The legal code devised by Shang Yang for the state of Qin was applied to every person in the Qin Empire. The primary objective of applying punishments and standardized rewards was to encourage the people to intensify their efforts in the sphere of agriculture and warfare. Early Chinese historians have vilified Qin's legal system, leveling the harshest criticism against both its cruel punishments and its totalitarian policy of group responsibility among family members and the five- and ten-person groups into which the Qin state organized the entire population. The discovery of more than 600 bamboo legal documents from the Qin dynasty, excavated at Shuihudi in Hubei Province in 1975, has provided a somewhat more measured view of the legal system.

The Standardization of Law

Scholars who have studied the bamboo documents note the extreme care with which Qin officials carried out their tasks of investigating cases, conducting interrogations, preparing written reports, and arraying evidence. The documents also show evidence of concern with the intentions of the accused to determine, for example, whether the crime was premeditated or involuntary. In addition, there is evidence that all those who knew about a certain crime were to be punished along with the offender. In contrast to what is said in received texts, about the universal application of the law to all individuals, the bamboo texts show that people of higher rank generally received lighter punishments than their inferiors.

In addition to criminal law, the excavated texts also cover administrative statutes concerned with managing conscript labor and reporting on local agricultural output, as well as grain storage and distribution. The complexity and legal sophistication of these texts are yet more evidence to disprove the idea that the Qin state, positioned on the periphery of the old feudal states, was backward and barbarous.

The Standardization of Script

The First Emperor also initiated the standardization of script as another important part of cultural unification. With such great emphasis placed on law and bureaucratic procedure, it is not surprising that the First Emperor took such a measure to insure that state documents could be read by all concerned.

language reform, it is unlikely that China would have enjoyed its astonishing cultural and political continuity, as a common written language was the foundation on which it was built.

Standardization of Weights, Measures, and Currency

The Qin state could maintain its supremacy only by strict husbanding of human, military, and natural resources. The First Emperor's call for the standardization of weights, measures, and currency was one more aspect of the imperial obsession with knowing precise numbers of men who could be drafted for military or conscript labor, the value of taxes they were expected to pay, the amount of grain they would consume, and the kinds of equipment they would be issued for public work projects. The legal documents from Shuihudi contain many laws stating the system of fines and punishments for issuing grain that was over or under weight and for the loss or damage of tools.

Standardization of weights, measures, and language also facilitated trade and commerce throughout the empire. In various places across China, archaeologists have found Qin bronze measuring vessels, and have determined that they are indeed uniform.

Currency was also standardized under the Qin state. Before the Qin dynasty, different states had minted their own, different shaped coins, but these were replaced by just two types of coins, of bronze and gold. The more common bronze coins were round with square holes and were inscribed with the words "one liang" (half an ounce or 14 g), which is also how much they actually weighed.

LEFT **The top character is the word for** "forest" and looks rather like two trees; the bottom charcter, the word "to drip," contains the same characters to indicate the pronunciation.

Contrary to widespread belief, written Chinese is, for the most part, not pictographic, although there are pictographic elements in the language. Chinese is also not a phonetic script, although there is a phonetic element to the language. For example, consider the word for "forest". It is pronounced *lin* and the written characters for the word are somewhat pictographic, being made up of two identical graphs that denote "tree." There is nothing in the graph, however, that tells the reader how to pronounce the word; the pronunciation just has to be learned. *Lin* is also the spoken word for the verb "to drip." The written word combines the two tree characters in *lin*, but only to show that the sound of the word is "lin". Next to the two trees is a graph denoting water. This element is called the radical and hints at the meaning of the word, whereas the two trees simply hint at the pronunciation. Thus, the reader is told that the word is pronounced *lin* and that it has something to do with water.

In spite of the complexities inherent in this system, the non-phonetic nature of the language allowed people across a wide area of East Asia who spoke different dialects (and later different languages, as was the case in China and Korea) to all use one writing system. The trouble in China was that as time passed, variations on the written language began to emerge so that there was no accepted standard form.

One of the first tasks the First Emperor set Li Si was to unify the script. This seems to have involved standardizing forms that had varied over time and geographical region, and simplification (by reducing the number of strokes for writing certain elements in the character). Without Qin's

BELOW **Qin replaced the odd-shaped coins** used previously and introduced round coins. The square holes allowed people to string them together.

The Control of Knowledge

In 213 BCE, the First Emperor made unlawful the private possession of all books apart from those concerning agriculture, divination, and medicine. All other books were proscribed and the people of Qin were ordered to burn them on pain of death.

Legalism formed the ideological foundation of the Qin state, teaching that the stability of the state rests not on the ruler's virtue and charisma, as the Confucians taught, but on a system of rewards and punishments spelled out clearly and upheld uniformly in a legal code. Nevertheless, the prestige connected with higher learning and state rituals was so great that even an empire predicated upon Legalist thought could not afford to neglect a body of learning associated with classical Confucian scholarship.

The Scholars

The First Emperor employed a body of some 72 specialists in classical texts, who were called "erudites," to advise him on religious rituals as well as matters of state. The employment of erudites was not a Qin innovation but had been commonplace in a number of states before the Qin conquest. Forming the basis of scholarship were The Five Classics. These were a compilation comprising the *Book of Odes*, the *Book of Rites*, the *Book of Documents*, the *Book of Changes,* and the *Spring and Autumn Annals.* Scholars of the Warring States era (453–221 BCE) were particularly fond of quoting, as historical precedent, passages from the *Book of Odes* and The *Book of Documents*—thus using the past to indirectly criticize current policies.

Criticizing the Emperor

During a feast held by the First Emperor in his palace in 213 BCE, 70 erudites came forward to toast his longevity. One man stepped forward and praised the emperor for his virtue and power. The emperor was pleased, but then another man, called Chunyu Yue, came forward and criticized the emperor for having broken with tradition by not ennobling imperial family members in the manner of the former Zhou kings. Moreover, he called the first man a disloyal flatterer, pointing out that the man's praise only served to perpetuate the emperor's errors.

At this point, the chancellor, Li Si, stepped in and castigated Chunyu Yue, explaining to the emperor that only a "stupid Confucian" would attempt to model government on antiquity rather than changing with the times and adopting policies that were more suited to contemporary

EXECUTION OF THE SCHOLARS

More heinous than the burning of the books is the charge that the First Emperor ordered the execution of some 460 scholars who had criticized of him. The incident is made more gruesome by the claim that the scholars were buried alive as a punishment. Close study of the historical accounts, however, prompts many scholars to doubt that the First Emperor ever ordered this mass execution. Even scholars who believe that the purge actually took place, tend to discredit the claim that the scholars were buried alive, and interpret the text to mean that they were executed in a more conventional manner.

RIGHT **This etching portrays a Westerner's view** of the First Emperor in the process of burning books and executing scholars. The name of the artist is unknown.

that were bound together like Venetian blinds. The characters were written vertically on each strip and the text was read from right to left. When not in use, the books were rolled up for storage.

In addition to the confiscation and burning of the books, anyone who merely discussed the *Book of Odes* or the *Book of Documents*, would be subject to execution in the marketplace. Anyone who criticized the present by using ancient precedents would also suffer execution, together with all of his or her family members. Those who did not deliver books to government offices for destruction would be liable to tattooing and forced convict labor duty.

Most modern scholars believe that the effects of the burning of the books were not, in fact, quite as devastating as once thought. After all, the decree did not call for the total destruction of targeted literature; the collections in the imperial library were to remain intact. Furthermore, scholars tended to memorize texts such as the *Book of Odes*, so that textual versions could be reconstituted from memory. In the next dynasty, Emperor Wu initiated an empire-wide recovery of the ancient texts. Books by the cartload sent to the capital as part of this effort are said to have formed mounds as high as mountains.

LEFT **Following the book burnings,** new histories were written. Sima Qian was to complain that his work was made difficult because these Qin histories were inaccurate and vague.

BELOW **Carefully recorded on bamboo strips,** the thoughts of generations of writers were believed to have been lost in the fires.

concerns and conditions. Li Si also claimed that Confucians made criticizing the ruler a point of pride, warning that such a practice would only embolden lesser officials to oppose their own superiors and dispute the law. Li Si argued that just as the First Emperor had unified all of China, he had also established a single source of authority, and to allow dissenting opinions based on classical scholarship would compromise both. In order to remedy the situation, Li Si proposed the famous Qin bibliocaust.

The Burning of the Books

It was decreed by the First Emperor that all historical records apart from those of the state of Qin be burned. An important exception was made for the erudites, whose official duties required use of these texts. Any person who had in their possession private copies of the *Book of Odes*, the *Book of Documents*, or any other schools of philosophy were ordered to deliver them to state officials for incineration. Books concerning forestry, medicine, or divination were exempt from these prohibitions.

The burning of the books must have caused a huge conflagration. Prior to the invention of paper, most books were made of bamboo strips

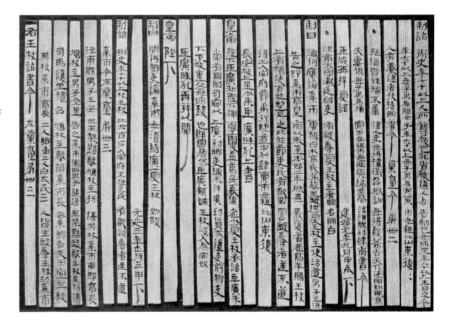

The Tomb of Qin Shihuang

The Power and Prestige of an Emperor

The terracotta army represents the emperor's control over the resources of his newly unified empire, and his attempt to recreate and maintain that empire in the afterlife.

For millennia, readers of Chinese history have read with a mixture of horror and delight accounts of the massive tomb complex constructed by Qin Shihuang, the First Emperor, for his final resting place.

Work began on the tomb when Qin Shihuang became King of Qin in 246 BCE. It was the standard practice of monarchs of the time, who needed plenty of lead-time to build their imposing final resting places, to begin work early in their reign. In 212 BCE, the First Emperor sent 700,000 convicts condemned to castration and hard labor to Mt. Li to work on the mausoleum. This number does not include the skilled craftsmen, artisans and engineers who must also have contributed their labor to the project. The tomb was finally finished, 36 years later, soon after Qin's death.

The tomb is situated beneath a man-made hill. Originally measuring some 1,675 by 1,575 ft (510 by 480 m), the tomb mound has eroded somewhat over the centuries. Inside, the tomb was equipped with replicas of palaces and towers as well as statues of civil and military officials. Crossbows were rigged to shoot anyone who broke into the tomb. The tomb was also made to represent the entire world, including rivers and seas made of mercury that seemed to move and flow, and a ceiling decorated with representations of the heavens.

While the tomb chamber itself has not been excavated, the scale and number of the artifacts in the surrounding area is staggering. More than 7,000 terracotta statues, interestingly not mentioned in early historical accounts of the tomb, have been excavated from the site.

Concealing the Army

The warriors were placed in corridors constructed with earthen walls. Wooden planks placed over the walls and covered with mats acted as roofing. The whole was then covered with earth.

Most of the statues portray soldiers, complete with horses, armor, and weapons, arranged in military formations ready for battle. Scholars speculate that the terracotta warriors were originally painted in bright colors and were equipped with real weapons, which may have been plundered by rebels at the end of the Qin. However, some bronze arrowheads, crossbow triggers, and swords have been found. An astonishing feature of the warrior statues is the individual modeling of their faces, hair, and head-gear, with no two the same. Entertainers are also included among the emperor's retinue, including acrobats, musicians and wrestlers. Scientists who have studied the site have also discovered unnaturally high concentrations of mercury in the soil, a result consistent with early records describing mercury rivers and seas that formed part of the mausoleum.

Archaeologists working on the First Emperor's mausoleum are far from finished with their work. The most important task will be to excavate his actual tomb. For the time being, scholars have advised patience and caution, wanting no attempts to be made to disturb one of the world's most significant archaeological finds until they have the technical skills that will allow excavations to proceed without danger of destroying any part of the site. Historical evidence suggests that the tomb has been looted more than once, probably after the fall of the Qin and again several centuries later. Archaeologists have also found signs of breakage and fire damage around the periphery of the tomb. However, studies suggest that the actual tomb chamber is still intact and has probably not been looted.

An Army of Individuals

Each soldier and official in the tomb is unique, with its own style of dress and individual face. The figures were originally painted in bright colors.

Wanted: A Few Good Men

The sheer number of condemned men (some 700,000) at the disposal of the First Emperor for this construction project is in itself an indictment of the Qin legal system. The site has yielded numerous graves of men aged 20 to 40 years who must have died during the building of the tomb. Concubines who had not given birth were also buried with the emperor, as were the craftsmen who knew the secret entrances to the tomb. The emperor also sent 30,000 households to tend his tomb site at Mt. Li. These families were rewarded with exemption of taxes and labor service for ten years, motivated, no doubt, for reasons other than his kind concern for the people.

The Overthrow of the Qin

The First Emperor died in 210 BCE and his incompetent son Hu Hai, known as the
Second Emperor, came to the throne, worsening an already tense political climate.
In a matter of months, the people prepared for revolt.

RIGHT **Qin Shihuang,**
who probably died from
swallowing mercury pills
intended to give him
immortal life, feared death
and never wrote a will. Hu
Hai, therefore, forged one.

The First Emperor died unexpectedly in the
summer of 210 BCE, during an imperial
progress on which he was accompanied by
one of his favorite younger sons, Hu Hai; the
chancellor, Li Si; and a eunuch named Zhao Gao.
Because they were far from the capital, Zhao,
Hu, and Li feared unrest if news of the emperor's
death became known. They therefore kept his
death secret until they were able to return. The
delayed announcement provided the three men
with an opportunity to lay plans to seize control.

Succession Conspiracy

Two years before the First Emperor's death, the
emperor had quarreled with his eldest son, the
heir apparent Fu Su, over the execution of
scholars critical of his reign. Fu Su had gently
urged moderation on his father. The First
Emperor's response had been to send Fu Su
away from the capital to the northern frontier
to oversee operations with General Meng Tian.

Fu Su remained heir apparent, but his official
designation as the next ruler was known only to
Zhao Gao, since the emperor refused to speak
to anyone about his own death. It was also Zhao
Gao who held in his possession the official
documents concerning Fu Su's appointment. On
the emperor's death, Zhao Gao proposed to Li Si
and Hu Hai that Hu Hai succeed his father rather
than Fu Su. In addition, Zhao Gao proposed that
he should become chief of palace attendants and
that Li Si should remain chancellor.

Knowing that they would not be able to
maintain their positions of power under the rule
of Fu Su, Hu Hai and Li Si reluctantly agreed to
Zhao Gao's scheme. Next, they forged an imperial decree naming Hu Hai as the heir apparent,
as well as a letter charging Fu Su with various
crimes and ordering him to take his own life.
When Fu Su received the letter he accepted
unquestioningly that the decree had come from
his father's hand and committed suicide.

Li Si, Hu Hai, and Zhao Gao then returned to
the capital, adding a cart full of dried fish to their
retinue to disguise the odor of the emperor's
decomposing body. They announced the death
of the emperor when they arrived in Xianyang.
At 20 years old, Hu Hai assumed the throne as
the Second Emperor but he was little more than
a pawn of Zhao Gao.

The Second Emperor

At the suggestion of Zhao Gao, one of the first
acts of the Second Emperor's brief reign was to
strike fear in the minds of anyone who might
challenge his rule. He therefore laid trumped-up
charges against chief ministers of state, the
imperial princes, and palace attendants. He also
put six imperial princes (his brothers) to death.

In the seventh month of the Second Emperor's
reign, officials reported that the leader of a rebel
force, Chen She, had set himself up as king. The
official who reported the revolt to the Second
Emperor was charged with slander and punished.
Thereafter, whenever the Second Emperor
questioned officials about the area outside the

In 207 BCE, Zhao Gao realized he would soon suffer the same fate as Li Si if he did not take matters into his own hands. Zhao Gao therefore confronted the Second Emperor and forced him to commit suicide. He then set up as ruler Ziying, one of the emperor's nephews. Several days later, Ziying murdered Zhao Gao along with his three sets of relatives. However, Ziying's reign was to last a mere 46 days. It was brought to an end by another rebel leader, Liu Bang, who tendered Ziying's abdication. The empire was now divided among a shifting series of rebel kings.

Chen She

The rebellion against the Qin had begun in 209 BCE with Chen She, an ordinary man who had been assigned for garrison duty on the northern frontier along with nine hundred other men from his region. The men encountered heavy rains along the way which frequently made the roads impassable, and they had no hope of arriving in Yuyang on time. Since the punishment for late arrival was death, Chen decided that he might as well take the opportunity to rebel as he would probably end up

capital, they concealed the truth and told him that there was nothing to worry about. Across the realm, the oppressed rose up and murdered Qin officials and joined Chen She's revolt. When chaos was so widespread that the Second Emperor could no longer be deceived, he blamed the rebellion on Li Si. He had him executed and made Zhao Gao chancellor.

LEFT **The first emperor,** fearing assassination, became secretive on tours of his empire, hiring doubles and moving constantly. This habit made concealing his death very easy.

BELOW **Weaponry in the Qin and Han dynasties** included bows, spears, sabers, and war chariots, as depicted on this clay tomb brick relief.

RIGHT **Before Liu Bang's final battle with Xiang Yu,** Zhang Liang climbed Mt. Ji Ming and played tunes from the homelands of Xiang's troops, causing 6,000 homesick soldiers to desert.

XIANG YU'S BIBLIOCAUST

Though the First Emperor of Qin is known for the burning of the books in 213 BCE, in fact, Xiang Yu's torching of the Qin capital in 207 BCE was far more destructive of book culture. Although the First Emperor had prohibited the private ownership of almost all books during the Qin, he still retained copies of the proscribed books for use by the officials who required access to these texts as part of their jobs. Since the last Qin king had already surrendered, the destructiveness of Xiang Yu's act is all the more abhorrent for its utter senselessness.

dead in either case. He killed his commanding officer and invited the men of his garrison to join his uprising. All of the men joined the rebellion, eventually mobilizing a force of 700 chariots, 1,000 horsemen, and 30,000 soldiers.

Chen She's men made him king of Chu, after which people in even more provinces murdered Qin officials and joined his cause. Chen She was assassinated only six months later by a Qin loyalist, but by that time the entire empire was convulsed in revolution. Among a series of short-lived kings, two men emerged as the final combatants for the imperial throne. They were Xiang Yu, an aristocratic general, and Liu Bang, a man of peasant background who served in a minor bureaucratic post as village head.

Xiang Yu

Xiang Yu came from a long line of generals in the state of Chu. His grandfather had been forced to commit suicide by a Qin general. When Chen She's rebellion spread, Xiang Yu seized the opportunity to avenge his grandfather and bring about Qin's destruction.

Considered to be one of the greatest generals of his day, Xiang Yu was extremely tall and possessed great physical strength. However, he was also known to be arrogant, impulsive, cruel, and vindictive. Despite his negative qualities,

other rebel leaders grudgingly cooperated with him because of his stellar success in fighting the Qin and the enormous number of men who had joined his ranks.

By 206 BCE, Xiang Yu had almost solidified his position to become the next ruler of the Chinese empire. He wanted to rule China from one powerful kingdom as a hegemon-king. To maintain the cooperation of rebel generals, and also to restore the old feudal states of China, Xiang Yu divided up the territory of China and set up 18 kings over these territories. However, the newly minted kings soon began to attack each other. In particular, Liu Bang, now King of Han, felt that Xiang Yu had cheated him of the territory he had fairly won. He therefore seized the region of Qin. Liu Bang and Xiang Yu then fought for the next four years until Liu Bang emerged as the unlikely victor.

Liu Bang

In contrast to Xiang Yu, Liu Bang hailed from a humble background. He was lenient, approachable, generous, and loved wine. He was able to inspire intense loyalty among his men, but could also be ruthless and boorish. Chinese historians generally praise him for his ability to accept criticism, admit error, and understand and avail himself of each person's best skills and qualities.

In 207 BCE, when Liu Bang defeated the Qin army and was about to enter its capital, he sent messengers to Ziying, the last king of Qin, urging him to surrender. Ziying agreed and presented Liu Bang with his seals of authority. One of Liu Bang's men urged him to kill Ziying, but Liu Bang refused, saying that it would bring bad luck to kill someone who had already surrendered.

When Liu Bang entered the capital, he refrained from enjoying the spoils. Instead he sealed up the palaces and treasuries. Before returning to his camp, he assembled the elders and officials of the area. He told them that he had made an agreement with Xiang Yu that whoever first conquered the area of the Qin capital would become king of that territory. He told them that he was now their king, and in recognition of their suffering under the Qin, promised a law code that consisted of only three articles: the death penalty was to be reserved for murders alone, that those who stole would be judged according to the severity of the crime, as would those who injured others. He assured the officials that he had become king so that he could protect them from further harm, not in order to exploit them.

However, Xiang Yu went back on his promise to give Qin to Liu Bang if Liu was first to seize it. Since Liu's forces were outnumbered by Xiang Yu's, Liu had no choice but to cede the area to Xiang Yu who thereupon entered Xianyang, killed Ziying, massacred the inhabitants and burned the city and palaces. It was not until 202 BCE that Liu Bang finally defeated

ABOVE **Terracotta horses** were stabled in the Qin emperor's tomb. Fighting was largely on horseback, and the Qin wall was built just high enough to prevent cavalry jumping over it.

Xiang Yu. Surrounded on all sides by Liu Bang's troops, Xiang Yu cut his own throat and was subsequently torn limb from limb by soldiers who were eager to claim the reward for bringing his head to Liu Bang.

Reasons for the Fall of Qin

Traditional Chinese accounts of why Qin fell tend to blame to the First Emperor's inability to tolerate criticism, his harsh laws and punishments, his ruthless mobilization of staggering numbers of conscript laborers for his construction projects, his scorn for Confucian moral values, and his ignorance of history. Most important of all was his failure to understand that the ability to wage war and the ability to maintain an empire in peace time are not the same thing. Historians argue that the people would have gladly embraced the Second Emperor if he had made only modest efforts to correct his father's excesses. Instead, he made the situation even worse by multiplying the laws, increasing taxes, and making punishments even harsher. The hungry, accused, and exploited became so numerous, that the rebellion of one man was enough to stir the entire nation to join him.

LEFT **Liu Bang's success** owes much to his skills as a leader. Born of peasant parents, he was apparently pleasant and generous. Men flocked to Liu Bang's side to join him in the rebellion.

Imperial Rule

Liu Bang, who reigned from 202 to 195 BCE, won the empire through his military genius. The more abstract project of establishing symbols of his authority required the specialized services of Confucian advisers and officials skilled in civil affairs.

Liu Bang, who reigned as Emperor Gaozu, had made his way to the throne using his ability as a general on the battlefield. Although he had served as village head, he was of peasant background and had received little or no formal education. He therefore had little patience with Confucian scholars who stressed the importance of ancient history, institutions, and rituals. In fact, there is a story that when a Confucian scholar once offered him advice, Liu Bang snatched the man's hat and urinated in it to show his contempt.

Establishing a Civil Society

Once Liu Bang became emperor, however, he began to understand the utility of Confucian learning. He was impressed, for example, with the diplomatic skills of Lu Jia, who had persuaded a renegade king to acknowledge his allegiance to the Han and thereby prevented an armed conflict. However, when Lu Jia began lecturing the emperor on lessons drawn from various classical texts, the emperor told Lu that since everything he had achieved had been done on horseback, why should he have any need for book learning? Lu's famous reply was, "An empire can be won on horseback, but it can't be ruled on horseback." Lu Jia also pointed out that the Qin dynasty had collapsed because it had stressed military conquest, strict laws, and a system of rewards and punishments at the expense of creating a moral and civil society.

Impressed with his argument, the emperor asked Lu Jia to write a series of essays explaining why Qin had lost, why Han had won, and how various states in antiquity had failed or managed to survive. The resulting essays seem to have made Emperor Gaozu receptive to Confucian teachings. Whether he was heeding the advice of Lu Jia or simply following Qin precedent, Emperor Gaozu decided to appoint a number of learned men to serve as erudites.

Establishing a New Court

Although the nobles conferred upon Liu Bang the title of emperor, he refused to follow the elaborate ceremonies that the Qin had followed. He also simplified court rituals. However, his courtiers and ministers, many of whom had been military men, were prone to drinking and brawling in the palace. One had actually taken to hacking away at the wooden pillars of the palace with his sword.

Even the emperor was disgusted with the behavior of his court. Consequently, an erudite named Shusun Tong offered to draw up new court rituals for their use. Gaozu's only comment was, "Just don't make it too difficult! It has to be something I can actually do!" Shusun Tong brought a group of scholars together. Over the course of a month they experimented in a roped-off enclosure using stand-ins for the emperor and court. When Shusun presented the new ritual to Gaozu, the emperor was pleased, and was confident he would be able to follow it.

BELOW **A lacquered wooden chamber pot with silver inlays like this one, would have been a more fitting receptacle for an emperor than the scholar's hat he once used in court.**

After the completion of the Palace of Enduring Joy, Emperor Gaozu summoned various nobles and officials to his court to witness the ceremony. The new ritual was performed without any difficulty, and any who did not perform their role correctly were promptly thrown out. Even after the drinking began, all of the guests behaved with perfect decorum. So pleased was Gaozu with the changed atmosphere at court, that he told his asembled guests that it was on this occasion that he understood for the first time the honor and dignity that came with being an emperor.

The palace itself had been planned by Gaozu's prime minister, Xiao He, who had also been charged with setting up a dynastic temple, altars, and various bureaucratic offices. Xiao He completed the palace in 199 BCE. When he presented it to Gaozu, the emperor was furious. "The empire is far from secure, why on earth have you built something so excessively opulent?" Xiao He explained that he had constructed the palace on such a magnificent scale precisely because the empire was still in such turmoil. With no outward symbol of his power and authority, the whole world would come to regard Gaozu as just another self-proclaimed warlord. Moreover, the palace would establish a firm legacy for his heirs and the dynasty as a whole.

In the end, Gaozu was pleased, although his father—a simple peasant—refused to move in until a section of the palace had been redesigned to look exactly like his native village, complete with chickens, dogs, and all of his neighbors, who had been moved there to keep him company.

Establishing a Bureaucracy

Another challenge for the early Han state was that of finding an adequate number of suitable men to staff the bureaucracy. In 196 BCE, Emperor Gaozu sent out an edict urging qualified men to send their qualifications to provincial offices for review. He sought men who were capable, virtuous and of good reputation. Officials who knew of such candidates were ordered to provide them with transport to local government offices where their appearance, age, and achievements, were to be recorded and then forwarded to the capital. As a legalist twist on this rather Confucian call for worthy officials, the emperor added that any official who knew of such qualified men, but did not see fit to recommend them, would be dismissed.

With an apparatus now in place for finding men to staff the Han bureaucracy, the construction of an imposing palace to display his power, and the creation of new dignified court rituals, and Emperor Gaozu had laid a firm foundation for one of China's longest and most glorious dynasties.

ABOVE **Cavalry** were a vital part of Han armies and horses came to be regarded as symbols of the empire's power and outstanding achievement. This image is from a Han tomb.

LEFT **This terracotta figure** displays the style of dress and armor worn by Han generals. The Han dynasty's greatest general and founder was Liu Bang.

Consolidation

After the military victory of the Han, Emperor Gaozu and his close advisers turned their attention to consolidating Han power, designing a new administrative structure for their empire, and strengthening their bonds with the common people.

ABOVE **Tomb bricks** were often impressed with scenes of entertainment to amuse the departed in the afterlife.

BELOW RIGHT **Dependency on agriculture** is reflected in the placing of replicas of farm tools and animals in tombs to ensure the survival of the occupants.

When Emperor Gaozu assumed the imperial throne in 202 BCE, he was forced to recognize seven kings who were not members of the imperial Liu clan. Moreover, not one member of the imperial clan held the title of king. As the seven kings soon proved a threat to Han stability, Gaozu had to devote much of his eight-year reign to quashing their rebellions. By the time of his death in 195 BCE, Gaozu's endeavours had reversed the situation. Now nine of his relatives held kingdoms.

Threat from the Lü Clan

After Gaozu's death, Han supremacy was again under threat. Gaozu's son, a minor, reigned as Emperor Hui for only eight years before he died. During this time Gaozu's widow, Empress Lü, served as de facto ruler. She appointed four of her nephews as kings despite her deceased husband's rule excluding from kingship all who were not members of the Liu imperial family.

After Emperor Hui's death in 188 BCE, Empress Lü installed two boys she claimed were sons of Emperor Hui. This enabled her to remain in her position as ruler. She worked quickly to ennoble as many Lü males as possible as a means of shoring up her own power. When she died in 180 BCE, the Lü family saw its chance and rebelled. However, within a relatively short period, Liu loyalists eliminated the rebels.

The Lü rebellion, Empress Lü's domination of court politics, and the installation of two minors of indeterminate parentage alerted the Han dynasty to the importance of maintaining strict control over imperial consort families and the selection of heirs to the throne. Some scholars believe that Emperor Wen (reigned 180–157 BCE) was chosen to succeed Emperor Hui, at least in part, because of the scarcity of his mother's and his wife's male kin.

Winning the Allegiance of the Common People

The imperial family made a concerted effort to garner support for newly installed heirs to the throne in various ways. For example, in 179 BCE and 150 BCE, on the occasion of naming a new

EMPEROR WEN'S COMPASSION FOR THE COMMON PEOPLE

Emperor Wen seemed sincere in his belief that it was the duty of the ruler to provide for the welfare of the common people. In addition to reducing taxes and dispensing with mandatory military service (apart from the defense of the frontier), he lived in a frugal manner, dispensing with the demand for tribute and going as far as to wear straw sandals to court. He understood the importance of agriculture by plowing the imperial fields himself, and abolished land tax on cultivated fields. He actively sought, and gracefully accepted, criticism of his policies. His edicts show him to be a man who blamed himself first went things went wrong. Later Han emperors owe much to him for the good will and foundation of prosperity he generated.

heir to the throne, the government proclaimed that all successor sons in the empire would be elevated in rank by one step. This practice fostered a bond between the common people and the heir apparent that was crucial to the continuity and long life of the dynasty.

In the early years of the Han dynasty, the efforts of Emperor Gaozu to win the people's support included the freeing of slaves and the granting of amnesties. In addition, he did away with mutilating punishments, paid for the funerals and coffins of fallen soldiers, pardoned criminals, and reduced and standardized poll taxes. Because of the geography and climate of China it was not possible to avoid famine altogether; however, the Han government put in place granaries that could issue relief rations in times of need.

In the early years of the Han, the imperial family also understood that the common people needed a time of rest and recuperation after the long civil war following the fall of the Qin. Sima Qian, the greatest historian of the time, wrote in praise of Empress Lü who, in spite of the plots that rocked the imperial court during her reign, maintained a laissez-faire government that allowed the people to apply themselves to their normal agricultural tasks so that food and clothing once again became abundant.

Establishing Administrative Precedents

The Han managed its large populace through a bureaucratic system that appointed officials charged with a broad array of responsibilities. Officials at the local level collected taxes, kept census records and records of land use, drafted men for labor and military service, investigated crimes and heard lawsuits, officiated over state religious ceremonies, and recommended candidates for civil service positions. They also maintained records and submitted reports to the central government on all of these matters.

Clearly, these officials wielded great power over the people. One of the three main branches of government, called the Censorate (the other two were the Civil and Military branches), was therefore designed specifically to maintain close tabs on officials. In addition, the emperor himself sent out memoranda to officials about new policies or to remedy difficulties that might damage the bond between the common people and the throne. Emperor Wen, for example, frequently issued proclamations urging local magistrates to reduce their demands on the people for labor and, in times of want, to relax prohibitions against hunting and fishing in restricted areas. These efforts were instrumental in securing the stability of the new dynasty.

Qin and Han Law

Until recent archaeological excavations, there were few specific examples that would help us understand the nature of either Qin or Han law, or how the two legal systems were related.

Law as practised in the Qin dynasty has traditionally been decried as cruel and complex; however, legal texts excavated at Shuihudi in Hubei province in 1975 give us a more accurate picture. They allow us to see with great clarity how law was actually practiced. Rather than reflecting arbitrary cruelty, the texts demonstrate cautious legal reasoning and wise administrative management. Although these texts represent only a small sampling of the whole Qin legal code, much can be surmised from them. In 1984, an incomplete copy of the Han legal statutes was excavated at Jiangling in Hubei Province and these reveal a striking similarity between the two codes.

RIGHT **A tablet found in the First Emperor's tomb** is a declaration by his son that he will continue the policies established by Qin Shihuang.

Qin Law

The Qin legal and administrative documents were found in the tomb of a prefectural clerk and are dated to 217 BCE. They were written on some 625 of the 1,155 bamboo strips recovered from the tomb. They were probably used by the tomb occupant for his work managing conscript laborers and government grain distribution.

The laws recorded in the bamboo texts are without question strict and complicated. They also illustrate, however, a very sophisticated and well-developed legal system, which helps to dispel any lingering notion about Qin being a culturally backward state.

A Test Case: Infanticide

A look at one particular Qin law—the legal status of infanticide—serves to illustrate many of the features of the text as a whole. The Qin law states the following:

To kill a child without authorization is punishable by tattooing and being made a wall-builder or a grain-pounder. When a child is newly born and its body is deformed or not whole, to kill it is not to be considered a crime. If when a child is born and the child's body is whole and not deformed—merely for the reason that one has too many children and does not wish that it should live—and consequently not to lift it up but to kill it, how is this to be sentenced? This is a case of killing a child.

The inclusion of the phrase "not to lift it up" in this passage suggests an attempt to provide the broadest possible definition of infanticide and thus clarify any uncertainty as to whether leaving a child to die is as culpable as actively killing it. Early Chinese texts indicate that parents frequently abandoned their unwanted newborns rather than actually killing them outright and, since the killing of a healthy child was illegal in Qin times, it seems logical that the Qin law should be stated in such a way as to prevent

Han and Qin Law Compared

Scholars have tried to reconstruct the Han legal code, which has been lost for thousands of years, from anecdotal accounts found in Han historical texts. It is from these sources we know that in 200 BCE, Xiao He, who was Liu Bang's chancellor, compiled a new legal code for the Han state which was an expanded version of the Qin code. Other anecdotal evidence also supports the notion that there was a general continuity between Qin and Han law. Since the discovery of the incomplete copy of the Han legal statutes at Jiangling, we are much closer to understanding how Qin and Han codes were related. The statutes reveal a striking similarity between the two codes.

To return to our infanticide test case: while the excavated Han statutes do not contain any specific statements about the killing of children, they do refer to assault on a pregnant woman who consequently miscarries. The punishment for such an assault is the third most severe hard-labor sentence. Furthermore, in one particular recorded case, the pregnant woman herself was punished with a fine of four measures of gold for fighting and thereby endangering her unborn child. Thus we can see that, in both Qin and Han law, crimes of infanticide were liable to be given the most drastic forms of punishment under the law except for the death sentence.

Although there are many similarities between the two legal codes, Han rulers continued to make changes to the laws, while many other laws stayed on the books but were not enforced. For example, Han histories tell us that in 167 BCE punishment by mutilation was abolished, in 179 BCE Emperor Wen revoked the law banning criticism of the government, and 191 BCE books banned by the First Emperor were allowed to circulate again. The effort of the Han to present their system of law as being radically different from the legal codes of the Qin may have had more to do with legitimizing a new dynasty than it did with presenting the reality of the situation.

RIGHT **Xiao He, greatly respected by Liu Bang,** was one of the few officials allowed to enter the imperial palace with his sword and wooden shoes.

LEFT **As this candlestick from a Han tomb indicates,** the wealthy expected to require wet nurses in the afterlife just as they had in their earthly life.

a parent who caused the death of an infant by abandonment from pleading not guilty on the grounds that he or she did not actually kill the child. The legal documents found at Shuihudi characteristically include details such as this which anticipate unfair manipulation of the letter of the law.

In the formulation of the infanticide law, as in other Qin laws, the principal concern is not for the protection of individual rights but for the maintenance of a population that the ruler could rightfully tap for his own purposes. Thus, killing or abandoning infants is condemned not for humane reasons, but because these practices rob the state of a child that is actually its due. This attitude is also revealed in the fact that the law prohibits exposure and infanticide in cases where the infant is healthy, but permits the disposal of deformed infants who would be of no future use to the state.

Provincial Government

As the Former Han kingdoms became increasingly powerful and wealthy, they posed an ever greater threat to the imperial government and were steadily eliminated in favor of the commandery, a provincial unit administered by centrally appointed non-hereditary officials.

RIGHT **Watch towers** were built to survey landholders' property. They were also used for entertainment. Miniatures like this glazed ceramic model were often included in tombs.

In 202 BCE the first Han emperor, Gaozu, reorganized the administrative units of the empire. In central China, he adopted the Qin dynasty unit of the commandery, to be controlled by centrally appointed, non-hereditary governors. In the east and north China, the unit of government was to be the kingdom.

Weakening of the Kingdoms

The kingdoms were reestablished in the civil wars following the fall of the Qin in 206 BCE, when rebels occupied the regions associated with the pre-imperial states and set themselves up as kings. At this time, the kingdoms occupied a much larger area than that area organized into commanderies, and also controlled valuable natural resources.

Although the kingdoms posed a serious threat to the Han imperial family's control of the empire, Gaozu had been forced to acknowledge them. It soon became clear that the only way to ensure the loyalty of the kingdoms was to grant the honor of kingship to Liu family members alone. Thus, by 196 BCE, only one of the kings acknowledged in 202 BCE remained in control of their kingdom, while the other kingdoms came under the control of close male relatives of the imperial Liu family. However, after the death

of Gaozu, the policy of granting kingship only to Liu family members was ignored. Four men of the Lü family were made kings by Gaozu's widow, the Empress Lü, although these were later eliminated after their abortive attempt to overthrow the Liu family which followed the empress's death.

During the reigns of both Emperor Wen (reigned 180–157 BCE) and Emperor Jing (reigned 157–141 BCE), the autonomy of the kingdoms, and the increasingly distant connection of the kings to the reigning emperor, continued to threaten imperial stability. To combat this, a large number of kingdoms were eliminated or greatly reduced in size when a king failed to produce an heir to the throne, or in response to a king's revolt, as in 154 BCE when the king of Wu, along with six other kings, led a large-scale but unsuccessful rebellion. Emperor Jing made strenuous efforts to weaken political power in the kingdoms. By 145 BCE, he had reduced the size of the kings' administrative staff, required their senior officials be appointed by the central government, and eliminated their independent control of fiscal affairs.

During Emperor Wu's reign (141–87 BCE) the number and size of the kingdoms were so drastically diminished that they ceased to threaten the dynastic stability of the Former Han.

BELOW **Liu Sheng, a feudal lord and son of Emperor Jing,** was entombed, as was his wife Dou Wan, in jade burial suits in order to preserve their bodies.

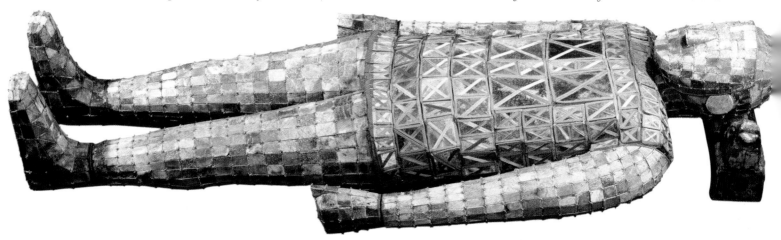

The Commanderies

By 108 BCE, China was divided into 84 commanderies and 18 small kingdoms, in addition to the capital. Because traditional historical sources tend to focus on the upper levels of society, until relatively recently, efforts to understand the administration of the commanderies during the Former Han have been thwarted by very limited available sources. However, in 1993, archaeologists recovered documents from Yinwan, Jiangsu Province, that shed light on this poorly understood area.

Dating from around the end of the Former Han, the bamboo texts detail the administration of the Donghai commandery, one of the largest commanderies of the Former Han. This unit was divided into 38 subunits in the form of counties, nobilities, and estates. The bamboo texts record a population of 1,397,343 individuals in Donghai, governed by 2,203 officials out of an estimated total of 130,285 officials in the central and provincial government.

Commandery Officials

As the kingdoms were eliminated, and the number of commanderies requiring centrally appointed officials increased, the imperial government needed to develop a system for the training and recruiting of men to fill the burgeoning numbers of positions to be filled in the bureaucracy.

The duties of an official varied widely and included such tasks as administering staff, disseminating information from the central government, advising on imperial policy, filing, duplicating and forwarding records, and making reports on population, taxes, and the disbursement of government funds. In addition, commandery officials might be required to respond to local emergencies, such as floods or earthquakes, or to report on cases of official corruption. They might also be charged with making legal decisions or appointing others to administer government enterprises such as mining or textile production.

Generally, officials were recruited from the local population to serve as low-level clerks in

the commanderies. The most talented were identified and recommended for office based on their fulfillment of various qualities such as "filial and responsible," "upright," or "flourishing talent." These men would then be tested or interviewed in the capital. The test generally involved a question set by the emperor concerning some matter of state. Archaeological texts from the tombs at Mawangdui, in Hubei Province, suggest that the government also provided training for low-level clerks that included the recitation of texts and study of several forms of script.

ABOVE **Buried in Emperor Jing's tomb** were naked and armless terracotta figures about 27–35 in (70–90 cm) high. Presumably, they originally had clothing and movable wooden arms.

THE MERITOCRACY

With the ever-increasing need for officials to staff the growing bureaucracy, determined and skilled men of humble backgrounds could rise to the highest ranks of government service. Ni Kuan was one such man. He worked as a wage laborer and is said to have carried copies of the classics as he hoed. Recognizing his brilliance, his commandery selected him to study in the capital under the erudites. He later assumed one of the highest posts in the government and was known, not only for his learning, but also for his efforts to improve agriculture and to reduce punishments, as well as for his proposal to improve irrigation by renovating the Zhengguo Canal.

Tombs of the Former Han

Looking Good in the Afterlife

This double-decker, lacquered dressing case, measuring 14 in (35 cm) in diameter, was found among Lady Dai's possessions in her tomb. Silk towels, a pair of gloves, and a mirror bag were in the top deck while nine small lacquer boxes of various shapes were in the bottom deck. These held wigs, combs, brushes, and cosmetics. Also found in the tomb were many dresses, skirts, shoes, socks, and gloves. Draped over her elaborately decorated coffin was a silk painting thought to be a portrait of the marchioness arrayed in all her glory.

Intensified archaeological activity in China from the mid-twentieth century onward has brought to light hundreds of Han dynasty tombs. Between 1974 and 1975, at Mawangdui, in the eastern suburb of Changsha in Hunan Province, archaeologists excavated three tombs which were unprecedented in the richness and cultural significance of the burial goods. Documents which were found among the burial goods reveal the occupants of the tombs were Li Cang, the Marquis of Dai, and his wife and son. The burials were dated to around 168 BCE.

The marquisate of Dai was relatively small, consisting of only about 700 households. Considering the very small revenue Li Cang must have received from his marquisate, the richness of the tomb is intriguing. The Marquis of Dai was the last prime minister to be appointed by the king of Changsha. After his tenure, the central government appointed staff of their own choosing.

The elaborate method of burial proved an effective measure against the ravages of time. Each person was buried in a series of four large nested coffins, with the innermost of the four holding the body. The coffins were surrounded with layers of white clay and charcoal, and buried in a pit some 52 ft (16 m) deep. The body of the marchioness was so well preserved, scientists were able to

Final Resting Place

A nest of four coffins, of which this black lacquered coffin was the second, helped to preserve Lady Dai's body. Scenes of Heaven, including spirits and animals, are painted on the coffin.

perform an autopsy which revealed that she died of coronary thrombosis and arteriosclerosis, and that she suffered acute back pain due to a fused spinal disc. Her skin was still soft and flexible upon discovery and her stomach still held the contents of her final meal. Her body was wrapped in some 20 fine robes tied with silk ribbons. The clothing was of exceptionally fine quality, represented by airy silks, embroidered gauze, and taffetas. The garments were dyed a great variety of colors—vermillion, deep red, yellow, purple, brown, grey, green, blue, silver, gold, and black.

In addition to the well-preserved corpse of the marchioness, the tombs contained an amazing array of other possessions which present a vivid picture of the luxury of elite life in the Former Han dynasty. As well as silk clothing, the tombs contained woven silk patterned with clouds, birds and scrolling spirals, lacquer dishes (some still containing food), furniture, musical instruments, board games, bronze wares, gold ingots, ceramics, pearls, statues of servants and entertainers, finely-wrought weapons, bamboo mats, decorated wooden screens, baskets, boxes, wall hangings, and toilet articles.

Food for the Soul
Three hundred and sixteen pieces of lacquer-ware, including dishes suitable for food service, together with food and wine for the soul's earthly part, were found in storerooms at Mawangdui.

With its stores of medicinal herbs and food, the tombs also provide a great deal of information about diet in the Former Han and the kind of pharmacopeia available to the upper echelons of society. The most spectacular discovery of all was a large array of books and maps. Unlike most Han texts excavated at the time, these books were written on silk rather than bamboo. The silk books represent some of the earliest copies of well-known texts, such as the *Daodejing*, as well as other works whose titles had not been transmitted to later generations, including texts on medicine, astronomy, divination, philosophy, and meteorology. The maps include a topographical map of southern Changsha, a military map, and another map that appears to be a plan for a town.

All Comforts Provided
Beautiful works of art, such as this terracotta vase featuring acrobats, were also a common addition to tomb furnishings.

Medical treatises that were previously unknown to scholars included a book of prescriptions. Another was a discourse on sexual techniques for improving fertility and longevity, and included illustrations of callisthenic exercises. A text relating to childbirth explained a ritual for proper disposal of the placenta.

Expansion and Trade

The reign of Emperor Wu began in an era of prosperity and colonial expansion that increased the territory of the Han empire to its largest extent ever. This expansion was achieved at a huge cost of both human lives and resources.

ABOVE **The walled city of Dunhuang** was a military outpost on the Silk Road. It was built around an oasis in the second century BCE.

The frugal reigns of Emperor Hui, Empress Lü and Emperor Wen had replenished the state treasury. As kingdoms were eliminated in favor of commanderies, their wealth, provided by taxes and natural resources, went entirely to the central government without having to be apportioned in any way to the various kingdoms.

Revenue Raising

To raise additional funds, Emperor Wu raised the poll tax, levied a new sales tax, and imposed taxes on property and vehicles. In addition, he created government monopolies for salt, iron, and alcohol. The new taxes, which people paid on top of poll and produce taxes, were mainly to support military operations, but were also used for public services, such as the construction and maintenance of roads and waterways, and the development of a new bureau that controlled profiteering in grain and managed the transport of grain to areas suffering from shortages.

Currency was also now controlled solely by the government. Previously, people had been allowed to mint their own copper coins, but in 120 BCE, after various wealthy individuals who owned extensive mining operations cornered the market in metal coins, Emperor Wu decided to prohibit private mintage. In addition, official titles were sold to raise money, especially for defense. All of these measures produced a period of wealth and surplus. Contemporary accounts claim that in this age of prosperity, even ordinary people rode horses and regularly dined on fine grain and meat.

Foreign Affairs

From the fourth century BCE, Xiongnu nomads had plagued China. Highly mobile, they lived in tents and were masterful horsemen. With their ability to launch a fierce attack and disappear quickly, they were formidable opponents for the large and cumbersome military operations of Han forces. The Xiongnu threat escalated in 209 BCE, when a new Xiongnu leader named Maodun united previously disparate tribes. In 200 BCE, the Xiongnu attacked and soundly defeated Han troops with an army of 300,000 men.

With other pressing domestic issues to attend to, Emperor Gaozu decided to sign a peace treaty with the Xiongnu. To appease them, he sent gifts of wine, silk, rice, and the hand of a Chinese princess in marriage. This solution came to be known as the "peace and friendship" strategy and seemed to work well.

In 133 BCE, however, Emperor Wu attacked the Xiongnu in order to extend his territory, fortify garrisons in the north, open new commanderies in conquered territories, and control trade routes that had developed in the western part of the empire. He also enlarged his empire to the southeast and in Korea. In 108 BCE, Korea was divided up into four Han commanderies.

One of the greatest adventurers of the period was Zhang Qian who explored the far west on two separate occasions, first in 139 BCE and again in 115 BCE. In 139 BCE, he volunteered to head a diplomatic mission to the Yuezhi people who lived to the west of the Xiongnu. It occurred to Zhang Qian that the Han would benefit from befriending other peoples in the area who might be willing to ally themselves with the Chinese against the Xiongnu. After spending ten years as a prisoner of the Xiongnu,

LEFT **The statue of Zhang Qian at Yangguan, Gansu Province,** celebrates Zhang's return to China via the Silk Road. His report to Emperor Wu led to the opening up for trade of the Silk Road.

Zhang Qian resumed his journey. He traveled as far as Bactria, in present-day, northwestern Afghanistan, returning home in 126 BCE.

As a result of Zhang Qian's reports, Emperor Wu initiated more wall-building activity in the northwest, regulated illegal border-crossing in both directions, and provided a route along which valuable trade goods could be securely transported. West of the wall, travelers followed the Silk Routes to the north and south of the Taklamakan Desert. Here the Chinese relied upon diplomatic relations with the various peoples who could help ensure the safe passage of caravans.

Foreign Trade

Exploration of China's periphery was fueled by the desire for border security, foreign conquest and trade. While Zhang Qian was exploring Bactria, he had been surprised to see Chinese goods being traded there. Although silk was traded between the Chinese and the Romans, these two great empires probably never dealt directly with each other. Chinese silk was traded in a system that included Central Asia, India, Indonesia, Africa, and the Middle East. In return, the Chinese purchased horses and jade from Central Asia.

In the southwest, where the kingdom of Dian was conquered by the Han in 109 BCE, trade focused on Dian's rich supplies of gold, silver, tin, and lead. The Yue people in the north of present-day Vietnam were assimilated into Chinese territory in 111 BCE and from them the Chinese purchased such items as pearls, fruit, rhinoceros horns, and textiles in exchange for weapons and iron tools.

Though Emperor Wu had made tremendous gains in extending his power and authority, the cost in human lives and other resources was staggering. Records show that the battles waged in the one year of 119 BCE alone claimed the lives of 100,000 horses. By the end of Emperor Wu's reign, the great vitality that had energized China when he first ascended the throne had begun to flag and the great surpluses were gone. What had once been praised was now viewed as so much extravagance and hubris.

BELOW **A statue of a general serving under Emperor Wu** stands near the wall at Jiayugan, a key pass on the Silk Road. This part of the wall, however, was built during the Ming dynasty.

Cultural Revival

With the political turmoil and exhausted resources of the opening years of the Han dynasty, there was little time for cultural pursuits until the consolidation of China's central power under Emperor Jing.

The reign of Emperor Jing (157–141 BCE), sees the beginning of a prosperous and expanding empire and the first signs of a newly burgeoning interest in literature and scholarship.

Poetry

For reasons that are unclear, there are almost no surviving examples of Chinese poetry between the fourth century BCE and the reign of Emperor Wen (180–157 BCE). Then, quite suddenly, a new poet emerged on China's literary scene, one who employed a new form called the *fu* or "rhapsody."

Sima Xiangru (179–117 BCE) is virtually the creator of the rhapsody, which usually takes as its subject matter the grandeur of the capital with its hunts, rituals, and palaces, the profusion of beauty in the natural world—birds, beast, rivers, and mountains—and fantastical journeys in which the poet roams through antiquity or soars above the world in a shaman-like flight. Rhapsodies tend to be long and the tone is often bombastic, assailing the reader with dazzling descriptions of exotica, dense with rhyme, onomatopoeia, alliteration, and assonance. The genre captures the exuberance of a new, prosperous, and expanding empire. Just as the Han rulers consolidated "All under Heaven," the rhapsody also aimed at being all-encompassing.

Sima Xiangru also epitomizes the ideal of the literati-bureaucrat. He served in the court of Emperor Jing and was commissioned to travel to the southwest and to bring the peoples who lived there under Han authority.

History

The *Records of the Grand Historian* by Sima Qian was the first history to cover all of China's past, from the very dawn of civilization to (what was then) the present. It was also the first history that was written by a known author whose life history is well documented. For the next 2,000 years, the *Records* provided the model for all dynastic histories.

Sima Qian (*c.* 145–86 BCE) used a five-part structure which included the basic annals of each dynastic ruler, chronological tables listing the principal events in the feudal states in tabular form, a series of treatises on topics such as astronomy, economy, and ritual, the "hereditary houses," which narrate the history of the Zhou dynasty feudal states, and the biographies, which include a select group of historical figures who represent the major trends of their times. This form allowed Sima Qian to give coherence to his complex subject matter without the constraints of a strictly chronological account.

In the *Records*, Sima Qian frequently relates historical events by means of fictional dialogs into which realistic, factual accounts are interwoven with

BELOW **The Temple of Sima Qian,** near Hancheng in Shaanxi Province, was built beside his tomb in CE 310 by his descendants. It contains records of Sima Qian's life and achievements.

LEFT **Sima Qian,** considered to be the father of Chinese historiography, recorded history as a series of biographies. This was an innovative style unlike that of any of his predecessors'.

having promised his father he would complete the history, Sima Qian chose to live on in humiliation in order to finish his life's work.

Like the all-encompassing rhapsody, the *Records of the Grand Historian* reflects the early Han passion for political and intellectual unification in its attempt to bring together all of China's history and culture in a single book.

Classical Learning

The revival of classical learning in Former Han times was the result of the growing numbers of influential Confucian statesmen at court, the need to train an increasingly large bureaucracy, and an effort to avoid the errors of the Qin's empire which toppled, in part, due to the First Emperor's failure to surround himself with wise counselors and learn the lessons of history.

In 136 BCE, Emperor Wu established an academy staffed with Erudites specializing in the five Confucian classics—the *Book of Odes*, the *Spring and Autumn Annals*, the *Book of Documents*, the *Book of Changes*, and the *Book of Rites*. Scholars who specialized in other texts were excluded. In earlier times, classical learning had flourished at the courts of a number of wealthy kings, and the establishment of the imperial academy may have been Emperor Wu's effort to enhance the prestige of his own court by patronizing the best minds and talents of the day.

In 124 BCE, a small number of well-qualified students were placed in the academy to study with the Erudites. Toward the end of the Former Han, the number of students in the academy reached 3,000. The Confucian classics remained the cornerstone of education in China until the early twentieth century.

elements of myth, dream, and legend. For all its imperfections as a mirror of ages past, it remains the single most important source for early Chinese history.

It was Sima Qian's misfortune to become embroiled in a political controversy at the court of Emperor Wu when he tried to defend a general who, upon being faced with overwhelming odds, had surrendered to the Xiongnu. The emperor, infuriated by Sima's response, punished him with castration. In Sima Qian's world, the honorable response to such a punishment was suicide, which the emperor would have expected. But,

BELOW **Emperor Wu,** who gathered young, educated advisors around him and founded schools for his administrators, established Confucianism as the official imperial doctrine.

LEARNING, NOT ALWAYS EASY

In the rarefied world of the elite, the last thing an aristocratic boy wanted was a strict tutor to interfere with his pursuit of pleasure. When Liu Wu, the third king of Chu, occupied the position of crown prince, his tutor was Shen Pei, an eminent scholar of the *Book of Odes*. Liu Wu's dislike of study and hatred for his tutor was so great that when he came to the throne, he had Shen fettered and sentenced to hard labor. Liu Qu, king of Guangchuan, went a step further. Once he became king he secured the services of a slave to murder the tutor who had several times admonished and corrected him.

Han Thought

Though increasingly Confucian as the dynasty progressed, Former Han thought was a unique amalgam of Daoist, Legalist, Confucian, and correlative cosmological thought.

Though never fully realized, the elevation of Confucianism as the state creed during Emperor Wu's reign ushered in a feeling of optimism about the ability of a Confucian emperor and bureaucracy to establish a new order of high morals and advanced civilization. The emperor, it was thought, would be able to promote the moral development of the general population not only metaphysically through the benevolent influence of his personal virtue, but also institutionally by the furtherance of Confucian instruction. From the start, the dual projects of shaping the emperor and morally informing the general populace were connected as elements of a program of social reform.

Confucianism and Han Policy

Han Confucian thinkers, such as Dong Zhongshu, were intent on correcting what they perceived to be the Qin's mistakes. The practical expression of their influence on imperial policy, though still limited in scope at this point, can be seen in two measures in particular. Confucian tutors were appointed for all heirs apparent from the time of Emperor Wu (141–87 BCE) onward, and schools and academies were established throughout the empire dedicated to the education of youths

BELOW **Confucius is shown here with his disciples.** Confucianism was tailored to fit comfortably with the prevailing social and political goals of the Han dynasty.

beyond the sphere of court culture. Confucian schemes to transform the morals of the general populace relied on the charisma and the good example of emperor, officials, and teachers who were instructed in canonical texts and who embodied and propagated their teachings. While the emphasis on education derived from idealistic hopes of forging an era of "Great Peace," and the practical necessity of educating large numbers of youths to staff an increasingly complex bureaucracy, there were other concerns that made promoting early education seem equally crucial.

The Importance of Education

The precipitous collapse of the preceding dynasty had rekindled the old Confucian distrust of law as the primary means of sustaining the state and preventing antisocial behavior. Although the Han preserved much of the apparatus of the Legalist Qin state, Confucian thinkers believed that moral education would be a more effective deterrent to crime than the strict laws and punishments of the Qin regime. Moreover, a Confucian form of education that would promote both morals and literacy would go far beyond the Qin agenda aimed at strengthening warfare, agriculture, and social control.

In early China, questions about the genesis and control of evil in the conduct of humans were an integral part of the ongoing debate about human nature. In the Han era there appears to have been little overt support for the views of Mencius, the fourth century BCE sage who, while stressing the necessity for moral cultivation, regarded human nature as essentially good. Rather, it was the third century BCE philosopher Xunzi with his emphasis on classical education and the notion that goodness was the result of the gradual accumulation of deeds and habits, who dominated Han notions about how to make people moral. Han critics, however, tended to disagree with a notion regularly imputed to Xunzi, namely, the doctrine that human nature is essentially

LEFT **Mencius, a Confucian philosoper,** believed that all humans are innately good. The Han, however, preferred Xunzi's belief that humans became good through their actions and education.

evil. On the contrary, most Han thinkers concluded that human nature was, for the most part, malleable and, in some sense, undeveloped or incomplete at birth and therefore in need of the transforming power of education.

Legalist Thought in Imperial Policy

The focus on education made selection of an imperial tutor a highly politicized issue. In the first half of the Former Han, men with various philosophical perspectives served as imperial tutors, and many of them were Legalists. As he particularly favored *xingming*—the Legalist teachings on personnel organization and control—Emperor Wen (reigned 180–157 BCE) appointed Zhang Shu as instructor for his heir apparent (the future Emperor Jing). Zhang was a *xingming* specialist known for his fairness and compassion in applying the law.

The Confucian reforms of Emperor Wu in early Former Han times had also been carried out for largely pragmatic purposes. It was not until the reign of Emperor Yuan (reigned 48–33 BCE) that a form of Confucian idealism

prevailed that had been promoted earlier by philosophers such as Dong Zhongshu. This led to Confucian projects such as educational reform being embraced with the quixotic goal of realizing the era of "Great Peace."

During the reigns of the emperors Xuan (74–48 BCE), Yuan, and Cheng (33–7 BCE), Confucian advisers at court advocated a "reformist" agenda; that is, a codification of the practices of the former sage-kings and a formalization of Confucian education as a means of social control. This philosophical, political, and religious stance was opposed to (and eventually replaced) the "modernist" perspective which favored the laws and religious conventions of the Legalist state of Qin, and which were represented by the statist policies that characterized much of Emperor Wu's reign.

A debate that took place in 81 BCE between critics and government spokesmen was later rewritten in the *Salt and Iron Discussions* and clearly represents the views of the two opposing groups. The title refers to the state monopoly that Emperor Wu established around 119 BCE to gain revenue to fund his expansionist policies.

Correlative Cosmology

Confucianism, in many of its Han inflections, had also absorbed modes of thought not originally associated with that philosophy, most notably cosmological speculation. This theory is based on

ABOVE **Ceramic entertainers,** such as these acrobats, were often placed in Han tombs to provide comfort for that part of the soul believed not to ascend to heaven but to remain earthbound.

a belief that the three spheres of Heaven, Earth, and Man are interrelated by way of a primal substance, called *qi*, of which all things are composed. In this system, all things move and develop in accordance with the patterns of nature, which are the quintessential expressions of the Dao (the "Way"). These patterns generally refer to the regular movements of the four seasons, the waxing and waning of the two primordial principles (Yin and Yang), or the revolving cycle of the Five Phases (Fire, Earth, Water, Metal, and Wood). Human beings who aligned their activities with these natural cycles were thought to work with, rather than against nature, and therefore maximized their potential for various forms of well-being, such as health, good fortune, and fertility.

Essential to acting in harmony with nature is the ability to discern which cosmic force governs which activity. For example, state executions are, according to one theory, permitted only during the "killing season" of the year; that is, during autumn and winter when nature kills plant life; while, on the other hand, capital punishment performed in spring violates the pattern of nature and therefore causes disequilibrium expressed in anomalous phenomena such as eclipses, plagues, and earthquakes. Furthermore, all things that belong to one category, Yin for example (associated with darkness, death, winter, and the like), are thought to be linked. This means that, when one component is affected, all things in that category are affected as well. This belief gave rise to the notion of *ganying*, "stimulus and response", whereby a drought (categorized as Yang) could be remedied by commanding women (categorized as Yin) to congregate in public which, through the stimulus of Yin, would bring rain.

Human Life as a Microcosm

Within the system of correlative thought, human life was understood, not as a series of descendants issuing from one distant ancestor, but as a microcosm that shared the same essence and obeyed the same natural laws that pervaded the entire universe.

Images, such as the roundness of a human being's head corresponding to the roundness of the dome of Heaven, and the squareness of a person's feet corresponding to the four corners of the earth, were not intended as simple figures of speech but as evidence of the actual links between human life and the cosmic powers and, by extension, the interconnectedness of Heaven, Earth, and Man.

Han belief systems led to many linked beliefs. For example, it was believed that triplets as well as all children born in the first and fifth months were innately bad. This view was based on the notion that because these months were the most intensely active and aggressive phases of the yearly Yin–Yang cycle, infants born during these times were imbued with similarly dangerous traits. Han texts state that parents often refused to rear their offspring born in the first or fifth month because of a commonly held belief that such children would be likely to grow up to murder one or both of their parents.

The desire to reorient human life in a past that transcended family ties, and to reintegrate it with new theories that embraced the entire cosmos, may well have reflected contemporary political aspirations toward a unified empire that was governed by one ruler, as opposed to a lineage-based, multi-state system.

ABOVE **Lady Dai's funeral banner** depicts the cosmos and afterlife, with Heaven at the top, her family offering sacrifices to Heaven under that, then the Earth, and the underworld at the bottom.

RIGHT **Immortals**—"patron saints" of the Daoists—were idolized and respected for their wisdom, humor, and moral lessons. Reverence for various immortals escalated during the Han era.

POETRY AS A MORAL FORCE

Under the Han, an almost supernatural power was attributed to the Confucian classics, in particular to *The Book of Odes*. In 74 BCE, when the young Emperor Xuan came to the throne, one of his first acts was to issue an imperial edict to all the officials in the commanderies and kingdoms ordering them to develop the virtue of the common people through the dissemination of the *Odes*. This edict reflects a claim made in the preface to this canonical text, which states that by hearing the odes people would become careful in their conduct. The importance of the *Odes* in court culture is also demonstrated by the fact that among the tutors assigned to Han imperial princes, the majority were known for specialization in the *Odes*.

Huang–Lao Thought

Another form of correlative cosmology that developed in Han times is called *Huang–Lao*, a name derived from the mythical sage king, Huangdi, and the Daoist philosopher, Laozi. Huang–Lao generally eschewed any discussion of virtues, made little use of the Confucian classics in its writings, and concentrated on minimalist methods of government to increase the military and political power of the ruler. Huang–Lao thought, as it is expressed in texts such as the *Huainanzi*, also draws upon the correlative cosmologies of Yin–Yang and Five

Phase theories which promote an understanding of the Dao as the highest and most primary expression of universal order and power, and the cosmos as a unity where no distinction is made between natural and human affairs.

Thus, Huang–Lao seems to have included a wide range of philosophies, such as Legalism and Daoism, but also have advocated various hygiene and meditation techniques. The Grand Empress Dowager Dou, Consort of Emperor Wen, mother of Emperor Jing, and grandmother of Emperor Wu, is said to have been devoted to the writings of Huang–Lao and required her son (as well as her husband and other members of her family) to study the texts of that school. Emperor Wu's initial purge of all but Confucian scholars in the imperial academy may have been at least partially prompted by a desire to be free from the control his grandmother had exerted over the philosophical tone of the court.

ABOVE **Laozi is referred to as the father of Daoism.** Whereas Confucianism is concerned with social relations, conduct, and society, Daoism is more individualistic and mystical.

Interregnum: The Xin

In 6 BCE, after Emperor Ping's death, Wang Mang named an infant of the Liu family as heir apparent. But instead of enthroning this child as emperor, Wang Mang usurped the title of emperor and established the Xin dynasty, also known as the Interregnum.

ABOVE **Wang Mang,** known in Chinese history as "The Usurper", aimed to found a dynasty of his own, claiming that the Han no longer held the "Mandate of Heaven."

The Path to Power

Because he had usurped the imperial throne, Wang Mang is presented in the Han histories as an incompetent and somewhat cruel fraud. On the other hand, histories credit him with improving provincial schools, sponsoring learned conferences, enlarging the imperial academy, as well as keeping peace on China's borders.

However, there are many negative accounts as well. We are told, for example, of Wang Mang's treatment of both imperial consort relatives and his own son. When Emperor Ping came to the throne, Wang Mang tried to prevent Ping's mother and her clan (the Wei) from coming to court in order to forestall the possibility of Wei power eclipsing his own. Emperor Ping's mother was naturally vexed at being separated from her young son and Wang Mang's own son, Wang Yu, sensed that if she were not allowed to come to court, more serious trouble would soon follow. Wang Yu tried to counteract his father's plans and Wang Mang had him sent to prison where he drank poison and died. His pregnant wife was kept alive only until she had given birth and was then promptly executed.

In fact, Wang Mang's actions where his family was concerned were no different from those of the Former Han emperors who frequently dispatched their own kin when it was expedient.

The Imperial Father-In-Law

In CE 4, Wang Mang married his 12-year-old daughter to Emperor Ping. When she achieved menarche in CE 5, Wang Mang was delighted since she would now be able (at least in theory) to produce a male child for the 13-year-old Emperor Ping. To mark the occasion he constructed the Ziwu road, a highway that ran from north to south. The two terms, *zi* and *wu*, were used in calendrics and were associated in China's cosmological system with North and South, Water and Fire, and Male and Female. As noted by a third-century commentator, "Fire is the consort of Water. *Zi* and *wu* were connected as a road as a means to assist her in producing heirs."

In 6 BCE, at the age of 18, Emperor Ai ascended the throne for his brief reign which lasted only until 1 BCE. He died at 24 years old without heirs. In 1 BCE, his successor, the eight-year-old grandson of Emperor Yuan, began his reign as Emperor Ping under the regency of Wang Mang (45 BCE–CE 23). Wang Mang was the nephew of Emperor Yuan's empress, Wang Zhengjun.

By building a road that conjoined Yin and Yang, Wang Mang hoped to establish a sympathetic resonance that would promote the fertility of the young couple, which would not only ensure the continuation of the dynasty but also his own continued presence at court.

Given the taboo nature of female bodily functions, the account of the incident in which Wang Mang paraded such an unmentionable fact as the reaching of menarche by his young daughter, was most likely recorded to illustrate the heterodox nature and impropriety of the rite, and Wang Mang's overweening ambition.

Suffering from respiratory problems, Emperor Ping was delicate and died in CE 5. There were rumors circulating that Wang Mang had poisoned the emperor, but many scholars doubt this. They argue that because Emperor Ping's empress was Wang Mang's daughter, it is more likely that Wang Mang would have regarded Emperor Ping's death as an event that would endanger rather than bolster his power.

After Emperor Ping's death, Wang Mang, in his role as regent, selected a one-year-old infant to ascend the throne. This was a transparent ploy to retain his hold over the empire.

The Rise and Fall of the Xin Dynasty

In CE 9, despite the years of proclaiming his devotion to the Liu imperial clan, Wang Mang announced the end of the Han and ascended the throne as the first ruler of his own Xin dynasty. In CE 10, Han nobles were stripped of their ranks and, with only two brief uprisings in protest against his new rule, the new dynasty continued with little upheaval. Wang Mang's policies were largely consistent with the established practices of the Former Han, and his reign proceeded smoothly. His officials seemed to support him, and there is no evidence that anyone ever tried to assassinate him. His fall, modern historians generally agree, was largely due to the catastrophic conditions that prevailed when the Yellow River changed course some time around CE 11, rather than to his own incompetence.

Starving peasants, who had been displaced by the floods when the Yellow River changed course, began to migrate south. Government relief agencies were unable to contain the masses who roamed from town to town, looting, robbing, and killing in search of food. Disorder prevailed and the peasants soon organized themselves into a rebel army known as the "Red Eyebrows," so named for the vermillion marks they painted on their foreheads. The government troops tried to restore order but met with repeated failure.

Finally, in CE 22, the Red Eyebrows approached Nanyang, a stronghold of the imperial Liu kinsmen, and the place where, soon after Wang Mang declared himself emperor, the first uprising against him had occurred. The Liu family saw their opportunity and joined forces with the rebel army in hope of restoring the Han. In CE 23, the armies invaded the capital and Wang Mang was beheaded by Han loyalists. After a long series of power struggles, Liu Xiu, a distant descendant of Emperor Jing, finally ascended the throne in CE 25 as the founder of the Later Han dynasty.

RIGHT **Bronze knife-shaped coins** had circulated in the Zhou dynasty 200 years earlier, but Wang Mang reissued them, along with some 20 other kinds of coins.

LEFT **The cover of this bronze censer**, from the Wang Mang era, represents Mt. Penglai, which is the central mountain in the Daoist paradise.

Women and Gender

Ideas about women's roles that emerged in the Former Han and Later Han set standards for feminine virtue that would prevail for the next 2,000 years.

RIGHT **This tomb figure** of a graceful and elegant female dancer is poised to entertain her master in the afterlife.

We can think of the position of women in Later Han times as the culmination of a long process of social, political, and doctrinal change that began in the Eastern Zhou (771–256 BCE). It is particularly in the sphere of elite marriage that we see the emergence of practices that would go on to affect women at all levels of society.

Changes in Imperial Marriage Patterns

BELOW **The tranquil and composed posture** of this female servant reflects the Confucian ideal for women, of all classes.

Prior to the Han dynasty, extending back in time at least as far as the Spring and Autumn period (770–476 BCE), the king typically selected consorts from elite families outside his own lineage and state. In this multi-state system, a royal marriage served the primary purpose of forging alliances between the king and the politically powerful family of the queen. But with the Qin's unification of all the states into one centralized empire in 221 BCE, rulers were no longer compelled to marry with the specific purpose of maintaining a balance of power between competing states.

Most significantly, the transformation from a multi-state system into a centralized empire resulted in marriages between rulers and their social inferiors, as no family had status equal to that of the emperor but were from within the realm. These families were thus positioned to amass power at court.

Empresses from Humble Backgrounds

In contrast to the elite women who were chosen as wives and consorts by rulers in earlier periods, the first Han emperor, Gaozu (206–195 BCE), himself of common origins, chose as empress, Lü Zhi. Of similar humble background, she rose with him from obscurity. After Gaozu's death, Empress Lü was able to dominate the government and

pave the way for her male relatives to accrue enough power to revolt (though unsuccessfully) after her death.

In an attempt to prevent the possibility of another similar uprising, Liu loyalists chose Emperor Wen (180–157 BCE) to be the new emperor, at least partially on the basis of the obscurity of his wife, Empress Dou, and the relative scarcity of her male kin.

The next several reigns saw equally ordinary women named empress. Wei Zifu, the second empress of Emperor Wu (141–87 BCE), emerged from the lowest strata of Han society. As such, she was the first of three women of slave origins to become empress in the Former Han dynasty.

The Harem as Imperial Sanctuary

The second change affecting women's roles came about as a result of the increasingly large amount of time the emperor spent in his harem. From the time of Emperor Wu onward, rulers would increasingly conduct business from within the confines of their harems where male presence was limited to the emperor and his eunuchs. The members of the imperial consort families happily filled the ensuing power vacuum, serving as the emperor's chief allies, and buffers against any antagonistic power-holders in the bureaucracy. Under these conditions, even an imperial concubine of humble status was in a stronger position to improve the fortunes of her family than a man of a similar social background. After all, it was only a daughter who could marry an emperor, give birth to his heir, and, following her imperial husband's death, rule the empire as empress dowager to an under-aged son.

Bureaucratic Opportunities for Women

The expansion of the bureaucracy generated more numerous and lucrative bureaucratic positions for women. In Qin and early Han times, the most efficient route to high government positions for men of low-born status lay in the acquisition of either military or administrative skills, and later, literacy and textual mastery. Freeborn women of low status, on the other hand, could gain entry into government service by occupying what were, with few exceptions, the only positions available to them—those of palace servant, entertainer, or concubine. By the time of Emperor Yuan (48–33 BCE), imperial concubines were graded into 14 different ranks that were correlated with the bureaucratic positions that men occupied. Thus, a woman who was ranked as Brilliant Companion had the equivalent rank of a man who filled the office of the Chancellor, and she received an equivalent income to him.

Female Education

Despite the rise in their status, women continued to play a fairly small role in the civil service and the military. Consequently, female education did not attract nearly the same level of attention as that devoted to the intellectual development of men. Nevertheless, from the reign of Emperor Xuan (74–48 BCE) onward, an increasing anxiety over the influence of women in political events, and the threat they posed to dynastic stability, resulted in efforts to educate girls about their proper roles in society. The earliest extant text for this sort of education is the *Traditions of Exemplary Women* by Liu Xiang which sets forth the biographies of appropriate female exemplars.

The goals of female education differed from those for men in several respects. Women were not educated to further their own ambitions but in order to acquire learning for the sake of the moral, intellectual, and professional development of their fathers, brothers, husbands, and sons. Nevertheless, toward the end of the Former Han, as ambitious men of the gentry were appraised increasingly for their Confucian morals, their

BELOW **Emperor Wu's grandmother and mother** held great power in the early years of his reign. Below is an artist's impression of Wu visiting the harem.

ABOVE **The role of a woman** of common status revolved around domestic chores that would contribute to the family unit. Her prime duty was to her husband and male relatives.

womenfolk also came under closer scrutiny. The government also made sporadic efforts to recognize morally accomplished women by way of special grants and awards for values such as chastity and obedience.

Approaches to female education ranged from promoting strict separation of the sexes and subservient roles for women to stressing literacy for girls as preparation for their future vocations as advisers to husbands, and teachers to children. In general, intensive literary education appears to have remained restricted to a small number of upper-class women and those who served in the imperial palace. Although a few low-born girl might receive a courtesan's training in music and dance, the life of most girls was centered on their roles as wives, mothers, and textile producers.

Because the importance of Yin–Yang thought was increasing in official Confucian ideology, a number of Han thinkers viewed the yin, or the female sphere, as an essential component in their efforts to achieve and maintain cosmic balance. To this end, they encouraged certain normative behaviors in the female populace. These views were generally linked to the Confucian utopian goal of creating an era of "Great Peace." Thus, any ordinary woman could now view herself as an active contributor to the improvement of family, state, and cosmic harmony. However, her involvement was often paid for by assuming an increasingly subservient position to her father, brother, husband, or other male family member.

Women in the Later Han

The Former Han dynasty ended when Wang Mang, a male relative of Emperor Cheng's mother, usurped the throne in CE 9. Later Han intellectuals, who were now deeply conscious of the threat posed by imperial affines (kin related by marriage), tried to prevent the resurgence of consort power in their own reigns. In CE 25, for example, when the Han dynasty was restored to the Liu imperial family, one of the policies that was adopted by Emperor Guangwu (as well as by his successor) prohibited the relatives of his own women from participating in government and from holding the rank of marquis. However, these measures soon proved ineffective in limiting the power of imperial consort families.

In contrast to the practices in the Former Han, empresses in the Later Han dynasty came from elite families. They were chosen, not for the emperor's personal pleasure but for the political connections they had to powerful families. (The scant attention paid to the matter of a couple's compatibility in imperial marriages may account for the fact that eight of the 11 Later Han empresses were childless.) By serving as regents and controlling the appointment of countless officials, those families whose daughters had married into the imperial clan had once again managed to reposition themselves to influence political affairs at the empire's highest level.

The most impressive imperial consort of the period was Empress Deng (81–121). After the death of Emperor He in 106, Empress Deng served as regent, dominating court politics until her death in 121. She is praised for her learning, frugality, and compassion for those less fortunate. For example, she visited prisons, reviewed cases of those who claimed to have been incarcerated unfairly, and established a school for boys and girls of the imperial family aged five and above. On the occasion of her being named empress, she eschewed the traditional luxurious tribute and asked instead for gifts of paper and ink. Later historians, however, criticize her for enthroning a minor in order to extend the influence of her family at court for as long as possible.

A Woman's Place

Empress Deng is also notable for having studied the classics, history, mathematics, and astronomy with the eminent female historian, Ban Zhao. Ban Zhao, who was the sister of the great historian, Ban Gu, is known for her work titled *Lessons for Daughters*. This text, while advocating literacy for women, nevertheless encourages them to be obedient to their husbands and fathers. Confucianism generally stresses the importance of submitting to one's hierarchical superiors and in classical texts men are similarly enjoined to submit to their rulers, parents, and elder brothers. It can be argued, therefore, that the requirement for a woman to subordinate her own interests to others was not a burden placed on women alone, but was placed on men too.

LEFT "**Let a woman retire late to bed,** but rise early to duties; let her not dread tasks by day or by night. Let her not refuse to perform domestic duties whether easy or difficult. That which must be done, let her finish completely, tidily, and systematically." — Ban Zhao's *Lessons for Daughters*.

However, men—unlike women—were never asked to deny the importance of their natal families, to remain faithful to a spouse with multiple live-in partners, to choose death over remarriage, nor to limit their scholarly attainments to an acknowledgment of their inherently inferior status in the family, state, and cosmos.

Lessons for Daughters, together with *Traditions of Exemplary Women*, set the tone for female education for the next two millennia, and thus ensured that the goal of educating women would always be bound up in the subordination of the woman's own interests to the well-being of her husband and his family. On the other hand, these two texts did provide important survival skills for women and girls, whether they were headed for the ruthless politics of the imperial court or the alien territory of their husband's family, and they became the foundation of almost all of female education throughout the remainder of imperial Chinese history.

LEFT **Ban Zhao, China's first female historian,** took a public role in the politics of the imperial court as adviser to the Empress Dowager Deng. She was also a notable poet.

The Power of the Eunuchs

Eunuchs are generally despised by Chinese historians because of their extra-constitutional manipulation of state affairs. They are also condemned as sycophants who gained power and influence by means of unquestioning, over-indulgent approval of imperial whim.

Of the many politically powerful eunuchs in early China, one of the most famous was Zhao Gao (died 207 BCE), who served the First Emperor. Zhao's political power, like that of many eunuchs, derived from his ready access to the emperor that resulted from his official position. This access enabled him to wield power that had not been formally granted to him. It was Zhao Gao, for example, who was in attendance on the First Emperor at the time of his death and who used that opportunity to change the succession and steer policy to his own advantage.

Eunuchs in the Former Han

The practice of employing eunuchs as private secretaries began under the reign of Emperor Wu (141–87 BCE), who spent much of his time in the imperial harem where male officials were not admitted. The presence of eunuchs in political affairs, however, did not become pronounced until the reign of Emperor Yuan (48–33 BCE).

In addition to having no real interest in governing, Emperor Yuan was in poor health and relied heavily on two of his eunuchs, Shi Xian and Hong Gong, to manage affairs. Another strong presence at the court was Xiao Wangzhi, an eminent Confucian scholar who had once served as Emperor Yuan's tutor and who held a key position in the imperial government. Shi Xian, jealous of Xiao Wangzhi's Confucian influence on the emperor, sought to eliminate him. As eunuchs were men who had been castrated for running foul of the law, Xiao Wangzhi fought back by suggesting that felons should not be employed in determining critical matters of state. The eunuch faction responded by slandering some members of the Confucian clique, which eventually led to the suicide of Xiao Wangzhi and many others.

ABOVE **Sima Qian chose the disgrace of castration** over death as punishment for displeasing the emperor so that he could complete his great history of China.

Because Shi Xian wielded such great power, people feared him, and his misdeeds were not brought to light until the next reign. After Shi Xian's death, the imperial government made an effort to keep eunuchs out of politics and little more is heard about them until their resurgence in the Later Han dynasty.

Eunuchs in the Later Han

The power of the eunuchs was unprecedented in the Later Han era as their numbers increased in important government positions. Instrumental in their rise were events that occurred in the reign of Emperor He (reigned CE 88–106).

Empress Dou (who was childless) had adopted Prince Zhao, the son of imperial consort Liang. Empress Dou then arranged for the demotion of the heir apparent—the son of another imperial concubine, Consort Song—and the death of his mother. When Prince Zhao assumed the throne as Emperor He, he was still a minor and Empress Dowager Dou effectively reigned on his behalf. However, she delegated much of her power to her eldest brother, Dou Xian, naming him as regent.

In CE 91, when Emperor He came of age and no longer required a regent, Dou Xian would not budge. With the help of a eunuch named Zheng

EUNUCH TERROR

In CE 168, consort families, officials, and some 30,000 students at the imperial academy formed an alliance against the eunuchs. The eunuchs struck back, executing over 100 of these officials and another 600 were banned for life from holding office. Four years later, another 1,000 students were arrested for their anti-eunuch demonstrations. In CE 189, anti-eunuch partisans stormed the imperial palace, closed all gates, and exterminated more than 2,000 eunuchs. The histories tell us that during the massacre, a number of men who were not eunuchs, but who had no beards, were mistakenly murdered as well.

LEFT **Cai Lun, a chief eunuch in Emperor He's court,** became rich and titled after developing paper. He later became the patron deity of papermaking.

of the civil administration of the state, and soon began to infiltrate the military.

Because eunuchs were not simply protecting their own interests but also those of an emperor who was constantly the target of feuding clans of various consorts, any victory for the eunuchs was also a victory for the throne.

Despite this support, eunuch power soon came to an end. Beyond the capital, frequent rebellions, raids by foreigners, as well as religious uprisings meant that the provincial governors had to be granted greater power to cope with quickly changing circumstances. When Emperor Ling died in CE 189, the regional warlords used their newly acquired powers to join forces and massacre the eunuchs. From this point on, until the Later Han's fall in CE 220, confusion reigned in the Empire.

Zhong, Emperor He accused Dou Xian of plotting to murder him and Dou Xian subsequently commited suicide, thus leaving Emperor He free of interference from the Dou faction. As with other Later Han reigns, court politics was so dominated by factional disputes among the powerful families of various consorts, that emperors naturally sought allies among the eunuchs. Indeed, Emperor He rewarded Zheng Zhong with a marquisate and later allowed his adopted son to inherit his fief. Elevations such as these were previously unheard of in the Han era.

The End of Eunuch Power

In CE 168, Dou Wu, who acted as regent for the 13-year old Emperor Ling (reigned CE 168–189), mustered the support of high-ranking civil officials and students at the imperial academy to demand the arrest of two powerful and corrupt eunuch officials. However, word leaked out and the eunuchs were prepared for the challenge. Ultimately out-maneuvered by the eunuchs, Dou took his own life. For the remainder of Emperor Ling's reign, the eunuchs took complete control

LEFT **Cao Cao was not himself a eunuch,** but it was the influence of a powerful court eunuch who had adopted Cao Cao's father that assisted Cao's own rise to power.

Uprisings and Rebellions

By 184, a large mass of China's peasantry had come to believe that the Han had lost its mandate to rule and it was time to establish a new order. The two most important rebel groups that took part in uprisings were the Yellow Turbans and the Five Pecks of Grain movement.

After 166, China's administration began to disintegrate as provincial warlords gained strength and eunuchs blocked from official appointment anyone who criticized their policies. Poverty-stricken peasants began increasingly to look for deliverance from leaders of popular religious movements. In 184, China was plunged into even greater chaos by two Daoist uprisings.

The Yellow Turbans

The Yellow Turbans, named for their distinctive yellow headgear, were centered in eastern China under the leadership of three brothers from a family of physicians—Zhang Jue, Zhang Liang, and Zhang Bao. They took as their divine patrons the Daoist sage Laozi and the mythical Yellow Emperor. The scripture associated with the Yellow Turban movement, which survives only in fragmentary form, is known as the *Classic of Great Peace*. "Great Peace" referred to a utopian era that would emerge after the fall of the Han. Scholars surmise that the teachings associated with this text included traditional values such as loyalty and filial piety, magical and medical teachings, meditation, and sexual and breathing techniques for prolonging life.

The Yellow Turbans organized themselves into 36 districts, each headed by a healer or "master of techniques," who could heal the sick. The three brothers who led the movement were referred to as the General of Heaven, General of Earth, and General of Mankind— names which derive from the traditional representation of

RIGHT **The Yellow Turbans took Huangdi (the Yellow Emperor)** as their patron. In this 350-ft (106-m) sculpture he is beside Yandi. Both are revered as ancestors in China.

the cosmos as a unity of Heaven, Earth and Man. The confession of sins, abstention from alcohol, the performance of charitable acts and other religious practices associated with the Yellow Turbans, suggest a Buddhist influence, which was beginning to spread in China at that time.

In 184, the Yellow Turbans, with an army of several hundred thousand men, mounted simultaneous insurrections in 16 commanderies. However, by the end of the year, all three leaders had been killed, and the movement more or less died out with its leaders.

The Five Pecks of Grain Movement

The Five Pecks of Grain movement was centered in Sichuan and Shanxi, in western China. The name derives from the rule that every year each member was to provide five pecks of grain for community use. Their communities, which were organized into 24 units, were headed by officials called "libationers." The movement's leaders were Zhang Daoling, his son Zhang Heng, and his grandson Zhang Lu. Called the Celestial Masters, these three were considered to be the earthly representatives of the Daoist philosopher Laozi, who was worshipped as the Most High Lord Lao.

These western rebels followed a religious path called the "Way of the Celestial Masters," and, like the Yellow Turbans, preached the utopian ideal of the age of great peace. They were also known for reciting the text of the Laozi for its protective magical power, and the extant version of *Classic of Great Peace* may well represent the sacred text associated with the Five Pecks movement.

The Five Pecks of Grain movement includes a number of religious elements that may have originated with Buddhism. An example of this is that illness was regarded by practitioners as a punishment for misdeeds, and absolution was sought through confession and good deeds. The Five Pecks of Grain movement may have also incorporated into their ideology ideas of the non-Chinese communities in west China.

Zhang Lu eventually surrendered to the Han general Cao Cao in 215 and resettled in the north where the religion continued to spread.

From Insurrection to Anarchy

Although the Yellow Turban insurrection of 184 was contained within ten months, the eunuchs and the Han court were no longer in control of the provinces, which were now headed by increasingly autonomous governors. Emperor Xian had been ousted from the capital in 190, but returned in 196 to find a ruined city littered with the corpses of those who had starved or had been murdered by rampaging militia. Those few officials who still remained were forced to live on wild grains.

Cao Cao, a military man and former dissident who had managed to recruit some 300,000 Yellow Turbans to his ranks, took command from Xian's generals. He urged Emperor Xian to move from the capital to Xu in the Yingchuan commandery, which was now under Cao Cao's jurisdiction. There, Cao Cao established the new Han court. The presence of Emperor Xian lent Cao Cao an authority that had previously evaded him, as well as access to prominent officials who had not been willing to serve the military upstart Cao Cao but who obliged in the case of the Han emperor.

Despite various efforts to restore the Han dynasty and unify China under one rule, by 215 three men divided China's territory. They were Cao Cao in the north, Liu Bei in the southwest, and Sun Quan in the southeast. Cao Cao died in 220 and the same year, Emperor Xian abdicated in favor of Cao Cao's son, Cao Pi, who then set himself up as emperor. However, as Cao Pi shared this honor with two other men, China remained, for the next 40 years, divided into the three kingdoms of Wei, Wu and Shu.

LEFT **Although Cao Cao held power** over the emperor, he never attempted to usurp the throne. After his death, he was named Emperor Wu of Wei by his son.

BELOW **Laozi's philosophy,** followed by both the Yellow Turbans and the Five Pecks of Grain movement, stressed individual freedom and spontaneity, as well as laissez-faire government.

Han Technology

Advances in metallurgy represent the single most important factor in the development of science and technology in Han times. These advances are demonstrated most clearly in the areas of agriculture, warfare, and timekeeping.

While iron was plentiful in China, the technology for producing it required metallurgical techniques, such as producing extremely high temperatures for the forging process. Once these techniques were acquired, production of iron soon replaced the less complex bronze production.

Agricultural Technology

The most important agricultural innovation in the period between the fourth century BCE and the second century CE was the introduction of iron picks, spades, and plows to replace inferior tools of bone, wood, and stone, or prohibitively costly bronze implements. These innovations increased the yield of crops and somewhat lightened the farmer's burden.

The shape of plows was also refined so that soil could be cut through more efficiently. Han tool makers attached moldboards to plows which streamlined plowing by simultaneously lifting, crushing, and turning over the soil, thus saving the farmer from additional hoe and spade work. Han plows also featured a vertical strut that could be adjusted to regulate the depth of the furrow.

Prior to the Han, farmers sowed seed using the method of "broadcasting"—throwing the seed by hand as they walked along their fields. This method is inefficient because it wastes much seed and makes for unevenly spaced crops. In Han times, farmers began to use deep furrows edged with broad ridges to protect seedlings from too much rain or sun exposure. This system also facilitated crop rotation, allowing one year's ridges to be used as the following year's furrows.

For blowing the chaff from the grain, farmers employed rotary-fan winnowing machines, which used the first crank in world history. The genius of the crank lay in its ability to connect two kinds of motion. By using a handle placed at right angles to the wheel's plane, the wheel could be turned much more easily.

Military Technology

Before the Han dynasty, bronze was the primary medium for weaponry. In Han times, spears, axes,

RIGHT **This replica of the armor of King Zhao Mei of Nanyue** was created from the original, seen at the front of the image. The cords tying the iron plates together had disintegrated.

INSTRUMENTS OF EFFICIENCY

The Han saw the introduction of an instrument called the "triple seed plow." This man-and ox-driven seeding machine plowed three rows at once. It was also equipped with adjustable funnels that distributed seed, and a wooden plank at the back that leveled the soil and covered the seed. Emperor Wu (141–87 BCE) decreed that the triple seed plow was to be used throughout the empire. Han technicians also devised an irrigation device called the "square-pallet chain-pump." This pump used man-powered treading pedals that moved pallet boards along a wooden trough connected to a source of water, such as a lake or river. The wheel moved the boards, which scooped up water into ditches that directed it into fields for irrigation.

swords, and knives of iron and steel became widespread. A steel knife dating from the Later Han, proudly inscribed in gold with the words, "This knife has been forged thirty times," was discovered by archaeologists. The makers of this sword clearly realized that repeated heating and forging strengthens steel implements by removing impurities.

Iron also replaced leather in armor. Iron armor was made by tying together iron plates with fine cords. The plates were smaller and lighter than the former leather ones, and could therefore cover a larger surface of the body.

Another innovation was the use of maps in warfare. Generals were advised that, before they engaged in a military campaign, they should attend closely to maps to gain information about difficult terrain that might hamper their mobility or provide cover for enemy ambush. Maps also provided crucial information about the condition of routes, the size and populations of cities, and about topographical features that might aid the army's advance. The tombs of Former Han at Mawangdui yielded three maps painted on silk that represent the oldest surveying examples found in China. One is a military map showing the configuration of forces stationed throughout the marquisate. Another is a topographical map that clearly depicts all mountains (including their contour lines and relative heights), rivers, roads, and population centers. The placement of rivers on this map corresponds well to modern cartographic representations, suggesting the existence of sophisticated surveying techniques.

Scientific Instruments

Many scientific instruments were developed in the Han era to keep track of time and other natural events, such as comets and eclipses. Hours were counted using sundials or water clocks, known as clepsydra. The most ancient clepsydra, the "outflow" variety, measured time by the gradual draining of water from a large metal vessel. During the Han dynasty, this simple instrument was replaced with the "inflow" clepsydra which corrected for the gradually slower timekeeping function of outflow clocks as pressure fell by adding tanks between the water reservoir and the inflow vessel. The inflow clepsydra also utilized an indicator rod attached to a float. As the water level sank, the indicator rod moved down to indicate the hour. A calendar of 365¼ days was also developed during this era.

The scholar Zhang Heng (78–139) invented the world's first seismograph. His interest in earthquakes was not related to an interest in geology in general. Instead, Zhang Heng viewed earthquakes as a sign of Heaven's displeasure in the mismanagement of dynastic affairs. Thus, the first response to an earthquake was to look into the bureaucratic misdeeds that prompted this disruption of cosmic harmony.

The Invention of Paper

The first writing in China is found on Shang dynasty oracle bones. This divination procedure involved inscribing turtle plastrons or ox scapulae with questions and then casting the bones into a fire where the heat produced cracks that were later interpreted by diviners. Slightly later, bronze vessels inscribed with characters were used in rituals. Wooden and bamboo tablets were probably also in use in very early times, but because these materials are so perishable, the earliest excavated examples are much later than those in bronze and bone.

Artifacts in early China that we classify as books were made of bamboo and wooden strips bound together with cords in the manner of a Venetian blind. Many texts of this sort have been found in recent times, including the bamboo manuscript of Qin dynasty legal documents excavated at Shuihudi. In some cases, the bindings of these books have disintegrated, which has left archaeologists with the unenviable task of trying to determine the correct sequence of hundreds of strips. Wooden text with "page"

Help with Important Matters
Kings sought guidance through divination, asking questions about such matters as sacrifices, weather, war, hunting, travel, and good fortune.

numbers inscribed at the bottom of the strips have only rarely been found by archaeologists.

Archaeologists have also uncovered, in the arid climate of northwest China, thousands of wooden strips, some still with their bindings intact. Most remarkable are the 20,000 wooden strips discovered in the area surrounding the modern-day city of Juyan, in Gansu Province, the site of a Han dynasty border settlement. The texts excavated in this area document concern mostly of military and administrative issues.

In early China, books were also made of silk, usually in the form of scrolls. The most famous examples are those found at Mawangdui in the Former Han tomb of the Marquis of Dai. Silk is not only lighter than wood or bamboo, but its soft, absorbent surface is more suited to writing. In addition, unlike strips of bamboo, which need to be bound together, strip by strip, silk provides a large flat area for writing. However, bamboo was preferred for writing drafts because the author could easily shave any errors off the surface of the bamboo.

In the Later Han, writers complained that bamboo was too heavy and silk too expensive for daily use. Alternatives were sought. In 105, Cai Lun, a eunuch of the Later Han presented Emperor He with paper made from tree bark, rags, hemp, and fishing nets. Scholars generally believe that paper was in use prior to 105 and

Recorded History
Answers to questions about weather and good fortune were often recorded on bones. Much has been learned about the Shang as a result of deciphering the text.

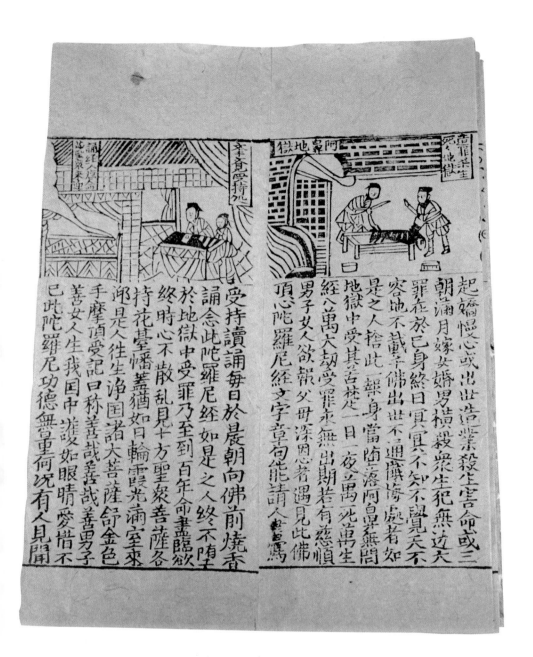

A Better Class of Paper

Until Cai Lun invented a new composition for paper and refined the papermaking process, paper was used only by the poor. Cai's paper was thin, strong, and could be mass-produced cheaply.

First Paper, Then Books

Buddhist sutras were among the first books to be produced, first by woodblock printing and then, in the eleventh century, by movable type printing technology. Inexpensive printed books became widely available in China during the Song dynasty.

that Cai Lun's paper was more of a refinement than an invention. Others suggest that the significance of Cai Lun's innovation is that the quality of paper he developed was finally adequate for writing official communications.

Cai Lun was employed by Empress Deng as the official in charge of manufacturing various instruments and weapons. As part of Deng Sui's general policy of frugality, she limited tribute gifts to ink and paper, and may well have set Cai Lun the task of developing a cheaper and more durable form of paper for official use. Some scholars have labeled Cai Lun's invention "quasi-paper" because it is not made entirely of vegetable fibers. Still, it represents an important phase in the development of true paper.

An Ode to Paper

After Cai Lun's invention, the use of paper for writing became more commonplace. But its beauty and pleasures were still novel enough to have inspired a poem about paper by Fu Xian (234–294).

> *Paper, so beautiful and precious,*
> *Yet frugal in principle.*
> *Expanding when it opens,*
> *Compact, when stored,*
> *It expands and contracts…*
> *Expressing one's love from a distance of ten thousand miles,*
> *Or crystallizing one's thoughts on one of its corners.*

In the third century, paper was used for producing multiple copies of works, such as the "best-seller" of Zuo Si, the *Rhapsody on the Three Capitals*, which raised the price of paper because it generated so many copies.

Han Medicine

The medical texts (*c.* 168 BCE) unearthed at Mawangdui reveal the extensive use in Han times of drugs, massage, cupping, fumigation, cauterization, magic rituals, gymnastics, sexual practices, and spells to induce good health.

RIGHT **Acupuncture** is a very ancient form of healing that predates the Han.

Two different kinds of medical treatment were practiced in early China: one that imposed responsibility on the individual for his or her physical health, and was thus grounded in moral conduct; and one that attributed illness to demonic agents that could be warded off with therapies unrelated to questions of morality.

Ethics-Based Medicine

The ethics-linked system of beliefs about medical treatment is associated with acupuncture and the concept of health found in texts such as the first century BCE document *Huangdi Neijing Suwen* (*Yellow Emperor's Inner Classic: Basic Questions*). Therapies included not only diet, exercise, and the effects of weather and climate, but also those which concerned a person's morals and emotions. For example, according to the correlative cosmology recorded in the *Huangdi Neijing Suwen*, anxiety is associated with the lungs, and the

BELOW **Organs of the body** were considered either Yin or Yang. They were believed to function more efficiently at certain times of the year and were linked with a season and its element.

圖六十八——仿明版古圖（十四）

weakening of that organ was thought to be caused by intense anxiety which resulting in a depletion of *qi* in the lungs. Similarly, imbalances brought about by sexual excess were thought to harm the liver. It is because of the concession to the moral dimension that medical texts such as the *Huangdi Neijing Suwen* are given a place of preeminence in Confucian culture.

When early Chinese physicians located the human body within the general pattern of the natural order, health became viewed as a process governed by predictable laws. Much Han dynasty medical advice, therefore, counseled regimens that were in keeping with natural patterns and cycles. This perspective reveals the optimistic belief that by aligning all aspects of one's daily life with the cycles of nature, it is possible to assert control over one's health. Thus, acupuncture, which is believed to regulate the flow of *qi* (or cosmic energy) throughout the body, is based upon this principle.

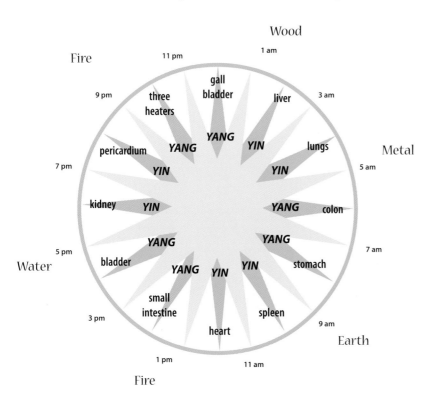

Acupuncture seems to have been developed from the two therapies of cauterization (the external application of heat to remedy internal imbalances of *qi*) and lancing. Documenting the early use of medical lancing are the gold and silver lancing needles discovered in the tomb of Liu Sheng, the king of Zhongshan (died 113 BCE), in present-day Mancheng, Hebei Province.

Demonic and Exorcistic Medicine

In contrast to ethics-based medicine, the amoral medical prescriptions of *Recipes for Fifty-Two Ailments*, which was found at Mawangdui, often present disease personified as baleful spirits and able to be dispelled by the use of demon-repelling drugs, exorcistic spitting, and incantation. Among the various remedies for urine retention, one text enjoins the sufferer to shout, face east, and urinate. To cure inguinal swelling (swelling in the stomach), the afflicted should rise at dawn and get an amputee, while facing east, to stamp with his/her peg leg on the afflicted one. Another method said to cure inguinal swelling was to rise early and shoot arrows fashioned of kudzu wood from a bow made of straw and cord.

The prescriptions in the *Recipes for Fifty-Two Ailments* also frequently recommend the use of exorcistic curses that threaten the demonic agent that is believed to cause the disease. The curse "I stab you with an oak stick, and stab you with a knife," for example, addresses the offending agent directly. Various objects, such as brooms, gourds, water, and plants, were also used to "absorb" evil spirits which were then discarded. To cure warts, for example, the afflicted is directed to brush the warts seven times with an old broom while saying, "I brush the warts to the north," and then drop the broom down a well.

Drug-Based Medicine

Alongside the magico-religious rites designed to produce health, the Mawangdui texts include a wide range of therapies based on drugs. Food items such as leeks, asparagus, ginger, cinnamon, and eggs were used—often cooked and consumed, or applied topically. Other non-food items were also recommended, such as the mineral mica and the menstrual cloths of virgins.

The *Recipes for Fifty-Two Ailments* includes a prescription to cure infants suffering from spasms which requires bathing the child with a mixture of water, bamboo truffle, and fried pig lard. A rather alarming cure for seizures is to make an incision in the patient's head from the top of the head to the nape of the neck, apply dog feces, and then cover the incision with half a white chicken. While this treatment is primarily drug-based, the use of feces—which were frequently used in exorcistic practices in early China—suggests a connection between pharmacological and exorcistic practices. However, these two therapies have one feature in common; they both supply relatively simple and instantaneous solutions that are unrelated to the moral status of the afflicted patient.

SEXUAL TECHNIQUES

In addition to various methods used to "nurture life," such as breathing exercises, dietary regimens, and calisthenics, the Mawangdui medical texts include manuals that detail the health benefits of certain kinds of sexual activities. These practices were thought to enhance the *qi*, conceived of as a kind of life-force or energy, while ignorance of the correct methods was thought to lead to ill health or death. In breath cultivation, the goal was to imbibe *qi* from the environment, which would circulate its healthful influences throughout the body. In sexual cultivation, the man was thought to imbibe the Yin essence of his female partner which complemented and strengthened his Yang, or male nature. The various forms of physical and spiritual cultivation thus did not seek to repress sexual appetites but to utilize them as a means to obtain good health and self-mastery.

LEFT **Hua Tuo was a famous Han dynasty physician.** He was expert in several fields, including acupuncture, gynecology, pediatrics, and surgery. He invented several effective herbal anesthetics.

Partition and Conflict: The Period of Division

Introduction

The collapse of Han government saw the formation of three contending states.
A short-lived unification under the Jin dynasty was followed by barbarian incursions
that divided China between a series of northern and southern dynasties.

By the late second century CE, 400 years of government under the house of Liu meant that the people of China saw the Han dynasty as their natural ruler. The brief interregnum of Wang Mang was considered an aberration, and though the regime of Emperor Ling—dominated by eunuchs—was confused and corrupt, the forms of administration were intact and the sovereign, regardless of personal failings, was the center of the civilized world.

Below the apparent unity, however, there was potential for division, notably in the growing independence of the wealthy landed families.

The End of the Han

The alliance of the central government with this provincial gentry, which provided the educated men who served in the bureaucracy, lay at the heart of the imperial system. Such a system meant that Later Han could never enforce an adequate system of land registration and taxation, while leading local families gained increasing power in their communities. The self-confidence of the gentry became so great that many gentlemen refused to serve a government they considered corrupt, while the proscription against ideal Confucians did much to alienate the dynasty from the very class on which it depended for support.

The devastating religious rebellion of the Yellow Turbans of 184 was followed by a collapse of power at the capital. The civil war which followed demolished the structures of imperial government and saw the formation of three rival states. The great warlord Cao Cao sought to reconstruct a government in the authoritarian fashion of Han, but his state of Wei failed to unify the Chinese world, and though he and his successors held splendid court they lacked the prestige of the past. In a strange way, memory of the glories of Han was an obstacle to any government that sought to revive its authority.

Southern Expansion and Northern Invasion

The two centuries of Later Han rule had also seen a substantial change in the balance of the population of China. Many peasant farmers abandoned the vulnerable territory of the

THE THREE KINGDOMS

MONGOLIA
MONGOLIAN STEPPE
INNER MONGOLIA
Yellow
Sanggan Valley
Pincheng
NORTH KOREA
Liang
QINGHAI
Ye
Yellow
Qi
SOUTH KOREA
Jin
Guandu
Yellow
Sea
GANSU
Chang'an
Luoyang
Song
Chen
Huai
SHAANXI
Jiankang
SICHUAN
CHINA
Han
Chengdu
Yangzi
Yangzi
East China Sea
Red Cliffs
Fei River
HUNAN
Yangzi
MYANMAR
VIETNAM
LAOS
South China Sea

KEY
- Archaeological site
- Battle site
- International border
- Kingdom of Shu Han
- Kingdom of Wei
- Kingdom of Wu

0   400 km
0   400 miles

N

northern frontier, leaving the region to non-Chinese herdsmen, while south of the Yangzi a steady process of colonization incorporated new and formerly inaccessible areas and people into the Chinese sphere of influence. As a result, when the central government collapsed, the south of the Yangzi was able to establish a balance of power against the north, and the Three Kingdoms state of Wu maintained its independence for 80 years.

The demographic potential developed under the Later Han, and its realization by Wu, meant that in the early fourth century, as non-Chinese regimes took advantage of the ruinous disorder of Jin, remnants of the imperial Sima family were able to find safety in the south. The refugee rulers of Eastern Jin settled in the city of Nanjing, founded by Wu, and began a period of division between non-Chinese states in the north and Chinese dynasties in the south.

In last resort, governments rely upon military strength. The long-lived Han dynasty concealed this reality better than most, but the Jin state and its successors, Song, Qi, Liang, and Chen, were dominated by fighting men, while the Tuoba Wei and other states in the north were clearly dynasties of conquest.

At the same time, however, the gentry kept aloof, accumulating land and followers and dominating their local communities. There were no bonds of reciprocity such as those which held feudal states together in the medieval West, and great landed families were unwilling to allow any central power to interfere in their affairs. They were, however, prepared to support the state in their own interests, and they presented a successful, stable alternative to the weak and erratic regimes that succeeded one another in nominal authority.

Splendors of Division

Such a history of political disorder and alien rule appears strange to those accustomed to a powerful and unified China, but the Period of Division was not an age of darkness. Freed from the sometimes stultifying authority of a unified empire, and with wealth in private hands, the scholars, artists, and people of China engaged in the remarkable development of new forms of aesthetic and philosophical expression.

During the early third century the state of Wei, in particular, attracted a brilliant court; its founder, Cao Cao, was a noted poet, his son Cao Zhi is one of the finest writers in Chinese literature, and others including Xi Kang and Yuan Ji became celebrated for their freedom of thought and expression. Two centuries later came Xie Lingyun. A member of a great southern family, he composed romantic landscape poetry that inspired some of the greatest works of later literature and art. Among his contemporaries were artists such as Gu Kaizhi and the calligrapher Wang Xizhi, both of whom became objects of admiration for later generations.

Confucianism was still influential, and great families boasted of their ancestry, but in this time of trouble its traditional philosophy was challenged by Daoism and Buddhism. Zhang Lu (founder of the Daoist church, who ruled in northern Sichuan until his surrender with honors to Cao Cao) and his followers erected temples and monasteries; the religion flourishes to this day.

Still more notable were the teachings of Buddhism that arrived in China during the Later Han time. A somewhat esoteric cult to start with, Buddhism developed a wide variety of philosophies, sects, and schools, and monks such as Huiyuan began to lead educated opinion. Patronized by many rulers, Buddhism became wealthy and influential, and this initially foreign religion was adopted so deeply by China that it has played a leading role in its civilization since that time.

LEFT **This carved stone heavenly musician** (c. 470–480) is from the Northern Wei dynasty. It is part of the elaborately carved decoration of the Buddhist cave temple site in Yungang, Shanxi Province.

BELOW **This stele features the Buddha Sakyamuni** as Abhayadana, or bestower of fearlessness. It is from Lincheng, Hebei Province, and dates to the Northern Qi dynasty, 550–577.

Wei, Wu, and Shu Han

The fall of Han may be dated almost precisely to an evening in September of the year 189. Formally, the Han dynasty survived a further thirty years, but the civil war begun by the frontier general Dong Zhuo and his opponents destroyed the unity of the empire and inaugurated four centuries of division.

On that September evening, from his camp outside the imperial capital of Luoyang, Dong Zhuo saw flames in the sky and led his army in to take control. He had no authority for such action, but there was no power in the city to withstand him, and another military force would be required to drive him away.

BELOW **This flying or galloping "celestial" horse** standing on a swallow is from the Eastern Han dynasty, second century CE, Wuwei, Gansu Province.

Political Balance Collapses

Dong Zhuo's opportunity came through the collapse of the political balance that had been established during the reigns of the last two emperors, Huan and Ling. When Emperor Huan took power at the expense of his consort Liang's family in 159, he was aided by the eunuchs of his harem, and these trusted men rose to great political influence. They retained power through the reign of Emperor Ling, but when that ruler died in 189 they were faced with the hostility of a new consort family, led by He Jin (the brother of the Empress, now Dowager), and urged on by men of the family such as Yuan Shao and his cousin Yuan Shu. The eunuchs hoped to remove the threat by killing He Jin, but Yuan and their allies broke into the palace and slaughtered them. As Dong Zhuo arrived, the two sons of Emperor Ling came into his hands, and he promptly replaced the new emperor with his younger brother.

Such usurpation of power brought an immediate response from the landed gentry who had traditionally served the imperial bureaucracy, and by the end of the year an army of "loyal rebels" had formed in the east of the empire. They gained some success, and Dong Zhuo was forced west to Chang'an, previous capital of Former Han, but the allies soon quarreled, and the various leaders who had claimed to support the Han turned into local warlords fighting for power against their rivals. Dong Zhuo's protégé Liu Xie, Emperor Xian of Han, reigned for 30 years, but he never held power of his own, and his empire was a gigantic battleground.

Warlord Armies

The Later Han had maintained a system of conscription in the territories of the frontier but unlike the former dynasty, men of the inner empire received no formal training in war: in case of rebellion or banditry it was considered better that the troublemakers be amateurs. The Yellow Turban rebellion of 184, however, had brought mass levies of troops, and although it was short-lived the disruption of that brutal campaign made large numbers of people homeless. Since that time bandits had been ravaging the east of

LEFT **These figurines of a groom, horse, and rider** made from painted terracotta date from the Three Kingdoms period, CE 220–280.

the empire, but the civil war against Dong Zhuo introduced a new level of disorder.

The first troops were raised by press-gangs, relying upon the notional authority of the ruined imperial government, but the various warlords later attracted support from wandering refugees and even bandit groups, looking for some form of security, while the soldiers were accompanied by camp-followers, wives, and children. Such wandering hordes, sometimes numbering in the tens or even hundreds of thousands, had little organization. After the years of disorder, many recruits had fighting experience, but they were grouped in comparatively small units, each dependent on a leader.

The Chinese had had bows and crossbows since early times, but their use required training and skill. Much fighting was hand-to-hand, with the leaders of troops seeking to break and disrupt an enemy line, aided by their skill and strength in martial arts. They were bold, strong, and charismatic—and often also a little mad, for it took a special cast of mind to face a mass of opponents without certainty that your men would follow you. If one of these chieftains was killed or injured, his men became vulnerable to confusion and panic, which spread easily.

Individual heroes, moreover, seldom possessed a broad grasp of strategy or tactics, and in the heat of battle there were limited means of communication. A general had to plan his battle in advance, and then hope his subordinates would follow instructions. An ambush or other surprise might disrupt the enemy, but the main thing was to keep one's own army intact; many battles were resolved by the sudden collapse and flight of one side.

The Decisive Battles

The first ten years of civil war saw an erratic and incoherent conflict across the greater part of China, increasingly dominated by experienced fighting men at the expense of the land-owning gentry who had formerly controlled the countryside through their economic power and their bands of retainers. At the battle of Guandu in 200, however, the warlord Cao Cao defeated Yuan Shao, his chief rival on the North China Plain, and after his enemy's death two years later, Cao Cao destroyed his family and took over his territory.

By 208 Cao Cao was the dominant figure in the north. In that year Liu Biao, the ruler of central China, died, and Cao Cao forced the surrender of his heir and took control of his territory. As he approached the Yangzi River, however, Cao Cao was faced by the combined forces of Sun Quan, warlord of the lower Yangzi, and Liu Bei, a soldier of fortune and refugee from the north. At the battle of the Red Cliffs, in the region of present-day Wuhan, the allies defeated Cao Cao's army and fleet and drove him back north up the Han River. Cao

BELOW **A bronze figurine of a horseman** carries a *chi* halberd, Eastern Han dynasty, second century CE, Wuwei, Gansu Province. It took strength and advanced training to wield the halberd effectively.

ABOVE **Liu Bei was one of three warlords** who claimed parts of the old Han empire, the others being Cao Cao and Sun Quan. This statue of Liu Bei is from Wuhou Temple, Sichuan Province.

CAO CAO THE HERO-VILLAIN

The founder of the state of Wei, Cao Cao (155–220), is celebrated in Chinese history. His father Cao Song, who was adopted by the palace eunuch Cao Teng, gained great wealth and rose to the highest office in the bureaucracy of Han. Cao Cao served against the Yellow Turbans, then joined the alliance against Dong Zhuo and became a provincial governor on the north China plain. From there he expanded his power across all north China.

A fine poet, Cao Cao was also a strong administrator, accepting any competent man, with no questions about morality. A scholar of Sunzi, he was the only man of family to achieve success in the civil war. His exceptional military skill and capacity for the unexpected were commemorated in the popular saying "Speak of Cao Cao, and Cao Cao is here"; and he is remembered as the great but flawed genius of Chinese tradition.

Cao swiftly recovered and he extended his control over the north, but his troops never crossed the Yangzi.

In 219 Liu Bei, who had taken over present-day Sichuan, defeated Cao Cao's army in the upper Han valley and set the border between them in the Qinling ranges. Later that year, however, as Liu Bei's chief general Guan Yu launched an offensive north from the middle Yangzi, he was halted by Cao Cao's defenses and then taken from behind by Sun Quan. Sun Quan seized the territory, and in 222 a revenge attack from Liu Bei was defeated in the Yangzi Gorges.

The division of China for the next 40 years was thus largely settled: Cao Cao and his state of Wei controlled the north, Sun Quan, ruler of Wu, held the middle and lower Yangzi and the far south, while Liu Bei occupied present-day Sichuan and Yunnan.

Three Empires
Cao Cao, King of Wei, died early in 220, and at the end of that year his son Cao Pi forced the abdication of Emperor Xian of Han and took the imperial title. Liu Bei in Sichuan, relying upon a

most distant descent from Former Han, promptly matched him, but Sun Quan waited until 229 before lodging his own claim.

Liu Bei died soon afterwards, and despite Sun Quan's seizure of the middle Yangzi, Liu Bei's son Liu Chan, guided by his chief minister Zhuge Liang, renewed the alliance with Wu against the north. There was endemic frontier conflict, but the forces of the Shu were unable to establish a position north of the Qin Ling, the lines on the Han River did not change, and while Wu could gain no ground along the Huai, Wei never crossed the Yangzi.

Of the three states, only Wei restored a measure of real government, notably through resettlement of many displaced people in agricultural colonies. Shu remained essentially a warlord state, and though Sun Quan and his family held power for 80 years, their court was overshadowed by the great families of the region. In similar fashion, the ruling Cao family of Wei was gradually isolated from the leading clans of the state, and was eventually subverted and replaced by the general Sima Yi and his descendants; in 266 Sima Yan proclaimed the empire of Jin.

The fortunes of Shu Han declined after the death of Zhuge Liang in 234, and after 20 years of gradual success the armies of Wei destroyed the rival state in 264. Wu, beset with succession troubles after the death of long-lived Sun Quan in 252, was overwhelmed in 280, and the empire of Jin restored a brief unity to the Chinese world.

Cultural Achievements

The comparative brevity and weakness of the Three Kingdoms was balanced by the splendor of their courts and by flourishing artistic and scientific achievements, from astronomy and mathematics to pottery, philosophy, and literature. Seven Masters at the end of Han were succeeded by Eight Sages in the time of Wei, and Cao Zhi, son of Cao Cao, is recognized as one of the greatest poets of China, working in a new style of personal, emotional, and spectacular expression.

The Division of China

In the civil war that followed the fall of Wang Mang 200 years earlier, the man who gained north China, Emperor Guangwu, found small difficulty in subduing the lands south of the Yangzi and then the region of Sichuan. During Later Han, however, constant trouble on the northern frontier drove people from that region, and a steady migration to the south increased the population of the middle and lower Yangzi.

As a result of this, by the time Cao Cao had control of north China, the warlords Sun Quan and Liu Bei, aided by the natural barriers of river and mountains, had sufficient resources to resist his attacks. Their states were not as strong as Wei, but Wu in particular maintained an aggressive policy of colonial conquest against the non-Chinese of the hills, so that it preserved its independence for many years. The combination of demographic change and economic development strengthened the south against the north, and increased the possibility of future division; the conquering dynasty of Jin would later have cause to be grateful to the achievements of Wu.

ABOVE **The Yungang Caves** (386–534), carved by the Northern Wei, comprise more than 53 grottoes and 50,000 statues that include Buddhas and Bodhisattvas.

BELOW **This detail from a painted scroll,** *Admonition of the Instructress of the Palace Ladies,* ink on silk, is attributed to Gu Kaizhi (*c.* 344–406).

The Three Kingdoms in Art

The sudden fall of China's first long-lived empire, and the complex struggle that followed, captured the imagination of later generations and has inspired storytellers for almost 2000 years. In particular, the conflict between the oppressive Dong Zhuo and the usurper Cao Cao against Liu Bei, self-styled heir of the legitimate imperial house, presented themes of courage and loyalty that lent themselves readily to epic romance and fantasy.

Many legends and anecdotes of the dramatic events and their protagonists were preserved in the formal history of the period, *Sanguozhi*, completed in the early fifth century. References from the Tang dynasty indicate that the deeds of that time were common knowledge, and the great Song poet Su Dongpo recalled the gallantry of Zhou Yu, general of Sun Quan, at the Battle of the Red Cliffs:

*With laughter and jest, holding a yellow
fan and wearing a silk scarf,
Amidst smoke and flying ash he destroyed
his great enemy.*

Incidents from the history formed the basis for popular story-cycles, and these in turn became the subject of many plays and operas. Identified by masks and flags, the heroes of the Three Kingdoms still strut the stage to the

Romance of the Three Kingdoms
Films and television based on the *Romance of the Three Kingdoms* now attract a widespread audience. Above is an opera staging of the *Romance*, a novel by Luo Guanzhong.

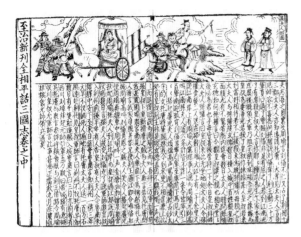

A Page from the *Sanguo zhi pinghua*, a Prompt Book
Prompt books were originally designed for professional public storytellers, to remind them of the plot. The story shown is from the *Romance of the Three Kingdoms* and features an illustration of the Lady Sun.

sound of drums and cymbals, and the traditional repertoire may be found in formal theaters and performed by strolling players.

Most popular versions embellish the achievements of Liu Bei and his comrades, fighting against great odds, and *Romance of the Three Kingdoms*, the great novel of Luo Guanzhong that took final form in the fourteenth century, confirmed the view of Cao Cao as the powerful villain. In modern times, moreover, there has been scholarly debate about events and personalities of the Three Kingdoms, and in the early 1960s Cao Cao attracted Maoist controversy.

In popular opinion, the genius of the Three Kingdoms is Liu Bei's great minister Zhuge Liang, who is credited with technical skill as the inventor of the wheelbarrow and of a repeating crossbow, and with a strategic brilliance to rival Cao Cao.

The battle of the Red Cliffs, central event of the *Romance*, celebrates his wisdom and skill. History tells that it was Zhou Yu, commander of Sun Quan's forces, who sent fireships against Cao Cao's fleet and camps, but the *Romance* presents Zhuge Liang as a wizard who summons the wind to destroy the enemy, giving him a romanticized reputation beyond his real, albeit considerable, achievements.

Guan Yu

While Zhuge Liang is praised as the great scholar and counselor, Guan Yu is seen as the epitome of knightly virtue and valor.

A close companion of Liu Bei, who treated him as a brother, Guan Yu was renowned for strength, loyalty, and prowess in single combat. On one occasion he was pouring a goblet of warm wine when he was challenged by an enemy champion. He slew his foe and returned before the wine had cooled.

Arrogant and aggressive, in 219 Guan Yu was surprised and killed by Sun Quan's general Lü Meng as he sought to break Cao Cao's defenses on the Han River. Guan Yu, however, remains a beloved hero to posterity, as Sun Quan and Lü Meng are reviled for their treachery.

In later generations Guan Yu's reputation grew further. With title as an emperor, he is worshipped by Buddhists and Daoists, and was canonized by the Qing dynasty. There are temples in his honor, and he serves as a guardian for others.

The Two Jin Dynasties

A member of a noted aristocratic family from Henei, Sima Yi entered Cao Cao's service in 208, and became a friend of his son Cao Pi, first Emperor of Wei. Sima Yi held high office and was a successful general against Shu Han and Wu, and in the northeast. When Cao Pi's son Cao Rui died in 239, Sima Yi was named a regent for his infant successor.

In 249 Sima Yi murdered his colleague and rival Cao Shuang and seized full power. There followed a series of puppet rulers, but the Sima continued to dominate the court of Wei, and in 266, after the conquest of Shu Han, Sima Yi's grandson Sima Yan proclaimed himself emperor of the new Jin dynasty.

The Sima Family and the War of the Princes

Wu was taken in 280, and a brief period of unity followed, but Sima Yan's son Sima Zhong, or Emperor Hui, who came to the throne in 290, was mentally incompetent, and his reign was marked by increasing turmoil.

A struggle between consort families resulted in ten years' rule by the murderous Empress Jia, but members of the Sima clan, who held military power in the provinces, seized the capital in the year 300 and eliminated the Jia family. Then, however, the cousins turned on one another, and in the War of the Eight Princes the leaders of the Sima destroyed themselves.

The last man standing, Sima Yue, ruled as regent for his kinsman, the puppet Sima Zhi, but the credit of the imperial house had been ruined by its history of bloodshed and treachery, and central government was no more than a façade. The years of war, moreover, had exhausted the military power of the Jin, and they were now

BELOW **The Shentongsi monastery**, in Qianfoyan, Shandong, flourished during the Tang era. It was founded during the Eastern Jin dynasty (317–420).

no match for their northern neighbors. In 311 the Xiongnu leader, Shi Le, sacked the imperial capital of Luoyang, and though a remnant court survived a few more years, the fall of Chang'an in 316 marked the end of the Jin dynasty in northern China.

Northern Invaders

Even during the Later Han, Chinese authority along the steppe frontier had been weakened by a steady emigration of people to the south, and peasant farmers were replaced by non-Chinese pastoralists. Divided and weak, the Xiongnu were driven from the Mongolian steppe by the Xianbi people, whose warleader Tanshihuai ravaged Han territory in the late second century, but the tribes were still too disorganized to pose a major threat. Cao Cao and the Wei recovered the northeast, but the lands northwest of the Fen River were occupied by the Xiongnu, while the Xianbi controlled the Sanggan valley and the Ordos loop of the Yellow River.

Early in the fourth century, as the Sima fought among themselves, the chieftain Liu Yuan, descended on one side from a princess of Han, and on the other from a Shanyu of the Xiongnu, proclaimed himself a king in 304 and then emperor in 308. He died in 310, but his son Liu Cong kept the title; it was his general Shi Le who stormed Luoyang. Liu Cong's forces captured Chang'an and drove the Jin to the south.

For many of the common people, non-Chinese rule was an improvement on the chaos of the Sima family, but there was still no settled government. In 329 Shi Le overthrew his former patrons and occupied north China, but his state was defeated in 352 by the Murong Xianbi, who were in turn replaced in 370 by the Qiang leader Fujian. Though militarily powerful, such short-lived regimes were unable to deal effectively with the refugee Jin dynasty based on the Yangzi.

Survival in the South

In 307 the prince Sima Rui had been sent as military governor of the southeast. The region was almost as disorganized as the north, but with the aid of the military chieftain Wang Dun he established a measure of control over the great local families, and in 318, after the fall

of Chang'an, he took the title of Emperor Yuan of Eastern Jin, and the dynasty ruled another hundred years.

Great numbers of émigrés from the north added to pressure on the exiled state. Although they strengthened the administration, the émigrés were resented by the local gentry. At the same time, the state itself depended heavily upon warlord families of northern origin. The Wang family was succeeded in power by the Yu and then by Huan Wen, whose plans to seize the throne were interrupted only by his death in 373.

Despite internal conflict, the state had sufficient resources and energy to hold the north at bay, and in 383 the regime of Huan Wen's successor, Xie An, gained decisive success over the great army of Fujian at the Fei River, tributary of the Huai. Soon afterwards Sima Daozi restored power to the imperial clan, but he was grossly incompetent and at the turn of the century there was a great rebellion of protest led by the Daoist Sun En.

In 403 Huan Wen's son, Huan Xuan, deposed the Jin emperor and, although he was swiftly destroyed, the savior of the dynasty, Liu Yu, held such control that in 420 the Jin ruler himself offered him the throne, as the Mandate of Heaven had clearly changed. So the Liu Song dynasty maintained a tradition by which military power brought imperial authority, while the division of China continued for almost three centuries.

LEFT **This glazed stoneware vase** of the Western Jin type depicts a scene of immortals or Daoist deities and features two-tiered buildings.

BELOW **Ox carts** became a common means of transportation, used as an alternative to horse-drawn carriages. This example is a Western Jin dynasty terracotta model.

The "Barbarian" Invasions

China's first empire, the Han dynasty (*c.* 206 BCE–CE 220), came crashing down in the first years of the third century CE, as non-Chinese peoples emerged to become the lords of northern China. But a careful examination of these peoples and their relations to the empire makes it somewhat difficult to call this an invasion.

BELOW **Wori Tusi castle,** Sichuan, was built by a lord of the Qiang, a people that emerged after 315.

The term often employed to categorize the Period of Division (fourth to sixth centuries), the "barbarian" invasion, must be used with care. There is a real meaning to the term.

During this time, with the collapse of China's first empire, political control of its old heartlands—the Yellow River region—fell into the hands of the leaders of non-Chinese groups, whom the Chinese considered to be "barbaric." But the term is also problematic, in two ways. First, and most obviously—terms such as "barbarian" are highly subjective epithets, which humans have used across the ages to denigrate their neighbors and their foes. As for "invasion," there certainly have been in human history a few examples of previously unknown peoples who came crashing into other worlds. One such group of invaders was the Mongols, with their sack of Baghdad in 1258 that shocked the Islamic world, or their appearance in Europe, where they were likened to Gog and Magog. But the events of the Period of Division are somewhat different.

The Strangers Within

The various non-Chinese peoples who took center stage in northern China with the collapse of the last successor to the Han's unified empire, the Western Jin (265–316), did not come from lands far away. Most, in fact, had long dwelt within the empire, or along its frontiers; some had themselves been displaced from the empire's rich farmlands and forced into uplands and peripheral zones, as has of course happened with many societies in human history. Although they had frequently raided Chinese territory, they had also been captured and sold by Chinese slavers. Despite differing from the Chinese farmer in the languages they spoke, and the clothes they wore, they were certainly not strangers.

The "Five Barbarian Peoples"

Chinese sources speak of "five barbarian peoples" that rose to prominence in the Sixteen Kingdoms of the fourth and fifth centuries. To the west, in Sichuan, Qinghai, Gansu, and western Shaanxi, were the Qiang, ancestors of the Tibetans; and scattered throughout the same region was a

THE EMERGENCE OF THE EASTERN JIN

By the fourth century CE, the largest armies were those of the emerging frontier kingdoms. They, however, were not the forces that brought about the empire's collapse; those forces came from the interior, beginning with the widespread Daoist millenarian rebellions of the late second century CE, which brought down the Han dynasty and led to the rise of a series of short-lived, volatile Chinese warlord regimes.

The tale of self-destruction is epitomized by the last of these, the Western Jin, whose princes in 291 turned on each other in a fierce and protracted civil war called the "Rebellion of the Eight Princes." Finally, into the vacuum stepped a Xiongnu prince, who in 311 seized Luoyang. A branch of the Jin ruling house now fled south to the Yangzi region, where as "Eastern Jin" it reestablished itself as the first of a series of native dynasties that would rule southern China until 589.

related people, the Di. Both groups had lived in these regions from time immemorial. Always overlapping, non-Chinese populations had in the early centuries CE begun to immigrate more and more into imperial territory (or perhaps assert their presence there), to the great consternation of the empire's officials.

Northeast of this, in what is now Shanxi province, were the Xiongnu. They were descendants of the lords of the great Xiongnu steppe empire, which had during the reign of the Han organized the horsemen of the northern grasslands for systematized extortion of the rich agrarian empire to the south. With the decay of the Xiongnu empire, part of the Xiongnu population had been allowed to move into Chinese territory. Giving up their nomadic ways, they were at least partly integrated into the Han system, serving as auxiliary troops in imperial armies. In the hills of Shanxi they lived among another non-Chinese people, the Jie, highlanders whose history in this region stretched back into the preimperial period.

The last of the groups, the one which might best be described as invaders, were the Särbi (Xianbi) people, ancestors of

the Mongols, who had replaced the Xiongnu on the steppe in a series of short-lived tribal confederations. At the beginning of the events discussed in this chapter, most of the Särbi remained nomadic pastoralists on the grasslands of what are now Mongolia and the Chinese province of Inner Mongolia, although this later changed.

Kingdoms at the Edge of the Empire

During the early centuries CE, these groups were drawn upon more and more regularly as auxiliaries for the imperial armies. At the same time, we see among them the growth of new forms of political organization: rudimentary frontier monarchies, which provided a rough order as the empire faded. Similar developments were certainly taking place among the Chinese populations, as provincial landholders with personal militias grew increasingly aloof from the capital, Luoyang. But with the emergence of the "barbarian kingdoms" at the edge came the militarization of entire societies, that were capable of calling up far more troops than the militias of the atomized interior. In fact, increasingly among their troops we find Chinese, seeking protec-tion from the endless civil wars of the interior.

ABOVE **The Särbi (Xianbi) people of the grasslands of Mongolia** lived as nomadic pastoralists, much like this Mongolian horseman herding horses on the Hulun Buir grassland of Inner Mongolia today.

LEFT **The ceramics made at the Deqing kilns** in Zhejian Province, such as this Deqing-ware ewer (317–420), are known for their monochrome black or dark brown glazes.

The Sixteen Kingdoms

A series of "sixteen kingdoms" rose and fell in northern China during the fourth and fifth centuries. During this volatile and complex period, the lines on the map changed often. Local lords on the edge of the empire who had hammered together unstable coalition regimes made up of various tribal groups engaged in a scramble for power.

The first of the Sixteen Kingdoms was founded by the Xiongnu, descendants of nomads who by the beginning of the fourth century lived within the empire for some 250 years. "In the past 40 years," said the Xiongnu lord in 88 to the Han emperor, "your subjects have been born and reared in Han territory and have depended entirely on China for food." In 304, during the course of the War of the Eight Princes and a devastating famine that accom-

BELOW **The Yangguan Pass,** south of Dunhuang, Western Gansu province, was a military command post from the Han to the Yuan dynasty but is now just a wall submerged in desert sands.

panied it, the Xiongnu lord Liu Yuan announced the reestablishment of the old Han dynasty, with which he claimed relationship through marriage and whose surname, Liu, had long before been bestowed upon his family. Liu died in 310 without successfully establishing his "capital" in Shanxi. In 311 his successor seized the Jin capital at Luoyang, putting a final and formal end to the empire. In 318 the regime was redesignated Zhao (as with most of the Sixteen Kingdoms, the name

was borrowed from one of the Chinese states of the Warring States period). The regime founded by Liu Yuan has come to be called the Former Zhao (304–329).

The Former Zhao

In the shaky and short-lived Former Zhao, we see features of most of the Sixteen Kingdoms. Liu Yuan was an educated man, who had lived much of his youth at the Luoyang. His wish was to recreate the empire under his own rule, drawing upon the institutions and practices of the old regime. But he and his heirs based their efforts on a coalition of armies, each of which was assembled and led by leaders with their own ambitions. One of these commanders was a Jie from Shanxi, Shi Le, who growing up in poverty had become a slave in the army of one of Jin's Eight Princes. Escaping from this bondage, he went on to form his own fighting force and become a follower of Liu Yuan. In 319, however, he declared his own regime, also named the Zhao—called by historians the "Later Zhao" (319–351); a decade later, in 329, he put an end to the Xiongnu Former Zhao.

Weaknesses of the Kingdoms

The reigns of the lords of the Sixteen Kingdoms were often brief, and their deaths violent. Of the seven monarchs of the Later Zhao, Shi Le and one other died in bed; the rest died through infighting. This infighting led to the end of the dynasty itself, which in 351 was overthrown by Ran Min, an ethnic Chinese who had been adopted into the Shi clan. Having risen to become a key military commander within the Later Zhao, he then turned upon it, initiating a slaughter of

the "barbarians." Despite the fact that relations between Chinese and non Chinese were important in these regimes, and intermarriage frequent, tensions clearly existed.

Appearance of the Särbi on the Northern Frontier

Just a year later, however, Ran Min was in turn swept away by a new force in the Central Plains. A branch of the Särbi (Xianbi), the Murong lords had originally built their state in Lower Manchuria before pushing south into the Central Plain. From this lineage came a series of regimes called the Yan, which appeared and disappeared depending on internal struggles and fighting with neighbors—the most important are called by later historians the Former Yan (337–370), and the Later Yan (384–409).

The Murong state took shape in the valley of the Liao River during the last years of the Western Jin. The Murong lord accepted titles from the Jin, while at the same time building up his armies. He also developed a solid agricultural base by resettling Chinese peasants fleeing the wars of the interior to the relative security of the frontier. In 352, the third Former Yan monarch, Murong Jun, led his armies down into the Yellow River plains, capturing Ran Min and establishing a capital from which—for almost twenty years—the Murong would dominate the Central Plain.

Trouble was brewing. West of Manchuria, in the grasslands of Inner Mongolia, had emerged a confederation of nomadic peoples led by

LEFT **This engraving of a man, children, and a horse** is from a Buddhist votive stele. During the Sixteen Kingdoms period Buddhism continued to spread to every part of China.

BELOW **Musicians playing horns and beating drums,** such as these mounted drummers, accompanied military campaigns. Northern tribesmen from the steppes introduced music of this kind into China.

RIGHT **This domestic scene** is carved into a limestone offering shrine from the Northern Wei dynasty, *c.* 386–535.

another branch of the Särbi, the Tabgatch (Tuoba). Fifty years later, the Tabgatch would reunify northern China under a stable regime, as the Northern Wei, first of the Northern dynasties. Of more immediate importance, however, was the rise to power in the west of several regimes of Tibetan peoples, Di and Qiang. The first of these, a purely local regime, had emerged in Sichuan in 304, the same year as Liu Yuan's regime. Interestingly, it also eventually took the same name, Han (*c.* 304–347). Founded by a member of the Di people, it lasted for more than 40 years before being taken by the Eastern Jin.

Emergence of Power in the Wei River Valley

Just to the north, however, in the Wei River valley, was emerging the far more powerful Di regime of the Fu clan, the Former Qin (351–394). Originally from the upper Wei region, in modern Gansu, the founder of this dynasty was Fu Hong (*c.* 285–350), who in the mid-fourth century served the Later Zhao as it extended its power into these western regions. Among the titles that he held in these turbulent times was "commander-in-chief of refugee populations." When the Zhao fell soon after, Fu Hong gave himself the title "King of Qin" (referring back to the Qin dynasty that in 221 created China's first empire).

In 357 Hong's great-nephew, Fu Jian, became lord of the Qin after seizing the throne from, and killing, his cousin. During the late 350s and 360s, while the Murong were extending their power from Manchuria into the Central Plain, Fu Jian took his time to strengthen his power base in the Wei River valley. Curbing the power of the landholders, he asserted control over the peasantry and taxed them efficiently. Having thus enriched the treasury, he was able greatly to strengthen his armies. These he sent forth in 370. After conquering the Former Yan and unifying the Yellow River region, armies were sent to bring the northwestern territories under control (temporarily suppressing the sequence of minor, local regimes that throughout this period rose and fell in the Gansu corridor, between mountains to the south and desert to the north, all with variants of the regional name "Liang"). In the south, Qin armies seized Sichuan and pushed the border with the Eastern Jin much closer to the Yangtze region.

In 383, Fu Jian went on to launch an expedition against the Eastern Jin itself. Southern sources tell us that almost a million men were sent south. This is almost certainly a gross exaggeration, but in any event, the Qin armies were defeated at the famous Battle of the Fei River; the Southern Dynasties would remain independent

RIGHT **This funerary statue,** in gray and polychrome terracotta, shows a horse almost totally covered in armor, a necessity during the volatile period of the Sixteen Kingdoms.

for another two centuries. Whether because of the Fei River defeat or not, the Former Qin now itself began to unravel. Murong armies that had fought under the Qin turned on Fu, driving him out of Chang'an; and in Manchuria, the Murong regime was revived, as Later Yan (384–409). Qiang groups had also been forced into submission to Former Qin; now, led by the Yao clan, they turned on their overlord as well. In 385, having been captured by the Qiang, Fu Jian killed his daughter to save her honor, and then killed himself. Though much weaker, the Yao family now established at Chang'an its own, much weaker, Later Qin regime.

The Rise of the Tabgatch

The first lord of the Later Yan, Murong Chui, had in 370 assisted Fu Jian in defeating the Former Yan. In 386, with the sudden decline of Qin, he declared himself emperor and established a capital in the Central Plain.

Within a few years, it was clear that the Murong were seriously threatened by their western cousins, the Tabgatch. More removed from the politics and fighting of the Sixteen Kingdoms than most of the other groups discussed above, the Tabgatch were originally a confederation of nomadic tribes that had emerged in the grasslands of Inner Mongolia in the third century. By the middle of the fourth century, they had clearly begun to move from chieftainship to a monarchy with the name of Dai, again a borrowing from preimperial Chinese history. These processes of state-building were, however, interrupted in 376 by the armies of Qin, which scattered the Tabgatch and put an end to the Dai, carrying its ruling family off to Chang'an.

With the decay of Former Qin in the 380s, the Tabgatch heir, Gui, returned to the north and regathered his traditional vassal tribes. In 386 he named the revived regime Wei, known by later historians as the Northern Wei. In 397 he routed the Later Yan and seized its capital in the Central Plain and in the next year established his own capital at Pingcheng, on the site of the modern city of Datong, on the northern edge of the Chinese world. The period of the Northern dynasties had now begun.

BELOW **Military funerary figures** such as these were used as tomb guardians during the Northern Wei dynasty. The figures are wearing elaborate armor.

The Southern Dynasties

Though troubled by often bitter struggles between locals and northern refugees, commoners, and aristocrats, the Southern dynasties were an age of wealth: the real wealth of extraordinary commercial growth in south China, and the cultural wealth of China's first great epoch of poetry writing.

ABOVE **This large chicken-headed ewer** with squared lugs and blackish-brown glaze dates to the Eastern Jin dynasty. This type of ewer was a speciality of the Deqing or Yuhang kilns of Zhejiang Province.

Seeking peace, hundreds of thousands of Chinese refugees fled south to escape the turmoil set off on the Central Plain by the Rebellion of the Eight Princes and the rising of the Sixteen Kingdoms. Among the refugees was a branch of the Jin dynasty, who went on to establish the Eastern Jin (317–420) at Jiankang (modern Nanjing) along the Yangzi.

The Struggle for Power

Resentment grew among the locals as the favored northern aristocrats seized lands to build up their new estates. This led in 399 to a rebellion, staged with the support of local gentry, which signaled the end of the Eastern Jin. Although the rebellion was put down, one of the generals involved became the power behind the throne, and in the year 420 took the throne himself as emperor of the Liu-Song dynasty (420–479).

A local man of humble origin, the general put an end to privileged treatment of the northern refugees. His heirs maintained stability for a generation or more. But with increasing pressure from the Northern Wei and growing resistance from large landholders, peace could not last. In 479 another general staged a putsch, to establish the Southern Qi dynasty (479–502). Yet another general, 20 years later, established the Southern Liang dynasty (502–557).

The Golden Age of the Southern Dynasties

The long reign of Liang's founder, Emperor Wu, would be the golden age of the Southern dynasties. Seeking to build and maintain harmony, the emperor drew more and more commoners into his government.

Great shows were made of patronizing Buddhism. In 548 a rebel general from the Eastern Wei, Hou Jing—who had defected to Liang—staged yet another putsch. The great city of Jiankang was taken and the 85 year old Liang monarch died soon after. Hou Jing was eventually killed by Liang forces. Once again power fell to one of the "loyalist" generals, who established his own dynasty, the Chen (557–589), last of the Southern dynasties.

By now the state was much reduced, with large parts having been seized by the northern powers. Conquest of the south by the Sui a generation later cannot have come as a great surprise.

Economic Development

The development in the fifth and sixth centuries of maritime trade routes connecting China with

LEFT **This covered dish with lotus pattern** is Yue-ware from the Southern dynasties period. The crackled, yellowish-green glaze is typical of the period and the southern provenance of the dish.

Japan, Southeast Asia, and India—together with the vast networks of navigable rivers in central and southern China—set the stage for dramatic economic development. As a city of one million people, probably the largest in the world at this time, Jiankang was the hub of a vast international trade network. Many of the inhabitants made their living as merchants and traders, as markets were abundant in the city.

Jiankang filled its treasury with sales taxes and tolls. Nevertheless, government control in the south was generally looser than in the north. The inhabitants of Luoyang or Chang'an were subject to strict curfews. These did not exist in Jiankang, upon whose streets wealthy commodity traders rubbed shoulders with peddlers selling snacks or knick-knacks. Thieves and robbers abounded as well. Above them, of course, were the privileged aristocrats and imperial princes. Although the groups lived off salaries and endowments, and looked down upon the shopkeepers, they too become engaged in the southern commercial revolution. A brother of Liang's Emperor Wu, in fact, was said to have operated dozens of pawnshops in Jiankang. Those who failed to repay would lose the shops or houses they had put up as collateral.

Poetry

During the period of the Southern dynasties, poetry emerged as a central cultural phenomenon, a role it would continue to play throughout the spread of Chinese history. While some fine verse had been written during the Han, it was for the most part the work of a self-selected few. In the third century, poetic composition became much more widespread, as we see with the late Han warlord Cao Cao, and his sons, Cao Pei—who established the Cao Wei dynasty (220–265)—and Cao Zhi. By the fifth and sixth centuries, under the Southern dynasties, it was expected that the upper class gentleman could and would write verse.

One of the most famous poets of this period was Xie Lingyun, scion of a prestigious aristocratic family, who is known particularly for his landscape poetry—poetry of "mountains and streams"—which mirrored developments in painting in China at this time.

Though not of such eminent birth, Xie's contemporary Tao Qian has come to be even more esteemed in the Chinese tradition, with his bucolic poetry of "fields and streams," in

which he celebrated the life of the simple farmer. Thematically, the two poets both expressed a deep wish to get away from the fetters of state control. Tao expressed this in his famous "Peach Blossom Spring" essay, a utopian tale of the discovery of a people in an inaccessible valley who had not even known of the Han, much less the minor dynasties that followed; Xie for his part fled to the mountains to escape the service expected of him at Jiankang, and was eventually sentenced to death in exile.

ABOVE **Buddhism grew in popularity** during the Southern dynasties period. This gilt bronze seated Buddha is dated *c*. 220–589.

The Northern Dynasties

The rise of the Tabgatch (Tuoba) under the Northern Wei in the late fourth century is an important event in Chinese history. A century of fragmentation in northern China would be brought to an end by Wei's highly effective armies.

RIGHT **This gilded bronze cup** was unearthed at Datong, Shanxi Province. It is from the Northern Wei dynasty (386–535).

Wei helped build the foundation for eventual reunification of all Chinese lands by the Sui (581–618) and the Tang (618–907) dynasties with his reforms of local administration, taxation, and land allocation.

Conquest of the North

In 386, having escaped Former Qin control, the Tabgatch lord Daowudi (reigned 386–409)—known as "the Emperor who Makes a Way of War"—established the Northern Wei (386–535) in the grasslands of Inner Mongolia. Eleven years later he led his cavalry south to defeat the Later Yan and occupy the lands north of the Yellow River. With his capital at Pingcheng (modern Datong, Shanxi), Daowudi broke up and reorganized the nomadic tribes to provide manpower for his armies. Hundreds of thousands of Chinese craftsmen and peasants were also forced to move

BELOW **The high altitude and harsh winters** of the Pingcheng region of Shanxi Province could only support so many people, causing famines to break out during the Northern Wei period.

north into the Pingcheng area to feed and supply the court and its armies.

Daowudi's successor, Taiwudi (reigned 423–452), brought an end to the last of the Sixteen Kingdoms by conquering the regimes in Manchuria, the Wei River valley, and the Gansu corridor who had been holding out until this time. With the north united, Wei's interests turned toward the Southern dynasties (though Wei never conquered the south). At the same time, the Tabgatch had lost control of the steppe, and were increasingly plagued by raiding from the new steppe confederation of the Rouran.

A NEW CULTURAL IDENTITY

Cultural reforms were also put in place seeking to merge the Chinese and the non-Chinese populations of the empire. It was now prohibited to wear Särbi clothes at court, or to speak the Särbi tongue. Intermarriage between Chinese and non-Chinese aristocratic clans was actively encouraged. In the midst of this, in 494, Emperor Xiaowen announced his decision to move his capital to Luoyang, deep in the Chinese heartland. For 40 years the city he built there thrived, with a population of more than half a million, magnificent Buddhist pagodas that reached up to the sky, and the great Longmen Buddhist cave temples. These temples or grottoes contain many carved figures, steles, and examples of various calligraphic styles.

RIGHT **The colossal Buddhist sculptures** at the Longmen cave temples were carved and decorated in the Northern Wei style.

Remaking the Monarchy

Located in the far north, Pingcheng was on the edge in multiple ways. Although Tabgatch lords showed interest in the culture and books of the Chinese—establishing an Imperial University at Pingcheng, with Masters of the Five Confucian Classics—the capital was essentially a base for non-Chinese armies. Chinese envoys from the Southern dynasties described what seemed to them to be bizarre rituals, in which horses were sacrificed while mounted drummers and horn-players galloped around the altar.

Pingcheng was also on the edge geographically. High, dry, and in the winter extremely cold, the Pingcheng region could only support a limited population. As the population grew over time, famines broke out. At the same time, control over the conquered territories of the Central Plain was still limited, local administration being in the hands of Chinese landholders who understandably sent as little as they could to the foreign lords at Pingcheng.

Reforms were needed, and these began in earnest during the reign of Emperor Xiaowen (reigned 471–499). Of the practical reforms, by far the most important was the Equal-Fields system. Under this bold new assertion of direct state control of the economy's base, arable land was divided, allocated to every farm family, and taxed on the basis of censuses. An innovation of the Tabgatch, unprecedented in Chinese history, this was intended to break the power of local Chinese landholders and strengthen the central state. The system was continued during the later Northern dynasties, providing the foundation for strong regimes into the early Tang period.

Alienation of the Armies and Northern Wei's Successors

In the move to Luoyang, Xiaowen brought with him almost all of the Särbi aristocracy and a part of its army. However, most of the troops stayed in the far north, where their situation rapidly deteriorated. Increasingly neglected by the court, these men served in a string of garrisons set up to guard against incursions by the Rouran steppe confederation. In 523, under pressure from the Rouran, the troops abandoned the garrisons and fled into the interior, setting off a civil war that lasted for decades and led to the destruction and abandonment of Luoyang in the 530s.

Out of these civil wars emerged two distinct new regimes, founded by warlords from the garrisons. In the east, controlling the great Central Plain, was the Eastern Wei (534–550), with a Wei puppet leader, which soon gave way to the Northern Qi (550–577). In the Wei River valley to the west was the Western Wei (535–557), from which developed first the Northern Zhou (557–581), then the Sui. The Sui dynasty unified all the Chinese lands, and from the Sui in turn came the great Tang empire.

Great Changes: The Tang–Song Transition

Introduction

During nearly eight centuries, from the rise of the Sui dynasty (581–618) until the expulsion of the Mongols, China underwent profound social, cultural, and economic transformation. The entire society was transformed.

China's reunification, after a long period of division and foreign conquest, signaled the beginning of an extended Chinese golden age. The Sui continued to be based in the north and acted as the conduit of dynastic power held by great aristocratic families since ancient times. The Sui dynasty was not that much different from the Han (206 BCE–CE 220) or Western Jin (265–316), both of which had unified old China. Although the Sui's successor, the Tang dynasty (618–907), had more in common with the past, there was much that was new. The breakdown of traditional patterns of culture brought in change.

Under the Tang, for example, China achieved unprecedented territorial expansion. Its influence extended as far as Afghanistan and northern India, both visited by Xuanzang (died 664), a celebrated Buddhist traveler. For the first time in Chinese history, a woman became emperor and was known as the Empress Wu (reigned 690–705). Tang dynasty cultural figures invented new forms of literature, including Du Fu (712–770), considered China's greatest poet, and the painter Wu Daozi (680–759), who experimented with new forms of painting. China's first dramas were supposedly performed before Emperor Xuanzong who ruled

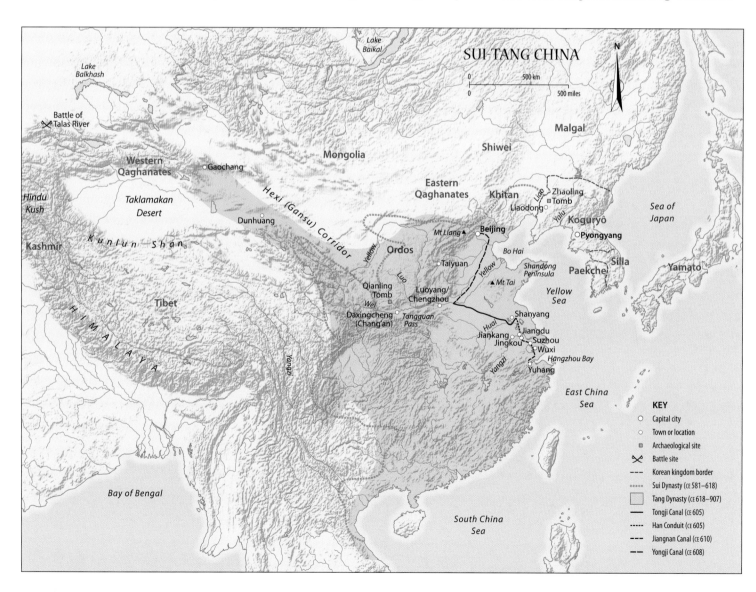

in 712–756, and there were important developments in Chinese literature. Economically, the Tang made tangible progress in absorbing the Chinese south and they also introduced new forms of taxation and financing, including "flying money," China's first banknotes. The Tang rulers also became cultural leaders, and had a strong impact on Japanese, Korean, and Vietnamese cultures, which still today preserve features of Tang dynasty life including classical music, dance, and clothing.

A New Era

Change accelerated during China's Five Dynasties period (907–960) and Northern Song (960–1127) dynasty. By the twelfth century, China's true economic base lay in the south. There it was dominated by special varieties of rapid-growing rice, and by tea, one of China's most important commercial crops and a major base of Song prosperity. Supplementing the highly productive agricultural sector was a sophisticated domestic and international trade with almost modern payments and financing systems. By this stage, the great aristocratic families had declined and power lay in the hands of a landed gentry. Its membership was determined not by heredity, but by wealth, and participation in a highly evolved imperial examination system based on the Confucian classics. Classical texts were no longer circulated as rare manuscripts and interpreted in accordance with arcane family traditions. Instead, printing had developed in China, starting with the printing of a few Buddhist charms during the Tang period and moving to entire books. As well as the Confucian classics, the Buddhist canon was in print from the tenth century onwards, one of the great accomplishments of the Five Dynasties period. Also printed in standard editions, using the new print technology, were medical texts disseminated throughout China. In the centuries that followed, official printers were joined by commercial publishers, producing large editions of China's first popular novels. Most were written in vernacular Chinese. The whole basis of the Chinese language changed after the Tang, leading to early modern languages directly related to modern Chinese. Although militarily weak and disunited after the collapse of the Tang dynasty, culturally and economically China enjoyed a high watermark, felt by much of the population.

The Mongols

Around the late thirteenth century, the Mongols reunified China. How far China had come is witnessed by impressions made on a foreigner, the Venetian Marco Polo (1254–1324). Polo visited south China in the late thirteenth century, just after the Mongol conquest of the Southern Song (1127–1279). He was amazed by everything he saw, including great and flourishing cities and highly sophisticated trading. Under the rule of the Mongols, China had not only reached out to Europeans but, as part of a greater Mongol world order, it also sponsored a flow of cultural goods from East to West and West to East. Mongol China, for example, preferred much the same medical system, based in Greek medicine, that was in the process of becoming the standard in the Christian West. Likewise, the Mongols promoted a cross-cultural exchange of foods in a court cuisine that was a mixture of the best that East and West had to offer. In art, the Mongols helped to spread Chinese painting and calligraphic techniques to the West, and also Western motifs to China. They patronized the first world-scale art craze, for blue and white pottery. It combined skillful Chinese porcelain techniques with the preferred Mongol (and Persian) color, a cobalt blue underglazing, and used a West Asian decoration alongside delicate Chinese illustrations. The first blue-and-white ceramics reached Europe by the early fourteenth century and became incredibly popular. This commercial success was the beginning of a brave new world for China.

ABOVE **A painted scroll from the Tang dynasty** shows the escape in 756 of Emperor Xuanzong during the An Lushan Rebellion.

BELOW **A porcelain ewer** from the early Ming dynasty shows the influence of the Mongol cobalt blue glaze and brushwork.

The Founding of Chang'an

As the founding sovereign of the Sui dynasty, one of the major achievements of Sui Wendi was the creation of Chang'an, a world-class capital city in the present-day greater Xi'an area, in central south Shaanxi, an area that had played host to Chinese capitals from Western Zhou times.

ABOVE **The Sui emperor Wendi** features in this detail, "Emperor with Attendants," from the painted scroll entitled *Portraits of Thirteen Emperors*, attributed to You Liben (died. 673).

After geomantic (*fengshui*) surveys of prospective areas, it was decided to locate the new city southwest of the old capital. There Yuwen Kai (555–612), the leading architect of the city, detected six east–west edges dominating the terrain, so he matched them with the six lines of the *qian* hexagram in the *Book of Changes*. *Qian* is the most potent of all 64 hexagrams, and is symbolic of the *yang* force, heaven, and the male principle.

The Layout of the City

Based on the canonical interpretations of the six lines in the *Book of Changes*, and taking into consideration past conventions in city planning, Yuwen Kai set out to locate different functional quarters in the city, with the royal quarter (the

RIGHT **The outer walls of Chang'an** (modern-day Xi'an), a section of which can be seen here, were made of pounded earth. In places the walls were up to 15 ft (4.5 m) thick.

Palace City) in the central north, and the government quarter to its immediate south. The two marketplaces were placed south of the government quarter. The area still south of the marketplaces was, however, of great significance in royal

symbolism, thus posing a challenge to the throne. Two prominent monasteries, one Buddhist and one Daoist, were therefore placed in the center of the area, in an attempt to suppress any incidents that might arise.

Less related to the theory of geomancy was the distribution of the residential quarters. They filled up the rest of the city as wards (*fang* or *li*). Each ward was virtually a mini town, with its own ward walls, gates, and regulations.

The Residents of Chang'an

The city population of Daxingcheng (better known as Chang'an) was estimated to be slightly under half a million at the height of the Sui. Under the Tang, in the early eighth century, the population would eventually reach one million. This made Daxingcheng-Chang'an by far the most populous urban center in the world.

Modern archaeologists have revealed a walled area of about 32 sq miles (84 sq km). Because of the vastness of the urban expanse, some of the residential wards laid out at the founding of the city, especially those wards lying in the far south, were too remote from the vital functional areas of the city to attract residents. Even as the city matured in the following Tang dynasty, these southern wards remained sparsely populated. They functioned as locales for religious institutions, parks, and private temples. A large part of the area was actually arable land under cultivation.

Ritual and Religion

As the capital city, Daxingcheng became the venue for a rich array of regular ritual activities. Urban-based national ritual centers were planned from the very beginning. The most prominent ones were the Ancestral Temple where the emperor made sacrificial offerings to the ancestral spirits of the imperial family, and the Altars of State, where the Gods of Soil and Grains—as guardians of the dynastic fortune—were worshipped. In the suburbs there were ritual centers in honor of the more highly ranked gods. Of these, the Lord on High, the nation's most revered celestial god, was worshipped at the Round Mound, a ritual center in the southern suburb. The rulers sought blessing and sanction from the gods.

Outside of state-sanctioned ritual activities, the religious life of Daxingcheng was divided. Within the city boundaries, Buddhism boasted 120 monasteries under Yangdi (reigned 604–618), while Daoism boasted at least ten. Although the Sui court sanctioned both religions, Buddhism was far more popular. In the wake of the proscription it suffered under the Northern Zhou emperor Wudi (reigned 560–578), the first Sui emperor; Wendi (reigned 581–604) was himself instrumental in reviving and promoting Buddhism. In the Tang dynasty that followed, the religious life of Chang'an was enriched by the arrival of three Western religions: specifically Zoroastrianism, Manichaeism, and Nestorian Christianity. With the endorsement of the Tang court, they built their religious centers in the city as well. Throughout the Tang period, Buddhism remained the dominant religion in Chang'an as well as throughout the nation.

Widespread destruction of the church properties of all religions except Daoism happened during the worst religious proscription campaign in Chinese history, between 843–845. Chang'an survived this catastrophe for almost 60 years, until 904, when the whole city was systematically taken apart as the penultimate Tang emperor was forced to move to Luoyang in the east.

LEFT **This bronze Buddha** of the Sui dynasty (*c.* 581–618) is a representation of the Cosmic Buddha or Mahavairocana, a form associated with the sect of Shingon Buddhism.

SUI LUOYANG

Sui Luoyang, founded in 605 on the site of present-day Luoyang (in Henan), was Yangdi's answer to Daxingcheng-Chang'an, created by his father. Like Chang'an in the west, Luoyang was an area rich in cultural heritage and political significance. As recently as the early fourth century it had been the site of the national capital. The new Luoyang of the Sui was designed by the architect Yuwen Kai. Smaller than Daxingcheng in walled area, it was nonetheless more extravagantly constructed. As the second city in Sui China, it resembled Daxingcheng in many aspects, having its own residential wards, Palace City, separate government quarter, and enclosed marketplaces. It also departed from its predecessor in its overall layout by placing the palace–government area in the northwest corner and by situating its marketplaces near rivers or canals.

The Reunification

After the fall of the Han in the early third century, China remained divided apart from the period *c.* 280–311. Under the Sui dynasty, Wendi launched the southern expedition in 589 to achieve reunification.

BELOW **Tomb figures** reflect the social life of a period. This ceramic figure of a late Sui or early Tang soldier, *c.* 581–650, comes from a period with many military campaigns.

In 581, when Sui Wendi (né Yang Jian) usurped the Northern Zhou throne and founded the Sui dynasty, based in the Yellow River drainage area in the north, China proper was under the rule of three political entities. Rivaling the Sui in the south was the Chen. In between there was a much smaller state—the Later Liang—in south central Hubei.

The Rise of Wendi

A man of great political ambition, Wendi set as his long-term objective the reunification of China. In demographic, economic, and military terms, the Sui was far superior to its rival in the south. The rising Turkic qaghanates north of China proper in Mongolia and beyond, however, had the potential to upset Wendi's plan.

Previous rulers of north China had adopted an appeasement strategy towards the Turks. Wendi abandoned that in favor of a more forcible policy at a time when internal strife greatly weakened the Turkish military threat to north China.

Preparation for War

Domestically, Wendi introduced drastic reforms to streamline central and local governments and create a more efficient military and a stronger economy. These reforms underpinned Wendi's military action against the south.

The person most intimately involved in the planning and execution of the war effort was Gao Jiong, co-head of the Department of State Affairs, and at that time the most powerful chief minister. He had been Wendi's steadfast supporter from the earliest days of the dynasty. Before his

ABOVE **These figures of late Sui or early Tang officials,** *c.* 581–650, represent members of the administrative class. Effective administrators were central to Wendi's reforms.

downfall, Gao was involved in most key policy moves at the center: from building the capital Daxingcheng to fighting the Turks. After reunification, he led a major military action against Koguryô (in Manchuria and north Korea) in 598. An able administrator in his own right, Gao Jiong enjoyed special favors because of the close ties between the imperial families and his own, ties that were strengthened by the marriage between his son and a daughter of Yang Yong, Wendi's eldest son and heir apparent. Gao also recommended a number of talented leaders to the court. One such recommendation was Su Wei, the son of Su Chuo, the architect of the Northern

Zhou administrative reform. Wendi greatly appreciated Su Wei's administrative talent, and appointed him to assist Jiong in running the central government. After reunification, he would serve as co-president of the Department of State Affairs.

The most promising leader Gao recommended was Yang Su, a general who distinguished himself in the campaign against the south and in suppressing insurgency in the south after the Sui annexation. Promoted co-head of the Department of State Affairs not long after reunification, Yang Su played a pivotal role in helping Yang Guang seize power.

Supported by a cohort of outstanding administrators and strategists, Wendi made the first strategic move towards reunification: he annexed the central Yangzi state of Later Liang in 587 and increased the Sui's military presence throughout the region.

The Sui Invasion Campaign

Wendi launched the Sui invasion campaign with a force of about half a million in late 588. Regarding himself as the ecumenical sovereign, he justified the invasion in terms of delivering the people of the south from the tyranny of the Chen sovereign.

The south seems to have been oblivious to the northern threat. The Yangzi River, serving as a natural barrier, gave the southerners a false sense of security. Their ruler, Chen Houzhu (Last Sovereign), was discovered indulging in sensual pleasures within his palace while the capital Jiankang (present day Nanjing, Jiangsu) fell in early 589. The Sui troops eventually captured Houzhu from a well, where he was taking shelter in the company of his favorite concubines.

The de facto commander of the Sui campaign was Gao Jiong. The man who received the most credit for the victory, however, was Wendi's second son Yang Guang, the nominal commander-in-chief of the Sui expedition forces. The southern invasion created a great opportunity for him to prove his worth. Subsequently, he was appointed the top administrator of the south. His decade-long successful tenure there proved to be a great political asset later when he competed for the position of heir apparent.

Reunification and a New Era of Empire

The reunification that took place in 589 was a momentous event in medieval Chinese history. It effectively ended the political, economic, and cultural division that had persisted following the 311 sack of Luoyang by the Huns. It marked the beginning of a new era of unitary empire that would lead to a period of extraordinary cultural development, eventually giving rise to one of the most brilliant periods in premodern Chinese history: the period of the Tang dynasty.

ABOVE **This stoneware funerary figure** is from the tomb of the General Chang Sheng of the Sui dynasty. His tomb, found at Anyang, was excavated in 1959.

WENDI'S REFORMS

The reformed central leadership was comprised of three branches: the Department of State Affairs with its Six Boards (in charge of the implementation of government policy), along with the Chancellory, and the Secretariat (these last two were in charge of policy initiation). The heads of these Three Departments—the "chief ministers"—were the top leaders of the bureaucracy.

In the military arena, Wendi greatly enhanced central control through reorganizing the militia (*fubing*) system. The *fubing* troops were farmers who received military training. When they were periodically called up for military duty on a rotational basis, they were responsible for their own logistics and light weaponry.

Economically, Wendi continued the existing Equal-Fields (*juntian*) system under which eligible farmers and their dependents received arable lands (a smaller portion of which were inheritable) from the state and were responsible for paying annual taxes in grain and textile.

The Reign of Emperor Yang

The second ruler of the Sui dynasty, Emperor Yang came to power under suspect circumstances. He energetically pursued his overambitious goals in domestic and foreign policies, and ruined the dynastic fortune in the process.

RIGHT **The Sui emperor Yangdi** (left) and his father Wendi (right) feature in this detail from the painted scroll entitled *Portraits of Thirteen Emperors*, attributed to Yan Liben.

To traditional historians, when Emperor Yang or Yangdi (previously known as Yang Guang) ascended the throne in 604, his reputation was stained with two unpardonable crimes: incest and patricide-regicide. He was suspected of having played a hand in the death of his father Wendi; and on coming to power he also took a consort of his father to bed, breaking the sex taboo. With sufficient support from the civil bureaucracy and the military, he took over the court without having to face serious challenge (the one exception being the rebellion staged by his brother Yang Liang, which was soon put down).

Stifling Criticism

Determined to show himself to be different from his father, whose dominance he intensely resented, Yangdi populated the court with his cronies. Deviating from his father's reasonably prudent approach to spending, he initiated new building projects not long after coming to power and went on a number of grandiose land and river tours. On the 607 land tour of inspection to the strategic

Ordos region on the bend of the Yellow River where the Sui land bordered on Turkish territory, he brought with him a host of top officials. One of them was Gao Jiong. As the most powerful bureaucrat in the first reign, Gao had been ousted by Wendi, but was reinstated by Yangdi. To Yangdi's chagrin, Gao expressed concern over Yangdi's irresponsible behavior. Another ranking official and a top general of the first reign also voiced their criticism. Yangdi had all three summarily executed. Through this action, he showed his intolerance of criticism.

Yangdi's Extravagances

Thanks to the relatively sound economic basis of his father's reign, Yangdi was able to carry out a number of large-scale public works projects. The first one was the building of the second Sui capital at Luoyang in present-day Henan. Practical utility seems to have trumped compliance with ritual requirements and architectural conventions. The population of Luoyang during Yangdi's reign in the early seventh century was estimated to be in the 400,000–500,000 range, which places it in direct competition with Daxingcheng as the most populous city in China and the world. Under the succeeding Tang dynasty, Luoyang continued its role as the second city most of the time, except during the reign of Wu Zetian (reigned 690–705) when Luoyang was made the primary capital and renamed the "Divine Capital."

Some of the strategic advantages for setting up the eastern capital were that it afforded more effective control of east China and closer access to the Yangzi River valley in the south, Hebei in the north, and Manchuria. The Grand Canal built by Yangdi, which comprised several long waterways, served as the transportation highway system that linked up these areas. Yangdi built palaces along the main canal routes, and near transportation hubs such as Luoyang and Jiangdu (in present-day Yangzhou, Jiangsu). Some of them were stand-alone touring palaces that served as way-stations for the imperial progress, while others were uniquely designed "mega-palaces," each of which was made up of a host of smaller palaces clustered together.

Yangdi's Reforms

The costly construction projects were indicative of Yangdi's penchant for extravagance. They do not, however, necessarily suggest that Yangdi neglected to govern, as in the case of Chen Houzhu. On the contrary, Yangdi was actively involved in government, and introduced sweeping reforms. The Six Boards—second-tier central government agencies in charge of personnel, revenue, ritual, works, justice, and war—had as their competing agencies the Nine Courts, which often had similar responsibilities.

Yangdi provided administrative clarity by ranking the Six Boards higher than the Nine Courts.

Under Yangdi's father, a prefecture-county two-level local administrative system was devised to replace the cumbersome three-tier system (prefecture; commandery; county) of the previous age. Yangdi retained the two-tier system, but substituted "commanderies" for "prefectures" while giving the commandery governors a lower bureaucratic rank.

Military structure stayed essentially the same under Yangdi. The *fubing* troops continued to be the main defense force, but Yangdi shifted the focus of their deployment from the Wei River valley (Xi'an, Shaanxi and its surrounding areas) to the Luoyang area in the east and demoted all *fubing* garrison commanders.

ABOVE: **The Grand Canal** (Yangzhou, Jiangsu Province) was constructed from 604–611, during the reign of Yangdi.

BELOW **This terracotta tomb statue** of a female traveler is from the Sui dynasty (c. 581–618).

THE EQUAL-FIELDS SYSTEM

The Equal-Fields (*juntian*) system was the prevailing land tenure system first introduced under the Northern Wei in 485. It was practiced by the Northern Qi, Northern Zhou, Sui, and Tang dynasties. A salient feature of the system was a more equitable distribution of land resources among landholders. Arable lands were mainly divided into two classes: non-inheritable and inheritable, and were granted based on age and gender. People in different age groups and of both genders could receive non-inheritable lands, which were returnable when they reached the legally defined old age. But only adult males were entitled to inheritable lands, lands they could pass down to descendents. Land quotas varied according to land availability. Residents in a "restricted locality" would receive much less land per grant than their counterparts in an "unrestricted locality."

Under Wendi, local military forces had been organized under area commands (*zongguan fubing*). Dozens of area commands had been centralized under one of the four superior area commands (*da zongguan*). Yangdi had been commander of two of these commands, and as emperor he abolished superior area commands as a potential threat to the throne.

In law, the Sui is noted for its *Kaihuang Code*, compiled under Wendi, which was considered a worthy attempt to bring order and leniency to the legal systems of the previous age. For example, in the area of capital punishment alone, it abolished 81 offenses. Not satisfied with the *Kaihuang Code*, Yangdi created his *Daye Code* under the guidance of "benevolent government."

Yangdi's reforms were one way in which he distinguished his reign from that of his father. But they also enhanced the centralizing measures introduced by his father by making the central government even stronger at the expense of the commandery governors and local commanders.

Sui Religion

There were important religious developments during the Sui dynasty, despite its relatively short duration. One influential Buddhist sect was that of the Three Stages, founded by Xinxing. This sect's gloomy and apocalyptic view of the epoch over which the Sui held sway finally led to its proscription in 600. The Tiantai sect of Buddhism in the south—which divided Buddhist doctrines and sutras into periods and established hierarchies of influence, with a focus on the *Lotus Sutra*—fared much better. The founder Zhiyi was a close friend of Yangdi when he was governor of the south. Daoism, considered a lesser religion by the court, was nonetheless respected, and went through sustained growth, especially its Shangqing (Highest Clarity) school favored by Yangdi, a school based on scriptures from transcendents revealed to mediums that had taken shape in the south in the previous age.

Wendi was one of the most enthusiastic royal sponsors of religion in Chinese history. His patronage of Buddhism was unprecedented in scope and national influence. His religious policy was essentially one of indulgence, although his rule did not blur the boundary between the secular and the sacred. By and large, Yangdi continued his father's positive policy, but he took a more proactive stand toward the religious communities, demanding that the clergies should not be exempt from showing due respect to lay authority figures. Later Yangdi withdrew this demand under pressure, but eventually carried out a campaign to reduce the number of Buddhist monasteries in the capital, and perhaps elsewhere.

BELOW **This Buddha is carved into the wall** of Cave 3 of the Yungang Caves. Cave 3 is the largest of the Yungang Caves and was carved by artists of the Sui and Tang dynasties.

THE SUI TAX SYSTEM

The Sui essentially implemented a flat tax system. Taxes were levied only on commoners who received land grants from the state. Ranked officials and non recipients of land grants were exempt from paying tax. There were three main components of the tax system: a grain tax, a cloth tax, and corvée labor. Both the grain and cloth taxes were payable in kind at fixed rates. Corvée labor was annual free labor service performed for government projects, lasting about 20 days for each adult male per year. In addition, there was a small toll tax for charity, imposed progressively. The overall tax burden as a percentage of a household's annual income was not onerous. But the abuse of the corvée labor part of the tax system under Yangdi brought about the collapse of the dynasty.

Foreign Relations

One area that really sets the first Sui reign by Wendi apart from the second reign of Yangdi is foreign policy and its broader implications. Wendi's foreign policy objectives aimed at projecting Sui power in areas that were traditionally within the Chinese cultural sphere. Within this framework, Wendi regarded containing the Turkic Qaghanates (Khanates) to the north as his top priority, and focused on weakening their power and limiting their threat, through diplomatic maneuverings accompanied by military action. One move that departed from this policy was his failed invasion of Koguryô in 598. But Wendi made no follow-up action. Yangdi, in contrast, was not constrained by the boundary set by his father and ventured much farther afield into such distant areas as Japan, Taiwan, north Vietnam, and Malaya. Having ruined by trickery the benign relationship with the Eastern Turks his father had worked hard to foster, he shifted his foreign policy focus to Koguryô and launched three large-scale campaigns against it between 612 and 614 when the economy was brought treacherously close to collapse, and rebellion by commoners and disgruntled officers was spreading.

The Fall

Yangdi turned a blind eye to serious domestic issues and remained single-mindedly focused on his Koguryô exploits, until China was embroiled in widespread insurgency. When Luoyang was no

longer safe, Yangdi had two obvious choices: to move west to Daxingcheng in the Wei Valley or to move south to Jiangdu in the lower Yangzi Valley. Although the prevailing view was that the Daxingcheng offered the best chance for dynastic revival, Yangdi adamantly opposed this possibility, instead choosing to move permanently to Jiangdu with his entourage in 616.

When Li Mi—the most formidable rebel, who commanded an army of a million—threatened Luoyang, Yangdi sent his most trusted general in Jiangdu, Wang Shichong, to the north to safeguard the city. The departure of Wang, who had been in charge of Yangdi's security detail, seriously compromised Yangdi's personal safety.

In early 618, a group of court officials and palace guard officers staged a coup and executed Yangdi by hanging. After that, the mighty Sui dynasty crumbled. Meanwhile, a Daxingcheng-based regime arose in the Wei valley. Under Li Yuan, an ex-Sui aristocrat, it defeated rival claimants for national power to reunite China again under the dynastic name "Tang."

ABOVE **The Wei River valley** was one of the cradles of Chinese civilization, with the capitals of the Qin, Han, and Tang dynasties all situated there.

RIGHT **This statue from the Sui dynasty,** 589–618, depicts the Bodhisattva Samantabhaddra riding an elephant. The statue is made of marble and has traces of polychrome decoration.

The Grand Canal

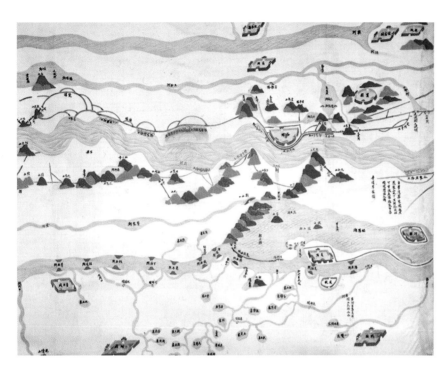

A Bird's-eye View of the Grand Canal

China's Grand Canal, completed in 611, stretches from Hangzhou in the south to Beijing in the north. This section of an eighteenth-century picture map shows the whole length of the canal on a long roll. Towns are illustrated from a bird's-eye view by their walls and gates.

Yangdi's Building Projects

In his short reign of less than 14 years, Yangdi reshaped China's landscape through his numerous building projects. Some of them, for example, the Eastern Capital at Luoyang and the Grand Canal, would provide immense benefit to posterity. But others would not, including the Sui Great Wall and a slew of palaces, located at major transportation hubs like Luoyang in the north and Jiangdu (present-day Yangzhou) in the south, or alongside the Grand Canal. One salient feature of Yangdi's palaces was their complexity, as embodied in the design of a megapalace, a palace composed of a number of subpalaces clustered together. These projects were completed at great human and financial cost to Sui's China, and were in part responsible for breaking the back of the economy.

The Grand Canal of China was a water transportation network that took shape in the early seventh century during the second reign of the Sui dynasty under Emperor Yang (Yangdi).

With an estimated length of 1,465 miles (2,357 km), it closely integrated, for the first time in history, such key strategic, political, and economic areas as the lower Yellow River valley (Hebei in the northeast and Henan in the Central Plain), the Huai valley, and the lower Yangzi valley. Part of the Sui Grand Canal was made up of existing, often derelict, canals, which, after dredging and repair, were merged into the system. But significant sections of the network were built from scratch. It took six years, from 605–611, for the four canals of the system to be completed. A labor force of more than one million each is recorded for the construction of two sections (Tongji and Yongji) at the time when Sui's registered population was just 46 million.

The first waterway of the Grand Canal was known as the Tongji Canal, which provided a vital link between the Yellow River valley and the Huai valley to the south. Construction began under Yangdi in 605. Previously it was believed that Tongji was completed and ready for use in the same year. Recent research suggests 611 as the more feasible completion date. Tongji originated from the Western Park of Luoyang. Passing through the urban area of Luoyang, it joined the Luo River as it was about to exit the east part of the city. From there the Luo River flowed east and north to join the Yellow River. Further down, the main section of Tongji began as an eastward branch off the Yellow River and turned southeast to join the Huai River.

The second waterway, known as the Han Conduit, was constructed in 605. It represented the southern extension of the Grand Canal into the Yangzi valley. Before the Sui there had been

Yangdi on the Grand Canal

This painting on silk from the eighteenth century depicts the Sui emperor Yangdi on his boat on the Grand Canal that was constructed during his reign.

Bridge over the Tongji Canal

The Tongji canal was buit to connect Luoyang with the Yellow River and to connect the Yellow River with the Huai River. It was the first canal in the Grand Canal system to be completed, and many lives were lost during its construction.

two Han conduits linking the Huai with the Yangzi valleys. Wendi had built his canal known as the Shanyang Conduit. Utilizing existing routes, Yangdi built his new Han Conduit that began at Shanyang (Huai'an, Anhui) and traveled south to go past Jiangdu (Yangzhou) before joining the Yangzi.

The third main waterway, the Jiangnan Canal, penetrated deep into areas south of the Yangzi to reach Yuhang (Hangzhou, Zhejiang). Built in 610, the Jiangnan Canal started at Jingkou (Zhenjiang, Jiangsu) and went south past Wuxi and Suzhou before emptying into Hangzhou Bay.

The fourth waterway, the Yongji Canal, was the northern extension of the Grand Canal. Built in 608, it incorporated the Hebei area north of the Yellow River into the system, and was of strategic significance for control of Manchuria. As the longest of the Grand Canal's four waterways, it made use of existing river routes and extended northward as far as the Beijing area.

After the fall of the Sui dynasty, later dynasties continued to repair the Grand Canal and modify its routes, as it evolved into China's national transportation network, indispensable for the economy of both north and south.

The Korean Campaigns

Among various northern neighbors of Sui China, Koguryŏ was a relatively small state. Historically, the Koguryŏ people had long been under Chinese influence. Both Wendi and Yangdi were interested in conquering Koguryŏ. Neither succeeded.

RIGHT **This cream-glazed terracotta figure** depicts a "barbarian" offering carrier. Although non-Chinese groups were often perceived as threats, at times they rejuvenated Chinese culture.

As the Sui began to project their might into Mongolia, Central Asia, and Manchuria, the powers that were most likely to stand in the way were the Eastern and Western Turkic Qaghanates (Khanates) in a vast area stretching from Mongolia to Central Asia.

The Sui and Northern Asia

During the first Sui reign, the Turkic challenge was managed by exploiting internal rivalry among Turkic qaghans. The Sui's long-term effort to prop up Qimin qaghan as a pro-Sui Turkic leader paid off handsomely in the early seventh century, as he came to dominate the Eastern Qaghanate.

To the east of the Eastern Turkic Qaghanate were lesser non-Han powers: Shiwei and Khitan (Qidan) in east Inner Mongolia. To their east were Malgal (Mohe) and Koguryŏ. With a territory that extended from south Manchuria to north Korea, the Koguryŏ were one of several peoples who are the ancestors of the modern Koreans. The ancient Koreans were distinguished by their long history of contact with Chinese regimes and their high degree of Sinification. According to legend, in the eleventh century BCE, Qizi—a Shang supporter—took shelter in north Korea when the Shang dynasty fell. In 108 BCE, Han troops under Wudi overran north Korea and south Manchuria and set up four regions there, including Rangrang (Lelang).

The "Three Korean Kingdoms"

Following the fall of the Han dynasty, Han influence in the area was in steady decline. By Sui times, Koguryŏ had emerged as the dominant local power. On the Korean peninsula and south of Koguryŏ, two rival powers coexisted, Paekche in the southwest and Silla in the southeast. For a long period, these "Three Kingdoms" were engaged in a three-way rivalry.

The Campaign of 598

The year 598 ushered in a new era in Sino–Koguryŏ relations. Across a span of 70 years, the Sui–Tang sovereigns made repeated attempts

THE WESTERN REGIONS

The Western Regions (Xiyu) encompassed the vast area west of Yumen Pass in western Gansu, especially present-day Xinjiang. Its geography was dominated by the Taklamakan Desert, with oasis states scattered along its northern and southern edges. Among these, Gaochang, located in Turfan Basin, had the closest ties with the Sui court. With an agrarian economy, Gaochang residents were predominantly of Han descent. Sui Yangdi courted Gaochang by marrying a princess to its king. Gaochang acknowledged its tributary position while remaining a vassal to Tiele, a Turkic power dominant in Central Asia. Like other oasis states, Gaochang was not brought into the fold until the following Tang dynasty.

LEFT **The city of Gaochang** became an important supply town and trading post on the Silk Road, and the capital of western China. The city was reduced to ruins in the fourteenth century.

LEFT **This is a replica of a mural** from a Koguryô tomb. Tomb complexes are almost the only remains of the Koguryô state that once ruled parts of northeast China and the northern Korean peninsula.

to contain the kingdom in Manchuria and north Korea. This ended in 688, when it was finally brought to heel under the Tang.

The event that triggered the first Sui campaign was a Koguryô–Malgal intrusion into Sui territory in southern Manchuria in early 598. Although the intrusion was halted, Wendi responded with a large-scale military campaign against Koguryô. Yang Liang, Wendi's youngest son, was appointed nominal commander-in-chief of the invading army, which numbered about 300,000. Gao Jiong, the most powerful court bureaucrat, served as the de facto commander. The Sui strategy was one of a two-pronged attack by land and sea: the land element of the campaign started out from present-day northeast Hebei, and advanced east; and the sea element led by General Zhou Luohou was launched from the Shandong peninsula to advance east to capture Pyongyang, the Koguryô capital. Bad timing inflicted a heavy toll on the Sui forces. The progress of the land troops

was impeded by excessive rain and inadequate food supplies, a situation made worse by widespread disease.

Meanwhile, much of the Sui fleet was destroyed by wind at sea. Wendi had no choice but to call off the campaign. The Koguryô king Yôngyang hurriedly sent a self-deprecating letter to appease Wendi. Apparently, Wendi decided to live with the status quo so long as Sui China's dominance was acknowledged. No long after, when Paekche offered its help in attacking Koguryô, Wendi turned it down. A balance of power was achieved as Koguryô continued to play its nominal role as a tributary to the Sui empire.

One upshot of the campaign was the rift between Yang Liang and Gao Jiong. During the campaign, Gao had always ignored suggestions by Liang. Liang complained to his mother, Empress Dugu, about this slight. This eventually led to Gao Jiong's removal at Dugu's insistence and paved the way for the rise of Yang Guang.

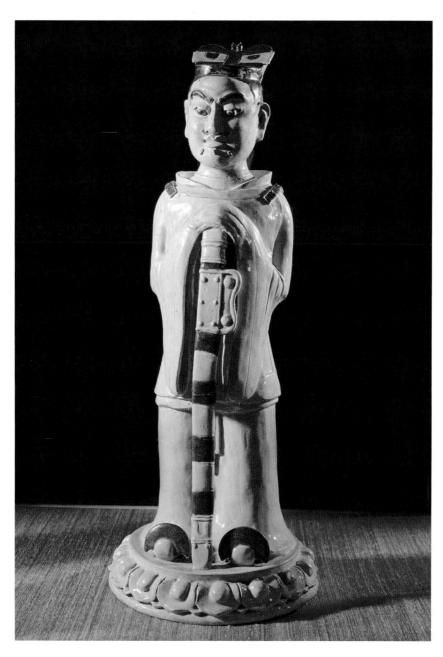

ABOVE **This glazed statue** is a figure from the tomb of General Chang Sheng. The making of tomb figures reached its developmental peak in the Tang dynasty.

After the king failed to respond, Yangdi sped up his war preparations.

Yangdi personally launched the campaign of 612 against Koguryô, his first, with an armed force of more than 1.13 million. After overcoming Koguryô resistance at the Liao River in present-day west Liaoning, the Sui troops started laying siege to the town of Liaodong (Liaoyang, Liaoning) but for an extended period failed to sack it.

While the Sui army made little progress on land, General Lai Huer led a Sui force by sea to land near Pyongyang. After Lai ordered 40,000 of his crack troops to penetrate deep into the city, they were ambushed and mostly killed.

Meanwhile, a Sui land force, comprised of nine armies under Generals Yu Zhongwen and Yuwen Shu, advanced east to reach the west bank of the Yalu River (today serving as the Sino–Korean border). On the order of Yu Zhongwei, Yuwen Shu led the force across the Yalu to reach as far as the outskirts of Pyongyang. As he realized that his troops were too stressed to sack the well-fortified Koguryô capital, Yuwen Shu made a decision to withdraw. While crossing the Sa River north of Pyongyang, his troops were routed midstream by a Koguryô ambush. By the time the remnants of the nine armies went west across the Liao River, less than 3,000 survived out of more than 300,000. With no hope of winning the war, Yangdi withdrew his invading army.

The Campaigns of 613 and 614

As soon as Yangdi arrived in Luoyang, he began to prepare for war again. In the campaign of 613, he personally directed a series of ferocious, unremitting assaults on the town of Liaodong (Liaoyang). After holding firm for weeks, the Koguryô defenders sustained a horrendous loss of lives. Just as the Sui forces were about to break through, Yangdi received news that Yang Xuangan, president of the Board of Rites, had rebelled in Liyang (Xunxian, north Henan), posing a direct threat to Luoyang. A worried Yangdi cut short the campaign and returned.

After the crushing of the Yang Xuangan rebellion, Yangdi focused attention again on Koguryô and launched the campaign of 614, his last one. By then, rebellion had spread nationwide in China proper. The Koguryô side was also exhausted. As General Lai Huer led the Sui forces to land from sea and oversaw a major victory against the Koguryô near Pyongyang, a terrified King Yôngyang sent his envoy to offer

The Campaign of 612

As has already been discussed, Yangdi took a much more forcible stand toward Koguryô. Unlike his father—who was provoked into knee-jerk military action—Yangdi spent years methodically planning for his invasion. The building of the Grand Canal, especially its northeast route (the Yongji Canal), greatly facilitated the movement of personnel, material, and provisions to the northeast front. In 607, while on his trip to meet with Qimin Qaghan of the Eastern Turkic Qaghanate in the Ordos area, a Koguryô secret envoy was also visiting Qimin. To Yangdi, a secret liaison between the Turks and Koguryô would be particularly alarming. So he issued a stern letter to summon the Koguryô king to court in the following year.

surrender. As a token of good
faith, he also returned the Sui
defector Husi Zheng. Yangdi
then decided to withdraw.

The three campaigns
Yangdi launched underscore
the strategic and political
importance he attached to
Koguryô, but he completely
ignored the social and
economic consequences. The
populace had to bear the high
cost in material, manpower,
and logistics in the form of
excessive levies, disruption of
livelihoods, and a tremendous
loss of life. The fact that the
campaigns came on the back
of a continuous string of
construction projects—
Luoyang, the Grand Canal, numerous palaces,
and the Great Wall—drove a large number of
his subjects to desperation and to rebellion,
bringing about the eventual downfall of Yangdi
and the Sui dynasty.

YAMATO

The Japanese state of Yamato, based in west Honshu, sent
several missions to the Sui court. Sui Wendi was scandalized
by a letter from the Japanese (female) sovereign Suiko, which
claimed that Heaven was her elder brother and the sun her
younger brother. Sui Yangdi was equally unimpressed with a
letter from the same Japanese sovereign referring to herself
as the "celestial sovereign of the east" and to Yangdi as the
"emperor of the west." Yangdi sent his own mission, headed
by Pei Shiqing and accompanied by the Japanese envoy
Ono no Imoko. In Tang times, Yamato sent more missions on
a much larger scale. They played a crucial role in transmitting
continental civilization to Japan.

RIGHT **Prince Shotoku Taishi (574–622)** was a Japanese Yamato period
ruler. He is depicted here with his sons Yamashiro Oe and Ekuri.

The Campaigns of Taizong

The Tang dynasty was on friendly terms with
three states on the Korean peninsula until early
642 when General Yôn Kaesomun usurped the
throne after murdering the king and began to
intrude into the territory of Silla to the south.
Taizong then made the personal decision to
intervene on moral grounds, despite strong
opposition from high-profile advisers. By that
time, Taizong's confidant and most outspoken
critic Wei Zheng had already died, and Taizong
became increasingly authoritarian.

Taizong (reigned 626–649) personally led the
campaign of 644–645, and captured a number
of Koguryô strongholds. But one strategic town,
Anshi (southeast of Haicheng, Liaoning), held its
own against Tang assaults for months. As winter
was approaching, Taizong withdrew in late 645.

After his return, Taizong became seriously ill
and was constantly in poor health until his death
in 649. Nevertheless, he kept the pressure on
Koguryô by launching more military campaigns
from 647 through 648.

The Campaigns of Gaozong

Gaozong (reigned 649–683) began to dispatch
Tang forces to rein in Koguryô in 655, after it

had assumed an increasingly hegemonic role in
the region. In 660, the Tang went to the aid of its
ally Silla, a kingdom in the southeast. At Silla's
request Tang conquered Paekche (now Koguryô's
ally) for its previous attacks on Silla, and went on
to invade Koguryô before withdrawal in 662.

The final campaign against Koguryô took place
in 668 after Yôn Kaesomun's death. Favored by
its control of Paekche, the support of Silla, and
by a weakened Koguryô leadership thanks to
internal strife, the Tang forces, led by Li Ji and
Xue Rengui, finally defeated Koguryô, which
was then annexed.

BELOW **White stoneware
from the Tang dynasty**
showed stylistic influences
from central Asia. Many
items had delicate lines
and simple incised or
molded ornamentation.

The Tang Conquest

Li Yuan, the Duke of Tang, a man of noble origins and a relative of the Sui imperial family, seized the throne in 618 and adopted the noble title of his clan as the name of a new dynasty. Within a decade, all of China had submitted to his rule.

The final years of the Sui dynasty witnessed the disintegration of the central imperial authority over much of the empire. By the fall of 616, when Emperor Yangdi decamped to the pleasure palaces of Jiangdu for a final time, traveling by way of the newly constructed Grand Canal, most of north China was in the hands of rebels. Yet these rebel bands, which numbered into the hundreds, were a disunited and diverse collection of disaffected Sui generals, regional warlords, local militias, and bandits. At the time, it was altogether unclear who would step into the power vacuum left by the ailing Sui dynasty.

The man who did was a Sui nobleman and general named Li Yuan (566–635). Scion of the Li clan, an aristocratic military family of mixed Han Chinese, Xianbi, and Turkish ancestry, and relative by marriage of the Sui imperial house, Li Yuan had distinguished himself in a series of important regional and court posts. These included service in the personal bodyguard of the first Sui emperor, Wendi, administration of strategic northwest commands, and, under Emperor Yangdi, command of the capital arsenal and supervision of the supply lines for the second Korean campaign in 613. By 615, he was stationed in Taiyuan, an important garrison on the empire's northern frontier, where he consolidated control by suppressing local uprisings and holding off Turkish incursions. His authority over Taiyuan, an area roughly equivalent to the modern-day province of Shanxi, was formally recognized in 617 by an appointment from Emperor Yangdi to the official post of Garrison Commander. The appointment was a tremendous test of loyalty, as Taiyuan extended into the heart of north China and lay within striking distance of the two great cities of Daxingcheng, the first capital of the Sui dynasty (later named Chang'an), and Luoyang.

The Rebel Leader

Li Yuan's loyalty did not survive this test. While his family had served the Sui since its rise to power, the rebellions seething throughout the northern territories made it clear that Yangdi's reign was faltering, and Li Yuan was not about to lose his power base. Within weeks of his appointment to the Taiyuan command, he had raised an army and set his sights on the capital. He was aided in this endeavor by three of his sons, who raised additional troops that swelled the ranks of the Taiyuan Garrison. In the seventh month of 617, together with his eldest son Li Jiancheng and his second son Li Shimin, he set out at the head of some 30,000 troops.

Historians have debated the degree to which Li Yuan should be credited with planning and leading the campaign. The official history of the Tang dynasty, written by state historians, characterizes him as a mediocre and lackluster general and credits his second son Li Shimin

BELOW **In the Sancai technique,** this pair of guardian figures is from the tomb of a highly skilled Tang dynasty military commander, Liu Tingxun, who died in 728.

(who would eventually become the second Tang emperor) for guiding the conquest. Other sources represent Li Yuan as playing a much more active, primary role. However, many suspect that the official record was doctored at the insistence of Li Shimin to elevate his father's role.

Whatever the case, the army suffered delays but no serious setbacks on the route to the city's capital, Daxingcheng. Along the way the army recruited large numbers of turncoat Sui forces whose loyalty they secured through a clever combination of promises, deception, and cash. By the time Li Yuan's army reached the gates of the capital, it was said to have numbered in excess of 200,000 men.

The siege lasted some five weeks. In the eleventh month of 617, the attacking forces finally overcame the Sui defenses and broke into the city. Initially, Li Yuan preserved the Sui dynasty, positioning himself as the power behind the throne, removing Yangdi to the position of Retired Emperor and installing his young grandson, Yang You, as the new emperor. In the fifth month of 618, Li Yuan deposed this puppet ruler and assumed the throne, formally creating the Tang dynasty. In a symbolic gesture to the grand days of the old empires, Li Yuan renamed the Sui capital Chang'an, which literally means "Perfect Peace," after the then-derelict former capital of the Han dynasty nearby.

The New Emperor

Even before personally assuming the throne, Li Yuan, who history remembers as Emperor Gaozu, began launching many battle campaigns to consolidate his rule. Although the capital occupied the most strategic region "between the passes" in what is now southern Shaanxi, shielded from the rest of the north China plains by a range of mountains, it occupied only a fraction of the former Sui territory and it contained less than a quarter of the territory's population. Serious rivals contested the new regime to the northwest, northeast, east, and southeast. The most serious threat was former Sui general Wang Shichong, who occupied the sister city of Luoyang to the east and who had, like Li Yuan, first installed a grandson of Yangdi as a puppet emperor and then deposed him to declare himself emperor of his own dynasty, in this case the Zheng. The Tang armies kept the pressure on the Zheng until 621, when Li Shimin sacked Luoyang. Over the next three years, the Tang progressively and strategically overcame each one of its remaining rivals, and by 624, the empire was reunified under Tang rule.

Everlasting Reforms

After consolidating his control over the empire, Emperor Gaozu implemented
a series of policies that provided a stable foundation for the new regime
which, in time, came to have a tremendous influence on the political
formations throughout East Asia.

One of the most effective things Gaozu did during his reign was to demobilize his armies, ensuring a ready supply of military forces for later conflicts while simultaneously preventing the rise of powerful regional generals (like himself) who might lay claim to the throne. In 623, the emperor dissolved the 12 armies that had carried him to power. Troops were organized into local military commands of 800, 1,000, or 1,200 soldiers each. The empire remained heavily militarized, and historical records indicate that, by the end of the dynasty, there was a total of 633 of these units. However, none of these units was large enough to constitute an independently viable threat to the throne. They were also placed under central, rather than local, command, with the groups of soldiers being rotated regularly to the capital to undermine local affiliations and preserve a common military culture.

Fiscal, Legal, and Educational Reforms

Although Gaozu handled the military in a manner distinct from, and ultimately far more successful than, that of the Sui dynasty, his other policies largely followed the models of his predecessors. He revived the Equal-Fields system of the Sui and earlier northern dynasties, which allocated farmland to adult male taxpayers on the basis of an annual census. The system limited private access to land and ensured the maintenance of equitable distribution. This was an extraordinarily ambitious attempt to assert centralized authority over land tenure, which would not be matched in scale until land reform under the Communists in the later half of the twentieth century. Most historians had thought that the Equal-Fields system was beyond the capacity of a premodern state. Discoveries of local land tenure documents at Dunhuang in the early twentieth century dispelled many of these doubts, for they demonstrated that the system had indeed been implemented in locales far from the capital until at least the mid-eighth century.

Gaozu also introduced a new penal and administrative law code. Based on the Sui code, which had, in turn, been compiled from the codes of the various northern regimes, the Tang code provided a set of 500 basic articles that laid down broad, rational principles and limited the death penalty to the most grievous crimes. The new code survived Gaozu's reign and outlasted the Tang dynasty, persisting as the foundation of Chinese legal practice until the fourteenth century. It also served as the ideal model for the earliest legal codes of Japan, Korea, and Vietnam.

In addition to the national land tenure and legal system, Gaozu reinstituted the Sui civil service examination and reestablished government schools. While these institutions would, in later dynasties, serve as important channels for recruiting capable men from beyond the nobility, in the Tang they were principally the preserve of the aristocratic elite. Literary talent and classical learning were part of a good pedigree, and the examination system institutionalized and codified these expectations. Admission to all government schools, in particular the prestigious capital city universities, was restricted to the sons of the imperial family, nobility, and the highest ranking officials. The principal function of this specific

BELOW **The Ba Xi'an An Monastery** is dedicated to the legendary Daoist eight immortals. This was one of the monasteries permitted in the Tang capital, Xi'an.

educational system was to unite the elite by providing them with the tools and the imperative to participate in literate high culture.

A Fatal Misstep against the Clergy

One of Emperor Gaozu's most controversial policies, one which may have contributed to his downfall, was his attempt to limit the power of the Buddhist and Daoist clerics. Monastic estates were formally beyond the reach of the imperial taxman, and this freedom from taxation, also combined with their popular appeal, had enabled monasteries during the Six Dynasties (220–589) to establish vast landholdings and absorb huge numbers of tenant farmers. These great estates belonged to many religious movements that transcended political boundaries, threatening the new imperial regime. Their landholdings, if divested, also represented a significant tax base that could be used to restore the imperial coffers, which Yangdi's Korean campaigns and public works had all but depleted.

In the fifth month of 626, the emperor duly proclaimed that only three Buddhist and one Daoist monastery were permitted in the capital, and only one of each faith in each prefecture. The scale of the restriction was stunning as Daoism and Buddhism had proliferated. At the time of the proclamation it is estimated that Chang'an and its environs held over 120 Buddhist and nearly a dozen Daoist monasteries. Gaozu's ruling threatened to decimate these institutions.

Yet the order was never fully enacted because in less than three months, Emperor Gaozu was deposed by his second son, Li Shimin. One of the first things that the new emperor undertook on

assuming the throne was to reverse the religious restrictions of his father. It has been suggested that the speed with which Li Shimin rescinded his father's original proclamation, together with his earlier submission of memorials defending the Buddhist clerics, strongly suggests that he was working closely with incensed Budddhist clergy and their supporters.

ABOVE **The Bodhisattva Avalokitesvara,** a painting depicting the Buddhist Saviour of all Perils. The practice of Buddhism was limited under Gaozu.

A NEW CURRENCY

One of Emperor Gaozu's most famous measures, and certainly the most enduring, was establishing a new bronze currency of standard size, weight, and metal content. This Chinese coinage had a decimal base, with each coin weighing a tenth of a Chinese ounce (about two-tenths of an ounce or 5½ grams) and measuring a tenth of a Chinese foot in diameter (about 1¼ inch or 32 millimeters). Known as the *Kaiyuan tongbao*, this new currency lasted for over 1,200 years, continuing to circulate for centuries after the fall of the Tang. *Kaiyuan tongbao* had a profound influence, and they continue to be found at later archaeological sites throughout East Asia. *Kaiyuan* means "new beginning" while *tongbao* means "circulating treasure" or "coin."

RIGHT **The Kaiyuan tongbao coin from the** Tang dynasty, 621, is an example of lettering originally written by Ouyang Xun, one of the dynasty's calligraphy masters. The coins were praised for their artistic merits.

Tang Taizong

Li Shimin, best remembered by his posthumous temple name Taizong, is widely regarded as one of the greatest rulers in Chinese history. Historically, he is considered a charismatic ruler whose reign from 626–649, known as "Excellent Governance of True Vision," made the Tang dynasty great.

ABOVE **Tang Taizong** is considered one of China's greatest emperors. Studying his exemplary reign became mandatory for future crown princes and emperors.

RIGHT **A silk scroll painting** shows the seventh-century pilgrim Xuanzang, responsible for bringing the Buddhist scriptures from India to China.

Building on the fine achievements of his father Li Yuan (Tang Gaozu), Emperor Taizong (599–649), tempering his innate martial spirit with an evergrowing awareness of all Confucian principles, embarked on an ambitious program of civil reform as well as vigorous military campaigns, allowing culture to flourish and the empire to expand dramatically.

The Making of an Emperor

Like many members of the military aristocracy in northwest China, Taizong, the second son of founding emperor Gaozu, had mixed Han Chinese and Central Asian blood. At four, a court physiognomist claimed he radiated the aura of a dragon and the sun, an appearance foretelling greatness. He was educated in the Confucian classics, but also excelled in hunting and archery, and his equestrian skills were legendary. Taizong's ascent to the throne was cutthroat and ruthless, as seen in the Xuanwumen Gate incident of 626: he murdered his brother and usurped the throne from his father, whom he forced into retirement.

Civil Achievements

Because he seized the throne by violence, Taizong worked diligently to show the people of the empire that he was not an unloyal son, but a ruler who valued Confucian ethics. In order to style himself as a champion of the Confucian ideology of order, Taizong first established a novel Bureau of Historiography, then set up a

School of Calligraphy, and organized a College for Magnifying Literature. He enthusiastically developed the examination system to recruit men of talent to staff his administrative ranks. To stabilize the newly formed dynasty, Taizong streamlined and reorganized the bureaucracy. He surrounded himself with competent, strong-willed prime ministers from eminent families—renowned men like Chu Suiliang, Zhangsun Wuji, and Wei Zheng—who offered blunt, straightforward advice and helped guide state policy. Though his court was divided by factions at times, Taizong usually managed them well. He proved a capable and circumspect politician willing to take advice and heed counsel, ruling as a "first among equals" rather than as an autocrat.

He devised other reforms including a detailed household registration system to help collect tax revenues, though it eventually proved ineffective. He set up relief granaries to feed the populace in the event of natural disasters. Under his sovereignty, in an effort to standardize all ceremonial practice and laws, Taizong compiled a new manual of rites and a comprehensive set of laws, *The Tang Code*. In 638, in an effort to put the imperial Li family on equal footing with the great clans, he ordered the compilation of a *Treatise of Surnames and Clans*.

Taizong was not a supporter of Buddhism. He sometimes ordered the quick execution of illegally ordained Buddhist monks. However, when the famous pilgrim Xuanzang, who made a 14-year pilgrimage to India, returned with a vast

ABOVE **The Tersey Alatoo mountains in Kyrgyzstan** were part of the Silk Road that became part of the Tang territory in 640, paving the way for future trade.

repository of Buddhist scriptures, Emperor Taizong received him, accepting him as a blood brother. Xuanzang wrote *Journey to the West in the Great Tang dynasty.*

A New Paradigm of Power

Taizong is best known for his strong military achievements. On the battlefield, a man was measured not by his ethnicity, but by his martial mettle. Therefore, in the multiethnic empire of the seventh century, he styled himself not only as a traditional Confucian Son of Heaven, which meant that the emperor was chosen by Heaven to enlighten his subjects and lead by example, but as a Heavenly Khan. Taizong took oaths of brotherhood with nomadic chieftains, making him an emperor who was determined to unify people whatever their ethnicity, which went against the thinking of the time. In 630, Taizong defeated the powerful Xieli Khan, leader of the Eastern Turks, and resettled the defeated Turks within Tang territories. In the early 640s, the Western Turks, divided by the discord sown by Taizong, became Tang vassals. The fall of the Western Turks enabled Taizong to establish the Four Garrisons, extending Chinese territory to modern-day Kyrgyzstan. This brought a long stretch of the Silk Road under Chinese control and, culturally and materially, greatly enriched the Tang empire. He also conquered smaller non-Chinese groups like the Xi, the Shiwei, the Tiele, and the Xueyantao in the north and northeast, further expanding the Tang borders. Despite his reputation as a martial conqueror, Taizong was considered humane and treated surrendered peoples well, cleverly incorporating them into the growing empire.

Trying to equal or excel the vast empire of the Han dynasty, in his later years Emperor Taizong repeatedly launched failed campaigns against the Korean kingdom of Koguryô. After his final and unsuccessful campaign in 645, Taizong tried again to conquer the weak Xueyantao, a confederation of nomadic tribes along the northern border. This move was geared to gloss over the aura of martial failure and to stifle a rival faction in court that opposed his policy of expansion. Taizong recast his martial legacy and, with spectacular pomp and fanfare, he gathered many non-Chinese chieftains at a frontier garrison where he was duly proclaimed once more a Heavenly Khan, the central military chieftain of all nations of the steppe.

Although Taizong was a vigorous warrior in his youth, his health rapidly deteriorated in his late forties. An ugly succession dispute between his two eldest sons by Empress Zhangsun led Tang Taizong to choose their youngest son, Li Zhi, as heir. To help the highly inexperienced Li Zhi with learning kingship and statescraft, Taizong crafted the *Plan for an Emperor*. He died in 649.

Foreign Affairs

Adopting a flexible, pragmatic policy that mixed appeasement with conquest, successive Tang emperors succeeded for over a century in defending the northern frontier and expanding dramatically into the deserts of Central Asia.

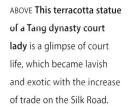

ABOVE **This terracotta statue of a Tang dynasty court lady** is a glimpse of court life, which became lavish and exotic with the increase of trade on the Silk Road.

The tribal alignments that confronted the Tang both as potential enemies and allies in the early decades included the Khitan, a nomadic tribe in the northeast of China, the Turks (Tujue) to the north, and the Tibetans to the west. The Tang dynasty began with a distinct disadvantage. Even before the dynasty was established, Emperor Gaozu had to buy off the Turks to ensure that they would not attack his supply lines and disrupt his drive to the Sui capital of Daxingchen. On the throne, he was forced to recognize the authority and declare himself a vassal of the Eastern Turkic Empire, which occupied the region of modern Mongolia and dominated the frontier. The arrangement changed under Emperor Taizong, who exploited divisions between the Turkish rulers and dissension among their subject tribes to undermine the integrity of the whole confederacy. By adding limited and well-prepared applications of direct military force to this strong revival of the classical Chinese policy of "using all the barbarians to fight barbarians," Taizong fractured the Turkic Empire and forced its component tribes to recognize his authority. The vassal was now the master.

While traditional historiography tends to emphasize the otherness of these Turkic "barbarians," it should be remembered that the Li royal family was itself descended from a mixed-blood lineage hailing from the northwest that shared many of the Turks' martial traditions. Horseback riding, hunting, and archery were skills esteemed on both sides of the frontier. Alliances were conducted and maintained on familial terms in that tribal leaders were brought into the fold through marriage to Tang princesses, and international diplomacy was conducted between the "elder brother" in Chang'an and "younger

RIGHT **A Sancai pottery archer on horseback** provides a historical record of tribes coming into China.

brothers" of the tribes. When the fragments of the Eastern Turkish Empire formally recognized Taizong's suzerainty in 630, they called him the Heavenly Khan, speaking not in Chinese idiom, but in the language of the steppe. This dual identity, as emperor to some and khan to others, is precisely how Taizong wanted to be known as it gave him authority in two worlds.

Expansion into Central Asia

Taizong used his new authority in a series of spectacular territorial acquisitions that were maintained and reinforced by his successors. The most noteworthy of these acquisitions were the oasis states of the Silk Road, which extended west from Chang'an, passed through the Hexi Corridor, and then split into two branches that skirted the vast Taklamakan Desert. Taizong

established garrisons in each of these oases and thereby extended Tang influence to the far-flung mountain passes of the Pamirs and Hindu Kush. The stability provided by these outer garrisons facilitated the thriving trans-Asian luxury trade, which had a tremendous influence on the consumption patterns of the Tang nobility. The Tang court drank the wine of Turfan poured from ewers of Persian glass into goblets of Byzantine gold. Culture and religion traveled with these luxuries, and the marketplaces of Chang'an echoed with the Sogdian and Indo-European tongues of Central Asia, while the prayers of the faithful emanated from Manichean temples, Zoroastrian fire shrines, and even the churches of the Nestorian Christians.

Over the course of the next century, Tang armies repeatedly clashed with the kingdom of Tibet and its affiliates for control over these lucrative trade routes. At times, the Tibetans succeeded in temporarily cutting off the Tang garrisons and isolating key Tang clients, such as the kingdom of Gilgit in what is today known as Pakistan. Yet these threats proved short-lived, and a succession of Tang rulers repeatedly mustered the financial resources and personnel necessary to reverse the Tibetan incursions. Ultimately, it was not the Tibetans, but rather the rise of the Arabs and the An Lushan Rebellion that turned the tide. In 751, the great Tang general Gao Xianzhi, who had in the preceding years expelled the Tibetans from Gilgit and reasserted Tang

influence over the Kashmir region, met and was soundly defeated by Arab armies at the Battle of the Talas River. These new opponents presented an unfamiliar threat, and it is quite likely that the Tang Empire could have, in other circumstances, raised the forces that were necessary to stem the advance, as they had with Tibetans so many times before. Yet the rebellion of An Lushan in 755 not only turned the court's attention away from the frontier, it also led to the recall of the Central Asian garrisons. Into this vacuum rode the triumphant Arabs and Tibetans, virtually uncontested. The spectacular Tang reign over Central Asia had finally come to an end.

ABOVE **Bamyan in the Hindu Kush, Afghanistan,** which was on the linking route between the markets of China and West Asia.

THE RISE OF THE UIGHURS

In the latter half of the eighth century a second Turkish confederacy, less powerful than the first, rose on the steppes of Mongolia. Initially an adversary, a peace settlement in 722 saw this confederacy transformed into a loyal tributary that rebuffed the overtures of the Tibetans in the west and the rebellious Qidan in the east, both of which sought to draw the Turks into their own struggles with the Tang. Disagreement within the ruling clan destabilized the confederacy, which collapsed into anarchy in the 740s. In their place, a new tribe appeared, the Uighurs, the largest group of Turkic-speaking people in Central Asia. Within a few years, the Uighurs consolidated their control over the steppe and, unlike their nomadic predecessors, established a fixed capital that they staffed with Chinese craftsmen and a literate bureaucracy of Sogdians and other Central Asians. The Uighurs remained supportive, if costly, allies of the Tang court, and played a central role in the restoration of the dynasty in the aftermath of the An Lushan Rebellion.

The Empress Wu

Wu Zhao (624–705), China's only female emperor, is better known as Empress Wu or Wu Zetian. Her ascent from provincial obscurity as the second daughter in the second marriage of a wealthy Taiyuan lumber merchant to her enthronement as emperor of the vast Chinese nation is a compelling historical drama.

ABOVE **Empress Wu** founded her own dynasty, the Zhou, in 690. After her death, her dynasty died with her and the Tang dynasty was restored to power.

A t age 13, Wu Zhao left her widowed mother to enter the women's quarters of the Imperial Palace as a Talent, one of nine fifth-ranked concubines in the harem of famous emperor Tang Taizong. Though she never gained Taizong's favor, he was impressed by her dazzling beauty and bestowed upon her the nickname, "Enchanting Miss Wu." When Taizong was on his deathbed and instructing his son and successor, Gaozong, in the arts of statecraft, Wu Zhao and the heir apparent formed a deep emotional attachment. Despite this, when Taizong died in 649, following ritual protocol Wu Zhao was sent with the rest of the women in the harem to a nearby Buddhist convent. Later, Emperor Gaozong recalled her to the inner palace and promoted her a higher position, known as the Lady of Luminous Demeanor. After she bore him several sons, Gaozong elevated her to become Empress Wu in 655. To make certain her two primary sexual rivals would not become favorites, Wu Zhao ordered the women to be beaten, then their hands and feet were severed, and they were cast intoa vat of fermented wine, and left to die agonizing deaths.

The Two Sages

Through much of his reign Gaozong was seriously ill and shared most of his imperial responsibilities with Wu Zhao. Beginning in 660, she often sat behind a purple curtain in the audience hall and deliberated upon administrative decisions, earning the royal pair the name the "Two Sages." From the very outset, she played an active public role as empress. In the spring of 656, she performed a very public sacrifice to the Silk Goddess, Leizu, leading eminent ladies of the state to pick mulberry leaves and feed them to silkworms. Traditionally the Empress had never

played a role in the *feng* and *shan* rites, the grand ceremonial offerings to Heaven and Earth. Wu Zhao persuaded Gaozong to allow her to perform the secondary *shan* offering at Mount Tai in 666. Her participation in such large-scale rites helped the court and country to become used to her strong and determined political presence.

In 676, after heir apparent Li Hong died of tuberculosis, ailing Gaozong offered to abdicate to Wu Zhao. Though she declined, Wu Zhao felt, after almost two decades of her deep involvement in matters of court administration, a proprietary sense toward the empire, and a taste for power. To help justify her increasing political role, she gathered a band of brilliant literary minds, talented Confucian scholars of low rank, known as the Scholars of the North Gate. These unofficial advisers compiled works geared toward consolidating Wu Zhao's political authority.

Grand Dowager and Caring Sage Mother

With Gaozong's death in 683, Wu Zhao's political authority diminished. When her son Li Xian, the inept and frivolous Emperor Zhongzong, rapidly fell under

sway of his Empress Wei, Whu Zao deposed him in 684. She also acted as regent, overshadowing her timid youngest son Li Dan (known as Emperor Ruizong). Wu Zhao "oversaw the court and issued all the imperial edicts."

Wu Zhao had many enemies. To intimidate and remove them, she used a group of cruel officials. Lai Junchen, the most notorious of these officials, wrote the *Manual of Entrapment*, an extensive work detailing the arts of ensnaring the innocent, fabricating the circumstances of conspiracy, creating a culture of terror.

But Wu Zhao preferred to use other persuasive measures. She cast herself in the role as a caring "Sage Mother" nurturing myriad "sons" within a wider empire. In 688, her supporters "discovered" a white stone in the Luo River that read, "When the Sage Mother is among the people, the realm will enjoy eternal prosperity." Shortly thereafter, she assumed the title Sage Mother, Divine, and August. To mark the occasion, military officials and foreign chieftains paraded before an altar set along the Luo River and offered a rich tribute of splendid birds, miraculous beasts, precious gemstones, and other exquisite rarities.

Symbols, Ritual, and Ceremony

Knowing that her role as a female emperor was unprecedented, Wu Zhao creatively used rituals,

ceremonies and symbols to reinforce her political legitimacy in the minds of the people she ruled.

The idea that "the male is honored and the female denigrated" is one deeply imbedded in Confucian thought, it was this ideology that made Empress Wu an ardent supporter of Buddhism, which offered her validation that Confucianism could not. Wu Zhao sponsored translations of Buddhist texts, construction of Buddhist temples, delegations of Buddhist monks, and magnificent Buddhist rites. With her own money, Wu Zhao helped fund the carving of Fengxian Temple at the Longmen Grottoes just south of Luoyang. The central Buddhist figure of the statuary ensemble, a 50-ft (14 m) Vairocana, is reportedly modeled on her image. On the eve of her inauguration as the emperor of her new dynasty, Buddhist monks promulgated the tome, *Commentary on the Great Cloud Sutra*, a meticulous catalogue of prophecies identifying Wu Zhao as both a bodhisattva (an enlightened being), and the Cakravartin,

BELOW **The Vairocana Buddhist statue** at the Fengxian Temple was funded by the Empress Wu.

a Buddhist universal wheel-turning monarch. She had the seven treasures of the Buddhist Cakravartin—a golden wheel, a white elephant, a woman, a horse, a pearl, a ruler's guardian warrior, and a ruler's hidden minister—displayed prominently in the audience hall of her court. The grandest Buddhist rite, the Pançavarsika, a massive ten-day communal vegetarian feast, was held in late 694. In 695, funded by Persian and Central Asian leaders, the Heavenly Pivot, a 100-ft (30 m) Buddhist pillar surrounded by mysterious guardian beasts and topped by a fire pearl set on a cloud canopy and held aloft by a quartet of dragons, was set up in the heart of Luoyang. Her lavish patronage won Wu Zhao the support of the Buddhist establishment, who realized that they had found a rich, charismatic imperial sponsor to promote their faith.

Wu Zhao built staggering architectural marvels. In 688, she built the Divine Palace of Myriad Images, a 300-ft (92 m) structure with rooms representing the four seasons and the 12 months, matched with their respective colors. A 975-foot, five-story, firmament-piercing Buddhist pagoda beside it housed a giant 880-ft (268 m) Buddha.

China's Only Female Emperor

On the ninth day of the ninth month of 690, Wu Zhao ascended the dragon throne as the first and only female emperor in Chinese history. She

WU ZHAO: A MISTRESS OF THE LANGUAGE

When Wu Zhao established herself as regent in 684, Lou Bin Wang, a disgruntled scholar, wrote a scathing statement, attacking the Grand Dowager: "Miss Wu, who has falsely usurped authority to run the court, is by nature cold and unyielding, by birth lowly and obscure. With embroidered sleeves and artful slander, her vulpine glamour beguiled the ruler. Beneath her pheasant's plumage, the former Empress was trampled. This musky doe once plunged my true Sovereign into rutting frenzy, vying with his own father. Her heart is half viper and half chameleon. Her disposition is that of a ravenous jackal or wolf ... Hated by men and spirits alike, neither Heaven nor Earth can stand her!"

When Wu Zhao learned of this elegant if caustic character assassination, she merely turned to her court and remarked, "Ministers, this is your fault! How is it that a man this talented isn't on my official payroll?"

built Luoyang, her "Divine Capital," into an international metropolis rivaling Chang'an.

In military affairs and foreign relations, she was neither soft nor weak. Unlike rulers of some later dynasties who denigrated the martial arts and prized civil courtly culture, Wu Zhao attached great importance to recruiting capable generals. In 692, General Wang Xiaojie defeated the Tibetans and reclaimed the Four Garrisons, rich oasis states along the Silk Road in western China, which strengthened Chinese control over Silk Road commerce and increased China's prestige among Central Asian peoples. She also managed to stave off a series of fierce incursions from the marauding Khitan and Turks.

Empress Wu's Fall and Final Days

Wu Zhao's later years were unremarkable. Realizing that her Wu nephews alienated court and country alike, she named her youngest son, Li Dan, heir apparent in 698, a decision that determined that the Zhou dynasty would not outlive her reign. As she became infirm, Wu Zhao turned to Daoism, performing rites of expiation and seeking immortality, frequently retreating to the hot springs and Daoist temples of Mt. Song.

She took solace in the brothers Zhang Changzong and Zhang Yizhi, handsome youths who turned her inner palace into a theatrical and ornate Daoist paradise. Dressed in bright, colorful silks and wearing vermilion rouge, the wily Zhangs turned their favored status into political influence. Confucian court ministers staged a coup in 705, brutally killing the Zhangs and forcing Wu Zhao into retirement in the Imperial Park, just outside the walls of the Imperial City. The Empress Wu died ten months later, disheveled, sick, and weary, in stark contrast to her shining persona when she was at the peak of her political powers.

She was buried with her husband Gaozong at Qianling, the only tomb in Chinese history to house two emperors.

ABOVE **The warriors of Qianling Mausoleum** guard the burial sites of Emperor Gaozong and Empress Wu.

LEFT **A female musician on a Tang dynasty fresco** fragment gives a glimpse into courtly life during the time of Empress Wu.

Printing and Ideas

The Bodhisattva Guanyin

This tenth-century painting depicts the deity of mercy and compassion accepting offerings. The Guanyin Sutra was one of the first Buddhist scriptures to be printed and distributed.

In 1907, the archaeologist and adventurer Sir Mark Aurel Stein, while rummaging through a horde of old manuscripts and documents found in a cave at the western Chinese oasis town of Dunhuang, discovered a long scroll bearing a transcription of a famous Buddhist scripture known as the Diamond Sutra.

The scripture itself was unremarkable; the horde had been the library of a medieval monastery, and it had been filled with thousands of religious texts that included many copies of the most famous scriptures. What was remarkable was that, unlike the vast majority of the manuscripts which were written by hand, this text was printed. The printing was of an exceptionally high standard, suggesting the use of an advanced woodblock printing technique and it had a finely carved pictographic frontispiece. It also bore a date (868 CE) that predated Gutenberg and the widespread adoption of printing in Europe by nearly six centuries. Stein brought the scroll (as well as several thousand other documents) back to England, and the transcription of the sutra remains in the collection of the British Museum, where it is recognized as the oldest printed book in the world.

The quality of the scroll strongly suggested that this was not just a tentative experiment with a new technique, but that it was the product of a well-established technical tradition. The scroll was made from seven strips of yellow stained paper printed from carved wooden blocks. The discoveries of other printed scriptures at Buddhist sites in Korea and Japan have pushed the beginning of printing in East Asia back to at least as early as the seventh century, possibly even earlier. Virtually all of these early printed texts are sutras (religious sermons), *dharani* (charms), and other Buddhist scriptures. Reproduction of these famed "words of the Buddha" was understood throughout medieval East Asia as a meritorious act that improved one's chances for a favorable reincarnation, and it is quite likely that such otherworldly motivations spurred on the rapid development of printing. Just as the reproduction of Buddhist images and the recitation of the name

The Diamond Sutra

This copy of the Diamond Sutra is the world's earliest record of a printed book. The illustration shows the Buddha expounding the sutra to an elderly disciple called Subhuti. Sutras were committed to memory and passed to others.

A Buddhist Woodcut with a Molding Board

The process of woodblock printing involves writing on thin paper, glueing it on to woodblocks, engraving the reverse characters into the wood and brushing the blocks with ink. Paper is placed on the block and carefully removed.

"Amitabha" recalled the vastness of the Buddhist cosmos and represented another step toward enlightenment, so too transcriptions of Buddhist scripture assisted one's progress on the Buddhist path. In all cases, quantity mattered, and by vastly increasing the rate at which scriptures could be reproduced, printing sped up achieving the much sought after religious merit.

Printing also facilitated Buddhist practice by aiding the wide dissemination of the *dharma* (Buddhist teachings), which was another meritorious activity. At least some of the early fragments found in Korea and Japan are believed to have been originally produced in China, and their location testifies to the role that the printing of important scriptures played in transmitting Buddhist theology throughout the East Asian teachings. One of the most frequently reported items obtained by Japanese and Korean monks on their pilgrimages to the Tang Empire was Buddhist scriptures. By lowering the cost of the transcription and standardizing the content of the text, printing made it possible for ever-expanding religious communities, throughout East Asia, to share the same bodies of religious text. Printing helped to create a common Buddhist ethos that transcended the political boundaries of any given state. The same dynamic is seen in the international efforts of the Church in Europe, and it is no coincidence that Gutenberg's most significant work—the Gutenberg Bible—was also religious in nature.

The new technique was used for the reproduction of non-Buddhist texts such as dictionaries, literary anthologies, encyclopedias, and the Daoist canon.

Bringing Confucian Classics to the People

By the tenth century, printing industries had sprung up at major population centers in both northern and southern China. Among the most significant of the projects undertaken by these industries was the printing of the Confucian classics, which for the first time standardized these texts and made them affordable to a much larger segment of the Chinese population. This, in turn, facilitated the expansion of the civil service examination system as the primary path of entry into government office and served as an engine for a faster rate of social mobility in the later half of the tenth century.

Tang Xuanzong

The first three decades of Xuanzong's reign, "The Splendid Age of Original Opening," was a high point of Chinese history marked by grand civil and military achievements. Often mentioned with Taizong's era of "Excellent Governance of the True Vision," this period is considered one of the Tang dynasty's twin peaks of imperial splendor.

Born Li Longji in 685, Xuanzong was the third son of the puppet emperor, Ruizong (reigned 684–690 and 710–712), and the grandson of Wu Zhao.

If Tang rule is considered a period of cultural renaissance, Xuanzong was a renaissance man, a master of calligraphy, music, and poetry; a man who developed a profound understanding of Daoism and esoteric Buddhism, and an ardent patron of the arts. He also venerated Laozi, the founder of Daoism and the fictive ancestor of the Tang rulers, naming the *Daodejing* as the most important canonical text, and then establishing a special examination based on Daoist scripture. His court included men like Yizing, the Buddhist astronomer and mathematician, and the Indian Tantric master Vajrapani. During the latter part of his reign, the famous Tang poets Li Bai (701–762) and Du Fu (712–770) served in his court. In 725, Xuanzong performed the *feng* and *shan* sacrifices at Taishan, the easternmost of China's

five sacred peaks. These rites confirmed Heaven's sanction of an emperor's rule, and were performed in the times of peace and prosperity, allowing a worthy sovereign to broadcast to entire empire and to neighboring lands a sense of cosmic harmony and order. Emperor Xuanzong streamlined the bureaucracy he had inherited. With the help of his minister Yuwen Rong, Xuanzong resuscitated the poorly administered household registration system from the provinces, which helped fill dwindling state coffers with tax revenues. He reformed the system of grain transport, in order to expedite the flow of grain tax from localities to the capital. The examination system was altered to allow provincial men to enter bureaucratic service more easily.

Military Expansion under Xuanzong

For most of his reign, Xuanzong was largely successful in military endeavors and managing

THE POWER WOMEN OF THE TANG DYNASTY

Xuanzong assumed the throne in a time of powerful women. His grandmother Wu Zhao dominated the court for half a century. After her death and the restoration of the Tang in 705, a quartet of women—Empress Wei, the Taiping Princess, the Anle Princess, and Shangguan Wan'er—competed to manipulate the corrupt, faction-ridden court, a hothouse of intrigue and treachery. In 710, the future emperor staged a palace coup that resulted in the execution of Empress Wei and the second enthronement of his father. Xuanzong assumed the throne in 712, but only the following year, after he exposed a plot to poison him by his scheming aunt, the Taiping Princess, executing her conspirators and forcing her to commit suicide in a monastery, was his position as emperor secure. In the Confucian paradigm, Xuanzong is regarded as a great ruler, in no small part, because he was an assertive male who restored the grandeur of the Tang, resuscitated patriarchal pride and restored a sense of proper order, ending 50 years of court domination by empresses, dowagers, and families of consorts.

LEFT **In this silk painting, Emperor Xuanzong is shown watching his favorite concubine,** Yang Guifei, mount a horse. It is said that the beauty of Yang Guifei, another powerful woman of the time, distracted the emperor and caused him to neglect his duties, contributing to the dynasty's collapse.

李白

LEFT **The Chinese poet Li Bai** was part of the group "Eight Immortals of the Wine Cup," and he benefited greatly from Xuanzong's patronage. He is regarded as one of China's greatest poets.

foreign relations. With the death of Eastern Turk leader Qapaghan in 716, many Turkish tribes had to submit to the Tang. This led other groups along the northeastern frontier, like the Xi and the Khitan, to become Tang vassal states. To cope with border incursions from the Tang's many formidable nomadic enemies—Xuanzong kept the Tang borders intact, by and large, managing the Arabs, Tibetans, Turks, and the Khitan—permanent military governors were garrisoned at critical frontier commands. Toward the end of his reign a weakness of this strategy became apparent: the best and most battle-hardened men of these professional armies were non-Chinese subjects of the Tang Empire who were under the control of the military governors on the frontier rather than the control of central government.

Yang Guifei and the An Lushan Rebellion

Chinese emperors often became used to the luxuries of palace life, and completely detached from the daily wranglings of court and the plight of their subjects. Such was the case with Emperor Xuanzong. Fascinated with esoteric Buddhism and Daoist mysticism, he lost his focus on the routine administrative matters of the Tang court. Mesmerized by the voluptuous and lovely spouse of his eighteenth son, Xuanzong took the young lady into his harem, making her Yang Guifei,

Precious Consort Yang. When this dazzling and beguiling woman, regarded today as one of the four famous beauties in Chinese history, entered Xuanzong's harem, the sovereign catered to her every need. On one occasion, when Yang Guifei craved lychees in the winter, the emperor sent riders to the far southern reaches of the empire to fetch the fruit. She maneuvered her relatives, like power-mongering Yang Guozhong, into positions of tremendous influence in the court and had a dubious friendship with the notorious Sogdian general An Lushan, whom she took as an adopted son. An Lushan's rebellion in 755 ended Xuanzong's reign, sending the Tang court into exile. During Xuanzong's flight to Sichuan, Precious Consort Yang and Yang Guozhong were killed, supposedly on orders from Xuanzong who suspected treason. His son and heir apparent Suzong claimed the throne, and the harried and beleaguered emperor surrendered the imperial regalia. Eventually, when the capital was restored to Tang control, he returned as a retired emperor to the city of Chang'an, where he died of old age in 761.

As magnificent as Xuanzong's noted accomplishments were during the first three decades of his reign, the Tang dynasty never completely recovered from the An Lushan Rebellion. His late reign marked the rise of a culture of militarism in the provinces, a weakening of central authority, as well as growing tensions between the Han Chinese of the center and the non Chinese of the periphery.

RIGHT **The painted terracotta statue of Yang Guifei** gives form to the daughter-in-law and later concubine of Emperor Xuanzong. This Tang woman is immortalized in Chinese art and literature.

The Rebellion of An Lushan

The An Lushan Rebellion was the axis upon which the fortunes of the Tang dynasty turned. While the dynasty ultimately recovered and survived for another century and a half, it never recovered the glory of its early days.

ABOVE **A Tibetan village in Sichuan Province** is an example of the outlying frontier areas of the Tang dynasty controlled by a decentralized regime.

An Lushan, like many of the military men that the Tang government appointed to guard the frontier, was descended from mixed Turkish and Sogdian parentage. While his precise heritage is unknown, he came from the sort of "barbarian" people that had been pacified by Taizong and used ever since as the mainstay of the imperial armies. An began his service in the Tang military while still a child, and although he later became an imperial favorite, it appears that he initially rose through the ranks purely on the basis of talent. In 742, he was appointed as the military governor of Pinglu, a very strategic command in the northeast and very close to the border with the troublesome Khitan. An's rise coincided with the deterioration of the earlier Tang system of rotating military appointments, in which generals were frequently shifted to new commands so that they could not develop power bases independent of the court. This relaxation of central authority gave frontier officials motivation and allowed them to develop all the resources needed to counter enemies like the Tibetans and Khitan, and indeed was one of the reasons that the Tang was able to maintain its widespread influence. It also revived the danger of regional governors developing dynastic ambitions. This was a factor that destabilized Xuangzong's power base, and created weak points in his authority to rule.

After his initial appointment, An Lushan moved swiftly to consolidate his new position, expanding his army and recruiting an unofficial bodyguard of some 8,000 troops who owed their loyalty to him personally. At the same time, he maintained a close relationship with the court, which granted him additional titles and enabled him to expand his official authority. By the early 750s, he was the de facto ruler of northeastern China. Throughout this process, he nevertheless remained a loyal servant of the imperial house. In 751, Emperor Xuanzong's favorite consort,

Yang Guifei, who had entered the imperial harem six years earlier and rapidly exerted her influence over the ageing emperor, decided to formally adopt An Lushan as her son.

An Lushan was not the only figure to benefit from his association with the "Precious Consort." In 752, Yang Guifei's cousin Yang Guozhong was appointed chief minister. The new minister's uncertain position at court made him suspicious of potential rivals in the provinces, and he and An Lushan soon grew suspicious of each other's intentions. An had long enjoyed the support of Emperor Xuanzong; Yang Guozhong's proximity to the throne and rival status made the continuity of this support increasingly uncertain. Within a few years, An Lushan was convinced that Yang Guozhong was actively plotting against him. His options were either to accept defeat, which at best, meant exile and ignominy, or to rebel. In the twelfth month of 755, he chose the latter.

The Course of the Rebellion

The rebellion advanced swiftly. By the first day of the lunar year 756, when An proclaimed himself emperor of a new dynasty known as the Greater Yan, his forces had captured the great city of Luoyang and marched all the way to the Tongguan Pass, which guarded the western approach to the capital. There they were finally blocked and outnumbered by an army loyal to the throne. For six months, the two armies eyed each other from either side of the pass, neither confident of its ability to defeat the other. The deadlock was finally broken when Yang Guozhong ordered the imperial forces to launch an all-out attack on the rebels, overriding the protests of the commanding general in the crowded battlefield.

The assault was an abject failure. Using the smoke from flaming carts to disorient the government forces, An Lushan's troops quickly out-maneuvered and trapped their enemy in the narrow confines of the pass. Within hours, the bulk of the loyalist army, which numbered some 180,000 men, was annihilated. From there, the rebels rode unchecked to the gates of Chang'an, the capital.

As An Lushan's army approached the city, Emperor Xuanzong and a small retinue that included Yang Guifei and Yang Guozhong fled the capital for the mountain sanctuary of Sichuan. While the emperor eventually escaped, his "Precious Consort" was not so fortunate. In an episode long remembered in poetry, song, and popular lore, the imperial guard, blaming Yang Guifei and her clan for the disaster, executed both her and her cousin on the road.

Imperial Recovery

Xuanzong's legitimacy was fatally undermined by the loss of the capital, and he was powerless to stop the heir apparent, Suzong, who had withdrawn to the northwest, from usurping the throne. Suzong recalled Tang armies from Central Asia, rallied loyalist forces, and succeeded at recapturing Chang'an in 757. By that time, An Lushan was killed by his own henchmen.

The rebellion raged for another five years, and while Chang'an remained in government hands, Luoyang was again lost and reconquered. One of the key factors aiding the imperial armies was the support of Uighur mercenaries, who played a particularly prominent role in the final recapture of Luoyang in 762. The service of these forces came at a heavy cost, for they claimed as their fee the right to loot the city. In the years to come, they continued to sell their "loyalty" in exchange for concessions from the weakened court.

ABOVE **Non-Sinitic (or "barbarian") tribes** became an important border resource for the imperial army.

LEFT **This painting of Chinese emperors** shows Emperor Xuanzong at home. He is surrounded by servants in the pavilion at the top of the painting.

Controlling the Provinces

The An Lushan Rebellion left the Tang Empire permanently changed. Regional military commands created to combat the rebellion remained in place, and their governors increasingly assumed what had once been the prerogatives of the central government, creating unstable shifts in the dynasty's power base.

ABOVE **A mural from the Dunhuang Caves** illustrates the Silk Road oasis state surrendering to Tibetan rule during the Tang dynasty.

The restored court faced many problems in the aftermath of the An Lushan Rebellion. The most pressing of these problems were financial. Huge sections of the most war-torn areas in the northeastern and central regions of Hebei and Henan were radically depopulated; many refugees had migrated to comparatively safer regions in the valleys of the southern Huai and Yangzi River systems. This huge demographic shift, combined with the widespread destruction of local tax records, made it all but impossible for the government to restore the Equal-Fields system, which was then predicated on detailed census registers and stable populations. The tax base that remained in Hebei and Henan, once the wealthiest and most productive regions in the empire, remained effectively outside the jurisdiction of the central government, which had essentially ceded control over these territories to rebel commanders in exchange for ending hostilities. This combination of southern migration and northern autonomy transformed the once marginal south, which remained firmly in government hands, into a vital breadbasket for the heavily populated but agriculturally unproductive capital region. Yet the use of this food larder required the maintenance of an elaborate canal system that represented a further drain on the imperial coffers.

The Diminishing Power of the Tang

In addition to creating these fiscal worries, the rebellion had reduced the empire's domains, undermined its prestige, and thereby emboldened its enemies. Once called back to fight the rebels, the Central Asian armies never returned, and many of the Silk Road oases states fell swiftly under the influence of the Tibetans, who also seized the Hexi Corridor and extended their border to within easy striking distance of Chang'an. The vulnerability of the capital was made abundantly clear when the Tibetans overcame the city's meager defenses and briefly occupied it in the fall of 763. Though they retreated due to the awareness of their inability to hold the city, this incident clearly demonstrated to all involved that the Tang court lacked the capacity to command the defenses of the empire.

Yet this military embarrassment was not due to a lack of troops. Indeed, by the end of the An Lushan Rebellion, it is estimated that nearly 800,000 men were under arms, in units at least

A TWO-EDGED SWORD: DIVIDED LOYALTIES

In an ironic sense, the post-An Lushan situation simultaneously saved and destabilized the Tang dynasty. Enormous regional armies stopped the revival of significant rebel forces and were checked by the coexistence of other armies. Substantial forces remained in the hands of men whose loyalty to the court was, at best, tenuous; no one person commanded more than a small fraction of the empire's total military capacity so power by the government was not strengthened by a single commander-in-chief. What suffered in the end was not governance as such, but the relative power of the central government. For the court, the problem became one of balancing the ambitions of military governors against one another and persuading enough regional powerholders that the fiscal solvency and military defense of the empire as a whole was in the interests of all.

ABOVE **A Tang dynasty statue** showing the practice of tribute offering. Tribute offerings were similar to a tax that various provinces paid for protection by the Tang Empire.

nominally loyal to the Tang court. The problem was not the availability of troops, but the various interests of their leaders, who were by and large regional military commanders who had, in the course of the rebellion, been granted considerable autonomy to raise and maintain what were effectively private armies. These new power-holders saw little advantage in vacating their territories and ceding control over their forces to a court of uncertain longevity.

The New Potentates

Recognizing the new balance of power, the Tang court integrated these generals and all of their commands into a tier of territorial administration interposed between the court, the existing prefecture, and the county hierarchy. This tier was divided into several dozen circuits. Officially speaking, these circuits were simply intended to coordinate the regional military units and inspect local administration, and were not granted the direct jurisdiction over the prefectures within their boundaries. In practice, these military governors (*jiedushi*) who oversaw the circuits were frequently able to win joint appointments as civil inspectors. This gave them the overall authority to rank the performance of local prefects and coordinate communication between the court and local governments. Many of the governors strategically turned these powers into de facto control over all local government and then transformed their circuits into private fiefdoms.

The result was a complex disposition of central and local authority that varied over time and space. In some places, particularly in the north, the military governors ruled as regional barons, exerting complete authority over their domains and forwarding tax revenues to the imperial court when and if they saw fit. In other places their powers were not as great, and they were rotated through a number of different regional commands like all other civil servants. The existence of these armies also gave governors the means to reduce banditry and reintegrate the individual localities into coherent, if informal, systems of administration and taxation. Reducing the distance between decision-makers and those in the field increased total efficiency.

Variations between the particular powers and the ambitions of individual governors made for many ad hoc decisions, and some unpredictable results. Yet the governors needed the court as well, not only as a source of abstract legitimacy, but also as a tool to hold in check the fierce ambitions of their powerful neighbors. The result was an extremely uneasy alliance that, despite its obvious flaws, per-sisted for more than a century.

LEFT **A painted stucco model** of a Tang dynasty soldier shows the military uniform worn by guards protecting the distant Silk Road outposts.

The Erosion of Power

The problem of banditry became widespread in the final half century of Tang rule, as increasing government exactions fueled popular resentment. This resentment culminated in a series of revolts that ultimately brought down the dynasty.

The An Lushan Rebellion affected the socio-economic landscape of the Tang Empire in three ways. First, it initiated a long period of sustained population growth in the Huai and Yangzi River valleys. Second, by placing taxation throughout most of north China in the hands of quasi-independent local potentates, it limited the central government's fiscal resources and forced it to focus its tax gathering measures on the Huai and Yangzi regions. Third, by ending the complex Equal-Fields system of land distribution, it also removed any checks on the creation of landed estates by local elites and exacerbated the dispossession of the peasantry.

For a time, the rising population and fertile agricultural potential of the southern valleys sustained the region as a stable imperial larder. Yet as the estates and resources of local landlords gradually increased, they developed the means to bribe and coerce the local officials either into resisting imperial tax demands or otherwise fulfilling their tax quotas on the backs of other, less advantaged segments of society. This trend impoverished the rural poor, who swelled the ranks of local bandit gangs. In many cases, these gangs limited their robberies to areas outside their home locale, and as a result enjoyed the support of the local gentry, who saw them as a means of redirecting crimes of desperation away from their own estates and as a way of defending the community against bandit incursions from neighboring regions.

The Huang Chao Rebellion

By the middle of the ninth century, the problem was widespread. Matters reached a head in 875 when gangs operating in the western portions of modern-day Shandong increased their numbers sufficient enough to expand their raids from local villages to walled prefectural cities. Within a year, several of these gangs formed a large confederation made up of several thousand men under the unifying command of Wang Xianzhi, a force large enough to pose an inter-regional threat and to attract the direct attention of the imperial court. The bandits proved surprisingly resilient, but the government finally gained the upper hand in 878 when its army won a victory over the confederation in the southern prefecture of Jizhou. Although Wang was killed in the battle, one of the leaders of the subsidiary gangs, Huang Chao, managed to escape with a portion of his

BELOW **Wheat and rapeseed fields** against the backdrop of mountains, in Qinghai Province, reflect the agricultural productivity of the region during Tang rule.

attempted to restore some order to the city, he soon found himself with little to command. Much of the city was in ruins, those with the means to escape had fled, and the flow of all the tax payments and foodstuffs from the provinces stopped. Huang Chao found himself the ruler of a near empty city that was starving to death.

Despite the scant economic base of Huang's regime, it took the Tang army over two years to recapture Chang'an. When they did, it was with the help of a substantial army of Turkic horsemen raised by Li Keyong, the feared autonomous warlord of Hebei in the northeast. Retaking the city, this fierce army proceeded to level most of the palaces that the rebels had left standing. Huang Chao escaped and another year passed before Li and his loyal allies succeeded in cornering him, at the aptly named Valley of Wolves and Tigers, where Chao turned his knife on himself, slitting his throat.

The Tang dynasty managed to limp on for another two decades. The regions under Tang rule formalized their de facto independence, proclaiming their own dynasties. The great city of Chang'an lay in desolate ruins and its rulers spent their days in shadowed halls.

LEFT **A Tang dynasty embroidery** illustrates the busyness of China's trading ports before it was destroyed by the rebel Huang Chao in 879.

forces still intact. Pursued by the imperial armies, Huang avoided being caught, recruited additional forces, and headed south. In the fifth month of 879, his army, which a few years earlier had been little more than a gang of thugs, sacked the great southern port of Canton, the primary gateway for trade with Southeast Asia, India, and the Middle East. Some figures suggest that more than half of the city's multiethnic population of 200,000 were killed. It took centuries for Canton to recover, and it lost its status as the major collection point for maritime trade to the ports of Fujian.

Huang then turned his attention to the north. After overcoming government armies in the Yangzi region, he crossed the Huai River, and, in the eleventh month of 880, captured the second capital of Luoyang without a fight. Although Huang had, by this point, amassed a sizable army, his victories were due to the reluctance of the Tang generals to commit to battles that might undermine their local positions. In the twelfth month of 880, Huang Chao's army overcame the meager defenses of the capital and put Chang'an to the sword.

Bandit Emperor of a Fallen City

The emperor escaped with a small retinue, while the rest of the city was left to the hands of Huang Chao's killers, who plundered indiscriminately, burnt the city's great markets to the grounds, slaughtering thousands. Helped by resentful townsfolk, they dragged the nobility and all the privileged officials from their homes, stripped them of their positions, and butchered them in the streets. Although Huang declared himself the emperor of a new dynasty—the Great Qi—and

BELOW **Tang dynasty military officials** offer a glimpse into the opulence of the once powerful dynasty, crushed by unrest.

The Five Dynasties

Usually seen as a brief transition from the Tang to the Song, the Period of the Five Dynasties and Ten Kingdoms (907–960) is important because it was the climax of half a century of militarism that had been developing since the eighth century.

ABOVE **A partridge and sparrow** are depicted in a tenth-century painting from the Five Dynasties period. It is attributed to Huang Zhucai, a landscape painter.

As indicated by the rapid change of government, the Period of the Five Dynasties and Ten Kingdoms was the final result of late Tang militarism. Beginning with the brutal An Lushan Rebellion (755–763), parts of northern China practiced military governance, which was a combination of Central Asian nomadism and the Tang system of military governorship. By the end of the eighth century, this military governance had spread so widely that the Tang Empire was practically divided into two halves, forming a military zone in the northeast and a civil zone in the central and southern parts of the country. The division of the two zones continued during the first half of the ninth century, and around the time of the Huang Cao Rebellion in 875–884, the military governors displaced the Tang court as the de facto rulers of China. When Zhu Wen, the military governor of Henan, brought the Tang dynasty to an end in 907, this represented the complete domination of the military machine over the civil.

Rapid Change of Power

Total military rule brought many drastic changes to the political, social, and cultural systems of China. During the Period of the Five Dynasties and Ten Kingdoms, political power changed hands many times, sometimes as frequently as once every ten to 15 years. Among the five northern dynasties, three of them (the Later Liang, Later Tang, and Later Jin) were founded by the Shatuo Turks, who had migrated into Tang China as military officers. To indicate and strengthen their link with the Tang Imperial Court, some of the Shatuo Turks carried the Tang royal family name Li, such as the first emperor of the Later Tang dynasty, Li Cunxu, who reigned from 923–926. This name was passed to the sons.

This period is given this particular name because there were five northern dynasties and ten southern kingdoms over 50 years. Located in the Yellow River valley and the Wei River region, the five northern dynasties included the Later Liang, Later Tang, Later Jin, Later Han, and Later Zhou. Clustered around or south of the Yangzi River valley, the ten southern kingdoms were Wu, Nan Tang, Wu Yue, Min, Nan Han, Chu, Early Shu, Later Shu, Nan Ping, and Bei Han.

With so many changes in political leadership in such a short time, the question for many of the leaders at the time was how to justify their right to rule. As former military generals, many leaders relied on portents as the true signs from Heaven. When auspicious portents like dragons, fragrant smoke, colored clouds, rare animals, and good dreams appeared, these were seen as giving heavenly blessings to the future rulers of China. Conversely, inauspicious portents such as the eclipses, droughts, locusts, and strange-looking animals indicated that Heaven was not pleased with the current ruler. This meant that either drastic reform was in order, or a new dynasty would soon be founded.

The importance of portents in politics is clearly shown in Zhu Wen's decision to end the Tang dynasty in 907. Unlike the other four first emperors of the Five Dynasties who replaced dynasties that lasted no more than 20 years, Zhu Wen distinguished himself as the military warlord who formally ended 300 years of Tang rule. The question for Zhu Wen then was why he was chosen by Heaven to undertake this great task of establishing a new dynasty.

For Zhu Wen his rise to power was due less to his military skills than his readiness to respond to heavenly signs. In his early life, Zhu was convinced that he was chosen by Heaven to be the next true emperor. As a child, he believed he saw dragons in his dreams and during the day. At one point in his life, an astrologer informed him that the realignment in the galaxy resembled a Chinese character that looked similar to his family name. Of course, portents alone did not make a great leader. Zhu Wen's star rose only after he "responded to Heaven and followed the time" by fighting bravely in battle and forging an anti-Tang alliance with other military generals. Yet, the heavenly signs had con-

vinced Zhu that he was the undisputed ruler of China. In his first announcement for establishing a new dynasty, Zhu Wen repeatedly referred to the auspicious portents to justify his rule. "When the heavenly mandate is rested upon you," he wrote, "the auspicious portents will match." He claimed that the Tang emperor had decided to transfer the right to rule to him after a careful examination of the oracle bones and bronzes.

ABOVE **This late Tang dynasty painting** shows musicians riding a white elephant. The influence of this particular style of artwork permeated Chinese cultural history for many centuries.

Kinship Based on Adoption

The total military rule also affected the family system. Rather than being based on the blood genealogy as prescribed by Confucianism, family ties during the Period of the Five Dynasties and Ten Kingdoms were modeled on the military custom of "joining hearts by sharing the same family name" between generals and soldiers. Originally, the practice was a means for military generals to build up an elite army known as the Army of the Adopted Sons. Directly responsible to the military generals, the Army of the Adopted Sons was the core army in battle as well as the principal administrators in occupied territories. Related as lords and vassals, the military generals and the Army of the Adopted Sons pledged to share all they gained in conquest. Once pledged, the gen-erals and the soldiers would treat one another as father and son. The adopted father

LEFT **Ceramic figures,** such as this from the eleventh century, were used in rituals to interpret signs from Heaven. These signs would determine who would rule a dynasty.

ABOVE *Sutra of the Ten Kings* from the Five Dynasties represents the "Ten Kings of Hell" passing judgment on souls going through the stages before rebirth.

would then regard his adopted son as if he were his son by blood, giving him full family privileges and property inheritance. Likewise, the adopted son would regard his adopted father as if he were his real father, cutting all connections with his biological parent.

A prime example of this practice is Li Keyong's family who founded the Later Tang—the second dynasty of the Five Dynasties. Originally the Shatuo Turks, the ancestors of Li Keyong were given the Li royal family name after participating in Tang Taizong's expedition to Korea. Later, Li Keyong rose as a prominent military officer in north China after helping the Tang court to suppress the Huang Cao Rebellion. In 923, Keyong's eldest son Li Cunxu was the founder of the Later Tang dynasty.

After Li Cunxu's death, his step-brother Li Siyuan (reigned 926–933) had to make a difficult decision on what to do next. As an adopted son, Li Siyuan's decision involved two parts. First, how he claimed to succeed his step-brother's throne, and second, after coming to the throne how he called his throne—a new dynasty or a continuation of the Later Tang. Explaining his decision in an elegantly crafted proclamation, Li Siyuan retraced his relations with the Li family: "Bearing the gusty wind and pouring rain, and risking my life in combat," Li Siyuan wrote, "the enterprise

of the Li family is my enterprise, and the world ruled by earlier Li emperors is my world." The heart of Li Siyuan's argument was that one's kinship was not given by birth, but was earned through sharing the hardship in achieving a common goal. Having been adopted by the Li family when he was a boy, Li Siyuan regarded himself to be a full-fledged member of the family. And throughout his whole adult life, he had always worked extremely hard to contribute to the family fortune. Therefore he was justified in succeeding his deceased step-brother's throne, and he would also prove his loyalty by continuing the dynastic line of the Later Tang.

Subservient Civil Officials

With more opportunities to show their talents, military officials performed much better than civil officials during the Period of the Five Dynasties and Ten Kingdoms. In general, military officials were brave in combat, responsible for their specific tasks, and clear about where their loyalty lay. In contrast, civil officials were selfish and calculating. They did whatever they could to pursue wealth, fame, and power.

On the other hand, as secondary players in politics, civil officials could do little but make themselves useful to the military rulers. One civil official, in particular, succeeded in mastering the arts of winning the trust of military rulers. His name was Feng Dao (882–954) and he served in four of the Five Dynasties. Apparently a skillful administrator and an erudite scholar, Feng Dao had such good relationships with all major military leaders that despite rapid dynastic changes, he always found a way to remain in power. Other than being good at winning over the trust of the military leaders, Feng Dao was also capable of serving as a bridge between the military and the civil.

A Hard Lesson Learned

Feng Dao's determination to serve the military rulers won him admiration and praise. To his contemporaries, he exemplified the standards of ancient gentlemen who followed closely the Confucian teachings. Nor was his decision to serve four dynasties seen as morally wrong, because it was Heaven that had changed its mind on the ruler of China, not a humble and public-minded civil official like him.

To Confucian scholars of later times, Feng Dao was the symbol of what had gone wrong under the total military rule. In *New History of the Five Dynasties*, for instance, the historian Ouyang Xiu (1007–1070) condemned Feng Dao for being "shameless" in not standing up to the military rulers. In condemning Feng Dao, Ouyang Xiu also condemned 53 years of military rule. To Ouyang Xiu, what Feng Dao had done revealed the seriousness of the militarization of China. Not only had militarization corrupted the Chinese state and the Chinese family, it had also corrupted the scholars—the self-proclaimed custodians of Confucian ethics and Confucian

LEFT **Bodhisattva Avalokitesvara** with 1,000 arms and 1,000 eyes is an example of a Buddhist deity assimilated into Chinese culture during this dynamic dynastic period.

culture. If both the state and society were corrupted, there was still hope that a cultural reawakening might occur through the examples of a few true scholars. When the scholars were corrupted, Ouyang found the Five Dynasties hopeless. It was this sense of urgency that drove many officials of the Northern Song (960–1127) to create a political system that would stop the military generals from gaining power again.

THE EVER-HAPPY OLD MAN

As the subservient civil official *par excellence* during the Five Dynasties period, Feng Dao saw himself as a follower of Confucian teachings. In the preface to his essay "A Self-Portrait of the Ever Happy Old Man," he presented himself as a contented old gentleman who was proud of watching his family flourish. He claimed that in public he might have shifted his loyalty from one imperial court to another, but in private he had done his utmost to maintain his family interests. For him, after Heaven had made its view known regarding who was the Son of Heaven, a civil official had to follow the Mandate of Heaven by serving the ruler whole-heartedly. Thus, it was perfectly acceptable to be subservient, because being a faithful official was one of the tenets of Confucianism.

LEFT **A rare ceramic from China's** Five Dynasties period was excavated from an an ancient vessel which sank more than 1,000 years ago in the Java Sea. Very few artworks from this period exist.

The Northern Song

Having seen the turmoil caused by militarism, the first two emperors of the
Northern Song (960–1127) made great efforts to reconstruct civil governance that
had a profound impact on the government and society of eleventh century China.

ABOVE *Evening Songs of the Fisherman* by Xu Daoning (970–c.1052). Xu was famous for his sublime landscapes; a hallmark of Northern Song artwork.

The first two Northern Song emperors—Taizu (reigned 960–976) and Taizong (reigned 976–997)—were determined to demolish the military governance that had shaped China since the ninth century, despite them being career military officers before coming to the throne. To limit the roles of military generals, the two emperors made three major changes. First, after the Song dynasty was established, all the major generals were asked to give up military power. Second, the military establishment was completely overhauled in such a way that the best army of the country was stationed around the capital, Kaifeng, leaving the feeble and the less trained to the provinces. Third, all the top military positions were filled by civil ministers certified by the expanded civil service examinations, setting the stage for civil officials to dominate military affairs.

Concomitant to the destruction of military governance was the rise in status of the civil bureaucrats. A major characteristic of these civil bureaucrats was their undivided loyalty to the emperors. To underscore the civil bureaucrats' direct link to them, the Northern Song emperors, beginning with Taizong, officiated over the palace examinations. As the ceremonial chief examiners who failed no one, the Northern Song emperors

RIGHT **The portrait of the priest Bu-Kong Zhang** is an example of the Song's adaption of Tang dynasty portrait painting. Northern Song artists reinvented historic art techniques.

performed the act of ordination. They granted titles, and the license to rule, to the successful examination candidates. In return, the civil bureaucrats were expected to serve the emperor with their hearts and souls. Hence, a partnership was formed: the civil bureaucrats would have the power to rule the country, on the condition that they pledged not to challenge the imperial authority at any time during their appointment.

Mid-Northern Song

Despite the structure of military governance being demolished in the first three and four decades into the Song dynasty, many military practices remained dominant in society. It took another half a century, through the emperors Renzong (reigned 1024–1063) and Shenzong (reigned 1068–1085), for new civil governance to flourish. Those 61 years from 1024 to 1085, commonly known as the mid-Northern Song, have long been regarded as the high point of the Northern Song period. In the area of thought, the first generation of the Neo-Confucian scholars such as Shao Yong (1011–1077), Zhou Dunyi (1017–1073), Zhang Zai (1020–1077), Cheng Hao (1032–1085), and Cheng Yi (1033–1107) began to make their marks on the intellectual landscape. In government, the three major Northern Song political thinkers Fan Zhongyan (989–1052), Sima Guang (1019–1086), and Wang Anshi (1021–1086) implemented drastic reforms to reshape the country. In the arts, the essayist Ouyang Xi (1007–1070), the painter Guo Xi (c. 1020–after 1090), the calligrapher Mi Fu (1051–1107), and the poet Su Shi (1037–1101) completed their masterpieces which are still admired today. All of these highly renowned practitioners enriched the cultural landscape.

One distinguishing characteristic of mid-Northern Song was the development of the self-identity of the educated elite. During the early Northern Song, members of the educated elite were still fighting against the old habit of mind that required civil officials to be subservient to the rulers. This changed during the mid-Northern Song and the elite became confident that they were the "co-rulers" of the empire. As the co-rulers, they thought that they were legitimate leaders of the empire, sharing with the emperor all his responsibilities of ordering the world.

Late Northern Song

The rise of power of the civil bureaucrats also caused tremendous political problems. With high expectations attributed to their strong participation in governing, the civil bureaucrats were often unwilling to yield in policy debates, regardless of whether the opposition came from their own kind or from the emperor. As the country confronted many internal and external problems, their strong reluctance to compromise produced bureaucratic factionalism that split the bureaucrats into a number of different groups.

With the various groups competing for power combined with the scope of reform expanding from the times of Fan Zhongyan to the times of Wang Anshi and Sima Guang, bureaucratic factionalism became increasingly intense. As a result, during the reigns of Zhezong (reigned 1086–1100), Huizong (reigned 1101–1125) and Qinzong (reigned 1126–1127), commonly known as the late Northern Song, officials in the central government were practically divided into two opposing camps. At the height of this partisan factionalism, when one group was in power, they expunged the other group from the government; when the other group held the upper hand, they returned the favor. As a result, almost all major cultural and political figures of the late Northern Song were involved in partisan factionalism. Many of them, most notably Cheng Yi and Su Shi, suffered humiliating banishments.

During the last 40 years of the Northern Song, when the body politic of China was threatened internally by partisan factionalism and externally by foreign invasion, some inquiring members of the educated elite began to question the validity of civil governance. They wondered whether civil governance was responsible for incapacitating the central government and weakening the military defense. Shortly before the Song court was to move south to Hangzhou to escape the invading Jurchen army, the discourse on civil governance had reached full circle. The high hopes in the early Northern Song for ordering the world gave way to end-of-the-dynasty pessimism about the human inability to control one's life. Although many members of the educated elite were not yet willing to let the military generals and aristocratic families take over the government, they had lost confidence in themselves to build a perfect human order based on classical learning and a long-lasting civil code of behavior.

LEFT; BELOW **Song-dynasty warming bowls,** shaped like lotus blossoms, were used to heat rice wine, a popular drink during the Northern Song dynasty.

The Threat from the Khitan

The Khitan were never numerous, and controlled only a small part of the Chinese north, mostly inhabited by Chinese subjects. Nonetheless, their mounted tribal armies seriously threatened the Song, forcing it to pay tribute.

RIGHT **A Jizhou stoneware vase** from the Northern Song dynasty is an example of the distinctive ceramics from the area where the Yellow River empties into the Yellow Sea.

The Khitan first appear in Chinese sources in the fourth century, becoming important during the rule of the Tang. By the end of the ninth century, they had begun to acquire a territorial base, primarily in Manchuria. By that time, a growing number of sedentary communities had come under their control. There were also large numbers of captives taken in raids. Despite this, the main Khitan striking force remained tribal and lived a pastoral life.

Abaoji: Leader of the Yila

Of the Khitan tribal groups, the most important were the "Eight Tribes" and, within them, the "Nine Tents" belonging to the Yila or the Yaolian lineage. Leader of this lineage in the early tenth century was Abaoji (872–926), son of a chieftain; in 901, Abaoji was elected as chieftain of the Yila. Abaoji is considered the founder of the Khitan Liao dynasty (916–1125). In fact he did more to

expand Khitan control into non-tribal areas of China and consolidate Khitan rule than any other Khitan chieftain before him. Abaoji's accomplishments lay in two areas. One was in conquest, in a series of well-led military campaigns that kept his enemies on the defense. The other was in the adoption of Chinese as an administrative language and the clever use of Chinese political culture to legitimate his "dynasty." The key conquest came after Abaoji's death, in the late 930s, when the aptly named "Sixteen Prefectures" of the frontier first came under Khitan–Liao control. Institutionally, the system put together by Abaoji and his successors was originally intended to provide the appropriate structures to govern both the tribal and Chinese sectors of the Liao Empire. The tribal sector included the Khitan tribesmen themselves and various pastoral allies. It was ruled in a more or less traditional manner from the Khitan Supreme Capital, partially built

BELOW **This tenth-century ceramic horse** was used as an incense holder. Horses were invaluable to pastoral nomads, such as the Khitan.

PASTORAL NOMADS

Throughout much of Chinese history, pastoral nomads have invaded and threatened China. The Khitan, so important as enemies of the Song, were only the latest in a succession of such peoples that included the Xiongnu and later the Mongols. The nomads owed their superiority to a higher level of social mobilization than possible in China, whole tribes went to war, and they possessed large numbers of horses. This important factor made their armies, even if smaller, nearly always superior to the less mobile armies of the Chinese, who always had trouble obtaining enough horses for their armies. The difficult herding life also produced superior generalship and the nomads were esteemed warlords and warriors, not always the case in China.

in the Chinese style. The non-tribal sector, primarily Chinese in culture, was governed from what were eventually four other capitals, also built in the Chinese style.

There were two parallel branches of government, a northern chancellery, and a southern chancellery. Both were kept firmly in the hands of the Khitan. The northern chancellery took charge of military and tribal matters, and tribute relationships, key areas from the standpoint of the Khitan elite. The southern chancellery had charge of a civil government that was effective in the sedentary areas of the empire and primarily involved with taxation. There was also a Chinese style central government.

Although Khitan raiding and intervention were always a problem for the Chinese states of the Five Dynasties period, and for the Song that succeeded them, Liao, as reorganized by Abaoji and his successors, reached a high watermark of its power during the first third of the eleventh century. Neither the Khitan, nor the Tanguts (tribal people from the northwest of China where they founded their own state called Xixia in the tenth century), were serious competitors with Northern Song for control of China. However, the Liao remained a threat. This was due to control over the "Sixteen Prefectures," which comprised the regions from Datong stretching eastwards to present day Beijing and offered an excellent advanced position for regular invasions of China.

In 979, the second Song ruler, Taizong (939–997), led imperial armies in person and began a major assault to recapture the "Sixteen Prefectures." The result was a disaster. Completely outclassed by the Liao cavalry, with the main part of the Liao army carefully held in reserve until the Song forces had committed themselves, as a result Song armies all but collapsed. They retreated, leaving behind great numbers of prisoners and massive amounts of booty, such as military supplies and equipment.

Treaty of Shanyuan

Other Song forces were able to halt a Liao counter invasion of the south, but a renewed Song attempt to retake the "Sixteen Prefectures" in 986 was also crushed by the powerful Liao. They remained completely out of Song reach. Under Taizong's successor, Zhenzong (reigned 997–1022), it was the Liao who took the offensive, penetrating almost to the surrounding walls of the Song capital, Kaifeng. Humiliated, the Song dynasty government was forced to make peace more or less on Liao terms in 1005, signing the Treaty of Shanyuan, one of the few treaties in traditional Chinese history signed by China on a basis of equality with another state. It stipulated a large annual tribute be paid indefinitely. Liao long enjoyed its tribute but was finally extinguished by the Jurchen (a tribe from Manchuria), founders of the Jin dynasty, in 1125.

ABOVE **The Iron Pagoda in Kaifeng**, the capital of the Song dynasty, was built in 1049. The rust-brown bricks give the impression it is made of iron.

Wang Anshi

The serious threats from Khitan Liao and Tangut Xixia faced by the Song forced them to maintain a large military force. This meant higher taxes and efforts to make the state and its tax system more efficient.

ABOVE **These figures of maidservants** were made during the Song dynasty for the Jinci Temple, Taiyuan.

The result was an extended reform effort associated with the names of Fan Zhongyan (989–1052) and Wang Anshi (1021–1086) but also involving a protracted struggle between peace and war factions. Both Fan and Wang were associated with the war faction, as were most Song dynasty reformers.

Fan Zhongyan

Fan, whose reforms, advanced between 1043 and 1045, are known as the "minor" reforms, to distinguish them from those of Wang, proposed changes in three major areas. One of these was personnel management. Fan wanted to stop rewarding those that were incompetent, and promote those with real ability. He also wanted to change the examination system to emphasize practical administration. Fan also wanted to strengthen local infrastructure. The salaries of officials were increased to eliminate corruption and enlist more competent candidates. Finally, Fan wanted to build a system of local defense based on militias.

Although Fan's reforms failed and Fan himself was forced into exile, the problems did not go away. A more serious effort was made by Wang Anshi, who first set down his program in a "Ten Thousand-word Memorial" in 1058 although at first his proposals fell on deaf ears.

The founders of the Song left one major task incomplete as they reunified China and consolidated power. Despite their best efforts, much of north China remained in the hands of their Tangut and Khitan enemies. Both peoples had established their own states, organized in the Chinese manner.

The Treaty of Shanyuan settled the boundaries between the Song and the Liao, but the threat of a simultaneous attack by both the Xixia and the Liao remained. This nearly materialized in 1040. To keep the peace, a large amount of tribute paid to Liao and Xixia became part of the tribute system. After 1044, it received allocations of silk, silver, tea, and various special "gifts."

These impositions imposed an enormous burden on the Song, coupled with the expense of maintaining a large army. As time went on, Song's tax system proved unable to sustain the demands placed on it. More tax revenue was needed and a more efficient imperial system.

Wang Anshi and the New Laws

Wang, who had gained his *jinshi* degree in 1042, was a native of Fuzhou, in Song Jiangxi, a hotbed of economic development. In 1068, after a successful local career, Wang was called to the court by the new emperor Shenzong (reigned 1067–1085). There he planned and implemented reforms that were among the most sweeping in Chinese history, but before he could complete them pressure from conservatives in 1076 forced him to resign.

The centerpiece of Wang's reforms was all about fiscal restructuring. Wang sought to lighten the burden placed on the peasants, to minimise the advantages enjoyed by the wealthy and powerful, and to eliminate widespread fraud and corruption. He wanted economic growth, but not at the expense of the poorest in society. Wang also sought to impose a managed economy in which government intervention was beneficial rather than disruptive. He ended the massive purchases of grain by the government, often at low prices forced on sellers, and attacked excessive stockpiling, a practice dear to the hearts of traditionalists.

Particularly important was Wang's attempt to control the price of grain. He wanted to make sure that the amount that a peasant family needed to produce each year to pay its taxes remained constant. As much as possible, taxes were to be collected in money, with many traditional exactions put on a cash basis. Wang offered state loans to peasants at reasonable interest rates to limit the impact of the high interest loans peasants had been forced to take out to pay taxes. Wang strongly encouraged increases in agricultural productivity. Through government investment in commerce he reduced the land tax and pressure on peasants.

To help govern his new fiscal structure, Wang encouraged the development of a well-paid, professional bureaucracy with a demonstrated competence. This went against the Confucian tradition that scholar–bureaucrats were to be generalists and not specialists. For the first time in Chinese history, the emphasis in recruitment examinations was on practical subjects, such as law and economics.

Running parallel to Wang's effort to create a professional and specialist bureaucracy was the major reform of the Song army. It had proven to be ineffective in resisting China's enemies, but Wang sought to introduce specialists into military offices, and to enhance the status and reputations of those serving. He sought to create a new militia system, the *baojia*, based upon organized units of ten families responsible for local security in times of peace and local defense in times of war. Such units could provide the basis for field armies that could be mobilized quickly by professional cadres. The new system had the potential for enormous savings. It might have provided an effective military force as well.

This was not the limit to the reforms Wang pushed in his brief eight years of power but they went against Chinese tradition, causing much friction in society. Wang also introduced his reforms with extreme rapidity, causing confusion. The existing government, overstretched and unable to do so many things at once, could not implement either the spirit or the letter of the reforms. In the end, all the problems that Wang had sought to counter returned. The dynasty began a downward spiral from which recovery would prove to be extremely difficult.

ABOVE **Detail from a twelfth-century silk scroll** gives a glimpse into farming life during the Song dynasty.

BELOW **This celadon tripod vessel** from the Song dynasty imitated bronze ware from earlier dynasties.

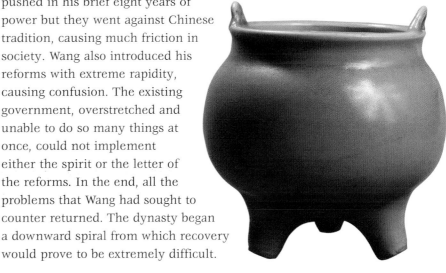

Industry and Innovation

Although unsuccessful at asserting itself militarily and politically, the Song dynasty was nonetheless an era of unparalleled growth and development. In cultural terms, it marked a true Chinese renaissance with a broad systemization of knowledge.

ABOVE **This 3,000-year-old rice terrace** in Yunnan Province is an example of the type of rice farming that boosted the production of rice during the Song dynasty.

Song economic growth had three roots. One lay in the complete mastery of the Chinese south, culminating in a process of internal colonization. A second was based upon China's first true maritime age and a burgeoning trade with the South Seas, Southeast Asia, and points beyond. The third area of growth lay in the truly amazing technological advances that took place under the Northern Song. Many had a direct and major impact upon the economy, for example, advances in metallurgy. Another major Northern Song accomplishment was the widespread and successful use of paper money and various modes of long-distance commercial exchange that were the precursors for modern day systems.

The South

Prior to the late Tang and Song, south China had largely remained *terra incognita*. Apart from a few islands of relatively concentrated Chinese culture such as Guangzhou (Canton), the rest was largely a land of legend and non-Han presence.

Three major developments gradually altered this situation. The first was the economic linkage of China's nearer south with the north through the extensive canal system built up from Sui times (581–618). It used China's many rivers to establish connections that extended far beyond the immediate areas serviced by the existing canal system. The second was the increasing colonization of the south by farmers from the north in search of economic opportunity in an environment far more favorable for agriculture than the arid north. Playing a key role in this development were the new crops and improved cultivation technology that characterized the Song dynasty. Foremost among these new crops were quick-ripening rice varieties, the Champa rices, named after the region in Vietnam from where they were supposedly introduced. With these new rice varieties, up to three crops a year were possible in some favored areas. As yields grew, the processing of agricultural commodities was also drastically improved, through an increased use of machinery and water power, often on a large industrial scale.

In addition to the cultivation of the new rice varieties, a whole new economic complex emerged, largely based on the rise in popularity of tea drinking in China's southeast. Areas once rejected for being too hilly, or malaria-ridden, or occupied by non-Chinese "barbarians," suddenly became preferred sites for tea plantations as demand for the new beverage increased. The "barbarians" (such as, Thai or Tibeto-Burman speakers) became a cheap agricultural labor force. Subjected to pressures to become more "cultured," many of them assimilated to the Han Chinese way of life, at least superficially. As a result, much of the coastal and interior south, land still stigmatized as a non-Chinese land during much of the Tang, became Sinicized and socially, economically, and politically integrated with the rest of China. For the first time in Chinese history, the distant domains comprising the provinces of Fujian, Jiangxi, and Guangdong became major foundations of Chinese power. Only the farther south and southwest had still to be integrated.

Maritime Expansion

Going hand in hand with the penetration of the interior and its integration with a greater China, was a maritime expansion by which Chinese cities located along the coast and navigable rivers were linked not only with each other but with the overseas world to the west, south, and southeast of China. Although China had long had relations with states beyond its borders, and although the trade supported by such relations was often important economically, the fiction was maintained that it was nothing more than "barbarians coming to court and bearing tribute." That is to say, ritual relationships were stressed over commercial ones, and any commercial contacts by foreigners with the government were understood in ritual terms. By the late Tang, this fiction had already worn very thin, and in Song times the body of trade had become so great that this fiction was no longer convincing. It became particularly important since Song China was now largely cut off from the traditional Silk Route commerce linking China and the West through Central Asia. Fortunately, the growth of maritime contacts more than compensated for this outstanding loss.

Making the important contribution to this particular achievement were major advances in all

ABOVE **A sword with Chinese design** was recovered from the Glass Wreck, a shipwreck dating back to the eleventh century. It is evidence of Chinese influence crossing the world's oceans.

THE BEGINNINGS OF TEA

Tea is the leaf, bud, and twig of *Camellia sinensis*. It is cultivated at moderate altitude under semitropical or tropical conditions in marginal soils unsuitable for growing rice, or other crops. Originally considered a medicinal herb, tea later caught on as a beverage. By Tang times (618–907), the most common form of tea was powdered but leaf teas had become common by the Song dynasty, although powdered teas continued to be popular. Powdered tea is still the preferred tea for the Japanese tea ceremony. More recently, oxidized leaf and pressed teas, known incorrectly as fermented teas (although some were), were the preferred form of tea for the European and American export market. During the Song, tea drinking became an important link between the literati and the monastic culture of Zen and was a hallmark of dynastic culture.

RIGHT *Camellia sinensis* produces white, green, and black tea, and oolong. The leaves are also used in Chinese medicine.

ABOVE **The Surging Wave Pavilion** was built by the Song poet, Su Sunqing. It was here that scholars, poets, and philosophers sought to encapsulate the grandeur of nature.

RIGHT **Genghis Khan (b.1167)** was a Mongol conqueror who became leader of his tribe. His rise to prominence began toward the end of the Song dynasty.

areas of maritime technology. By the twelfth and thirteenth centuries, Chinese ships were among the largest in the world. They had multiple masts with fore and aft rigging of highly efficient mat sails, and possessed watertight compartments, sternpost rudders, and the first compasses. All these vitally important technical advances seem to have been made on the China Sea, from where they spread to the West and elsewhere, although China's technological contacts with Southeast Asia were important too. Supporting these technical advances was a revolution in maps and map-making, including maps recording nautical lore. Judging by the surviving examples, the best Song maps, in their detail and accuracy, were up to the standards of nineteenth century Europe. Accompanying the maps, and also appearing independently, was a wealth of geographical literature, much of it printed, which made it generally accessible. The most famous example of this tradition, relating specifically to the Chinese trade with the Arabic and Persian worlds, comes from Southern Song times, with Zhao Rugua's *Zhufanji*, "Monograph on the Various Barbarians." The maritime expansion in light of the printed word that Europe witnessed in the sixteenth and seventeenth centuries began in China in the eleventh and twelfth centuries.

As a result of these developments, the great cities of the south became even larger and were transformed into commercial centers in the true sense of the word. They managed overseas, regional, and local trade on a large-scale basis. Some, including Quanzhou, in modern Fujian, and Guanzhou, even had large foreign colonies, principally consisting of Persian and Arabic traders. These colonies helped administer the trade. A Chinese trader of Arabic extraction, for example, actually had total charge of much of the trade in the thirteenth century. The colonies also introduced new ideas and even foods to China. China's sugar industry and sweets, for example, were largely developed under the direct influence of the Indian, Arabic, and Persian merchant communities of the south. Islam, which had first been introduced to China during Tang times, suddenly acquired major importance, and was to grow later due to Muslim help in colonizing the Chinese southwest after the thirteenth century.

Science and Technology

Northern Song technology and its impact upon agriculture and overseas commerce were by no means the only areas strongly affected by Song advances. Northern Song, for example, witnessed a veritable industrial revolution with iron, steel, and coal production attaining unprecedented heights, comparing favorably with production levels of nineteenth century Britain. Coal was especially important in the treeless Chinese

north, where it rapidly became the most important fuel. The Northern Song dynasty also saw the first serious experimentation with gunpowder and weapons of various types, including primitive handguns and war rockets. Various kinds of flame-throwers were also in use. The Song dynasty developed advanced mechanical clocks, paddle-wheel driven warships, and sophisticated building techniques and codes that promoted healthy and environmentally sound buildings. Northern Song intellectuals were among the world's first known archaeologists, producing catalogs of published artifacts, and also made substantial contributions to various fields of botany. Most of the results of Song dynasty research in this and other areas were published. This was a first for China.

Printing was, in fact, an important area of advance. It continued to gain ground, printing from movable type, clay, and metal. Whereas printing exclusively using carved wooden blocks was still relatively rare during the Five Dynasties period (907–960), book printing became a generalized phenomenon under the Song. Works produced included single volumes as well as huge encyclopedias that were generally accessible, many of them on scientific and technological topics. Shen Gua's *Mengqi bitan*, "Dream Torrent Essays," devoted to scientific topics, was among works printed. Also printed were standard editions of the Chinese medical classics, along with some new compendiums, specially created by the Song government to aid in maintaining the health of all its subjects. These efforts included the first large printed herbal reference books in Chinese history.

Cultural Life of the Song

Song innovation was not confined to economics and technology. Cultural life also changed. The most important poetic form of Song poetry was the *ci*. Originally the *ci* was intended to be sung, but soon the tradition of composing music for one's own *ci* was put aside. Poets used either existing melodies or simply took the verse pattern of some popular *ci* (for example, the *Pusaman*, "The Barbarian Bhodisattva"), and

imitated it as a poetic style, removing the text and music. Thus most Song dynasty *ci* are only very remotely connected with music, although musical versions continued to exist at a more popular and mass-market level, moving away from the high-end literary arena.

Because of its early association with music, and with popular female singers able to perform it, the *ci* was always more than a poetic form and influenced a whole way of life, principally the bright life of the capital, its brothels, bars, and restaurants. Even elite poets participated, and so their *ci* are rich sources of Song popular culture

Most famous among Northern Song poets was Su Shi (1036–1101), who wrote in all genres, including that of the *ci*. He was also a famous essayist in the new *guwen*, "ancient literature," tradition that exemplified the new Neo-Confucian humanism and sensitivity. Other important Northern Song poets were Ouyang Xiu (1007–1070), also a proponent of the *guwen* style, and Li Qingchao (1084–1141), China's most famous woman poet, and wife and assistant to Song archaeologist Zhao Mingcheng (1081–1129).

A key area of Song innovation were two other important areas of Song dynasty innovation, calligraphy and painting. These new styles were developed along with the rise of a literati culture.

ABOVE **Su Shi** was a writer, poet, artist, calligrapher, and statesman of the Song era. He is often referred to as Su Dongpo. This statue is located in his hometown of Meishan.

Art of the Song

Portraying Filial Piety

A twelfth-century handscroll is a homage to the Confucian concept of filial piety. This important virtue requires love and respect to be shown toward parents and ancestors.

Art of Ma Yuan

Bare Willows and Distant Mountains is a painting by the Song dynasty's most well-known landscape painter. Ma Yuan (1190–1225) lyrically expressed the strong simplicity and pure idealization of nature with bold and dramatic brushstrokes.

China looked inward during the Song dynasty, and so remained isolated from the rest of the world. It sought to find balance and time for reflection in the world of nature. Through nature, China sharpened her cultural and artistic senses. Artworks of this period aimed to refine nature, working toward creating simplicity and impression. In this manner, Chinese art was able to reinvent itself based upon the traditions of antiquity and established artistic legacies that were developed by later dynasties. This new aesthetic was most obvious in the landscape painting of the Song dynasty. The artist aimed to harmonize man and nature, which meant that humankind was part of the whole of the universe, not just an element outside of it. This was a philosophy described by Neo-Confucianism. In practice, this meant that the Song artist tried to produce realistic paintings that were previously unseen in Chinese history. The Song Academy painters developed this approach.

Song realism was truer to nature than earlier Chinese paintings. People were painted in the right perspective against mountains and trees, whereas before, people were painted as being the central feature, dwarfing the elements of nature around them. Plants and animals were treated with much more detail, in a manner that was almost scientific. The Song painter was often just as concerned with time as with place; that one should be able to work out the season and time of day from a painting, or perhaps a sequence of events. For example, plum blossoms represented the coming of spring. A boy running into his small hut with clouds overhead suggested that a light rain shower was about to fall. To express the pure quality of nature, an emphasis was placed on perfecting technique, through observing nature and copying the masters throughout the ages.

Realism did more than capture what one actually saw. Guo Xi (1000–1090), painter and critic, stated that when painting mountains, one should clearly distinguish between the light and the dark, that there should be no mountains without mists. He was hinting at a theory that believed emptiness, such as its representation by mist, places lucidity beyond everyday comprehension, something that the spirit can only hope to grasp. The popular monochrome painting style only strengthened the other-worldliness aspect of the Song dynasty aesthetic, where man contemplated the material and immaterial, engulfed by the Dao and silenced by the Buddhist *shunyata*, the "emptiness." Unlike the narrative painting prior to the Song, where figures were often part of a storyline, the Song excelled in mood painting that was meant to provoke the spirit to enter Daoist and Buddhist metaphysical realms through stylized detail.

During this period, a group of intellectuals began the Literati Movement. This was established by Su Shi to stress self-expression. This group was heavily influenced by the Chan (Zen) Buddhist doctrine of spontaneous and personal enlightenment. Just as the strokes of calligraphy were supposed to reflect the eight trigrams of the *Book of Changes*, and allow the mind intuitively to express the workings of the universe, the same approach was used for painting. Song dynasty literati painting is usually less approachable, with meaning not measured by how faithfully nature is rendered, but how the individual strokes or dots form a whole to express the mind.

Cut-Silk Painting

When the founding emperors of the Song defeated the courts of their rivals, they took over their court artists who specialized in bird and flower painting. This type of painting also became a specialty of the Song court.

The Popularity of Porcelain

Porcelain differs from other ceramics in its raw materials, and in high firing temperatures. It was not invented during the Song dynasty, but reached a high point under this era, as illustrated below in this Song-dynasty bowl. The most important types of Song porcelains were celadon, a glaze famous for its blue-green color applied to the delicate base. Black ware was considered popular but was still exclusively used by the elite. The black ware included Jian tea bowls, where the black glaze contrasted with the green color of the tea itself and where the body of the bowl helped maintain temperature. Such bowls were particularly popular at Chan (Zen) monasteries, and the culture of tea was shared by the literati and monks alike.

The Jurchen Invasion

The Jurchen, who replaced the Khitan as the dominant people in north China during the early twelfth century, proved a difficult adversary for the Song. Their attacks nearly ended the dynasty, and forced it to fall back on the south.

RIGHT **A gilded crown** was possibly worn by emperors of the Liao dynasty. The Liao borrowed from the Song to embellish and create intricate works of art.

BELOW **The relief of fighting horsemen** on this bronze mirror from the Jin dynasty shows how the Jurchen successfully adapted to war on horseback.

The founder of the new Jurchen state, Wanyan Aguda (1068–1123), chieftain of the Wanyan clan, was primarily a ruler of the "raw" Jurchen. He was well-known in his tribe for bravery and participated in numerous campaigns against rival Jurchen tribes at the command of the Liao dynasty (the Khitans). In 1109, during a widespread famine, he took care of starving warriors from other tribes to strengthen his own clan. It was his skill and diplomacy that helped to unify the disparate Jurchens under Wanyan rule. Aguda also knew how to use cavalry effectively in warfare, and borrowed aspects from different cultures. Horsemanship and war on horseback was not a part of the Jurchen native tradition, but they learned quickly and became adept at it. Liao sources credit Aguda with quite large armies, but the figures are exaggerated; it was the quality and effectiveness of Jurchen forces that counted, not their size. The loyalty that Aguda garnered from his earlier years helping out other tribes in times of need greatly assisted his cause.

The Might of Aguda

After initial raids all along Liao's western frontier, Wanyan Aguda went on attack. He began this by taking the Liao capitals one at a time, starting with the Eastern Capital in 1116, and then the Supreme or Northern Capital in 1120, the Central Capital in 1122, followed by the Southern Capital (close to modern Beijing) that same year. It was not held and later turned over to the Song, but only after it was pillaged. The Liao emperor, defeated in open battle with the Jurchen, had no choice but to flee to the last Liao center, the Western Capital, located near Datong in what is now Shanxi. Aguda died the next year, aged 55, but there was no pause in the relentless Jin advance under his successor Wuqimai, or Taizong (reigned 1123–1135), who now came into conflict with Song. It had formed an alliance with the Jurchen in 1220 hoping to recover the "Sixteen Prefectures" and other territories. This hope proved elusive as the Jurchen turned against the Song after the end of their sweep against Liao. They

RAW OR COOKED: THE JURCHEN

The Jurchen, ancestors of Manchu, were Tungus-speaking farmers and hunter–gatherers who overthrew the Khitan Liao dynasty in 1125 and then went on to considerably expand its domains and power in a new dynasty, the Jin (1125–1234), run by themselves. Although not a steppe people, the Jurchen had close relations with steppe peoples such as the Khitan, many of whom supported the Jurchen in their rise to power. The Jurchen also went about forming their new state in much the way that the Khitan and other Central Asian groups went about it, that is, by harboring a power base but also carefully adding elements to create a confederation. At the time of their rise to power, two groups of Jurchen were distinguished by Chinese observers: the "raw" or unassimilated Jurchen, living a mostly traditional life in the forests of Manchuria and southern Siberia; and the "cooked" Jurchen, those most influenced by Chinese culture as mediated by the Liao.

RIGHT **A peony and fish cup** is an example of Jizhou ware, a sturdy porcelain, that was produced when the Jurchen took over the Song kilns.

captured the last of the Liao holdouts including the Liao emperor in 1125. Only in Central Asia, beyond Jurchen reach, did any kind of a Liao regime survive, in the Qara-Khitan (Kara-Khitan or "Black Khitan") Empire in Central Asia founded by Yelü Dashi (1087–1143).

The War against the Song

The real war against the Song began even before the conquest of the last Liao centers of resistance. The Jurchen had found the Song a weak ally. Even remnant Liao forces were able to defeat Song armies. In 1125, Jurchen armies went over to a general assault on the Song. It proved a complete surprise and was successful. Two main Jurchen armies advanced south across the Yellow River toward the Song capital of Kaifeng, which was surrounded in February 1126. By that time the Song emperor, Huizong (reigned 1100–1126), known more for his painting and calligraphy than his governing ability, had abdicated under pressure in favor of his son, Qinzong (reigned 1126–1127). Qinzong proved unable to mount an effective defense against the invaders. He had no choice but to open surrender negotiations. Terms were agreed upon and the Jin force surrounding Kaifeng withdrew to reestablish contact with the other Jin invading force, but once this had been accomplished the united Jin army returned and resumed the siege. In January 1127, Qinzong surrendered the capital and his throne, and the Jurchen entered the city, taking Qinzong captive. The former emperor, Huizong, had already been captured trying to flee south. Jin forces raided former Song domains in the north and central China. Northern Song was at an end.

The Song barely survived the Jin assault of 1125–1131. The sheer size of China gave Song loyalists the time and space to organize new resistance to the invaders. The dynasty survived, but with much reduced boundaries that proved extremely difficult to defend. Jin armies were not prepared for the supreme effort that a conquest of the Chinese south would have entailed, and found the heat oppressive and debilitating. They also had no navy and could not catch the Song leaders that took to the seas. Ultimately, after protracted hostilities, Song and Jin were forced to make peace with an 1141–1142 treaty, known as the Shaoxing Treaty, but the outcome left Song with a far larger and more powerful northern competitor than Liao had ever been. During the Southern Song period that followed, China was divided with the boundary running right down the middle of the country.

The Jin Dynasty

The Jin dynasty, the Song's main competitor in the north, was powerful and well organized. It was too well entrenched for the Song to conquer but also proved itself unable to conquer the Song. The result—stalemate.

ABOVE **This head of a Monk** made of black marble from the Liao–Jin dynasty from northern China shows the blend of Chinese and Jurchen influence.

With two brief exceptions (the very unsuccessful Jin attacks during 1161 and 1216–1220, and a Song attack in 1207), the Shaoxing Treaty of 1141–1142 between the Song and the Jin marked the end of the major hostilities between the two. It also brought an end to the period of strong Jin dynastic consolidation. At first the Jin had only been able to conquer but not rule its new domains. Initially, the Jin had simply taken over and continued Liao or Song institutions, sometimes even under former Liao or Song officials. They also cooperated with the local military leaders, which further confused the governmental organization and the lines of authority. For all practical purposes, the armies in the field were the main Jin regime and real Jin power only existed in proximity to these military forces.

This situation changed as the Jurchen took the unprecedented step of controlling the newly conquered territories not just institutionally, but also directly, by encouraging a mass migration of the Jurchen and their allies. At first, the move was into former Liao domains. It then continued on south as territories were taken from the Song. Going along with the move of population was an extension of the Jin *meng'an* and *mouke* system. Under this system, most of the Jin's tribal population, an estimated three million, was organized into military units, *meng'an*, the real basis of Jin military power, and *mouke*, technically companies of 100 men that made up the *meng'an*. The *mouke* were social as well as military units and were clan based. The *meng'an* conquered but the *mouke* were responsible for administration as well as supporting conquest. They became the key effective base organizational units of Jurchen society and, by extension, of the local Chinese society, since the Jurchen government was represented by the *mouke* at the local level. The movement of millions of Jurchen and other tribal allies (including some Chinese) into the conquered territories not only meant the advance of non-Chinese ethnic groups, but also the complete transplantation of the social and organization system.

At a national level, the Jurchen continued running an institutional system similar to that of the Liao before them. The system, initially at least, proved well suited to the Jurchen. They needed the strong protection of their tribal sector from the population of Chinese people that their new state now encompassed. To the same end, the Jurchen sought to reorganize part of the conquered north into puppet states, including Qi in Shandong. These were later absorbed as the focus on consolidation of the empire proceeded.

Sinicization: Adopting Chinese Customs and Culture

Jin reliance on its tribal sector continued through the reign of Wuqimai but the latter, alarmed by the many conflicting lines of authority and the growing power of the clan authority of traditional Jurchen leadership, abolished its most significant manifestation. This was the Council of Chieftains (the *bojilie*). It had long remained the real center of Jurchen government and the basis of the Jin emperor's power as the greatest of the chieftains. Wuqimai's (Taizong) successor, Xizong (reigned 1135–1149) went still farther by putting into place a Sinicization of the government to counter the "feudalism" of the clan-based system of authority, although the system of dual institutions by and large remained. The Sinicization involved had never meant a slavish dependence upon Chinese culture, combining it with Jin. It was Xizong's regime that signed the treaty with Southern Song, ending all immediate and future confrontations.

Xizong was a tyrant and was murdered by enemies led by his cousin, Wanyan Liang. The latter then took the throne as Prince Hailing (reigned 1149–1161). Prince Hailing continued

Creating Capital Cities

Among the more successful measures of Prince Hailing was the movement of the Jin capital from Manchuria to a site near the present-day Beijing, called Zhongdu, "Middle Capital." This move had the advantage of bringing the Jurchen government closer to the larger body of its dislocated citizens of the *meng'an* and *mouke*. Along with the opening of facilities in the new capital, the old one, Shangjing, also known as the Manchurian "Upper Capital," was largely leveled to the ground to deprive the Jurchen elite of a base. Prince Hailing then intervened against the old Jurchen nobility, depriving some of their rank and privileges, while killing others. He also removed many *meng'an* and *mouke* organizations from princely control to imperial control. In addition to the empty "Upper Capital" and the city of Zhongdu, the Jin had an Eastern Capital in southern Manchuria (at Liaoyang), a Western Capital at Datong, and a Southern Capital at Kaifeng which Prince Hailing hoped to build up and establish the city as the primary Jin capital for him to rule from.

The Opposition to Prince Hailing and Sinicization

The Sinicization policies of Prince Hailing, who was never granted a proper dynastic name as a legitimate member of the Jurchen ruling house,

LEFT **Yue Fei** was a Chinese patriot and nationalist military leader who fought for the Southern Song dynasty against the Jurchen armies of the Jin dynasty.

BELOW **This Jizhou-style stoneware saucer** with pomegranates is the type of dish that was used by the Jin dynasty general population rather than the imperial court.

with the campaign to Sinicize the Jin central government, but abandoned most of the final remnants of the previous system of dual institutions. This was to reduce the power of the Jurchen tribal elite. The authority was centralized in the emperor's hands.

Prince Hailing used his new powers for aggrandizement, planning, and launching an invasion against the Song territories, this time not just with tribal cavalry but also with the enormous numbers of Chinese ground forces, and even naval units placed strategically on the rivers. Such units had been utilized effectively by the Song national hero Yue Fei (1103–1142) when resisting all Jin invasions several decades earlier. However, this time, the invasion was a fiasco and it led directly to the bloody murder of Prince Hailing. The Song had become a very different and much stronger adversary in 1161, when the invasion was launched, than it had been in the 1120s and 1130s when the previous attempts at invasion of the Song had occurred.

aroused considerable opposition. Prince Hailing's successor, Emperor Shizong who reigned from 1162–1189, coming into power with the strong support of the tribal elite, and set about undoing his predecessor's changes in favor of Chinese culture. This process continued with his grandson, the Emperor Zhangzong, who reigned from 1189–1208. The period saw the Jurchen elite regain its power in relation to the imperial institution. It also saw a return to traditional Jurchen symbols at a time when the symbols meant less after many years of Jurchen assimilation to the mixture of cultures from northern China.

Neither Shizong nor Zhangzong changed the centralization of Jin government, partly because of a series of domestic crises faced by the regime. These included a large Khitan uprising that continued until 1164. Both emperors were canny enough to realize that they could not depend too much on the traditional aristocracy to help them.

Among the genuine reforms of Shizong was a reorganization of the *meng'an* and *mouke*. They had become weak after more than half a century

occupying and governing China. The existing units were completely reconstituted and brought more effectively under government supervision between 1180–1183. The Jurchen of the *meng'an* and *mouke* were encouraged to go back to their traditional lives and livelihoods. The state hoped to secure a more effective military from these reforms. Even before this series of reforms, Shizong and his court had sought to rid all of the *meng'an* and *mouke* units of ethnic elements that were likely to pose a threat. These included the Chinese and Bohai people in Manchuria, and most tribal cavalry, principally the Khitan. The Jurchen no longer trusted them, in spite of the importance of the Khitan in the Jurchen rise to power. As a result, the *meng'an* and *mouke* became almost entirely Jurchen ethnically. Since the Jurchen were tied to local rather than national interests, this meant a considerable weakening of Jin military potential around the time that the Mongols were beginning to stir in spite of sporadic Jin efforts to control them by exacerbating conflict. This problem was all the more urgent due to the fact that the Jurchen had

BELOW **An archaeological dig in Xi'an**, historically a thriving metropolis and intermittently a dynastic capital city, unearthed coins from the Song dynasty.

THE DRAMA OF ZAJU

The Jin period is noted for its flourishing drama, based upon an old form, the *zaju*, now given new prominence. In the *zaju*, a "variety show," as in modern Chinese opera, arias alternate with short musical interludes, skits, some acrobatic, and dance, all to tell a story often with comments upon current events and interests. Although few of these *zaju* scripts survive, hundreds of plays were written by Jin writers, indicating the popularity and success of the genre with the general public. The *zaju* was later taken up in Mongol China and enjoyed great popularity under the Mongols when significant innovations enriched the tradition. For both Jin and Yuan times, the surviving *zaju* texts, far more numerous under the Mongols, are rich sources and examples of popular culture of the time. So important was the *zaju* that one of the major lyric forms of the period, the *qu*, was an attempt to imitate *zaju* arias.

LEFT **The spectacle of modern Chinese opera** is influenced by *zaju*. Originally, early forms of opera were performed for the Chinese emperors. *Zaju* introduced formal theater to the masses.

moved most of their people south into China and no longer had a "tribal reservoir" to draw upon.

These problems became even more pressing under Zhangzong since the court was becoming more and more assimilated to the north Chinese variants of Chinese culture, whatever the lip-service to Jurchen traditionalism. The army that advanced on Song invaders in 1207 was mostly Chinese. By that date even the Jurchen cavalry was a great deal less effective, despite all the government efforts to foster it. It was military weakness that explains the great success of the Mongols in a relatively few years. After losing the north, in 1215, partly by default, the Jin regime was extinguished in 1234 by the Mongols and their north Chinese allies, including some groups of the Jurchen.

The Economics of Industry, Resources, and Trade

Although long considered a "barbarian" dynasty and somehow less worthy of notice than the Chinese Southern Song, the Jin was in fact very powerful economically. It had a large population, two-thirds of which were Song. The Jin dynasty period also witnessed a number of important cultural advances for its Chinese subjects. Two forces propelled

the Jin economy. One was the continuation of trends already important under the Song, including large scale exploitation of local iron and coal resources, as well as the marshalling of large industries to produce consumer and export goods. Like the Song, the Jin empire was dotted with large cities, major commercial centers well linked by internal trade routes, some of them water based. It also had a sophisticated monetary system, even beginning to coin silver money, something that was rare in China, for a brief period of time. This reform of the currency system was an important milestone and would have a far-reaching influence on the currency of later dynasties. The Jin were also involved in many international trade exchanges, even though its primary trading partner was Song China and not distant barbarians groups, at least not directly. The Jin's trade with Song China was valuable and extremely well protected.

BELOW **A Jin dynasty ceramic pillow** was used by the living and was also placed in tombs. The bold decoration on the white stoneware is a feature of the artwork of this period.

The Southern Song

The Song, faced with the Jurchen assault, survived by taking refuge in the south, where a new Song dynasty was founded. Unexpectedly it flourished, thanks to the economic power of its remaining domains.

RIGHT **The Southern Song dynasty** was a period in which new forms and styles of mirrors were invented. This round bronze mirror is decorated with a unicorn, a symbol of good luck.

Faced with an overwhelming Jin attack, the Song was only able to fall back, regroup, and play for time. The primary leader of restoration efforts was the 20-year-old prince Zhao Gaou, Prince Gang, younger brother of the Emperor Qinzong who had surrendered to the Jin. After more than one harrowing escape and buoyed by popular resistance, Zhao Gaou was able to take advantage of the temporary retreat of Jin armies to avoid the heat. He ascended the throne as Gaozong (reigned 1127–1162) on June 12, 1127. In his fight against the invaders, the new emperor was ably seconded by Li Gang, one of the few Northern Song ministers to escape captivity. Although ultimately removed from power, Li Gang put the Song resistance on a firm basis and was largely responsible for survival of the Song.

As the Jin advance continued, Gaozong's court fled farther into the south, at first to Yangzhou on the Yangzi then to Hangzhou, where a temporary capital was established. Even this bastion proved too exposed. In 1130, as Jin forces roamed freely in the south, the court was forced to take to the seas, leaving Hangzhou to the mercy of the Jin. China's fierce summer weather intervened and saved the restoration, forcing a new Jin retreat north to Manchuria. The court finally returned to Hangzhou in 1133, where it remained until 1276. Subsequently, the Song court attempted, with a few exceptions, to keep peace with the Jin, and avoid invasions. The treaty of 1141–1142 recognized the Jurchen's conquest of the north. A permanent boundary was established that ran directly through central China and left the north in Jin hands.

As the Jurchen consolidated their rule in the north, the Southern Song developed their own position. Their success in defeating a renewed Jin invasion of 1161 showed, momentarily at least, that the old ineffectiveness of Song forces was a thing of the past. This was in spite of an obligation to pay a large tribute to the Jin, and the continual factional struggles occurring at court.

The Great Ministers

After Gaozong's death, a nephew, Xiaozong (reigned 1162–1189) came to the throne, the last strong Southern Song emperor. Xiaozong sought to balance the powers of civil officials to prevent any from gaining the power held by the Chief Councillor Qin Gui (1090–1155), who had been responsible for the disgrace and death of the Song national resistance leader Yue Fei (1103–1142). Nonetheless a tradition of strong ministerial rule continued. The most powerful of the chief ministers of Southern Song was Han Tuozhou (1152–1207), who dominated the court between 1195 and 1206, during the reign of Emperor Ningzong (reigned 1195–1224). Han was a relative by marriage of the emperor, and rose to power taking advantage of his royal connections. Because of his irregular route to power, Tuozhou hated the conventionally recruited scholarly bureaucrats and did everything possible to persecute them.

Unfortunately for Han Tuozhou, he went too far and began a war with the Jin, partly aiming to discredit his scholarly opponents, many of whom were adherents to the "peace" faction at court. The war, despite some initial successes, was a disaster for the Song. Jin forces counterattacked deeply in response to the Song advances. The Song court had no choice but to accept humiliating terms for peace. The Jin demanded Han Tuozhou's head in a box, an unprecedented affront to the Song. They had never treated a chief minister in that way before. The powerful minister was duly assassinated and his head

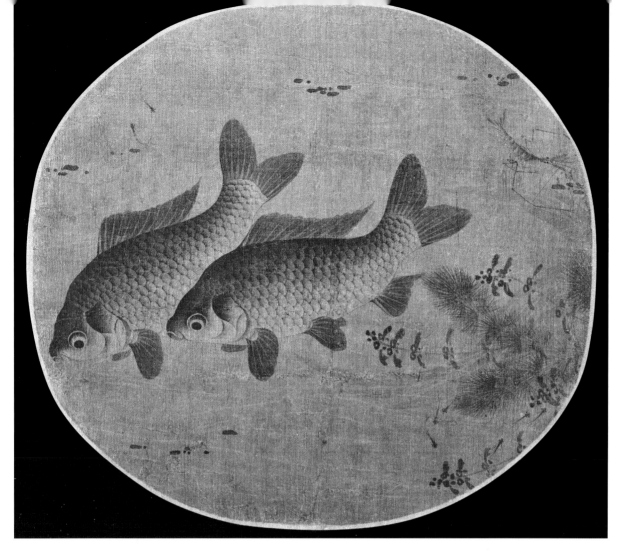

dispatched, seriously damaging Song traditions of government, but also creating a martyr for the Song cause.

Han Tuozhou's successor was Shi Miyuan (1164–1233), who operated under the shadow of the powerful Empress Yang, the consort of Ningzong. Shi Miyuan had a more conventional career than the previous emperor, although he was not always totally scrupulous, and favored the scholarly elite. After Shi Miyuan's period of dominance, events in the north dramatically changed the status of power in China forever. The Jin dynasty collapsed and a new power, the Mongols, appeared in their place.

Last of the Great Ministers: Jia Sidao

The last of the great ministers, who inherited the problem of the Mongols, was Jia Sidao (1213–1275). He dominated the court from 1259 until he was dismissed a few months before his execution, and has been held responsible for the collapse of the Song in the face of Mongol invasion as a "bad last minister," despite his actual merits.

The Song's political and military problems were insolvable. A thorough reform was needed to increase revenues, but reform went against ingrained political divisions, growing social divisions between a powerful elite, and a weakening peasantry. Jia Sidao made some progress, using new revenues to improve the financing of the military, which was already expensive to maintain. Unfortunately, the Song's war with the Mongols was lost. The Song had huge numbers of troops but its armies were immobile due to the shortage of horses. The Song had many well-held positions but they were easily isolated or turned. Despite resistance efforts led by Jia, the collapse of the dynasty was inevitable.

The Age of Zhu Xi

The Southern Song philosopher Zhu Xi (1130–1200) reinterpreted Confucian doctrine
to suit the needs of his class, the literati, China's new elite. As a result of his work,
this "new look" Confucianism permeated Chinese culture, influencing the arts,
literature, calligraphy, and painting.

Before Zhu Xi, Neo-Confucianism was pragmatic and forward looking. It had encouraged intellectual enterprise, and was not rigidly attached to the Confucian vision, certainly not to its classics. Zhu Xi placed the emphasis on individual meditation, the teacher's authority, and social hierarchy. He stressed the strict dictates of inherited texts, in particular Meng Zi (Mencius), another Chinese philospher, to whom Zhu Xi first gave prominence after centuries of relative neglect. Zhu Xi's version of Neo-Confucianism emphasized all the "proper" relations between ruler and subject, man and woman, elder and younger, with the first in each pair having authority over the second. To hammer home his ideological points, he even produced his own versions of Confucian and other scholarly texts. These included a synopsis of the *Zizhi tongjian*, "Comprehensive Mirror for Government," a general history of China by the scholar and statesman Sima Guang (1019–1086). Zhu Xi also prepared fully annotated versions of most of the Confucian classics. In so doing, Zhu Xi, it is claimed, became an architect of China's conservative social position in the late Song and also during subsequent dynasties. His influence was great.

The class that Zhu Xi served, known as the literati, replaced the old class of the landed aristocrats. Unlike their predecessors, the Song literati enjoyed an elite status solely because of their participation in the imperial exam system, in which they had to express their Confucian knowledge in carefully contrived essays. This is what the young Zhu Xi sought to train for. Some recommendation of candidates was allowed, which meant that family power could be perpetrated through patronage and wealth, but, in general, elite status was not hereditary. It had to be proven again and again by each new generation and the examinations were repeated.

LEFT **A *luohan,* or spiritual practitioner,** was painted by Liu Sognian, one of the four great masters of the Southern Song dynasty.

Examination System

The ostensible purpose of the Song examination system was to select talent but it became a form of indoctrination as well as selection. It tested moral orthodoxy as well as Confucian knowledge of participants. The earliest civil service examinations were those of the Han, but they did not become important until the Tang; at that time, Empress Wu used an expanded system of civil service exams to enlist a bureaucracy favorable to herself. In her time, the exams remained only one of several possible paths to power. During Song times, by contrast, the civil service exams quickly became the most important path to office. Those who gained office through other ways were looked down on by the scholar–bureaucrats.

Examinations took place at several levels. The highest level, the palace examination, was supervised by the emperor. It led to the award of the title *jinshi*, "scholar advanced [to the emperor]." Emphasis was almost entirely upon correct interpretation of canonical texts to be expressed in an "eight-legged" essay. The name refers to the required structure of the argument. A typical examination question might come from a passage from a classic text, for example, "the nature of man is good." The successful candidate would have to recognize the passage from Mencius (Meng Zi), interpret it, and develop Mencian ideas as a basis for general moral and government authority. Thousands took the examinations each year, but only a relatively few passed, and rarely at the highest level. Many had to take the examinations again and again before passing. Some candidates, the majority, never passed, in spite of many years of study and great expense but, due to the influence of the ideological

concerns inherent in the exams, even the failures came to share the same values and traditions. This made for a remarkably uniform upper crust at all levels of Chinese society, and became the glue holding Chinese society together. Even those not actively seeking to pass these examinations and gain government office were influenced by the values expressed in the examinations themselves, due to the high profile prestige of elite membership. The all-pervading Confucian examinations imposed a common worldview on the entire ruling class, some in government service, but more trying to pass their exams, and even on the many failures.

Shared Values

So pervasive were these shared values and traditions that even the arts of the time became expressions of these values. Two artforms were very important, calligraphy and painting. Every member of the literati was expected to know the classics. Likewise, each was expected to express their great learning through writing in a delicate hand, and painting. The literati also wrote poetry, another obligatory sign of class membership. A painting with one's own calligraphy, copying out one's own poem, became an expression of literati art. The only thing better was a painting with other inscriptions by highly placed friends and colleagues, the true expression of elite status.

A FAMOUS SCHOLAR: SU SHI

The literati scholar Su Shi (1036–1101) was Song China's greatest poet and a major statesman opposed to the reforms of Wang Anshi. Like other members of his class, he also became famous for his calligraphy and painting. At this time, Chinese calligraphers wanted to express themselves as individuals. They also wished to show their understanding of the roots of their art, specifically as seen in the calligraphy of the master Wang Xizhi (303–361). Su Shi did this in a bold yet subtle style, while mastering the difficult art of bamboo painting to produce some of the most famous examples of this genre. Later, like Wang, Su Shi became one of the masters imitated by others, down to modern times.

LEFT **This carved soapstone showing a scene from *Ode to Red Cliffs*** is a tribute to Su Shi's poem, with the poet Huang Tingjian, the monk Foyin, and a servant under the cliffs.

The Neo-Confucian Ethos

Neo-Confucianism of the Song dynasty (960–1276) was a philosophical movement of a dual nature. On the one hand, it was a response to the Buddhist and Daoist challenge; on the other hand, it was a reinvention of classical Confucianism.

As a response to the Buddhist and Daoist challenge, Neo-Confucianism was to come to terms with the sociopolitical situation in Song China. Since the fall of the Han dynasty in 221, the classical Confucian vision of a benevolent government ruling with the Mandate of Heaven had been discredited. For nearly seven centuries, the focus of Chinese philosophy had been dominated either by the Buddhist concern with the achievement of personal liberation from suffering, or by the main Daoist concern with transcending the particular view that humans are the center of the universe. The true goal of Neo-Confucianism was to make the Confucian doctrine relevant to the new and rigorous intellectual environment.

In terms of its contents, Confucianism in the Song is called "Neo-Confucianism" because it contained elements which differ from classical Confucianism founded by Confucius (551–479 BCE) and Mencius (331–289 BCE). One of the key differences was the redefinition of the Confucian canon. Replacing the Five Classics of classical Confucianism (namely: the *Book of Changes*; the *Book of Odes*; the *Book of Documents*; the *Book of Rites*; and the *Spring and Autumn Annals*), Neo-Confucianists had their own four books: the *Great Learning*; the *Analects*; the *Mencius*; and the *Doctrine of the Mean*. Furthermore, many terms in classical Confucianism, such as *ren* (humanity), received new meanings in the hands of the Neo-Confucian thinkers.

There were seven major Neo-Confucian thinkers during the Song period. Five of them lived in the Northern Song period (960–1127): Zhou Dunyi (1017–1073), Shao Yong (1011–1077), Zhang Zai (1020–1077), Cheng Hao (1032–1085), and Cheng Yi (1033–1107). The other two lived in the Southern Song period (1127–1279): Zhu Xi (1130–1200) and Lu Xiangshan (1139–1193).

The Cosmological Root of Human Morality

Among the five Northern Song masters, Zhou Dunyi and Shao Yong were closely linked to Daoism. For instance, Zhou Dunyi's magnum opus, *An Explanation of the Diagram of the Great Ultimate*, was based on a specific Daoist diagram for obtaining elixir. Likewise, Shao Yong spent the later part of his life living like a recluse in Luoyang, and he allegedly learned his numerology from the Daoist Chen Tuan (*c.* 906–989).

Despite their Daoist predisposition, Zhou Dunyi and Shao Yong were Neo-Confucian in one specific area. They both argued that humankind is related to the cosmos as a part to the whole. This co-dependence of the part and the whole was graphically represented in Zhou Dunyi's work *An Explanation of the Diagram of the Great Ultimate*. Modifying a Daoist diagram, Zhou used five circles to clearly illustrate the sequence by which the universe came into being. First, he traced the creation of people and objects back

BELOW **The Flying Horse of Gansu** is an example of the the Han dynasty craftsmanship at its peak.

chronological chart depicting how the universe had evolved in time. With this chart, he located human history in the long-term historical structures of the universe's self renewal.

Moral Metaphysics

While Zhou Dunyi and Shao Yong identified the cosmological root of human morality, it was Zhang Zai who first made a logical argument about the metaphysical nature of human morality, or the "moral-metaphysics." In his essay *Western Inscription*, Zhang Zai went beyond Zhou and Shao by abandoning cosmology. Instead of offering a detailed account of the development of the universe, he outlined morality as being human bonding with all beings in this universe. For him, ethical deeds are not just good deeds in the interest of human society, but also deeds in the interest of the universe as a whole. For instance, to be a good son is not just a son's duty to his parents, but is also his duty to the cosmos. Similarly, to be a dedicated minister or official is not just being faithful to the emperor, but also means being faithful to the universe as a whole. In short, what is moral is metaphysical.

Cheng Hao detailed the intimate connection of ethics and metaphysics by re-inventing the Confucian concept of *ren* (humanity). In classical terms of Confucianism, *ren* was understood as human relationships. Going beyond the classical interpretation of *ren*, Cheng Hao defined it as the relationship between humankind and the cosmos. In his essay *On Understanding the Nature of Ren*, Cheng Hao described *ren* as "forming one body with all things without any differentiation." He stated that to be humane, it was not just enough to love one's parents, kinsmen, and countrymen, but one had to love all things on earth. Given the complexity of humans on this earth, one needs to cultivate a relationship with those nearby before reaching out for those further away. Yet, one should always remember that the goal of cultivating relationships with those nearby was to achieve "forming one body with all things without any differentiation."

to the origin of the universe, the Supreme Ultimate (*Taiji*). Then turning from cosmology to ethics, he argued that as members of the cosmic family of beings, humankind will contribute to the unfolding of the universe by doing what it is good at: acting morally. Put simply, he identified the cosmological root of human morality.

Along this line, Shao Yong discussed the co-dependence of the part and whole in numerology. By rearranging the 64 hexagrams of the *Book of Changes* into a circle, and by dividing them into a series of the multiple of four, he demonstrated how people and objects were related to a gigantic cosmic system of ebb and flow, growth and decay. In his magnum opus, the *Supreme Principles Governing the World* (*Huangji Jingshi Shu*), he offered his readers a

LEFT **The disciples of Buddha,** as depicted in this artwork, gave alms to the poor. The easing of suffering was one of the key Buddhist ideas that influenced personal thinking during the Song.

BELOW **The pearl and the fishes** on the roof of this white glazed shrine from the Northern Song dynasty are representative of Buddhist architecture.

As much as Zhou Dunyi and Shao Yong were semi-Daoists in order to counter Daoism, Zhang Zai and Cheng Hao were semi-Buddhists in order to counter Buddhism. The key argument in the "moral metaphysics" of Zhang Zai and Cheng Hao is that the human mind is fully equipped with the potential for spiritual transcendence. To be enlightened, human beings do not need to seek from without, but to undergo an inward search to activate the innate potential in the human mind. For this reason, both Zhang Zai and Cheng Hao emphasized the simplicity and easiness in the human quest for enlightenment. For Zhang Zai, enlightenment comes when one realizes mentally that "all people are my brothers and sisters, and all things are my companions." Likewise, for Cheng Hao, there is no need for exhaustive search for enlightenment, because "if one preserves *ren* long enough, it will automatically dawn on him."

Co-Dependence of Intuition and Learning

Zhang Zai and Cheng Hao still had so much in common with the Buddhists that they caused alarm among some Neo-Confucian thinkers. Cheng Yi, Cheng Hao's younger brother, was among the first philosophers to attempt to steer Neo-Confucianism away from Buddhism. To balance the idealistic bent of Zhang Zai and Cheng Hao, Cheng Yi argued that one cannot rectify one's mind with intuition alone, and intuition has to be actualized in daily practices. For Cheng Yi, the path to enlightenment should include two parts: intuition and learning. While intuition informs learning, learning firmly cements intuition.

To highlight the co-dependence of intuition and learning, Cheng Yi coined the phrase "self-cultivation requires seriousness; the pursuit of learning depends on the extension of knowledge." The first half of the phrase "self-cultivation requires seriousness" was Cheng Yi's summary of Zhang Zai's and Cheng Hao's position, namely, the importance of cultivating the human mind. The second half of the phrase "the pursuit of learning depends on the extension of knowledge" was Cheng Yi's attempt at balancing intuition with learning. The key point in the second half of the phrase was the term "extension of knowledge." Originally one of the eightfold cultivation in the *Great Learning*, Cheng Yi used the "extension of knowledge" to highlight the importance of practicing one's thought in daily life. For him, the purpose of the "extension of knowledge" was not to lock oneself aimlessly in daily humdrum. Instead, it was a way of cultivating the mind so that it would accept things and situations as they were, not what they could be or a person wanted or wished them to be.

BELOW **This Reclining Buddha** is found at Baoding Shan, Dazu. The carvings incorporate a blend of Confuciansim, Daoism, and Buddhism—ideas at the core of Neo-Confuciansim.

Two Schools of Neo-Confucianism

In many ways, Cheng Yi's phrase "self-cultivation requires seriousness; the pursuit of learning depends on the extension of knowledge" helps to make clear the heated debate between the two Southern Song Neo-Confucian masters, Lu Xiangshan and Zhu Xi. As two philosophical rivals, Lu and Zhu wrote to each other many times, debating issues concerning cosmology, the method of moral cultivation, and interpretation of text. Once they even had a face-to-face encounter at the Goose Lake Monastery in present-day Jiangxi Province.

Following the position of Zhang Zai and Cheng Hao, Lu Xiangshan stressed "self cultivation requires seriousness." With a tendency to go directly into the fundamentals, he considered the perfect truth as a unity. Regardless of how vast and diverse the universe may be, he believed that its principle is one and it is the same as the principle endowed in the human mind. Based on his theory of the unity of mind and principle, he argued that the cultivation of the mind is the direct method in achieving the Neo-Confucian "moral metaphysics." To search for the cosmic principle, he suggested, one does not need to seek from without, but needs to cultivate one's mind from within oneself.

Following Cheng Yi's position of balancing intuition with formal learning, Zhu Xi stressed that "the pursuit of learning depends on the extension of knowledge." Not disputing with Lu with the ultimate unity of mind and principle, Zhu was keenly aware of the gap between what is potentially given and what is fully realised. Even if the human mind is endowed with the cosmic principle, a potential that is not fully realised remains an unused resource. So for him, a genuine theory of moral cultivation has to

THE GOOSE LAKE MONASTERY DEBATE

A landmark in the development of Neo-Confucianism, the Goose Lake Monastery debate between Lu Xiangshan and Zhu Xi in 1175 shows the fundamental difference between the main schools of Neo-Confucianism: the "Mind and Heart" school and the "Principle" school. Arguing for the unity of human mind and the cosmic principle, Lu paved the way for the emergence of the "Mind and Heart" school, which stressed the cultivation of the human mind as the only way for achieving spiritual transcendence. Likewise, arguing for a balance between intuition and learning, Zhu became the founding father of the "Principle" school, which took an attitude toward bridging the gap between what is potentially available and what is fully actualized.

RIGHT **Confucius** was a philospher whose teachings have deeply influenced Chinese, Korean, and Japanese thought and life.

address the technical problems and the human anxiety in realising the innately endowed potential in the human mind. For this reason, Zhu Xi considered the human mind as having two very distinct elements. He called the part of the human mind that has fully realised its potential as the storehouse of the cosmic principle, the "Mind of the Way." He called the other part of the human mind that has not actualized its potential, the "Mind of Man." To further emphasize the gap between the potential of the human mind and the realised, he created a series of dichotomies or arguments: firstly, the principle (*li*) versus the material force (*qi*), the above shape (*xing er shang*) versus the within shape (*xing er xia*), the principle of Heaven (*tianli*) versus the human desire (*renyu*), the mind (*xin*) versus the nature (*xing*). The aim for the loyal followers of Zhu Xi was to develop the potential that they were born with and to then overcome the "Mind of Man." The premise of Neo-Confucianism was a philosophy attempting to merge the intrinsic elements and also theories of Confucian, Daoist, and Buddhist thought.

LEFT **A sculpture of a Song dynasty priest** shows the simple robes that they were required to wear.

The Mongol Invasion

The appearance of the Mongols signaled the beginning of an era of unprecedented change for East Asia. By 1234, the Mongols had completely crushed the Jin and were posed to conquer the Song as well.

ABOVE **Genghis Khan** was a fierce tribal chieftain who changed the course of China's history. This fourteenth-century painting shows Genghis and his troops fighting rival tribes near a mountain pass.

The rise of the Mongols is inextricably linked with the name of the chieftain Temüjin (1167–1227). He was the son of a minor Mongol nobleman, and grew up in very difficult circumstances, including the poisoning of his father by Tartar enemies and the abandonment of himself, his brothers, and his mother on the open steppe, which was a virtual death sentence. Despite the setbacks, young Temüjin not only survived, but prospered, and became prominent in China's military and dynastic history.

By 1205, Temüjin had defeated his rivals in years of brutal conflict and his fierce conquering movement had begun to penetrate outside Mongolia. In 1206, in a great assembly or *khuriltai*, Temüjin was elected supreme khan (*qan*) of the Mongolian world as Genghis Khan (Chinggis Khan), "Universal Khan." The next year the new empire expanded its authority into what is now known as Inner Mongolia, directly threatening the Jin.

Assault on the Jin

Armed with a new base on the fringes of China, the Mongols stepped up their attacks. In 1209–1210, the Mongols advanced directly to the Xixia capital and brought Xixia into tribute-paying status. Next it was the Jin's turn. In 1211, the Mongols began a general assault. Much of it was on the territories in Inner Mongolia seized by the Mongols in 1207 and helped by the new allies recruited there.

Jin resistance proved surprisingly inept. Also, many groups within the Jin Empire were only too willing to ally themselves with the invaders. By 1214, after penetrating deeply into the Jin domains and defeating the best Jin forces, the Mongols besieged the capital of Zhongdu. The Mongols were unable to take the well-fortified city due to their lack of siege equipment. It was also summer and well past the usual Mongol campaigning season. The Jin were willing to make peace, and the Mongols returned home laden with booty.

LEFT **This tortoise sculpture** marks the site of Qaraqorum, the capital of Genghis Khan's Mongol Empire in the thirteenth century.

Jin court was once again forced to flee south, this time to Caizhou, the last Jin stronghold, where they attempted to resist the Mongols. Kaifeng fell in 1233, and in February 1234, Caizhou was taken. During the final Jin resistance, calls to Southern Song for help fell on deaf ears, proving detrimental to the isolated Song, who were yet to feel the wrath of Mongol invaders.

A Lucky Break for the Song

Luckily for the Song, in spite of sporadic hostilities, renewed Mongol preoccupations elsewhere and the need for the conquerors to absorb their north Chinese conquests put off the bloody day of reckoning. Only in the 1250s, after a fierce power struggle leading to the election of a new imperial line in Möngke (reigned 1251–1259), did the warlike Mongols turn once again to China as a primary target of their expansion. Between 1253 and 1254, an army led by Kublai (1215–1294), younger brother of the khan, advanced along the Sichuan border with Tibet into Yunnan, which was finally conquered by the Mongols. Then, in 1258, khan Möngke prepared for a major advance into Song domains from Sichuan, in coordination with the advances of other armies, including one from conquered Yunnan. Fortunately for the Song, Möngke died before completing this advance. The whole campaign was abandoned by his viceroy in China, Kublai, who had to rush back to north China to secure his position in a succession dispute that would destroy the unified Mongol Empire. The Mongol conquest of the Song was not achieved by the Mongol Empire but by its Chinese successor state, the late Yuan dynasty (1279–1368).

No sooner had the Mongols retreated, when the Jin court, alarmed by the rapid erosion of its power, suddenly and unexpectedly abandoned Zhongdu, fleeing south to the Jin Southern Capital (Kaifeng), leaving Zhongdu to its own devices. The city was besieged by Khitan allies of the Mongols, formerly part of the Jin emperor's personal army. The Mongols responded to this opportunity and sent reinforcements to take over the siege. Mongol forces and local allies were deployed against other Jin centers, including the subordinate Northern, Eastern, and Western capitals. Local allies proliferated and soon the Jurchen were fighting for the Mongols.

This time the Mongol siege was successful. Zhongdu fell in the spring of 1215. In addition to Zhongdu, the Mongols also seized the other Jin capitals, except for the Southern Capital. The Jin dynasty was now confined to the area north and south of the Yellow River, centering on Nanjing or Kaifeng. Its days seemed numbered.

Surprisingly, the Jin survived for another 19 years. The primary reason for this was the Mongols' preoccupation with the West. When Genghis Khan finally turned his attentions to East Asia again it was to chastise the recalcitrant vassal Xixia, which had taken the advantage of the absence of the main Mongol armies to rebel. In 1226, the Mongol troops led by Genghis Khan invaded, and within a year had completely destroyed Xixia. Their victory was complete, but unfortunately for the Mongols, Genghis Khan died soon after.

Once again the Jin were spared. Before the Mongols could resume their advance they had to elect a new khan, Ögödei (reigned 1229–1241), and assemble resources for renewed operations. In 1232, the Mongols advanced on Kaifeng. The

BELOW **Genghis Khan,** founder of the Mongolian Empire, is surrounded by his servants in a fourteenth-century Persian-influenced illumination.

Fall of the Southern Song

The Mongol empire collapsed after the death of Möngke Khan in 1259. In China, his brother, Kublai (reigned 1260–1294), built up a power base and prepared to conquer the south to expand his territory.

RIGHT **This *Guan* vase** is from the Southern Song dynasty. *Guan* ("Official") was the name given to the ceramic wares produced by the imperial household at the capital, Hangzhou.

BELOW RIGHT **Seven of the nine emperors** of the Song dynasty are buried with their spouses, concubines, and nobles at an imperial tomb in Gongyi City.

The final Mongol campaign against the Song began in 1267 and went on until 1279, when the last embers of resistance were crushed in the Canton delta. The attacking approach was to be along the Han River and then along the Yangzi River, eventually to the Southern Song capital of Hangzhou. This time the Mongols intended not just to isolate Song defenders but also, relying upon their experts in siege warfare and even naval units, to cut Song water supply lines, to take all of the major Song fortresses, and systematically destroy the Song field army piece by piece.

The key positions blocking the advance were Fancheng and Xiangyang, facing each other strategically across the Han River. It took Mongol forces six years to reduce these well-defended positions. It was late 1274 before the Mongols reached the Yangzi, attesting to the tenaciousness of the defense. It took an additional year and a half to make the final approach to the Song capital of Hangzhou. During this time, until his dismissal, and eventual execution, Jia Sidao took charge of the defense efforts, although mostly comfortably from the rear. The tensions between civil and military officials undermined his efforts. In March 1275, the Song minister took personal control of the Song forces at the front. Under his sole command, the Song suffered one of its greatest defeats, in a land and river battle that opened the way for the final Mongol advance on the city of Hangzhou.

On the Mongol side, the invading forces were capably led by Marshall Bayan (1237–1295), who was seconded by a variety of Mongolian and non-Mongolian figures. By this time the various armies controlled by Kublai, Mongol and Chinese, were working

SOUTHERN SONG STRATEGY AT THE END

The Song mobilized large armies to fight the Mongols backed up by a large population. It also sought to use the best available military technology including the latest pyrotechnics. Cannons had not yet been invented, but simple handguns were already in use. There were also rockets, flamethrowers, and various other deadly devices. Both sides had sophisticated engines using torsion power or thrown by human strength or by weights. These included the ubiquitous *huopao*, fire catapults (mangonels), hurling incendiaries and other loads, and later their counterweighted variant, *huihui pao* (Muslim catapults). Nonetheless, the lack of horses was a serious handicap for the Song defenders. Without a large cavalry force to face its extremely mobile enemies, Song forces were largely restricted to positional warfare in great fortresses. These were easily isolated. Such fortresses did often block Mongol access to the Song interior, and could cut off raiding parties from the north, but once Kublai Khan's China mobilized large armies of foot soldiers equipped with siege equipment as well as Mongol horsemen their value fell considerably.

well together. On the water, the wily Mongols proved to be capable, using large numbers of captured Song ships.

Despite sporadic Song resistance—at the Yangzi city of Changzhou, for example, the entire population was massacred in the traditional Mongolian style applied to cities that resisted for too long—the Mongol forces closed inexorably on Hangzhou. The Song Empress Dowager Xie, who had taken charge of the Song court during the rule of the puppet emperor Gongzong (reigned 1274–1276), finally surrendered the city and the Mongols entered it on February 10, 1276.

Song Resistance Movement

Before the Mongols entered Hangzhou, loyalists smuggled two young princes out of the palace to the naval base at Wenzhou and from there by sea to Fuzhou, in Fujian. This began three years of Song last-ditch resistance in the southeast. The resources available to the loyalists were insufficient to defeat the Mongols, who were able to take full advantage of their mobility in overrunning the last Song domains, but loyalist forces were able to achieve regional successes in 1277. In that year, the Mongols were preoccupied with their Central Asia frontier, site of invasion and rebellion.

Even before the crisis in Mongolia had subsided, Mongol forces began to counterattack the loyalists. On September 26, 1277, forces under the loyalist hero Wen Tianxiang (1236–1283) were decisively defeated in southeastern Jiangxi. Wen himself was nearly captured and his army almost totally destroyed. Elsewhere, Mongol forces crushed resistance in Fujian, forcing loyalist forces to fall back on Guangdong. Although loyalist armies recovered the following year, they never again achieved the success that they had in 1277. In late 1278, resolved to finally crush them, the Mongols began a three-pronged invasion of the loyalists' Guangdong base. Although there was spirited resistance, mostly by local militia units, loyalist armies were completely outmaneuvered and outfought at every turn. After securing most of the mainland, the Mongols began a final assault on March 19, 1279 against the Song fleet that was anchored off the coast near modern Macau. In the historic naval Battle of Yaishan, fought at a site between two islands, the powerful Song fleet was utterly defeated. A few ships survived to try to continue resistance, but the drowning of the loyalist leader Zhang Shijie on June 14, 1279, put an end to those hopes once and for all. After 319 years, the Song dynasty was extinct and Kublai Khan was the new emperor of a united China. A new era was to begin.

ABOVE **A Turkoman, or Mongol chief,** is depicted holding an arrow in this sixteenth-century painting. The Turkomans battled fiercely with the Song over control of the Silk Road.

The Court of Kublai Khan

Kublai Khan was the founder of the Mongol Yuan dynasty and reunited China
after centuries of division. It was his court and world that was visited and described
by Marco Polo (1254–1324). The legend of Kublai Khan captivated Europe.

ABOVE **Kublai Khan** was the
founding Yuan emperor.
Kublai's increased social
welfare spending won over
the Chinese warlords, which
was essential to the building
of the dynasty.

Kublai (reigned 1261–1294) was the second
of four sons of Tolui-noyan (1190–1232), the
youngest son of Genghis Khan (Chinggis
Khan). At first he was just one of many Mongolian princes holding land near China. The
accession of his elder brother, Möngke (reigned
1251–1259), to the imperial throne changed his
position. After a successful military campaign in

Yunnan, Kublai became his brother's
viceroy for Mongol China. Here Kublai
built up an independent power base. It
stood him in good stead when Möngke
died in 1259.

Kublai rushed back to north China
from Sichuan, where he had been very
involved in his brother's advance on the
Song, hastily convening a political and
military council, or *khuriltai*, of supporters, and had himself elected khan, as
the successor to Möngke. Based in China,
his new regime was staffed by the same
local advisers, mostly Chinese, whom
Kublai had acquired during his time
as Möngke's viceroy.

Kublai's hasty self-anointment as khan
was considered a blatant act of usurpation by most Mongols. Only a few
Mongol princes had participated in the
khuriltai electing him. His election did
not go unchallenged. Opposing Kublai
was a younger brother, Arigh Böke (died
1266), who enjoyed wide support among
the Mongol aristocracy and who also
controlled Qaraqorum, the old imperial
capital. He also convened a *khuriltai* and
had himself elected khan. The Mongol
world now had two competing rulers,
neither enjoying universal support,
although Arigh Böke had better claims
to legitimacy. He had been left in charge
of Mongolia by Möngke and had good
contacts in the Golden Horde and in the
Chagatay provinces or *ulus* of western
Turkistan. The Mongols of Iran, ruled
by Hülegü (1217–1265), another brother
of Kublai, supported him. The eruption of civil
war was inevitable, it was just a matter of time.

The war, fought mainly in Mongolia, went on
until 1264 and ended with Arigh Böke's defeat,
thanks to Kublai's superior resources. Kublai then
set about consolidating and expanding his control
of power in the Chinese north. He also continued
to press his case as the legitimate successor to

Möngke. To this end he maintained a very strong presence in Mongolia and Turkistan even securing the submission of the Chagatay *ulus*, as well as that of Mongol Iran.

Blending Mongolian and Chinese Culture

Although ultimately unsuccessful in his quest to reestablish a unified Mongolian empire under himself, Kublai paid careful attention to Mongolian symbolism throughout his long reign. He also, given his real heritage, had to appear Chinese as well, to the majority of Chinese subjects. Among the numerous Chinese symbols that became important for him were a coterie of "Confucian" show ministers (real power continued to be in the hands of Mongols), a Chinese-style government, backed up by a Mongolian sensibility, and a new permanent capital. This was the new city of Daidu, built from 1267 until 1276. Kublai also adopted a dynastic calendar, including Chinese-style year periods (*nianhao*) and in 1272 gave his new dynasty a name. It was Yuan, a name drawn from the *Yijing* or "The Book of Changes," a classic canon revered by the Chinese population.

As the next step, Kublai sought universality in Chinese terms by seeking to bring "all under Heaven" under his rule. This meant conquering the Song, a process completed by 1279. Kublai also launched campaigns against other areas loosely considered part of the Chinese world order, including Japan, Vietnam, Burma, and Java. Korea was also successfully ruled by the Mongols for a period longer than China, and strongly influenced the Koreans.

Kublai Khan, Emperor of China

Kublai was the first emperor of a fully united China since the Later Tang although he was and always remained a foreigner for his Chinese subjects, and much of his regime was tangential to China. Like Mongol rulers of the past, his court

never stayed in one place for long but trekked seasonally between Kublai's former residence, the Yuan summer capital of Shangdu, and the Mongol winter capital of Daidu (also known as Qanbaliq, "*Qan* City"), modern day Beijing. Kublai's court was not only nomadic, but we know from Marco Polo that Kublai personally participated in traditional Mongolian activities while on the trek. This included extensive hunting. Even when in Daidu, Kublai Khan preferred to live in a Mongolian tent, pitched on a lake in the middle of what is now known as the Forbidden City, a significant Mongol creation.

To govern a realm that was truly multinational, Kublai encouraged the creation of an international court culture. Officials spoke Mongolian, Persian, and Turkic dialects, as well as Chinese. The khan even ordered the creation of a universal script, the Aphags-pa script based upon Tibetan script. It was used to write down all the languages adopted by the Mongol court. To keep the culturally varied members of his court happy, Kublai and his successors encouraged the creation of a highly mixed official cuisine. It was based on Mongolian mutton soup but with additions and refinements from the world over, particularly from the Muslim world. This cuisine is described in the official Mongolian court dietary book, the *Yinshan zhengyao,* "Proper and Essential Things for the Emperor's Food and Drink," published in 1330.

Kublai's government was Chinese on the surface but at its center was a Mongolian reality. This was a Chinese version

of the Mongol government of empire. The pattern involved a system of dual administration with Mongolian officials, representing Kublai and his interests, working on every level. Also a feature in Kublai's new khanate was a system of branch administrations, to take charge of the regional government. Taking part in them were various imperial officials, appointed by the khan, along with the representatives of other interested parties, including princes. The latter held land throughout Mongol China and had a right to participate in regional government. Out of this system, China's province system developed.

To make sure that this imperial writ was carried out, Kublai extended the old Mongolian postal system, or *jam,* into China. Messages and sometimes goods were carried on horseback, by boat, even on foot from one end of China to the other, often in record time. To enhance the reliability of the system, Mongolian ponies, which could forage on their own, replaced the more dependent grain-fed Chinese horses.

In this and other ways, Kublai ruled China largely in the Mongol mold and lived a more or less Mongolian life. He trekked with the seasons, hunted the animals that the Mongols had always hunted in the traditional ways, drank fermented mare's milk, ate mutton soup, and generally lived on the margins of China near the steppe that he loved. As time went on, there were no real barriers to Chinese participation in government but the Chinese officials of the Yuan court had to assimilate to a court culture that was anything

BELOW **This scene from the thirteenth-century** *Mongol Invasions Scroll* depicts a Japanese warrior boarding a ship to kill the Mongolian leader of the second Mongolian invasion in 1281.

but Chinese. Some of it rubbed off on them and the Yuan dynasty was an important era of change for almost all aspects of Chinese culture.

The Weakening of the Yuan Dynasty

Kublai was entirely successful in creating a power base in China as well as a dynasty that was to rule much or all of China for almost a century. However, he never established himself as the ruler of a reconstituted Mongolian empire, recognized by all Mongolian groups. His constant quest for unity ended up seriously weakening his regime.

Primarily in pursuit of this unity, Kublai's armies twice invaded Japan, an island never within the reach of any Chinese dynasty, in 1274 and 1281. Both times, after their initial successes, Yuan armies, comprised of Mongols, Jurchen from Manchuria, Koreans, and Chinese, were heavily defeated, with a little extra help, according to Japanese tradition, from the wind. (This was the famous *kamikaze,* "divine wind," that was called upon again to save Japan in 1945 from the invading allies.) Mongol armies were much more successful in Burma, controlling it. Java, attacked in 1292, did not even come fully within the Chinese sphere of influence, although it had been visited by Chinese merchants.

The most protracted of all Yuan dynasty efforts to expand its control, and the bloodiest and most expensive in treasure, were efforts against Vietnam. The peninsula was, at the time, ruled by two states, Vietnamese Annam, under

the Tran dynasty in the north, and the city state of Champa, whose rulers spoke a Malayo–Polynesian language in what is now Central Vietnam. The Mongols warred against each, starting with an overland expedition against Annam that reached its capital in 1258. Later, in 1281, they moved against Champa itself, by sea, at the same time pressuring Annam to support the venture. The result was a complete disaster. Not only was the Mongol attack on Champa repulsed in very difficult terrain, but a struggle began with Vietnam that went almost to the end of Kublai's reign. It proved as much a quagmire for the Mongols as it did for the Americans and their allies centuries later.

ABOVE **This sheep and goat painting is by Zhao Mengfu,** a preeminent painter in the early Yuan dynasty. He gained favor with Kublai Khan as a regular official serving the Mongol court.

Kublai's Later Rule

Also weighing on Kublai in his old age were continual difficulties along his Central Asian frontier. Much of this was due to his civil war with Qaidu (1236–1301). Qaidu was a grandson of Ögödei (reigned 1229–1241) whose line had been excluded from succession in 1251. He nursed his grievances and built up a power base in Turkistan and Siberia, from which he attacked Kublai's armies and supporters. In 1277, Qaidu even seriously threatened Kublai's control over Mongolia, taking and pillaging the old Mongolian capital of Qaraqorum. It took Kublai until 1282 to restore final order but in 1292 Qaidu took over Qaraqorum for a second time, forcing the ageing Kublai to take the field to battle against him in person. Qaidu outlived Kublai, and continued to be a threat deep into the reign of Kublai's chosen successor, his grandson Temür Öljeitü (reigned 1294–1307).

Despite all of these difficulties, Kublai lived to the ripe old age of 80. No other Yuan dynasty ruler lived or ruled as long nor was as successful as Kublai, despite the continuing and extensive problems in Central Asia and with enormous foreign expansion. Thanks to the journals and reports from Marco Polo, the West was well informed about his rule and his empire.

CHABUI-QATUN

Chabui-qatun (died 1281) was the primary wife of Kublai and like other Mongolian imperial women before her was highly influential. She was the mother of three of Kublai's four sons, including the heir apparent, Zhenjin (1243–1285), and the grandmother of Kublai's successor, Temür Öljeitü. She encouraged her husband to accept Tibetan Buddhism as an official religion and supported the Tibetan monks who began converting the Mongol elite. To that end she maintained active connections with the prelates of the Sa-skya family who later established a special relationship with Kublai. Her interest in Tibetan Buddhism is witnessed by numerous letters and other documents in Tibetan collections. These documents show her as a woman with a mind of her own and a powerful force in Mongol China. She also protected the Song imperial family from any revengeful attacks.

RIGHT **Dhritarashtra, the Guardian King of the East** is shown using music to spread Buddhist teachings. Tibetan Buddhism was practiced among the Mongol nobility.

Religion and Culture

Mongol China was religiously and culturally diverse. This diversity was due to foreign
rulers and their willingness to consider more than purely Chinese traditions,
including the state religion of Lamaism and a new international art.

Before coming to China, the Mongols were mostly adherents to their own religious traditions. These focused on shamanism, rain-making, and fertility magic. Some Mongols were also Nestorian Christians. Even before moving beyond the steppe they had acquired some knowledge of Buddhism. Genghis Khan himself favored native religious practitioners, but he also showed his royal patronage and support to Chinese Daoists, Buddhist missionaries from Tibet, even a Zen monk. Later Mongol rulers continued this tradition of patronage of all the

BELOW **Sa-skya Pandita** was a Tibetan spiritual leader and Buddhist scholar who became well known throughout India, China, Mongolia, and Tibet.

religions with little preference shown to any. In spite of this, Tibetan Buddhism grew rapidly in importance.

At the time of Kublai, a number of competing Tibetan sects were active at court. The most important of these and directly patronized by Kublai and his primary wife, Chabui, were members of the Sa-skya sect. The Sa-skya had originally appeared among the Mongols in the 1240s when Kun-dga rgyal-mtshan (1182–1252), better known as the Sa-skya Pandita, went north to the court of the Mongol prince Köten, who was responsible for Mongol military operations in Tibet. The Pandita wanted to stop raids against Tibetan monastic groups. He took with him his two nephews, Phyag-na (1239–1267) and Aphags-pa (1235–1280), and they remained among the Mongols after the Pandita's death in 1251. The then Prince Kublai heard of them and brought both to his court where he established a personal relationship with the young but highly learned Aphags-pa.

When Kublai became the first ruler of the Mongol Khanate of China, he continued to patronize Aphags-pa. He adopted the Sa-skya variant of Tibetan Buddhism as the official religion for his khanate. According to Tibetan sources, Kublai established the *Mchod-gnas* relationship with the Tibetan lama, in which Kublai became the *Yon-bdag,* "giving lord," that is, patron and the protector of Buddhism, and Aphags-pa the *Mchod-gnas,* "sacrificer," responsible for religious practice. Kublai became a *chakravartin,* or "wheel [of the dharma] turning" king of Indian tradition, and Aphags-pa became a *dharmaraja,* "dharma king," the religious equivalent of a secular ruler, with powers in the religious realm equivalent to those of Kublai as secular monarch.

Although Buddhism had been favored at other times in Chinese history, there was no parallel to the role of Tibetan Buddhism in Mongol China in any other period of Chinese history. The Tibetans not only dominated the religious life of the time but also introduced Tibetan science, including Tibetan medicine. They also strongly influenced the Chinese art of the time, not just temple art over which they had direct control, but even secular painting that included a new use of colors and different ways to lay on paint.

Art from Mongol China

The art of Mongol China was a mixture of Chinese and other traditions. While painting and calligraphy continued the Song and Jin traditions, literati painting became less important (the Mongols used the imperial examination system only sporadically). Professional artists were more important than ever before. A significant difference between Song and Yuan painting was the predilection of the latter for strong color, this predilection perhaps showing west Asian or Tibetan influence. This style can be seen in the work of Zhao Mengfu (1254–1322), the greatest painter and calligrapher of the period. His paintings combined the impressions of the Song, with its empty spaces and hints of landscape, with rich use of color, producing an entirely new Yuan style of painting. Also new, but representing Chinese tradition rather than any foreign input, was Zhao's calligraphy. Although rooted in the past, it was strongly emotional and rejected the dry approaches of most Song literati calligraphers. During this period, Chinese calligraphy exerted its influence as far away as Mongol Iran, which saw the blossoming of a golden age of Islamic calligraphy. Chinese painting also arrived in Iran and Iranian miniaturists attempted to produce their own variants of Chinese landscapes, as well as using Chinese colors and brushstrokes.

ABOVE **Ancient medical illustrations** at the Lhasa Tibetan Medicine Hospital have diagrams representing traditional medical remedies found in ancient books.

Another art of Yuan times was its porcelain. Porcelain itself was an artform that had developed throughout the ages, the art of making it had flourished under the Song. Yuan improved on this artform by introducing their own particular variant of porcelain. This was blue and white porcelain, noted for its intense cobalt underglaze, reflecting the Mongol imperial color of sky blue. The artists also applied West Asian subjects, design elements, and even shapes. So successful was this new type of porcelain that it became widely sought after and imitated in the West, even in places as distant as the kingdom of fourteenth century Bulgaria, and gave rise to the first international art craze.

The Development of Literary Culture

Another important cultural development of Mongol times was secular literature. Drama was nothing new in Mongol China, but the Mongols developed drama to new heights. Some 167 Yuan plays survive, including the famous Yuan reworking of the *Xixiangji*, "Record of the Western Pavilion." Yuan is also noted for its vernacular fiction, made available to a wide range of people in cheap printed editions.

LEFT **This Yuan dynasty vase,** with dragon, phoenix, cloud, and floral motifs, would have held a single stem of plum blossom. The curves of the vase hinted at a female form.

The Liberalization of Trade

The Mongols strongly stimulated the Chinese economy. Their empire fostered international trade to levels that were never seen or experienced before. When land links were cut, sea trade expanded rapidly.

Before the Mongols, China's trade had mostly been internal, between Jin and Song China, for example, and within the two competing empires themselves. Overseas trade did exist, coming from the Song southeast. This had grown quickly under the Southern Song, but the old Silk Route had lost much of its importance. The Song were almost entirely cut off from this route and the Jin were blocked by Tangut Xixia. This situation changed as the Mongols expanded rapidly, and progressively brought north and west China under their control. By the 1250s, much of China was part of a world centered on the Mongol capital of Qaraqorum. Trade moved freely and in large quantities across Eurasia with few obstacles. Facilitating trade were *ortaq,* or associations of Mongol aristocrats and merchants. The former provided the financing, the latter provided the knowhow. The profits shared between the two groups were immense.

Although Mongol lengthy civil wars, including Kublai's wars to become the new Great Khan,

reduced the volume of land trade after 1260, they did not eliminate it entirely. It was too lucrative, and too well established. Land trade even enjoyed a highly renewed upsurge in the early fourteenth century after the Mongols made a temporary peace. In any case, more than compensating for any decline in traffic along the traditional Silk Route was an expansion of sea commerce.

Trade Goods: Tea and Porcelain

Within China, which was united after 1279, the main trade goods continued to be what they had been a century earlier. The Yuan continued the tea trade throughout China and transported large amounts of rice and other foodstuffs. The Yuan merchants also moved enormous quantities of porcelain and other consumer goods, including textiles, from one end of the Yuan Empire to the other. Externally, trade was focused on goods seen as exotics. These included fine Chinese textiles for which there was considerable demand in the rest of the Mongol world. Also traded extensively were spices and medicinals, including such rare commodities as grains-of-paradise, all the way from Africa. Exciting new commodities, at least as components of world trade, were tea and, of course, porcelain.

Exactly when tea drinking began to catch on in the West is unclear. By the time of the Mongol Empire, tea was widely available throughout Iran and in Turkistan as a rare medicinal and, more and more as time passed, as a common beverage. This led to the tea craze of the centuries that followed. The tea trade was primarily overland, with a maritime commerce in tea developing much more slowly. One primary customer for tea were the Mongols themselves. The earliest recipe for "Mongolian tea" made by boiling a tea brick in milk is dated from the fourteenth century. Soon such tea became a feature of Mongolian life.

The porcelain trade also began as a land trade but this specific commodity, for which demand grew rapidly over time, soon became an important component of goods shipped by sea. This fact is substantiated by a growing number of shipwrecks with loads of porcelain being recovered.

Managing the Trade

Managing the ocean trade for the Mongols were a variety of foreigners. Some came from Muslim families long resident in China. Their most well known representative was Pu Shougeng, a Perso–Chinese who managed overseas trade for the Song in the second half of the thirteenth century before taking up with the Mongols. He supplied ships to them for a fleet to fight his former masters as well as providing trade expertise.

Europeans too took an active part in helping the Mongols in China to organize their trade. Playing a lead role were merchants from the great trading city of Genoa, Italy. The Genoese, in fact, not only traded with Mongol China, but continued to maintain connections in southeast Asia long after the fall of the Yuan Empire. As a result, they set the stage for European economic expansion into the Indian Ocean in the sixteenth century. On land, Muslim merchants, many like Pu Shougeng, actually a resident in China, also played a key part in the extensive *ortaq* trade.

Among the most important trade ports for the overseas trade was Quanzhou in Fujian (the Zayton of Marco Polo), noted for its large foreign communities. Guangzhou, better known as Canton, later played an important role. The old Song capital, described in detail by Marco Polo,

LEFT **In this painting from the Yuan dynasty** of a nobleman on horseback, the flat use of color adds to the detachment and restraint typical of Yuan paintings.

was important as well. The sophistication of its economy completely flabbergasted the Venetian. Marco Polo had never seen anything like it. The amount of trade running through other Chinese cities was nearly as significant.

THE BEGINNINGS OF SEA TRADING AND EXPLORATION

Yuan China built upon foundations already laid down by the Song and expanded considerably. In the mid-fourteenth century, for the first time in Chinese history, a large portion of China's north–south commerce was carried by ships, to avoid rebel-infested areas. Kublai also, unsuccessfully, attempted to physically expand his political control, in part to gain control over the trade. The city state of Champa, for example, was correctly identified as the focus of the southern seas trade of the time. Kublai wanted to control this area in order to monopolise Indian Ocean trade. He failed to take Champa, but overseas trade continued to expand, reaching a high point under the Ming during the great voyages of Zheng He (1371–1433). These voyages were based upon early Yuan-era explorations, and the extensive geographical knowledge that was gained from visiting the Islamic world.

RIGHT **Ancient Chinese ships** salvaged from the bottom of the China and Java Seas contained cargoes of gold, silver, and porcelain, confirming centuries-old trade links between China and the West.

Contact with the West

The appearance of the Mongol Empire ushered in an era of intense international exchange. China, although remote, was not isolated and was visited frequently by Europeans, among other foreign guests, who returned with tales about China.

ABOVE **Franciscan monks** were sent as envoys of Pope Innocent IV. This fourteenth-century manuscript shows monks in China preparing herbal remedies.

By 1241, the Mongol Empire reached well into Eastern Europe. In that year the Mongols mounted a grand invasion, into Germany, Moravia, and Hungary, and through the Balkans. Well aware that a new power had emerged, Western powers hurried to make contact, gather intelligence, and possibly gain a new ally in the fight against Islam. Several major embassies were sent by the Pope. The first in 1245–1247 was led by the Franciscan, John of Plano Carpini. The embassy arrived in Mongolia in time to witness the election and coronation of Güyük Khan (reigned 1246–1248). After his return, John wrote up his adventures in a widely disseminated *Hystoria Mongolorum,* "History of the Mongols." This was the first substantial report of the Central Asian conquerors to reach the West. Also leaving behind a detailed and factual account of everything he saw or heard was another Franciscan envoy, William of Rubruck. He went to Mongolia during the years 1253 to 1255, and lived at the new Mongolian capital, Qaraqorum. Other envoys went to Mongol princes and official envoys were followed by merchants, few of whom have left behind detailed travel accounts of their travels.

Westerners in Mongol China

Although the establishment of Kublai's khanate of China marked the beginning of an era of civil war and the end of easy contacts across Eurasia, they continued nonetheless. A number of papal envoys, following in the pioneering footsteps of Plano Carpini and William of Rubruck, made their way to China. They even managed to establish a Catholic mission there. The envoys included John of Monte Corvino, who was the first archbishop, to Qanbaliq or Mongol Beijing. He is said to have translated the Psalter into Mongolian or more likely, a Turkic language. His translation has not survived. Also traveling to Mongol China was John of Marignolli, who reached Qanbaliq in 1342. He came bearing a gift of powerful warhorses for Toghon Temür (reigned 1333–1368), the last ruler of Mongol China. His visit is actually recorded in the official history of the dynasty, the *Yuan Shi*, "History of the Yuan." John of Marignolli survived to tell his tale and returned to papal headquarters in Avignon in 1353. Another Western visitor to inland China was Odoric of Pordenone (1265–1331), who left behind a short account reporting on the status of his Franciscan order in China.

Also traveling to China in numbers were soldiers and merchants. Kublai Khan had, for example, had a Russian guard, which existed for some years although cut off from its Russian homeland. Merchants included the famous Polo family. Marco (1254–1324) spent 17 years in Kublai's China (1275–1292), traveling quite extensively, and has left the most famous of all medieval travelogues, written in the Western *lingua franca* of Old French and widely disseminated. The Polo family were by no means the only Western merchants in China, as witnessed by the enormous amount of commercial intelligence researched in Europe about conditions in China and in nearby areas.

Cultural and Scientific Exchanges

In addition to the direct exchange of people (Mongols traveling to Europe, Europeans visiting China), also taking place were indirect exchanges of cultural goods. These included exchanges of science and technology between the two different parts of the world. An important part of the scientific connections were comprehensive exchanges of medical knowledge. Much of this took place through the Islamic world acting as an intermediary. At the time of the Mongol invasions, European medicine, although having its own folk traditions as well, was based in Greek humoral medicine, the ancient medicine of Hippocrates

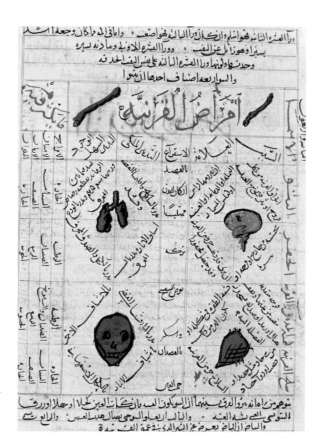

LEFT **This table of medical information** about the skull, lungs, stomach, and heart, is from the *Canon of Medicine* by Avicenna (990–1037), a Persian physician.

of Cos (*c.* 460–*c.* 370 BCE) and Galen (*c.* 130–200). Their works, along with other classics of Greek medicine, had been translated into Arabic where they formed the basis for the medieval Arabic as well as the Western medical tradition.

The Mongols had their own medicine, but began using the medical traditions of others as soon as expansion began. Mongol medicine emphasized a limited intake of herbs and the consumption of specific parts of animals to treat particular conditions. They also had methods for wound treatment and bone repair. None of the practices of the Mongols was as sophisticated or as well developed as the medical systems of the world outside Mongolia, with their rich written traditions, well-thought-out theories, and thousands of herbs and many other forms of treatment. This included Arabic medicine, with its numerous Greek components.

Although other forms of medicine were popular in Mongol China, including Chinese and Tibetan, it was Arabic medicine that ultimately became the preferred medicine of the elite there. This was also the case throughout the Mongol world as a whole. In China, the Mongols attempted to introduce Arabic medicine on a broad scale, establishing government offices officially promoting Arabic medicine, and even making it available to the people as a whole. They also

LEFT **Hippocrates, an ancient Greek physican,** is known as the father of medicine. His teachings were translated and used in Arabic medicine, which was adopted by the elite in Mongol China.

promoted a vast translation effort to make readily available the medical lore and specific treatments of Arabic medicine in China. This included the compilation of a huge encyclopedia, with more than 3,500 dense manuscript pages, of which major fragments still survive, called the *Huihui Yaofang*, "Muslim Medicinal Recipes." This is the only text in the Chinese tradition to quote Galen and other Western authorities by name. It was important enough for a new edition be made during the Ming period. Although the medicine in *Huihui Yaofang* draws extensively from Arabic medicine text, its working language was Persian. This was a language that was well known to most Westerners in China, including Marco Polo.

This text typically shows not pure Arabic medicine but carefully reworked and adapted Arabic medicine that uses many of the terms and categories of Chinese medicine. It shows Tibetan influence, in the humoral system, for example. Tibet, at the time, had its own Western medical traditions as well as Indian and even Central Asian ones. The Mongols promoted a cosmopolitan Eurasian tradition of medicine in which all the major traditions of medicine were integrated. As part of this, Chinese medical ideas were even transmitted across to Iran and ultimately to Europe. From this, Europe avidly translated Arabic texts for its own consumption.

Geographical Lore

Another area of active East–West exchange during the Mongol era was that of geographical knowledge. The Mongols were avid consumers of all different kinds of geographical information due to their strong focus on learning. This intense interest was reflected in Mongol China with the production of some of the world's finest maps. They were based on Greek knowledge from the astronomer Ptolemy (83–161) and others, as expanded by the Arabs. One result was the drawing up of the great atlas, the *Guang Yu Tu*, "Extended Map of the Earth," compiled by the cartographer Zhu Siben (1273–1337) from a variety of sources, many of them of clear Islamic origin. The atlas is not only remarkable for its detail for East Asia, but also for the extensive information that it relays about areas quite remote from East Asia, including Africa. It is shown in its correct shape, something in which Zhu Siben was centuries ahead of European mapmakers. Other Yuan sources do contain still more detail about Africa, including extensive information about interior west Africa, the land of medieval Mali. It was the source of much of the gold of

BELOW **Ptolemy** was a highly regarded mathematician, geographer, astrologer, and astronomer. His extensive knowledge influenced Mongol cartographers.

the Western world and the Middle East. Also shown on Zhu's maps is Europe, including many of its most important cities. Zhu's maps influenced future generations of cartographers.

Astronomy and Other Exchanges

As was the case with medicine and geography, the Arabic world also transmitted to China, Greek astronomy, which had been expanded upon by Arab and Persian thinkers. A typical product of the exchanges involved, besides the many astronomical instruments from the Mongol period still surviving in Beijing, there is a calendar now housed in the collection of a large Russian museum. It begins its dating system in 1206, the date of the formal establishment of Genghis Khan, and is written in Persian and also Chinese. The Persian writing style has been copied using a Chinese brush, showing the strong influence of Chinese calligraphy. The paper appears to be Chinese. A similar calendar shows an effort by the Mongols to create a universal dynasty that incorporated a wide range of teachings, practices, philosophies, and social ideologies.

The age was, in any case, a truly international one. For example, coins in the Mongol West, had Chinese, Mongolian, and Persian inscriptions. The Mongols in Iran also attempted, unsuccessfully, to introduce Chinese-style paper money. It was the first effort to print documents there and although printing was not followed up in the Islamic world, it certainly was pursued in the West. Another important Mongol-era contribution to Europe was gunpowder weapons and firearms, transmitted from China.

LEFT **Gunpowder weapons** became a highly sought after trade commodity during the Mongol Yuan dynasty.

FOOD AND MULTICULTURALISM

An important area of cultural exchange during the Mongol era was food. Mongol court cuisine—as witnessed in China by the imperial dietary manual *Yinshan zhengyao*, "Proper and Essential Things for the Emperor's Food and Drink," presented to the court in 1330—spread from one side of Eurasia to the other. Traveling along with it were the porcelain vessels in which the court cuisine, which emphasized soups and drinks, was consumed. Some of the same recipes found in China and apparently regularly consumed there also occur in the Middle Eastern cookbooks of the period. Some European recipes even made their way to China, such as piroshky, the subject of a recipe in the *Yinshan zhengyao* and possibly coming from Kublai's Russian guard. One celebrated dessert of the Mongol era is still with us, baklava, the earliest recipe for which is found in a Chinese encyclopedia, called there *güllach*, "flower bread food," and not by the later name for this pastry, derived from a Mongolian word.

RIGHT **Piroshky** were originally from Russia and are traditionally served with borscht (sugarbeet soup). The origins are Slavic but have been adapted by many East Asian cultures. Similar food is served as *jiaozi* in China and *gyoza* in Japan.

Marco Polo

A Chinese Vision of Marco Polo

A fourteenth-century statue of Marco Polo intricately carved and gilded in gold leaf shows him wearing traditional Chinese clothing. He is seated on a chair from the Mongol court.

Did Marco Polo Go to China?

Some have cast doubts on Marco Polo's veracity and have claimed that he never went to China at all, and his reports were taken from Arab and Persian records. There is much in his account that is truly fantastic, but much of his detail is confirmed by other reliable sources. Marco Polo (seen above in this Italian mosaic by Enrico Podio) has been criticized for his apparent ignorance of the Chinese language and for not mentioning such things as the Great Wall of China or footbinding, but this is unfair. He is more likely to have traveled using Persian, Mongolian, and a Turkic language rather than Chinese, given conditions in Mongol China and at Kublai's court. Also, the Great Wall was not built until the Ming period and footbinding only became important later.

Marco Polo (1254–1324) was the most famous European traveler of his time and left behind the best known and most influential travelogue in history. More than any other explorer, Marco Polo has formed our image of China.

Marco Polo grew up in the powerful Italian city state of Venice; a member of a great trading house. His family, represented by Polo's father, Niccolò, and uncle, Maffeo, took advantage of the security and ease of communication afforded by Mongol control in Eurasia and expanded its trade far into the interior, eventually reaching China in 1266. Sent back by Kublai with a Mongolian ambassador and a request for 100 Western missionaries, they returned to Venice to await the election of a new pope to reply to the Khan's letter. This took some time and only two missionaries were sent, neither of them braving the long journey east. The two brothers arrived in China again in 1274, this time bringing with them Niccolò's young son, Marco.

The Polos subsequently remained in China for 17 years from 1275 to 1292. Marco seems to have found the favor of Kublai, who appointed him to an official post, possibly as part of the imperial bodyguard. In any case, Marco moved in elite circles and gained an intimate knowledge of Mongol China and its workings. As part of his official tasks, he traveled extensively, apparently on the khan's business. Among places that were visited were the old Song capital of Hangzhou, described in some detail, and Mongol Yunnan. Marco was the first European to visit it. Marco heard of but did not visit Japan, but his notice of the Japanese islands is the first mention recorded in European literature.

Marco's greatest mission came in 1292, when the Polo family were finally permitted to return to Italy. The land route had by then been cut by Mongolian civil wars and Marco and his father and uncle were asked on their way back by sea to deliver a Mongol princess to Iran. They did this successfully and on the way Marco collected a wealth of information about Southeast Asia and the countries of the Indian Ocean. These foreign places were largely unknown in Europe.

Marco Polo Leaving Venice

The Venetian explorer's account of China inspired European navigators to venture into the unknown. This detail from the *Travels of Marco Polo*, was illuminated in England by the artist known as Johannes around 1400.

Finally returning to Italy in 1295, Marco heard about the death of his patron Kublai. Shortly thereafter, he was enlisted by Venice to fight in one of its many wars and became a prisoner of war. While imprisoned, Marco dictated his memoirs, in Old French, the great language of commerce, to a writer of romances, who embellished them. Several versions of the text exist today, which all differ quite substantially in detail and completeness. Some are even in languages other than the original Old French. Despite the variation, Marco Polo's memoirs were an immediate sensation and few books have been more translated or have had a greater impact upon the wider European intellect. Typically, Columbus is said to have taken a copy of Marco Polo's memoirs along as he sailed off to search out the exotic realm of the Great Khan as described in them in detail.

The Expulsion of the Mongols

The Mongols ruled China for another 74 years after the death of Kublai but their influence steadily declined. Ultimately they were expelled by Chinese rebels who first took over the south and then conquered the whole country.

ABOVE **Guanyin,** China's Bodhisattva of Compassion, is an example of the white porcelain figurines made during the Yuan dynasty.

The 30 years following the death of Kublai in 1294 were the high points of Mongol rule in China. During this time, the Yuan government remained highly effective, and the Mongols had few enemies, foreign or domestic. This situation slowly changed as conflict between members of the Mongol ruling elite limited Mongol abilities to respond to the problems occurring in China.

Kublai's successor was his grandson Temür Öljeitü (reigned 1294–1307). He continued his grandfather's existing policies, and maintained stability, ending further plans for more foreign expeditions. Temür is best known for brokering peace between feuding Mongol groups, and briefly restoring the vista of a united Mongolia. Not so successful was the rule of Temür's successor, Khaishan (reigned 1307–1311). Khaishan came to the throne as part of a reaction against the Sinification of Kublai and

Temür. Instead of uniting the old Mongolian empire, as his supporters had hoped, he proved ineffectual and tyrannical.

Following Khaishan came a succession of short-lived rulers. They included Ayurbarwada (reigned 1311–1320), one of the few Mongol emperors of China with the ability to speak and read Chinese, and Shidebala (reigned 1321–1323), just 18 at the time of his accession. He was pro-Chinese but his rule was ineffectual due to the Mongol conservatives at court.

Conflict and Decline (1323–1370)

Shidebala was assassinated in 1323 and the conservative Mongols placed their own candidate on the throne, Yesün Temür (reigned 1323–1328). He arrested and killed Shidebala's assassins, but was soon himself caught up in the violence. He died suddenly in 1328, leaving behind a nine-year-old successor, Aragibag (reigned 1328–1328), who disappeared during what became a fully-fledged and bloody civil war.

After some years of conflict, and frequent changes of rulers, Toghon Temür (reigned 1333–1370), the last emperor of Yuan, took the throne. Although ruling for some years, his reign

ZHU YUANZHANG AND THE WHITE LOTUS SOCIETY

Most important of the sectarian groups in rebellion against the Yuan was the White Lotus Society. It focused on the coming of the savior Buddha Maitreya and had branches scattered across central China, united by common ideological traditions. The founder of the Ming dynasty, Zhu Yuanzhang (reigned 1368–98) was involved with a rebel army growing out of this group.

Although not an early favorite to prosper and form a new dynasty, since his territories were not particularly rich and he had powerful neighbors, Zhu bided his time as most of his competitors eliminated themselves. Those surviving were attacked and overcome by Zhu. Although it took some years to secure the surrender of all Mongol holdouts in China, Zhu took Qanbaliq in 1368, forcing Toghon Temür to flee into the steppe. There he and his successors continued to claim succession to Kublai as Northern Yuan. Zhu established a new dynasty that was to become one of the most prosperous and successful in Chinese history.

RIGHT **Bodhisattva Maitreya,** shown in this eleventh-century bronze sculpture seated and waiting to become Buddha, was vital to the White Lotus Society, a type of Buddhist sectarianism that appealed to Chinese people.

witnessed the gradual loss of power in China by the Mongols, who soon controlled little more than the areas around their capital and a few outlying provinces.

Chinese Resistance to Mongol Rule

Mongol rule was relatively stable in the north, almost to the end of the dynasty. By contrast, south China never forgot its Song heritage and remained a bastion of Chinese conservatism and a protector of Chinese cultural values. At first, resistance was passive. Large parts of the south Chinese elite simply refused to acknowledge the existence of the Mongols or to take service with them. This deprived the Yuan of much needed cadres, although many did serve. During the Yuan dynasty, the Mongol rulers discriminated against the former Song Chinese, referring to them as *Manzi*, "southern Barbarians." The legal system favored Mongols, other non Chinese, and northerners, who received the lion's share of government posts.

By the 1330s, the weakening of the Yuan central authority, gripped by civil conflict, was becoming increasingly obvious. "Banditry" became a growing problem. Much of this "banditry" arose for local reasons, but there was

also a general sense of resistance to the Mongols as well. Stoking the fires of popular resistance were failed Mongol financial policies, what was perceived as a generalized corruption, and the favored position of the hated Tibetan Buddhists.

In the 1340s, "bandits" began to seize towns. They formed alliances with the local elite. The latter also formed private armies to deal with the "bandits." These armies quickly became a two-edged sword as the owners of private armies formed alliances with each other and also with "bandits" for self-protection. Local armies supported competition between regions for dominance as successors to the Mongols, who were becoming more and more irrelevant to the course of events.

Some regional associations were ruled by allies of the Mongols. Most were positioned along the coast and were accessible to Yuan fleets. Others were against them, mostly those of the interior. Among the major enemies of the court was the former salt smuggler Zhang Shicheng, who controlled the lower Yangzi River and established a dynasty called Great Zhou. Another infamous salt smuggler, Fang Guozhen, became the enemy of the Mongols when he and his men attacked Yuan dynasty officials on the coast of Zeijiang.

ABOVE **Buddha Maitreya,** is a key figure in the devotion to Buddhism. This statue at the Bingling Si Caves is an example of ancient Buddhist carvings.

Late Imperial China: The Ming and Qing Dynasties

Introduction

China's last dynasties, the Ming (1368–1644) and the Qing (1644–1911), marked a glorious end to the imperial tradition and heralded China's troubled entry into the modern world. Often treated as a unit, the Ming and Qing were fundamentally different.

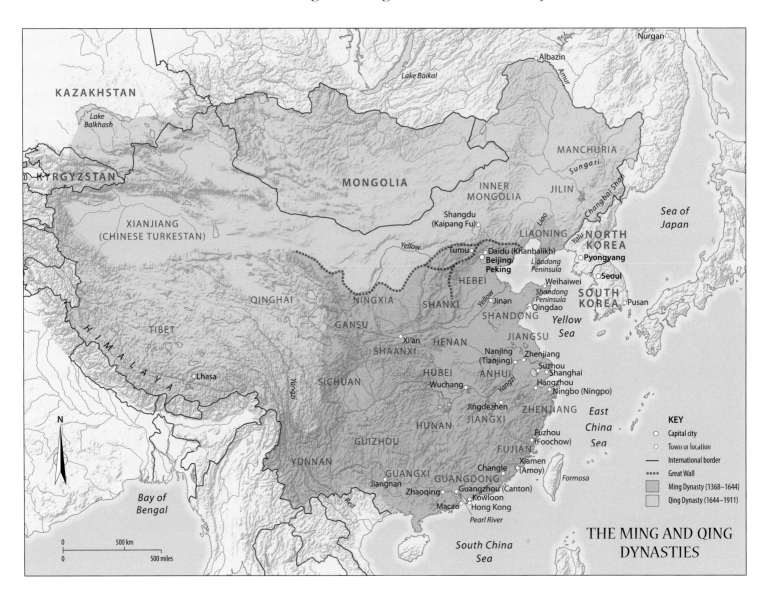

THE MING AND QING DYNASTIES

KEY
- ○ Capital city
- ○ Town or location
- — International border
- ···· Great Wall
- ▨ Ming Dynasty (1368–1644)
- ▨ Qing Dynasty (1644–1911)

Following the Mongol Yuan dynasty, the Ming dynasty can be seen as a response by the ethnic Han people to the experience of foreign rule. Efforts were made by the Ming founder to revive and strengthen traditional values and practices, and foreign contacts were discouraged. The Ming government was pre-occupied with defense of its northern frontier against the possibility of renewed invasion.

Ming China grew to be the wealthiest and most populous society in the world. During the fifteenth and sixteenth centuries, private and illegal commerce thrived as foreign demand for Chinese silk and porcelain brought an influx of silver from the emerging world trading system. As the economy flourished, wealthy urban centers developed, especially in the lower Yangzi region where the Ming elite developed a very sophisticated and luxurious lifestyle.

By the late 1500s, Jesuit reports to Europe described Ming China as a prosperous and orderly society ruled by learned scholar–officials, a vision of an alternative kind of polity that was seized on by Western Enlightenment thinkers who wished to transform their own societies. In the early seventeenth century, government

LEFT *One Hundred Flowers* by the Ming-dynasty artist Chen Jiayan (1539–1625) is painted on silk and shows the art motifs that were very popular during this highly creative period.

corruption and the neglect of rural problems led to widespread insurrections and the overthrow of the Ming emperor. This catastrophe was followed by the entry of Manchu forces from beyond the Great Wall and their occupation of Beijing, where a new dynasty was proclaimed.

Manchu Rule in the Qing Empire

The Qing Empire was a solution to the problem of the age-old conflict between the materially wealthy agricultural population of China and the militarily powerful peoples of the vast Asian heartland. Over the second millennium CE the military advantage tipped inexorably to the Inner Asian peoples. The Ming period was a heroic and generally successful effort to repel and resist the northern invaders. However, the Qing was the conquest dynasty that solved the problem completely, uniting Han China with a large part of Inner Asia.

Entering China, the Manchus claimed the Mandate of Heaven and portrayed themselves as champions of order. They called their new state the Qing (Pure or Uncorrupt), an antidote to all that was wrong in China. The Manchus, despite their small numbers, were able to create a stable order that governed China for more than two and a half centuries.

With careful study of Chinese history, the Manchus created institutions adapted to the rule of multiple ethnic groups. A bi-national state structure was set up that used dual staffing by Chinese and Manchu officials at the upper levels and documents written in both Chinese and Manchu. Patronage of Chinese culture, the promotion of Confucian orthodoxy, continuation of the Ming law code, and Ming bureaucratic institutions all enabled the Manchus to recruit talented Chinese officials through the examination system. Across a vast arc of Inner Asia, including Tibet, Xinjiang (Chinese Turkistan), Mongolia, and also Manchuria (the northeast), Qing emperors patronized local rulers and religious leaders directly.

The End of Imperial China

So successful was Qing rule that the population doubled to more than 300 million in the 1700s and rose to 450 million in the 1800s. Like their Ming predecessors, the Qing were more oriented toward Inner Asia than they were toward the sea and maritime affairs. The Manchus were to pay the price for their inattention to international affairs. By the 1840s, China's balance of trade was reversed and a series of wars with the Western powers and humiliating unequal treaties eroded Qing sovereignty. Internally, the dynasty was rocked by domestic rebellions that challenged Qing authority. The Manchus managed to survive for several more decades.

By the late nineteenth century, the traditional values and Qing institutions were no longer adequate in the modern world. The initial reform efforts were aimed at military modernization in the face of Western pressure. Defeat by the Japanese in the 1890s made it clear that more profound changes were needed. After 1900, a desperate Qing government turned to even more radical measures, such as ending the traditional examination system and even drafting a constitution. The Qing dynasty was overthrown in 1911, ending two millennia of imperial rule. It left behind a redefined, multinational China occupying more than twice the territory of the Ming dynasty.

LEFT **The brilliant copper red glaze** and exquisite workmanship of this peach blosson vase from the Qing dynasty was highly sought after in the West.

The Reconquest

Zhu Yuanzhang, founder of the Ming dynasty (1368–1644), was only the second peasant in all of Chinese history to become emperor. He brought an end to the first period during which all of China was subjected to foreign rule.

By the mid-1300s the Mongol Yuan dynasty, founded in 1279, was torn by internal rivalries, the rise of local rebellions, and eventually full-scale civil war. This was the world into which Zhu Yuanzhang was born, in central Anhui Province. He was the youngest son of a peasant family so poor that two of his older brothers were given up for adoption. Zhu was only 16 years old in 1344 when famine and plague killed his remaining family members. A destitute orphan, unable even to afford a burial plot for his parents, he joined a local Buddhist monastery. There, he learned to read and gained a basic understanding of Buddhist doctrines. Shortage of food compelled him, for a time, to wander as a begging monk, an experience that exposed him to the rebellion abroad in the land. He joined an insurgent group that was animated by an ideology that combined strong messianic ideas about the Maitreya, the Buddha of the Future, and the Manichean idea of a Prince of Brightness (Ming Wang), who would appear and deliver the world from its time of troubles.

Displaying aptitudes for military and political affairs, Zhu rose rapidly to leadership of an armed force and carved out a territory along the lower reaches of the Yangzi River. He established a regional state at Nanjing, recruited advisers, and organized a formal government. After a decade of fighting with rival regimes on all sides, Zhu Yuangzhang emerged triumphant, unified the Chinese heartland, captured the Yuan capital at Beijing, and drove the Mongols back into the northern grasslands. In an appeal to the people's expectations of an imminent world transformation and to cement a long-lasting legacy, he gave his new state the name Ming, and he took the reign name Hongwu, which translates to Vast Military Power.

Founding the Ming

Despite the name of his new dynasty Zhu Yuanzhang did not subscribe to the messianic beliefs of many of his followers. During his rise to power he recruited learned advisers and schooled himself in Confucian doctrine. His spectacular pronouncement claiming the Mandate of Heaven was a call for a conservative restoration of order. In an almost nationalistic indictment, he condemned the Mongols for their failure to observe Chinese moral standards, either in their familial relations or their political practices. He was particularly horrified by the Mongol marriage institutions in which a widow might be passed to other members of her husband's family, and by struggles for control of the throne where there

LEFT **An enamelled terracotta Ming-dynasty figure** from central China with its exaggerated hand is considered a revealing symbol of poverty.

MING AUTOCRACY

Zhu Yuanzhang's despotic style had important institutional consequences. When he suspected his chief minister of plotting to overthrow him, Zhu had the man executed along with hundreds of his relatives and associates. Furthermore, Zhu Yuanzhang abolished the central secretariat and eliminated the position of chief minister and decreed that anyone daring to recommend that such a position be reestablished should be executed. Thus administrative power that had traditionally been exercised by prime ministers passed to the emperor's hands, centralizing his control. This marked a significant expansion of imperial power at the expense of civil officialdom.

were no rules of succession. Once on the throne, Zhu outlawed the many unorthodox cults that had flourished during the time of civil war, and promoted, instead, orthodox Confucian notions about social hierarchy, filial piety, and undivided loyalty toward the ruler.

Despotic Rule

Emperor Yuanzhang left an indelible imprint on China. He was energetic, shrewd, pragmatic, and ruthless and he had a vision of what he wanted to accomplish. After 30 years of tireless legislation and adjustments, he fashioned an extensive set of institutions that would endure for centuries. His success came at a great price. The former peasant harbored a deep-seated hostility toward the many educated scholar–officials who surrounded him, the very people upon whom he depended to carry out his orders. His style of rule was far more harshly authoritarian than his predecessors in the Song or even the Yuan. His previous experience of warfare and political intrigue left him deeply scarred with paranoia and highly alert to threats, both real and imagined. On the throne his suspicious nature, intolerance of criticism, impatience, and lethal capacity for anger frequently led to bloody consequences.

Officials who felt his wrath were often beaten in the court in the presence of the emperor; those who remonstrated with him, even with the best of intentions, risked execution.

The Vision of an Emperor

The nature of Zhu Yuanzhang's vision for Chinese society can be gleaned from the many essays and texts he issued to guide his subjects. None are more revealing than a series of "Grand Pronouncements" or "Great Warnings" issued around the time of the 1380s. In these texts, litanies of crimes and insubordinations that had come to his attention, we can hear the emperor's anger and frustration across a wide spectrum of civil and military affairs. Increasingly aware of the limitations of his own power, Zhu used the Grand Pronouncements to reach out to the common people and to keep them on his side. To do this he declared that local schools be established so that sons of commoners could learn to read and write. Students learned the texts of the Grand Pronouncements and the Ming Code and groups were brought to the capital where they competed to recite what they had memorized from these lengthy tomes.

LEFT **A pair of courtesans,** realized in colored terracotta, demonstrate the courtesan's vital role in the culture of leisure and pleasure in the Ming courtly life.

BELOW **Zhu Yuanzhang (1328–1398)** was the authoritarian founder of the Ming dynasty.

National Reconstruction

China's national reconstruction in the wake of Mongol rule occupied the first three Ming emperors for half a century. The founder, Zhu Yuanzhang, completed the military pacification and occupation of Yuan territory, organized a comprehensive administrative structure, and undertook economic recovery measures.

Where warfare, famine, and disease had reduced the population of north China, Zhu Yuanzhang moved great numbers of people from the south. Peasant families were given livestock and excused from taxation for a number of years, criminals and their families were banished to the north for life, and soldiers were settled along the great frontier in military colonies that combined farming with manning outposts. Wealthy families from the lower Yangzi region, especially from areas that had supported the founder's rivals in the civil war, were moved to Nanjing where they both enriched the capital and could be kept under surveillance.

The new order the Ming founder created had two fundamental weaknesses that came to be related. The first was geopolitical. The new Ming capital at Nanjing on the south bank of the Yangzi River was a long way from the militarily sensitive northern frontier. This fact entailed a dangerous, strategic weakness: it obliged the emperor to entrust his largest military forces to commanders who were far away and hard to supervise. The emperor gave some thought to creating a second capital in the north so that he could maintain a tighter control over his field commanders, but nothing came of the proposal. The second issue, equally as dangerous to the dynasty, was the challenge of managing imperial offspring, princes who might compete for the throne. The solution was to

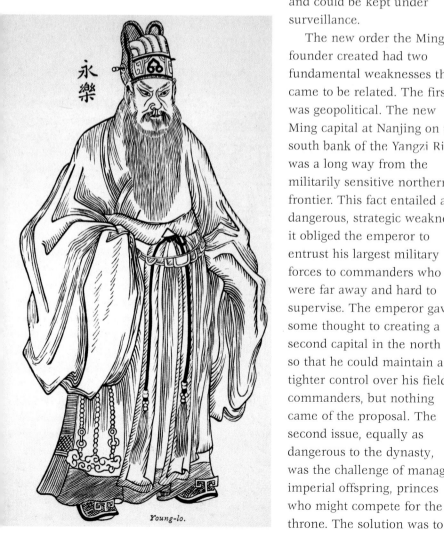

BELOW **Emperor Yongle** used Buddhism and its festivals to help calm the civil unrest of the Chinese frontiers.

Young-lo.

OBLIGATIONS TO THE STATE

The Ming population was divided into three hereditary categories with specified obligations to the state. The first group, the large majority, were the peasants, who were required to pay grain taxes and perform labor service. The next group included military households which provided sons for military service, and the third group were the artisan households sending craftsmen to work on large government projects such as the construction of palaces. Regulation of other occupations, such as merchants, was less formal. This arrangement provided for the defense and support of the government establishment. The Ming founder imagined his ideal society as a vast array of essentially self-sufficient agrarian villages. He also saw no need to promote commerce, urban development, or foreign trade. He explicitly warned his successors against military adventures or conquest of additional territory.

allow only the heir apparent, the emperor's oldest son, to remain in the capital. Other imperial princes were sent to estates in frontier regions where they could participate in defense and also oversee military commanders on the emperor's behalf. This arrangement appeared to solve two problems at once.

Civil War and Usurpation

Trouble arose, however, when the heir apparent died before taking the throne. In order to maintain the line of succession his oldest son, the founder's grandson, was named heir. When, in 1368, this grandson came to the throne at the age of 21, he was threatened by the existence of a number of armed uncles in princely establishments in strategic areas. The young emperor, acting on counsel from his senior advisers, began to slowly remove his uncles from their positions, stripping them of their powers and placing them under surveillance. This action provoked the

senior surviving uncle, Zhu Di, the Prince of Yan, who was stationed at Beijing, to revolt and march south under the guise of saving the emperor from the influence of evil underlings. A civil war ensued, concluding with the fall of Nanjing to Zhu Di who installed himself as emperor. He took the reign name Yongle (Eternal Happiness, 1402–1424), no doubt to put a good face on his usurpation.

A Second Founding: the Yongle Era

What followed was almost a second founding of the Ming dynasty. Once in power the Emperor Yongle proved an energetic and able ruler, becoming known as another great emperor of the Ming dynasty. He mobilized and unleashed enormous forces in a series of actions that transformed the empire in numerous ways. He acted quickly to execute those who remained loyal to his predecessor who had disappeared, and presumably died, in the seizure of the capital. He rewrote the historical records to erase the rule of his nephew and bolster his own legitimacy. He saw to it that imperial princes would no longer have military escorts. He solved the strategic problem by moving the capital to Beijing in the north, a heroic undertaking that entailed the rebuilding of the city and

reopening the Grand Canal in order to bring provisions from the south. From Beijing, Yongle was able to directly oversee military affairs along the frontier.

Domestically, Yongle upheld the policies and principles of his father but in external relations this was another matter altogether. In the north, he personally led five major military expeditions into Mongolia harassing and attacking the Mongol forces. In the south he sent an army to invade Annam in the Red River delta and attached it to China as a province. Today, the most famous of Yongle's external initiatives was his dispatch of naval expeditions to the South Seas and the Indian Ocean under the command of the eunuch admiral Zheng He. This initiative was designed to enhance China's standing and, by attracting many ambassadors from foreign lands, cast glory on Yongle himself. Domestically, it bolstered his claim to ruling legitimacy.

Zhu Di died in Mongolia during his fifth northern campaign. His career of aggressive and expansive rule did not survive him and many of his initiatives were not sustained: Ming power was never again projected into Mongolia, as spirited resistance caused the Annamese to be granted independence three years after Yongle's death, and the extensive maritime expeditions were discontinued.

ABOVE **The Imperial Ancestral Temple** was part of the former Imperial Palace built in 1420 during Emperor Yongle's rule.

LEFT **This sword from the Ming dynasty** is thought to date to the Yongle period. The sword is covered in the finest early Ming decoration and Buddhist symbols.

Beijing, the New Capital

The relocation of the capital from Nanjing to Beijing (Peking), a process that began in 1403 and took almost four decades to complete, constituted the single largest project undertaken by the Ming dynasty. The city, increasingly threatened by the incursions of modernity, represented the dynasty's most permanent legacy.

ABOVE **The Corner Towers** of the city are said to have been designed by an immortal master craftsman, Lu Ban, based on an intricate and elaborate cricketcage.

"Walls, walls, and yet again walls, form the framework of every Chinese city," wrote Osvald Siren, author of *The Walls and Gates of Peking* (1924), "They surround the city, they divide it into lots and compounds, they mark more than any other structures the basic features of the Chinese communities." To non-Chinese visitors to Beijing, the perfect north–south orientation, the grid-like regularity of nested squares and rectangles, and the symmetry that once characterized the city's form, as defined by its walls and its gates, made it one of the great wonders of the world. Marco Polo, the first Westerner to speak of it, observes, "Moreover I tell you that the whole city is set out by line; for the main streets from one side to the other of the town are drawn out straight as a thread, and are so straight and so broad that if anyone [was] mounted on the wall at one gate and looked straight one sees from the one side to the other the gate of the other side, opposite to that, and they are so planned that each gate is seen as the others along the town, by the roads."

To generation after generation of Chinese, such features hint at the attempt to partake of the perfect order and regularity of the Heavens above —the city was designed and built as a simulacrum within the human realm of the order of the Heavens themselves. As such, the layout of the city was believed to embody both the geometry of the cosmos itself ("Heaven is round, the Earth is square"), but also the power and centrality of Chinese civilization within universal hierarchies, that China was the center of culture and also of learning, with the Son of Heaven (the emperor) himself safely ensconced at its heart within his contained Forbidden City. The central idea of such a city came from one of the most revered of the Confucian canons (the *Rites of Zhou*), which influenced the form of all major Chinese capital cities. Never was this ideal to be so perfectly expressed than it was to be in Beijing (Peking).

Earlier Capitals

The path that led to Beijing becoming the inevitable and permanent capital of the Chinese world was neither a simple nor an easy one, however. "The history of Peking is the history of China in miniature," wrote Juliet Bredon in 1919 in her *Peking: A Historical and Intimate Description of its Chief Places of Interest,* a book that is an invaluable source on the history of the city, "for the town, like the country, has shown the same power of taking fresh masters and absorbing them. Both have passed through dark hours of anarchy and bloodshed. Happily both possess the vitality to survive them." Indeed, somewhat ironically for a city that is regarded as representing something that is quintessentially "Chinese," the site of the present city of Beijing (Peking) began its life as a capital under a series of "alien" masters, such as the Khitan Tartar Liao (916–1125), the Jurchen Jin (1115–1234), and the Mongol Yuan (1279–1368). Before the site had acquired its numinous quality as the "Roots of an August Enterprise," it had been recognized under a variety of names, the earliest records calling it Reeds (Ji), later records referring to it as Swallow Capital (Yanjing), or, under the Han dynasty, as Tranquil Town (Youzhou). Once it had become a capital, it took on names that referred to its location within specific and differently shaped empires; for the Liao, it was their Southern Capital (Nanjing), for the Jin it was known to them as the Middle Capital (Zhongdu).

In 1256, Kublai Khan (1215–1294), having occupied the Jin capital, was ordered to found a city to the northeast. Having chosen a site some ten days' ride from present-day Peking (Beijing), he commissioned his Chinese chief adviser Liu Bingzhong (1216–1274), the man who was said to have suggested the name Yuan ("First") for the dynasty, with the design of the city. Kaiping Fu, as the city was named, was modeled on time-honored Chinese imperial city plans, with even the placement of specific buildings being determined by reference to prescriptions found in the Daoist *Book of Changes*. In 1264, this city was elevated to central and capital status and renamed the Upper Capital, also known as Shangdu.

Eleven years later, in 1267, Kublai Khan was ready to build an even greater capital, known to the Chinese as Great Capital (Dadu) and to the Turks as City of the Khans (Qanbaliq). This city was explicitly Chinese in design—except, it is said, for Mongol touches such as the planting in the parks and gardens of the sweet grasses of the steppes—and again it was designed for the khan by Liu Bingzhong. All trace of the previous cities was removed, and the new city was built from scratch, with the help of Muslim architects, as a triple-walled city whose concentric boundaries each had a perfect (or nearly so) geometric form, and at the heart of these myriad number of walls was placed the imperial city.

Yongle's Usurpation

This capital city was rebuilt with certain modifications by the first emperor of the Ming soon after it had been taken away from the Mongols in 1368. After much debate at court, it was decided that the new dynasty's capital city would be established south of the Yangzi River at Nanjing (known as the Southern Capital). Beijing (the Northern Capital), that was renamed as Northern

THE WHITE DAGOBA: A REMNANT FROM THE MING DYNASTY

The White Dagoba has its own history of more than 700 years. It was initially built during the Yuan dynasty (1279–1368) and designed by the Nepalese architect A-ni-ge (1245–1306) under Kublai Khan. The White Dagoba Temple originally had the name "Temple of Great Holy Longevity and Eternal Peace." It was named "Miaoyingsi" after it was rebuilt in the Ming dynasty (1368–1644). The name "White Dagoba" refers to the old dagoba (temple) that is inside the bigger temple. The White Dagoba is one of the few traces left of Kublai Khan's great city, and one of the original remnants of Ming Beijing.

LEFT **The White Dagoba is** a 131-ft (40-m) high stupa of white stone. It is situated in Beihai Park, an imperial garden northwest of the Forbidden City.

Peace (Beiping), was given into the charge of the emperor's fourth son, Zhu Di (1360–1424), known as Prince of Yan. In 1402, when this prince usurped the throne—his brother, the ill-fated Jianwen emperor (1377–1402), was said to have perished in the fires that raged in Nanjing, along with his wife and son—the newly proclaim-ed emperor, Yongle ("Eternal Joy"), started on a project of consolidation and focused on fortifying the city that sat at the heart of his powerbase, in the face of continued internal and external threats to his authority.

A New Capital Constructed

The new emperor's plans for the relocation of his capital, announced publicly by his granting it the name Beijing in 1403, almost came to a halt when, in 1421, just a year after the city had been officially accorded the status of principal capital (Jingshi), a fire destroyed a substantial part of the restored and expanded Forbidden City. During the debate that the court held to examine the causes and implications of the disaster, the emperor faced blunt criticism over the cost and incon-venience of the project. These arguments came far too late and Yongle, who had already quit Nanjing for the last time in 1417, responded to the disapproval of his dissenting officials by having one imprisoned and another executed. The massive tasks of construction of palaces, walls, and gates, of bureaucratic reorganization, and of relocation of population, already well underway, continued to gather pace. It is esti-mated that by 1425 over a million people had

RIGHT **The Temple of Heaven, Beijing** was built by Emperor Yongle to make offerings to Heaven. This undertaking also showed his respect to higher authorities.

decided to transmigrate into the Northern Metropolitan Region, either of their own volition or at the explicit command. The city was built according to the detailed blueprint of the Yuan city, "walled and square," and in the words of the city's most recent historian, Susan Naquin in her *Peking: Temples and City Life, 1400–1900,* it was "carefully oriented to the points of the compass, flanked by sym-metrical gates, and organized around wide avenues that formed a regular north–south and east–west grid anchored by the emperor's residence at the centre." However, the new city gradually "swallowed up" its predecessor cities, Liao, Jin, and Yuan. After the death of Emperor Yongle in 1424, the destiny of the city was again threatened when his son and his successor decided that the centre of his empire was to return to Nanjing and Beijing was to be given the status of "Temporary Residence" or Xingzai. Fatefully, within a year, the new emperor died and his successor, the Xuande ("Propagating Virtue") emperor (1399–1435), a young man born in Beijing but who had been put

LEFT **This Ming-dynasty combination sundial and compass** was used in *feng shui*. This ancient practice of geometry and astronomy was used to map out the best position for Beijing.

A Lasting Legacy

As a capital of China, the city seems somewhat eccentrically sited, too close to China's northern border and too far removed from both the traditional site of Chinese capitals along the Yellow River or the increasingly important centers of economic power along the Yangzi River, forever dependent on the expensive supply of grain and water from elsewhere. For over half a millennium Beijing's role as capital of China has been all but uncontested. In 1688, writing in the "Preface" to his monumental documentary history of the city, entitled *Accounts of the Past Heard in the Precincts of the Sun,* the renowned Qing scholar Zhu Yizun (1629–1709) captured something of the melancholic fate of a city that seems particularly prone to the vicissitudes of history: "Alas, the sites of the palaces and mansions, the walls and the marketplaces change repeatedly, and only one in ten of the monasteries and temples are found where they once stood, and nine out of ten of these now bear different plaques. As that which once was there is ruined and disappears, and as the years follow, one after another, the physical traces of the past become harder to seek out." The Forbidden City is a survivor of history. It is also interesting to note that Zhu Yizun's residence beyond the Gate for the Promulgation of Martial Power was destroyed as part of the latest plan for urban renewal.

in charge of the relocation southwards, had revoked his father's decision. Gradually, Nanjing's claims as the rival capital dissipated as its bureaucratic structures were downgraded until, in 1441 the city's status as dual capital was removed and, it became known as "Former Capital" (Liudu), the memories of this city were all that remained.

The Forbidden City

A Palace Built by the People

The Forbidden City is a marvel built by unimaginable human persistence. The stone slabs required for building were moved in a boat along roads of ice, pulled by 1,000 mules and horses.

The Gate of Heavenly Peace

This is the main entrance into the Forbidden City to the north. A throne would be placed here for the emperor to give audience to government officials, showing the emperor's concerns for national affairs.

The Forbidden City, the Ming Imperial Palace complex in the heart of Beijing, now the designated home of the Palace Museum, was constructed in the early 1400s. Construction of the palace lasted for 15 years and this was achieved with over a million workers. As the residence of the emperor, it was the heart of the Ming government and its ruling dynasty from 1420 until 1644.

Exquisite care was taken in the design and construction of the complex to symbolically express the superhuman status of the ruling emperor, the Son of Heaven. The Forbidden City was square in shape to represent the Earth where the emperor resided in the center, facing south, toward the sun (*yang,* the bright, male force). Behind the palace lay an artificial mountain to shade his back from the northern cold (*yin,* the dark, female force).

The Tiananmen (Gate of Heavenly Peace) was the central gateway in the Imperial City wall leading to the Forbidden City. Just inside the Tiananmen to the west lay the Altar to the Gods of Soil and Grain where five kinds of colored soil stood for the four corners of the empire as well as the center. This altar was understood to represent the nation and its people. To the east lay the imperial ancestral hall, representing the dynasty.

Approaching from the south, one would pass through the Tiananmen, crossing the moat over one of five ceremonial bridges and passing through one of five arches in the gate. Here, as in all imperial structures, the central bridge and the larger, central archway were reserved for the emperor alone. The visitor might note in passing that on either side of the central walkway the paving stones were laid at an angle, slanting inward. This subtle indication of centrality, pointing to the locus of imperial authority, can be seen throughout all Ming imperial buildings. Less subtle symbols are the elaborate carvings of dragons and phoenix, representing the emperor and the empress, on the central stairways marking the route over which the emperor was carried in his sedan chair. Proceeding northward, the route leads to the massive rose-colored walls of the palace itself, surrounded by its own moat, its wall and buildings topped by yellow roof tiles, a color reserved by sumptuary regulations for imperial use.

In the center of the Forbidden City lies an elevated platform with three great halls aligned along the north–south axis. Southernmost is the largest, the Taihedian, Hall of Supreme Harmony. Behind it is the smallest, the Zhonghedian, Hall of Middle Harmony, and farthest to the north is the Baohedian, Hall of Preserving Harmony. These three

great halls, situated in the exact center of the Forbidden City, were the main venues in which Ming emperors held audiences, performed ceremonies, and conducted official business. The northern half of the palace complex held a maze of internal streets, passageways, and small buildings like the residences of the emperor, his principal wife the empress, together with imperial ladies, and imperial offspring. Inside the northern gateway lies the Imperial Garden with ponds, artificial mountains, fantastic-shaped rocks, fish ponds, and walkways.

Impressive Walkways and Buildings

The Forbidden City was the Chinese Imperial Palace from the mid-Ming dynasty to the end of the Qing dynasty. It is located in the middle of Beijing and now houses the Palace Museum. The complex consists of 800 buildings with 8,886 rooms. It is a UNESCO World Heritage Site.

The Spatial Manifestation of Imperial Authority

At dawn, passing through the Meridian Gate (Wumen), a Ming official or foreign dignitary could not help but be awed by what came next. Inside the gate was a vast sea of flat, gray paving stones bisected by a curving river with five arched bridges leading to yet another great wall and gate complex, the Taihemen, Gate of Supreme Harmony. The serenity and austerity of this vast and enormous space, unlike anything ever seen before, was designed to impress the viewer simultaneously with his own insignificance and with the unfathomable power of the emperor. Crossing this vast empty space, the visitor passed through the Tiananmen, only to encounter another empty space, larger than the first. The effect was to reinforce the sense of the emperor's remoteness, even as one approached his presence.

Zheng He and His Travels

In the early 1400s, Ming China sent seven great naval expeditions into the Indian Ocean, some reaching Arabia and Africa. This achievement reveals both the Ming's technological capabilities and political priorities.

ABOVE **Navigator Admiral Zheng He's** ship was recreated from historical records. He rose through the ranks to become one of China's leading sea explorers.

RIGHT **Zheng He** traveled as far as the western coast of Africa. He is immortalized in bronze.

The leader of the expeditions to what the Chinese called the Southern Oceans was a high-ranking eunuch named Zheng He (1371–1433). Zheng He was born Ma He to a prominent family in Yunnan Province in southwest China, ten years before the province was incorporated into the Ming Empire. His surname, Ma, was a quite common designation for Muslims. Both his grandfather and father were called Hajji, indicating that they had made the pilgrimage to Mecca. Ma He's father was killed resisting the Ming conquest of Yunnan in 1381. Ma He was captured, castrated, and presented to the Ming imperial family as part of the spoils of war. He was assigned to the service of the Prince of Yan, Zhu Di, who was the fourth son of the Ming founder. The fief of the Prince of Yan was in Beijing, which had, until recently, been the capital of the Mongol Yuan dynasty.

The young eunuch proved an able servant and gained his master's trust. He grew to be tall and stout, and he displayed a good capacity for state military affairs when the Prince of Yan led armed forces along the frontier. When the Prince of Yan revolted and marched on the capital in Nanjing, Ma He distinguished himself in the fighting. After the Prince triumphed in 1402, and took the reign name Yongle, Ma He emerged as a trusted lieutenant. In 1404, he was granted the surname Zheng and given the title of Director (*taijian*), implying the head of a eunuch agency in the imperial household. He was a person the emperor, who had just usurped the throne and faced considerable resistance among both civil and military officials, could always trust implicitly. This was the background that caused Zheng He to be placed in command of the expeditions to the southern oceans, although he had no naval experience.

The Fleets of Yongle

At Yongle's command, a frantic shipbuilding program was undertaken along the southern coast. Already, by the summer of 1405, when the first expedition set sail, more than 1,100 ships had been built or rebuilt as oceangoing craft. The vessels were of different sizes. The largest, called treasure ships (*bao chuan*), were built in a shipyard outside of Nanjing. They were 440 ft (134 m) long and 186 ft (57 m) wide, the largest wooden ships ever built. They were multi-mast, shallow-draft vessels composed of watertight compartments with a displacement of 25,000 to 30,000 tons. Besides the treasure ships, there were horse ships that were 370 ft (113 m) in length, supply ships 280 ft (38.1 m) in length, billet ships 240 ft (73.2 m) in length, and battleships 180 ft (54.9 m) in length and loaded armed with cannons.

The great and imposing size of these ships, and their numbers, allowed Zheng He's fleets to carry large amounts of Chinese goods for gifts and for barter, supplies of food, water, and equipment sufficient for months at sea. Besides the head commander and his officers, other crew such as navigators, interpreters, medical and religious specialists, and craftsmen along with substantial military forces—both foot soldiers and cavalry—were the passengers on board. The first voyage in 1405 was staffed by 27,800 men. It had 62 large ships and 255 smaller craft. The six voyages that followed were all similar in scale.

The Voyages and Expeditions

Altogether there were seven voyages from 1405 to 1433. They usually took two years because the fleet had to wait for the monsoon winds that made it easier to sail south in the winter and north in the summer. All voyages followed the same basic route, although some went farther than others, and in some cases the fleet broke up to send side expeditions. From the mouth of the Yangzi, the fleet sailed down the coast to stops at Changle in Fujian Province and at Qui Nohn in Champa (now part of Vietnam), and then continued southward to Sumatra and the Strait of Malacca. From the northern end of Sumatra, the route went westward, across open water, to Ceylon (now Sri Lanka) and then around to the major trading center of Calicut (Kozhikode) on the Malabar Coast of southeastern India. This was as far as the first three voyages went. The next four voyages went on from Calicut northwest to Hormuz, a great regional trading center, at

the mouth of the Persian Gulf in Iran. Beyond Hormuz the last three expeditions sent detached squadrons westward along the southern coast of Arabia to Aden, located at the mouth of the Red Sea. Zheng He and a handful of his subordinates went north from there to visit Mecca. The most distant points from China reached by Chinese ships were as far down as the east coast of Africa, including Mogadishu in Somalia, and as far south as Malindi in Kenya.

Military Force

On several voyages, Zheng He's forces engaged in combat. On the first expedition (1405–1407) the fleet came into conflict with a Chinese pirate, ensconced in Palembang in Sumatra. More than 5,000 pirates were killed in the fighting; their leader was captured, taken back to Nanjing and executed. On the second voyage (1407–1409), the fleet stopped in Java on the return route and intervened in local politics; the Chinese came into conflict with the local ruler and set up a regional rival before leaving. During the third voyage (1409–1411), the king in Ceylon attempted to capture the Chinese ships, but Zheng He and his men, after fighting hard against them,

BELOW **A copy of a map** that collector Liu Gang claims proves the controversial theories that Zheng He was the first to discover the Americas.

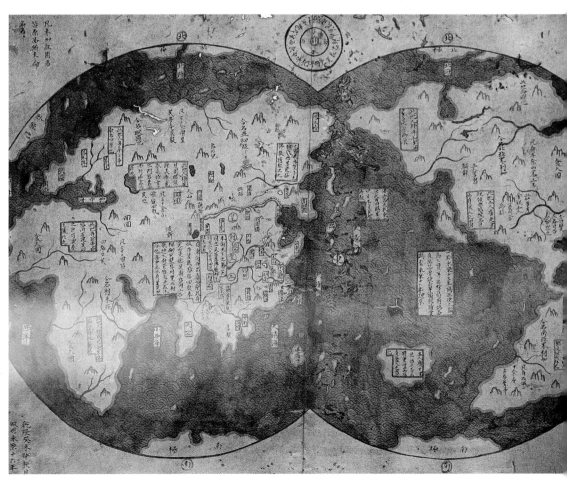

formal recognition of the superior status of the Ming emperor. The fourth voyage, the first that went beyond India to Iran, Arabia and Africa, was notably successful. It brought back tribute and envoys from 19 countries.

Chinese records indicate that Zheng He's voyages reached 30 countries from Southeast Asia to Africa. Some were sizable kingdoms, for example, Champa, Cambodia, Thailand, and Bengal; most were smaller island or coastal trading communities, some too small to identify definitively. By the 1420s, the voyages served their purpose in legitimizing Yongle's rule, and the court was moved to the new capital at Beijing. After a sixth voyage (1421–1422), the emperor ordered that the costly expeditions be temporarily suspended. Emperor Yongle never again returned to Nanjing and died while on a campaign in Mongolia. His son and successor listened to voices at court that opposed further voyages on account of the great expense. Zheng He was assigned to be a garrison commander of the now auxiliary capital at Nanjing. He was called back to action one last time, when the following emperor, Yongle's grandson, ordered a seventh voyage (1431–1433). After that, the voyages ended for good. Chinese attention focused on the northern border.

ABOVE **Chinese pirates** plundered ships for the treasures being plied on the lucrative maritime trade routes during the Ming dynasty.

captured the king and took him back to Nanjing. Emperor Yongle set him free and allowed him to return home. On the fourth voyage (1413–1415), Zheng He's forces fought with a local leader in northern Sumatra who was also captured and taken to Nanjing. These incidents illustrate that while the Ming government was not interested in acquiring territory overseas, it did not hesitate to use military power to intervene in local affairs and to keep order. The presence of Chinese pirates in Southeast Asia reveals that the Ming founder's ban on overseas trade had not stopped Chinese from going abroad; it really only served to criminalize any of those who decided to do so.

Diplomacy

It is clear from the Ming records that the purpose of the voyages was to demonstrate the Chinese wealth and power to the rulers of overseas states. Everywhere he went, Zheng He gave generous gifts of fine Chinese products, especially silks and porcelains, to the local rulers. These were to be seen as examples of China's sophistication and were tokens of the emperor's goodwill. What the Chinese wanted in return was ceremonial tribute, gifts of very distinctive local products, and the

The Director of Three Treasures

Zheng He's voyages provide a window on the complexities of religious life in the Ming dynasty. Although he came from a Muslim family, and despite the fact that he may have visited Mecca, Zheng He was a professed Buddhist. He is often referred to as the "San Bao Taijian", which closely translates as the Director of Three Treasures. The three treasures are the Three Jewels of Buddhism: the Buddha, the Dharma or law, and the Sangha or monastic community.

We can see other sides of Zheng He's religious life from the inscriptions on stone steles that he had erected at various times and places. In 1405, he asked the Minister of Rites to write an epitaph for his father's grave, and, in 1411, he went to his hometown in Yunnan to make an offering in person. Even though he was a eunuch in imperial service, Zheng He still honored his father as Confucianism would have a filial son do. At the start of his voyages and upon his return, Zheng He always made offerings at the temples of the Celestial Empress, Tian Hou, to whom he gave credit for his ongoing safety at sea. Zheng He was a modern man in that he embraced a number of religions that were prominent during this time.

In 1911, a stele erected by Zheng He was discovered in Ceylon. The inscription in Chinese, Tamil, and Persian reveals his official flexibility in all religious matters. It details the offerings Zheng He presented at the temple—gold, silver, silk, incense burners, lacquer utensils, and other symbolic objects. The Chinese text there records Emperor Yongle's reverence for Buddhism. The Tamil inscription clearly tells of his respect for the Hindu god of the Tamils. And the Persian inscription records that the offerings were made to Allah, the god of Islam. Zheng He provides a model for what China was capable of achieving.

Significance of the Expeditions

Today, Zheng He's great maritime expeditions are the accomplishments of the Ming period that enjoy the greatest attention in the field of world history. They have often been compared to the more modest voyages undertaken by Christopher Columbus some nine decades later. It is more a contrast than a comparison. The Ming dynasty expeditions were astounding in their scale and technical sophistication, and far surpassed any known in Europe or elsewhere up to that time. But Zheng He's many voyages were different in character from those of Columbus. He was not an explorer, nor did he lay claim to the territories he visited, and he did not alter the course of world history—he traveled and observed.

ABOVE **A carved *qilin*, or mythical beast**, is an example of the exotic animals brought back to the Ming court. It was considered a good omen that brought serenity or prosperity.

AUSPICIOUS BEASTS

Among the tribute gifts that Zheng He brought back to China from his travels, it was the animals from Africa that made the greatest impact at the Ming court. Nothing caused more excitement than the unearthly looking giraffes, which the Chinese took to be *qilin*, fabled creatures like unicorns, which were said to appear in conjunction with the arrival of a sage or signaled a good omen. The appearance of such creatures was apparently most welcome to Emperor Yongle because it implied divine approval for his reign. When the fifth expedition (1417–1419) took the envoys home, they let it be known what the emperor liked. More animals followed including antelopes, camels with one hump (Chinese camels have two humps), leopards, lions, ostriches, rhinoceroses, and zebras.

LEFT **This fifteenth-century Chinese painting,** *A Giraffe with an Attendant,* is by Shen Du.

Ming Law and Government

Ming China, the last era of Han Chinese self-rule before the twentieth century, saw indigenous legal and governmental institutions reach their highest and most extreme levels of development.

The Ming founder, Zhu Yuanzhang, was a tireless and inventive legislator. He codified rules governing many aspects of Ming society from the imperial clan down to the rural village community. The emperor's most enduring achievement was the Great Ming Code (known as *Da Ming lü*) of 1397. The Code had 460 articles organized by sections on personnel, revenue, rites, military affairs, penal affairs, and public works. It was essentially a penal code, specifying how the traditional five punishments (beating with a light stick, beating with a heavy stick, penal servitude, life exile, and finally death by

BELOW **This ceramic lid detail** from the seventeenth century shows a Chinese magistrate holding court in the provinces.

strangulation or decapitation) should be applied for specified transgressions. This Code was designed to uphold an idealized social hierarchy so the punishments were harshest for those who transgressed against their superiors. Special consideration was given to the young, the elderly, women, and persons with disabilities. Punishment was generally lighter for those who voluntarily confessed; in many cases payment of fines could reduce or eliminate punishment. Wishing to inhibit any social change, the Ming founder commanded that the Code could never be altered.

Enforcing the Code

The Ming dynasty did not have specialized judicial institutions; the Code was enforced by district magistrates who functioned as judges whenever legal cases arose. They were assisted by a local staff of constables, bailiffs, jailers, and coroners who handled prisoners and gathered information. There were no lawyers but some literate persons studied the codes and assisted in offering pleas before the magistrate. Guilt was assumed in most cases where the crime was alleged, and torture was often applied to extract confessions confirming the charges. Civil disputes involving property or kinship matters were meant to be resolved by arbitration under the supervision of community and lineage elders below the level of county government. Despite this, stubborn disagreements were often taken to the magistrate for resolution, frequently with disastrous results for both

parties. There was limited appeal to higher levels of government and all death sentences were reviewed at the capital. Pardons and reductions in punishment were constantly routine features of the legal system.

Civil Administration

The Ming government was the largest and most rationally organized administrative system in the world. It was divided into parallel military and civil hierarchies. Civil officials were recruited through a triennial examination system, military officials through a combination of examinations and heredity. Nine official ranks, each divided into two sub-ranks, from "a" at the top to "9b" at the bottom, were distinguished by brocaded squares worn on the uniform—birds for civil officials and animals for military officials. The number of the officials holding civil ranks rose to about 24,000 in the course of the dynasty. Perhaps 1,500 were stationed in the capital where they staffed the six government ministries of Personnel, Revenue, Rites, War, Justice, and Works. Once appointed, Ming officials were subjected to regular posting for long terms of duty away from their home province, so as to avoid conflicts of interest.Their careers were

centrally managed, often alternating service spent in the provinces with assignments in the capital. All officials were evaluated every three years; and those deficient were either demoted or punished. Also running parallel to the administrative and the military hierarchies was a censorial system that existed to monitor effectiveness, to detect any criminality and incompetence, and alert the emperor to the various problems.

The great majority of civil officials were assigned to the provincial, prefectural, sub-prefectural, and district (or county) offices throughout the Ming territory. In addition to northern and southern metropolitan areas around Beijing and Nanjing respectively, there were 13 provinces. Below the level of provinces, civil government, primarily the administration of justice and collection of taxes, was carried out by 159 prefectural and more than 1,000 district magistrates aided by a much larger number of local functionaries who lacked civil service degrees. The territory they administered was about 1.5 million square miles (3.9 million sq km), just under half the area of China today. A district magistrate would have had authority over 60,000 individuals making any kind of close and personal super-vision unthinkable. In the villages, responsibility lay in the hands of elders and tax captains overseeing the delivery of grain and labor service.

LEFT **A stone warrior** standing guard on the "Spirit Way," the road leading to the Ming dynasty tombs. The site was chosen by the Emperor Yongle.

BELOW **The crane on the tunic of a Ming dynasty** official indicates the figure is a civil official.

EUNUCHS

One of the flaws of Ming government was the interference of eunuchs in civil and military affairs. The palace was staffed by eunuchs, the only men allowed to wait on the emperor and his family for fear of interference with the dynastic line of succession. The eunuchs were ranked and organized into specialized agencies responsible for myriad household matters such as food, clothing, ritual regalia, and entertainment as well as document handling and care of imperial seals. Emperors found it convenient to give eunuchs sensitive assignments. In the capital city, they operated the notorious Eastern Depot to investigate and torture those suspected of treason or other offences, but they could be dispatched to the provinces or given special missions, as in the example of the famous admiral Zheng He. The numbers of eunuchs increased to more than 10,000 in the capital with others scattered around the empire on imperial business. Proximity to the emperor allowed some eunuchs to gain great influence over their masters. In a number of instances eunuchs became virtual dictators, controlling the entire imperial government.

The Ming Scholar

Sitting in his study, surrounded by his books, the Ming scholar was a member of a tiny and much privileged elite. As the dynasty drew to its close, the scholar preferred the safety of that study to the dangers of office.

Early in the seventeenth century, the eminent Chinese painter, art critic, and influential arbiter of good taste, Li Rihua (1565–1635), relayed the following sketch of the scholar's study:

His study will be situated there where the brook twists and turns its way through the hills. In total, the structure will not exceed two or three bays, with an upper story from which to observe the clouds and the mists. All around 100 slender bamboo plants will grow, to welcome the fresh wind, and to the south will stand a tall pine tree from which to hang the bright moon. A gnarled old prunus tree with low, twisting branches will jut in through the window, while fragrant herbs and thick moss will encircle the stone foundation. To the east will be housed all the Daoist and the Buddhist sutras, and to the west, the Confucian classics. In the center will be placed a bed and a desk, this latter strewn with examples of fine calligraphy and painting.

ABOVE **The road leading to the Ming dynasty** tombs is lined with officials, such as this statue of a scholar.

Morning and evening a meal of white rice and fish stew will be served, accompanied by fine wine and strong tea; a stout man will be posted at the gate to reject social callers.

This is a consciously idealized description of the late imperial Chinese world's most highly charged and ritualized space. It was only by years and years spent in such a study, his writing brush in hand, that scholars (the literati, in the chosen terminology of their early Jesuit interlocutors, the *shi* (scholar) or *wenren* (men of letters) in Chinese terms) could best provide for the material well being of their families, and, if luck and talent were theirs, this could ensure a name that would last forever.

Literacy, the Essay, and the Examinations

But such opportunities, although theoretically available to all men at all levels, in practice severely circumscribed by the luck of wealth and locality, were both rare and onerous, and also involved prodigious feats of study and memorization. From a very early age, the son of a family that was rich enough would set about the task of acquiring, through the memorization of Chinese characters, the very terse and difficult classical language. By the time he entered the clan school in his eighth year of life, he would be expected to know around 1,500 to 2,000 of these characters. He would then proceed to the memorization of the various books of the Confucian canon and to training in the art of composition. By the Ming dynasty, this last skill, also heavily dependant upon the use of memory, revolved around

LEFT **This painting from** *Album of Eight Landscape Paintings,* by Ming artist Shen Zhou (1427–1509), illustrates a scholar's idealized surroundings.

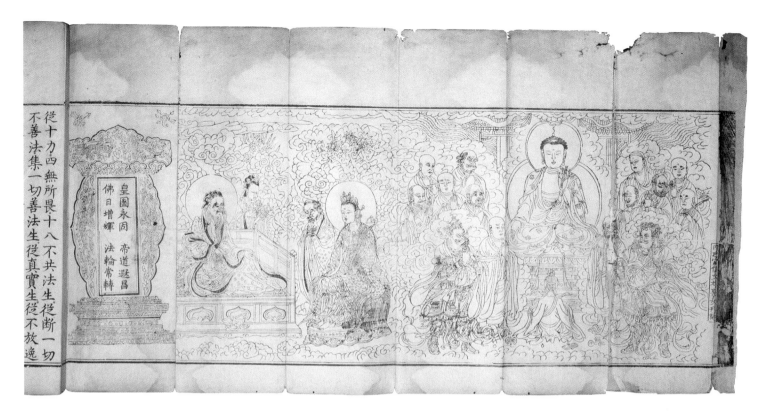

皇圖永固　帝道遐昌　佛日增輝　法輪常轉

從十力四無所畏十八不共法生從一切不善法集一切善法生從真實生從不放逸

acquiring the mastery of a tightly-defined form of composition, the much maligned "Eight-legged Essay" (or *baguwen*), where one would address, through a prescribed sequence of stages, the topic given to them. This process began with firstly "Broaching the Topic," and finally ended with a "Conclusion," which always included a series of antithetical statements (the eight "legs"). The command of these classical and rhetorical traditions required knowledge of upwards of 10,000 Chinese characters, which, once acquired, permitted one access to a civil service examination system that had reached its full maturity. During the eighth lunar month of every third year, all candidates for the first stage of the examinations would gather in the various provincial capitals and on the ninth, twelfth, and fifteenth days of that month would be sequestered in examination cells to produce their essays. The successful candidates, "Raised Men" (*juren*), would become eligible to embark upon the next stage, the Metropolitan Examination (*huishi*), held in the capital during the second month of the succeeding year, again to undertake the rigors of three day-long tests of learning, of memory, and of stamina. If he was successful, a candidate, now called a "Presented Scholar" (*jinshi*), would appear before the emperor (or his representative) on the first day of the third month of that year, to be allocated an appropriate ranking. In the course of the 90 occasions during the Ming dynasty on

which the examination were held, a sum total of 24,874 achieved the status of Presented Scholar.

A Constricted Curriculum

The Ming scholar had available to him more readily than ever before a wider range of texts, scholarly or otherwise, either in the form of a manuscript copy or, increasingly, a woodblock imprint, acquired from the many libraries (private, official, or monastery) or from the commercial book merchants. And yet, for the purposes of examination success, the actual curriculum became more and more narrowly defined, focusing on the commentaries to the Confucian canon developed by the Song dynasty Neo-Confucian scholar Zhu Xi (1130–1200). It was believed that this was the key to the wisdom of the sages of old, which, once understood and put into action, would move society toward universal peace and order.

Office and its Dangers

In a sense, eligibility for office was everything for the Ming scholar; as long as one maintained one's registration, one was exempt from tax (in money and labor), and from a variety of other sumptuary laws, was also immune from prosecution for various crimes, and would immediately became a member of a national elite. Although the actual salary levels were particularly low during the Ming dynasty, office holding could prove a parti-

ABOVE **Buddha and other religious figures** are depicted in an antique book illustration that is an example of the work cataloged by the Ming-dynasty scholars.

吹毛

悟空

ABOVE **The magic monkey Sun Wukong** from the Chinese story "Journey to the West," is one of the many stories preserved by scholars in woodblock records and paintings.

system and the public works of the locale, and, if circumstances required, the proper distribution of famine relief. Little wonder then that a man such as the eminent literary figure Yuan Hongdao (1568–1610) complained of his fate in the following terms in a letter to a friend shortly after he had taken up his post in Suzhou in 1595:

As for me, serving as Magistrate of Wu I have found myself forced to strike all the most ugly attitudes imaginable, such as are quite beyond description. To give you some impression of my torment, however, I'll try to do so now; when I encounter my superiors I am forced to grovel like a slave; entertaining passing guests I act the harlot; whilst managing the government treasury, I'm like an old granary keeper; seeking to instruct the populace under my charge in their rightful duties, I become an old maid! Blowing hot and then cold all in the space of a single day, one minute I'm yin and the next I'm yang. As magistrate, I have tasted all the worst flavors of this world. How very poisonous is my existence!

At the other end of the bureaucratic ladder, however, the dangers were even more immediate if one happened to be serving as one of the 1,500 officials in the capital; "...the Ming emperors," it has been argued, "through their agents among the palace eunuchs and in the Imperial Bodyguard, maintained a supreme reign of terror over the civil service," and in many humiliating instances the officials were subjected, in open court, to "vicious floggings on bared buttocks."

Travel and its Delights

Little wonder then, in the words of Zhu Yizun (1629–1709), that the "long years of peace from the reign of the Wanli emperor onwards have afforded men of learning the opportunity to turn their minds to painting and to calligraphy, to discussions about collecting, and to exchanging their writings with their friends." In a quite remarkable manner, they also turned their attentions to despised forms of vernacular and performance literature, the short story, the novel, and the opera in particular, to the arts and crafts (including that of garden design), and to the

cularly profitable venture; in any case, in a Confucianized world, learning and its validation through competitive examinations was the sole acceptable means of social mobility. Yet, holding of office had its drawbacks, even in a circumstance where, increasingly, the supply of these eligible officials far exceeded the needs of a bureaucratic system that was comprised, at most, of around 24,000 officials. For one thing, the intense factionalism at court and elsewhere, that became such a marked feature of the late Ming dynasty governance, meant that few men could enjoy a steady career free of the anxiety (if not the reality) of dismissal and disgrace. For another, the tasks required to be done were quite extraordinary in circumstances where an official's every action was susceptible to regular review and examination. Take the role of the District Magistrate, for instance, one of approximately 1,500 such officials responsible for the well being of perhaps some 90,000 people spread over an area of 1,300 sq miles (3,367 sq km); his duties, according to a highly influential handbook for magistrates, Huang Liuhong's (1633–1705) *Complete Book Concerning Happiness and Benevolence* (*Fuhui quanshu*), completed in 1699, highlighted tax collection, supervision of the census and cadastral survey, the administration of justice, the undertaking of local rites and ceremonies, the maintenance of the education

THE DYNASTIC PRIVATE LIBRARY

The Pavilion of Heaven's Oneness (Tianyi Pavilion Library) in Ningbo, established around 1561 by Fan Qin (1506–1585), an imperial governor who was passionate about books, became the most famous private library of the Ming and Qing dynasties, because of its reputation for being both fireproof and inaccessible to scholars. Fan Qin borrowed his idea for the library from *The Book of Changes*. The library sits beside the Moon Lake ensuring that water surrounds the library in case of fire. Fan Qin collected over 70,000 volumes. Today only 17,000 volumes remain but the local chronicles of the Ming dynasty are priceless treasures that give an insight into the day-to-day living during this period in history. It is China's oldest surviving library.

RIGHT **This is the entrance to the Tianyi Pavilion Library complex.** The library is a remarkable representation of the Chinese private book-collecting tradition and an example of Ming architecture.

connoisseurship of tea. Travel throughout the empire offered its delights for, if the Ming scholar was by definition peripatetic in his lifestyle, traveling in order to study, in order to sit the examinations, and, if successful, to take up office elsewhere in the empire (for he was forbidden ever to serve in his locality), by the late years of the dynasty there was a growing tendency for scholars to indulge in travel simply for its own sake. This occurred to such an extent that, particularly the men of Suzhou, Yuan Hongdao observed, somewhat enviously, that "their fondness for travel has become something of an obsession." His own younger brother, Yuan Zhongdao (1570–1624), although not a man from Suzhou, seems to have been especially prone to the delights of roaming the empire, judging by the following extract from his "Record of My Second Junk":

> For the six years now... I have spent much of my time aboard a junk. When my first junk fell into disrepair, I had another built. Whenever I live in town I become as inflamed as if being cauterized with moxa, only finding release when I climb upon my junk. If when studying at home I can understand not a word of what I happen to be reading, on board my junk I become intoxicated with the copiousness of my reading notes. Or if I haven't written a line of poetry during the course of a year spent on land, my poetic inspiration surges up again like a spring the moment I find myself within the cabin of a junk ..."

The achievement of the Ming scholars was founding libraries and producing anthologies that preserved numerous written works from extinction.

LEFT *Waiting to Cross a River in Autumn* by Zhang Lu gives an insight into the inspiring nature of travel for the Ming scholar.

Foreign Trade

The beginning of the Ming dynasty brought an end to the *Pax Mongolica* or "Mongol Peace" that had created long distance trade across the Eurasian landmass. By the end of this era, China was the center of maritime commerce.

Unlike his Mongol predecessors, the Ming founder was not interested in promoting foreign trade; he advocated defense of the northern frontier and discouraged his people from any maritime contact with other countries. Under his rule foreign trade fell to a low point.

The situation began to change in the early 1400s when Emperor Yongle (1402–1420), having just usurped the throne, greatly expanded China's external contacts. For the most part this was official trade both by land and by sea. Yongle was anxious to build up Ming military power and to do this he needed horses, which were in short supply in China. Consequently, he established "Tea-Horse Markets" along the northern frontier where Inner Asian horses were purchased in exchange for Chinese tea. There is substantial evidence that testifies to this strategic shift in Ming priorities. *The Veritable Record,* the most important account of the Yongle period, contains annual totals for the number of horses acquired, rising from just under 40,000 in 1403 to more than 1.5 million in 1423. Outsiders were made aware of Ming demand for horses both through tribute and trade. A surviving account of a Persian delegation describes Yongle's new court in Beijing and the Emperor's keen interest in procuring horses.

Emperor Yongle undertook a quite different trade initiative when he sent a series of great naval expeditions, led by the eunuch admiral Zheng He, to the Indian Ocean. The route to southeast Asia was well known to Chinese traders, and Arabs had conducted maritime commerce with China for centuries. Zheng He was able to recruit Chinese Muslims who spoke Arabic to act as

BELOW **Swatow porcelain** was commissioned for the southeast Asian market, during the heightened period of trade during the Ming dynasty.

interpreters when he reached the Indian Ocean. Yongle's expeditions were ostensibly for diplomatic purposes; their official exchanges of gifts can be characterized as "tributary trade." Nevertheless, there were some items, especially spices, that China could not produce, that could only be obtained by trade. These expeditions carried many fine pieces of porcelain, along with other valuables, to be given to the rulers of other states as gifts of the Ming emperor. Dated Ming porcelains were used to decorate the ceiling of the Ardebil Shrine in Safavid Iran. Other fine pieces can be seen among the treasures of the Ottoman Empire on display in the Topkapi Palace Museum in Istanbul. Alongside official exchanges it must be assumed that considerable private trading also occurred.

The Growth of Maritime Trade

After Emperor Yongle, when imperial policy again emphasized exclusion of foreign contact, the growth of foreign trade was in the private sphere. Despite the lack of imperial enthusiasm, and even in the face of government attempts to ban seafaring, maritime trade grew substantially. Chinese products were well known overseas and demand was strong. Again, thanks to its durability, porcelain provides evidence of what happened. Tributary trade was succeeded and eclipsed in volume by commercial trade as Ming kilns and merchants tried to satisfy the foreign demand from Japan, Southeast Asia, and the Indian Ocean. By the second half of the sixteenth century, Western ships, especially Portuguese and Dutch, were carrying ever increasing volumes of Chinese porcelains to Europe. A single vessel could carry as many as 70,000 items. It became possible for European customers to special order china services to be manufactured with a family coat of arms or other Western-style decoration.

In order to purchase Ming goods Japanese, Portuguese, and Dutch traders brought quantities of silver to Chinese ports. This flow of bullion was substantially increased when, in the second half of the sixteenth century, the canny Spanish

established a foothold in the Philippines. Unlike the Portuguese and Dutch, who came to China by sailing around Africa and across the Indian Ocean, the Spanish came to Asia by crossing the Pacific. Spanish vessels, laden with silver from the mines of the New World, left Acapulco and crossed the Pacific on favorable winds for Manila. Silver was exchanged with Chinese merchants from Guangdong and Fujian for everything the Spanish needed to build and sustain their new colonial outposts: food, livestock, furniture, tools, and daily use items. The "Manila galleons" soon returned to New Spain stuffed with quantities of silks and porcelains for sale in the Americas and trans-shipments to Iberia.

Ming Money

Early in the Ming dynasty, the government issued paper money in denominations equal to strings of copper coins, which were depicted on the front and back of the notes. Paper money was convenient for the government because it served to facilitate payments to soldiers and officials in the north. However, the notes were not supported and rapidly fell into disuse. Small transactions were carried out with copper cash but the larger payments required the use of ingots of silver, which were not coined, and were cumbersome. With China's commercial economy expanding, demand for silver soared. From the middle of the sixteenth century, the Chinese willingness to exchange fine products for silver precipitated a

global flow of silver to China, directly from Japan and New Spain, indirectly on the Portuguese and Dutch ships from Europe. Inside China, the silver was substituted for labor service or taxes in kind owed to the government, this greatly facilitating long distance transactions and commerce. The Chinese trading boom had begun and the empire's prosperity was guaranteed.

ABOVE **Portuguese and Dutch ships** braved the treacherous journey to China to trade in the riches available.

LEFT A **Ming-dynasty banknote** was worth 1,000 cash coins. The evolution of paper money revolutionized Chinese currency.

Mongol and Japanese Foes

Ming security was challenged by the remaining Mongol troops in the north and by piracy along the coast. Invasion from the north threatened the dynasty's existence; coastal incursions caused disruption and economic loss without endangering the empire.

ABOVE **The Great Wall of China** was extended and rebuilt during the Ming period for protection against the Mongols.

After the fall of the Yuan in 1368, Mongol remnants continued to pose a threat in the north, and some strategic positions taken at the Ming garrisons had to be abandoned. The Ming military defense in the north combined diplomacy with the use of military force. Tribal leaders were granted titles as the heads of guard units (*wei*) and were encouraged to settle in areas along the border as defensive buffers. At the same time, Ming military outposts were established in strategic areas and supported either by part-time farming or the costly transport of daily supplies from the south. These elements were unsatisfactory: the allegiance of tribal leaders to the Ming ruler was subject to change and soldiers in fixed outposts could not match the mobility of the raiders with their exceptional horses.

During the founding emperor's reign, imperial princes joined with Ming commanders to pursue and harass Mongol leaders. Zhu Di, the Prince of Yan stationed at Beijing, was the most active in this military task. In 1302, having marched south and taken the capital at Nanjing, he usurped the throne and took the reign name Yongle. He subsequently moved the capital north to Beijing and used it as a base from which to lead five major military campaigns into the grasslands. The largest of these campaigns mobilized half a million men, including more than 10,000 mounted cavalry and much larger numbers of foot soldiers and transport workers. In 1424, Emperor Yongle was killed in action in the field during the fifth campaign.

Subsequent emperors were unable to match Yongle's military prowess. One who did try, the ineffectual Emperor Yingzong, was captured and taken prisoner by Mongol forces at Tumu in 1449. Disaster was averted and the dynasty saved when officials in Beijing installed Yingzong's brother on the throne and organized an effective defense of the capital. Unable to raise the ransom for the captive emperor, the Mongols then returned him unharmed. Ming defense policy shifted away from campaigning to reliance on static walls, fortifications, and outposts. The Great Wall is an enduring and impressive artifact of this period.

The Increasing Threat of Piracy

After the middle of the fourteenth century, tributary trade declined in importance as the Ming court turned its attention to the defense of the northern border. Coastal and overseas trade, however, continued to grow and could not be confined within the few ports like Canton and Ningbo, where the government allowed foreign merchants to call. By the 1520s, illegal traders and desperate commoners formed small pirate bands that operated from offshore islands, making raids along the coast. They were soon joined by growing numbers of Japanese intent on trade and plunder. This led the Chinese officials to label all the outlaws "Japanese Pirates," *wokou*, a derogatory term that might be interpreted as "dwarf bandits." In actuality, a majority of those involved were Chinese, and they had many connections to wealthy merchant families and local officials. By the 1550s, the level of violence escalated dramatically. The whole area of the southern coast became a total war zone, as armed bands raided and plundered cities, and even established fortified bases. The government responded by trying to enforce its prohibition on maritime trade, remove the civilian population from the coast, build its own fortifications, and raise troops to do battle with the raiders. After a decade of confused and destructive fighting, a degree of order was restored, Ming government policy changed, and maritime trading was again permitted along the southern coast.

It was just at this point in time that Western ships began to reach Chinese waters in significant numbers. In 1557, the Portuguese were allowed a permanent trading post on a peninsula at Macao, near Canton, a facility they maintained down to the end of the twentieth century. The Spanish

took possession of the Philippines in the 1570s where they came into conflict with Chinese pirates. They fought the pirates and pleaded with Ming coastal officials to allow them to establish a trading post similar to Macao. When this request was denied, they settled for large volume trade with Chinese merchants in Manila. When the Dutch appeared on the scene it was as much in the role of pirates as of merchants. They looted Chinese ships, raided along the coast, and, in 1622, attacked the Portuguese at Macao. Two years later, they established a base, Fort Zeelandia, on the island of Taiwan beyond the reach of Ming authorities. By the early 1600s, the western Pacific became an active venue for international piracy and trade, a competition in which the English and Japanese played significant roles.

ABOVE **A painting of two warriors** illustrates how thirteenth-century China was shaken by invasions from without and within its borders.

JAPANESE INVASION OF KOREA

The Yi dynasty (founded 1392) in Korea was a loyal tributary and ally of the Ming. In a rare engagement beyond its borders, the Ming sent aid to Korea when it was threatened. In 1590, after a century of civil war, Japan was unified by Toyotomi Hideyoshi. Two years later, declaring that he was going to conquer China, Hideyoshi sent an army to invade China's tributary ally, Korea. Moving north from Pusan, his army quickly took Seoul and Pyongyang, and then pushed northward toward the Yalu River, but it did not enter Chinese territory. Ming China responded by sending tens of thousands of soldiers and substantial naval forces. Two rounds of fighting and negotiations led to a peaceful Japanese withdrawal after Hideyoshi's death in 1598.

RIGHT **Toyotomi Hideyoshi, the Samurai feudal lord** and chief imperial minister of Japan who invaded Korea, was seen as a enormous threat to China's security. Hideyoshi, son of a peasant warrior, became one of Japan's most powerful warlords.

An Empire in Decline

To some living during the early 1600s, the tokens of the impending collapse of their dynasty were all too obvious in the social, political, and moral ills coming from the increasing wealth and luxury of the material circumstances of their world.

RIGHT **Porcelain wine containers** became more ornate and more detailed toward the end of the Ming dynasty.

The end, when it eventually came on the nineteenth day of the third month of the *Jiashen* year (a date that corresponds to April 25, 1644 in the Gregorian calendar), a day upon which "Earth cracked open, Heaven crumbled, and the sun and moon darkened," proved to be one of the most dramatic and cataclysmic dynastic transitions in Chinese history. As the troops of the rebel leader Li Zicheng (1605–1645) entered the outer suburbs of his capital, the ill-fated Emperor Chongzhen (1611–1644), then in the seventeenth year of his reign, took himself to the Imperial Hat and Girdle Department on Coal Hill and hanged himself, having the night before, in a drunken rage, killed his consorts and injured his daughter with his own sword. Some later reports claimed that he left behind a suicide note in

BELOW **This engraving of the death of the last Ming dynasty emperor** shows the recovery of the body of Chongzhen and one of his murdered consorts.

which he begged that both the imperial tombs and that the citizens of Beijing be left in peace. Within six weeks of his arrival, however, Li Zicheng had withdrawn from the city, only to die in obscure circumstances the next year. His short-lived and unrecognized Shun dynasty had collapsed, and Beijing, now in flames, was occupied by yet another army, that of the Qing under the command of Prince Regent Dorgon (1612–1650). For his part, his first public act after securing the city, was to ensure and oversee the appropriate burial and respect the memory of the last emperor of the Ming dynasty.

What Had Gone Wrong?

The reverberations of this transition from Ming to Qing lasted for much of the next half century. As the various Southern Ming imperial aspirants withdrew further and further southwards (the last person was executed in Yunnan in 1662), the educated men and women who had chosen to live through the drama (rather than become martyrs to the cause of their dynasty) positioned themselves—if only very provisionally—along a spectrum of engagement that stretched from armed opposition, to retreat from public life to, close accommodation with the new Manchu masters of the empire. Understood moralistically, the essayist and historian Zhang Dai (1597–1684), writing in 1655 as a "remnant subject" (*yimin*), who had remained loyal to the memory of the Ming dynasty

saw the collapse as a "large touchstone fallen from Heaven" that served to reveal the "true face" of his contemporaries, a "grand year-end settling of all outstanding accounts." Others, such as the scholar Gu Yanwu (1613–1682), another who refused all connection with the Qing, offered somewhat more technical explanations of the collapse of the dynasty; to his mind the fall of the Ming had been the inevitable result of the sclerosis of the very arteries of the empire as a result of the serious misuse and under-funding of the official postal service; ensuring that communications were stalled.

Taxing Problems

To many historians, both contemporary and modern, it was the middle years of the almost sixty-year reign of the Wanli emperor (1563–1620) that marked the turning point. On the one hand, the late Ming was an age of explosive economic and commercial development, fueled by the growth of commodity markets, and the partial conversion to legal tender of the massive amounts of imported New World silver bullion; of a rapid rise in population (estimates range between 150 to 175 million by the end of the sixteenth century); and of increased levels of urbanization. On the other hand, such changes, brought with them increased levels of social mobility and of literacy, and served to unsettle China's ruling elite by undermining existing status relationships. An expanded and commercialized publishing industry took advantage of this mobility, and the flourishing popular culture of the urban centers of China displayed a greater willingness to question and undermine existing Neo-Confucian orthodoxies.

Accompanying such socioeconomic challenges were the age-old (and, to many contemporary observers, unmistakable) signs of severe dynastic decline; an incompetent and extravagant emperor increasingly uninterested in the administration of his empire, particularly once his own preferred arrangements for his succession had been cruelly thwarted at court, the consequent expansion of eunuch power, intense factionalism and widespread corruption among the officials both at court and out in the provinces, localized natural disasters and food shortages, increased expenditures on a number of wasteful and failed military campaigns, rampant inflation, and increasingly

obvious disparities of wealth. For the decade between 1572 and 1582, while the day-to-day administration of the empire was in the firm and resourceful hands of Zhang Juzheng (1525–1582), the emperor's erstwhile tutor and now the Grand Secretary, its plight seemed reversible. His introduction of the "Single Whip" method of taxation, in particular, whereby a uniform and consolidated form of tax was imposed on the basis of detailed knowledge of local circumstances, was payable in silver throughout the empire, served to improve the efficiency of the imperial bureaucracy and replenish the emperor's reserves of grain and bullion. Piecemeal measures imposed throughout the state by means of the considerable force of Zhang Juzheng's personality, however, could not serve to reform a government system committed to preserving the agrarian simplicity of a golden Confucian age long gone. With his death and the posthumous disgrace, and the repudiation of his more successful measures, the empire seemed finally incapable of dealing effectively with the various threats, both internal and external, to its political order. It was these continuing threats that eventually overran and destroy the dynasty.

ABOVE **Mandarins of the Ming dynasty court** wore embroidered plaques on their robes. These served as badges of rank on the robes of Chinese officials.

Ming Ceramics

Chinese Dragon Jar Teapot

At the beginning of the Ming dynasty, leaf infusion tea became popular. The earliest examples of teapots came from this period, made from the purple clay of the Yi Xing in Jiangsu Province.

Porcelain manufacture reached new heights, in both quality and volume of production, starting in the fifteenth century. In recent years Ming porcelains have been among the most prized art objects in the world in value at auction.

The greatest and biggest center of Ming porcelain production was at Jingdezhen in Jiangxi, thanks to ample deposits of *gaolin* (china clay). The most important consumer of porcelain was the Imperial Porcelain Depot through which eunuch overseers placed extremely large orders for the imperial household. Often, thousands of vessels were ordered at a time.

The monochrome vessels that had reigned supreme in the Song era continued to be made in the Ming dynasty. Pure white and celadon wares were often enhanced with barely visible molded or incised patterns of imperial dragons. Monochrome red, blue, and yellow bowls of elegant simplicity, in their lack of superfluous detail, appear modern to our eyes. But the greatest triumph was the blue and white decorations that have come to be regarded as emblematic

Ming Vase with Three-color Decoration

Although blue and white porcelain is the most recognizable from the Ming dynasty period, experimentation with three-color glazes become popular within China.

Blue and White Porcelain Bowl
The imagery painted on the side of this fifteenth-century Ming dynasty bowl includes pine, plum and bamboo, which are grouped together and commonly known as the "three friends of winter."

of the Ming dynasty. Blue and white porcelain was made in earlier periods but it had never before gained imperial favor as it did in the early Ming dynasty. Blue and whites emerged in full glory in the Xuande period (1426–35) when, with China at peace, there was a jump in both the quality and volume of wares produced. Ming blue and white ceramics surpassed their Yuan predecessors in two ways. One was the richness of the color of the blue underglaze. This depended on the care taken in firing, and the quality and availability of cobalt oxide that produced the blue. When supplies were short, cobalt had to be imported from the Middle East. The other difference from the Yuan dynasty style was the way decoration was applied to the vessels. Ming dynasty artisans achieved more with less, allowing bands and spaces of white to accent the areas of blue decoration.

Ming porcelains were made in many sizes, shapes, colors, and styles. Vessels procured for the imperial household ranged from tiny cups just big enough to hold a grape, to enormous pieces well over 4 ft (over 1 m) in height. In addition to utilitarian wares for daily use, many objects were made to imitate the form of objects originally made from other materials. The ritual vessels previously cast from bronze were cleverly reproduced in porcelain. Tall pitchers and shallow serving dishes with flat edges assumed the shapes of hammered metal vessels from the Middle East. Elegant flasks echoed the appearance of humble gourd water bottles, revealing Central Asian influence.

From the early fifteenth century it became standard practice to date porcelain vessels with the reign period when they were produced. This marking was usually applied to the underside of vessels in the form of six characters applied in two vertical rows and encircled by two narrow lines. A typical marking might say "Da Ming Xuande nian zhi"— meaning it was manufactured in the Xuande period of the Great Ming. On occasion the words, Great Ming, were omitted, or the whole phrase was placed on the side of a vessel. In later times, copies and forgeries routinely came to include dates that did not tally up with the traditional Ming dynasty wares.

A Many Splendored Thing: Ming Decorations

The most common decorations on Ming porcelains were flowers, trees, plants, animals, and birds. Some had political significance such as the five-clawed dragon that represented the emperor or the phoenix that stood for the empress. Many conveyed conventional, often religious, symbolism. The pine, bamboo, and plum were the "three friends of winter." Lotus flowers were a Buddhist symbol; the crane, a Daoist allusion. Just as the shape of Ming porcelains could mimic handicraft items in other materials, so the subject matter interacted with other arts. Paintings of immortals, or children at play, or panels with characters from well-known stories could appear on the surface of a vessel, and so too could text. A poem might float next to an illustration or a pious expression in Sanskrit or Arabic might be artfully worked into the intricate design.

The Jesuits in China

From the 1580s onwards as part of their mission to China, the Jesuits inaugurated an intercultural conversation between East and West that has continued, sometimes fitfully, until the present day.

ABOVE **Saint Ignatius of Loyola (1491–1556)** was the founder of the Jesuit Order, a religious order of the Catholic Church.

Quintessential products of Catholic Renaissance humanism, the loyal members of the order of the Society of Jesus (or the Jesuits), established in 1541 by Saint Ignatius Loyola (died 1556), were long dedicated to "procuring the progress of men's souls in their lives and in the Christian doctrine...by reasoning with the public and by teaching." Those Jesuits who journeyed eastward were an intellectual elite from throughout Europe, trained in an Aristotelian scholasticism that had only recently been challenged by new ideas and discoveries, disciplined and pious in their commitment to their mission to convert the Chinese to Catholicism. It was a mission, that, to the Jesuits' minds, involved a two-way exchange of knowledge; just as they sought to understand the history, geography, languages, and literatures of the peoples of the East and to spread this newly found knowledge, so too were they intent on making available to such peoples the best that European culture had to offer.

The story told of this mission usually focuses on the labors of one man. An Italian Jesuit, Matteo Ricci's (1552–1610) initial progress toward Beijing where the Wanli Emperor, the object of his mission, sat at the heart of an empire, was excruciatingly slow and filled with incident. Ricci was stoned, robbed, and arrested. His companions died, and his boat was shipwrecked. Throughout all of this, he was engaged in a heroic struggle to understand the spoken and written languages of China, a task that some among his fellow Jesuits believed to be a "hopeless enterprise," and for which he had available to him none of the usual tools of grammars and dictionaries. In this respect, Ricci's success was truly remarkable. Ill and dispirited, he began his study of Chinese in the early 1580s. Within a year or so he was able to hear confession in the language. By the 1590s he had begun to translate the five books of the Confucian canon into Latin, and in 1595 he issued his first full composition in Chinese, his authoritative *Treatise on Friendship.*

Communicating across Cultures

The textual and linguistic conditions for the work Ricci was engaged in were complex. Although the *lingua franca* for the Jesuit community in China was Portuguese, their letters back home (and to Rome in particular) telling of their experiences were written in a variety of European languages. Many of these letters were translated into Latin by their fellow Jesuit Nicolas Trigault (1577–1628) and circulated widely throughout Europe; tracts, excerpts, and summaries of these reports were made available to English readers as early as 1625. This attempt to communicate across many cultures and civilizations relied upon numerous conversations conducted in a wide variety of languages and dialects, both European and Chinese, and the production of volumes of text. The latter was a process that was dependent upon quite remarkable and sustained efforts of acquiring the language, of translation, and of interpretation between two of the world's great "sacred languages," classical Chinese and Latin, languages that are commonly understood to work at opposite ends of the spectrum of linguistics, and both of which had fallen silent a thousand or more years earlier.

Blending into the Landscape

The late imperial Chinese world that greeted Ricci and his companions was one governed by a set of time-honored sumptuary laws that sought to regulate all aspects of consumption: housing, food, and clothing. Although the commercial revolution of the times had served to loosen the grip of such controls, the rules that governed the

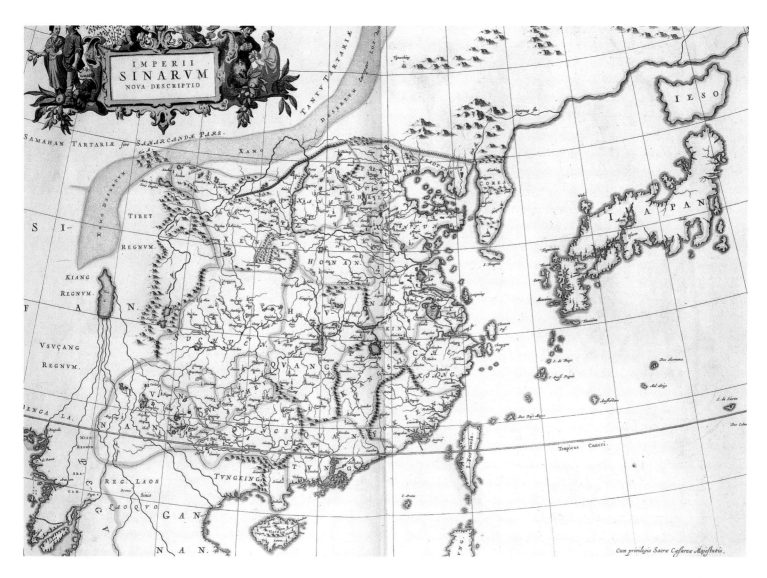

official robes and accoutrements of the scholar–official elite continued to be strictly observed. When Matteo Ricci accompanied his fellow Jesuit Michele Ruggieri (1543–1607) to the city of Zhaoqing (in Canton Province) to establish the first inland Chinese mission in 1583, they were dressed in the robes of a Buddhist monk, having also shaven their heads and faces. By the early 1590s, however, Ricci had begun to realize the severe disadvantage of this particular guise. Buddhist monks, almost by definition, had little status in educated society, and tended to be treated with contempt by both scholar and official alike. Buddhism, in any case, in China at this time, was only just recovering from a long phase of intellectual and organizational decline. On the advice of a Chinese acquaintance, the Jesuits decided that they should don the robes of the

Confucian scholar. Having obtained permission for this change from his superiors, Ricci first appeared in public in his new robes in 1595, later writing that: "Since persons receiving visitors dress, in accordance with their rank, in the same way, my prestige is greatly enhanced when I go visiting."

ABOVE **This map of Imperial China** was prepared in 1653–1658 by Jesuit missionary, historian, and cartographer, Martino Martini.

RIGHT **The Jesuit Cathedral façade** in Beijing is flanked by classic Chinese architecture. This is symbolic of the history of relations between China and the West and shows the contrast between the two sets of beliefs.

BREAKING DOWN RELIGIOUS BARRIERS

Just as the Jesuit reports about China were to have a remarkable and lasting impact on the thinking of many of the leading intellectual figures of the European Enlightenment (to the extent that one scholar has argued that Confucius became this movement's patron saint), the European texts that the Jesuits translated into Chinese, designated as "Learning from Heaven" (*tianxue*) or "Western Learning" (*xixue*), had a remarkable and lasting impact within Chinese scholarly circles. In his "Preface" to the fourth edition of Ricci's world map, the Chinese scholar Feng Yingjing (1555–1606) gave poignant expression to the hopes embodied in this remarkable instance of intercultural conversation. "Just as the Western countries have certainly never heard of the teachings of the Sages of the Middle Kingdom, so too have we never heard tell of the books of their ancient Saints and Scholars now circulating here. Now, however, both enlighten and benefit each other…so that misunderstandings between the people of the far-flung East and West will no longer exist."

LEFT **The Great Universal Geographic Map** was carried by the Jesuit, Matteo Ricci when he journeyed to China in 1608. This world view amazed the insular Chinese society.

The prevailing theme of Matteo Ricci's life in China is explained by the word "accommodation." He had become a "Western Confucian Scholar" (*xiru*), and dressed in a scholar's robes and also produced the text expected of such men, "as though we were men of China." As he changed his clothes—from the student clothes of his time in Rome, to the clerical habit of Christian Europe, to the Buddhist robes of his first few years in China, and finally to his scholar's gown—as a result, his entire frame of reference begin to shift from that of an outsider to that of an insider, from observer to participant.

China's Place in the World

Matteo Ricci carried with him to China a recently drawn world map. It instantly attracted the curiosity of the Chinese scholars he met with, and he was forever being asked for copies of the map. Many changes took place in the series of maps produced to satisfy such requests; the maps were made to "speak Chinese" in two distinct ways. First, all the place names and terms were transliterated into Chinese. Second, and more significantly, China increased in size and was placed toward the centre of the map, to better accord with the traditional Chinese views of their empire as being the Middle Kingdom, culturally and politically as much perhaps as merely geographically. Ricci's maps, far from representing the introduction of value-free scientific truth into China, are better understood as a technique in what has been better labeled as the "enterprise of seduction." Ricci understood that for his map to be accepted as "true," some considerable alteration in traditional Chinese conception of the world as flat and square would be required. He was traveling in China with the strong hope of converting the Chinese people to Christianity, however, and in this respect his scientific toolkit was simply a mere sideline to this particular mission—designed more to impress and interest people, perhaps, rather than to communicate the immutable and verifiable "truths" about the shape and state of the world.

Accepting Christianity

If the Jesuit engagement with Chinese cartography served to dispel

RIGHT **This blue and white Ming dynasty dish** was made for the Jesuits to take back to Europe.

certain myths about the imaginative geography of the world in general, and the shape of China in particular, their intensive effort to learn the language of China served also to dispel a number of powerful linguistic myths about the nature of the Chinese language and of Chinese characters in particular.

The Jesuits sought to perpetrate their own, and convenient, understanding of the prevailing religious circumstances of China. Dismissing both Daoism and Chinese Buddhism as irrelevant, Ricci argued that the Chinese believed a "Natural Religion" that was very much in keeping with Christianity. "Of all the pagan sects known to Europe," Ricci argued, "I know of no people who fell into fewer errors in the early ages of their antiquity than did the Chinese. From the very beginning of their history it is recorded in their writings that they recognized and worshipped one supreme being whom they called the King of Heaven...One can confidently hope that in the eyes and mercy of God, many of the ancient Chinese found salvation in the natural law..." In a way the Chinese had been Christians all along, it appeared, beliefs having found expression in Confucianism were presented by the Jesuits as being essentially secularist. This argument led to the Jesuit's greatest and significant aspect of accommodation, the use of pre-existing Chinese terminology for their Christian concepts, and their acceptance of the possibility that the Chinese could continue to undertake their own rites and rituals (particularly those associated with ancestor worship), and become Christians at the same time. In conversation with the Jesuit's great Chinese interlocutors and converts—with men such as Xu Guangqi (1562–1633) and also Li Zhizao (1565–1630)—the Catholicism that they brought to China seemed about to be transformed by its Chinese circumstances. In this respect, there exists an extraordinary historical irony in the fact that shortly after the Kangxi Emperor declared, in 1692, that Christianity was no longer to be listed as a ruinous

doctrine, a series of Papal Bulls of 1704, 1707, 1715, and again of 1742, condemned what it now labeled the "Chinese Rites" and banned any further "accommodation" of the type that Ricci had undertaken, a decision only reversed in 1939.

Death in Beijing

Matteo Ricci did not live to either celebrate the victory or to suffer the defeat of his lifetime's efforts. Having fallen ill in May 1610, the ministrations and comprehensive medical care of Beijing's best physicians proved to be unsuccessful. After taking the act of anointing, Ricci called his fellow priests to his bedside. His last words to them seemed almost prophetic: "I am leaving you on the threshold of an open door that leads to great reward, but only after labors endured and dangers encountered." At the time of his death, the estimated number of Chinese Catholics stood at around 2,500; by 1700, this figure had grown to 200,000. As a token of favor, Ricci was buried just beyond the inner walls of Beijing, an order that was specifically granted to him by the emperor.

BELOW **Founded by the Jesuits in 1602,** St. Paul's Cathedral is one of the major landmarks in Macao.

The Origins of the Manchus

In 1644 the Manchus, a semi-nomadic people from northeast of the Great Wall, conquered China and established the Qing dynasty. In the process, they expanded the territory of the former Ming dynasty to include new territories in Central Asia, Tibet, and Siberia.

ABOVE **Changbaishan,** near the North Korean border, is the mythical birthplace of Nurhaci and was considered sacred by the Manchus. Changbaishan means Perpetually White Mountain.

RIGHT **The Imperial Palace in Shenyang**, which Nurhaci began and son Hongtaiji completed, contains many objets d'art such as this blue cloisonne lion dog.

Prior to 1635, there was no group of people calling themselves the Manchus. The majority of their ancestors were the Jurchens, who had defeated the Liao dynasty in 1115 and, soon afterwards, formally established a new dynasty in northern China called the Jin. The Jin dynasty were constantly at war with the Southern Song dynasty, interspersed only intermittently with periods of uneasy coexistence.

The Jurchens

The Mongols defeated the Jin in 1234 and the Jurchens returned to their forests and mountains in the northeast. The Jurchen in the Sungari River region were hunters and fishermen; while some, who had a mixed agricultural and hunting economy, lived near Changbaishan, a mountain range which now separates China from North Korea. Other Jurchens lived as agriculturalists with Chinese emigrants along the Liao River (in present-day Liaoning Province), also establishing a lively business selling ginseng to China.

Ming strategy had been to gain the support of the Jurchens by including their territories in the Chinese defense system. The Jurchens were given honorary titles and trading privileges in exchange for recognition of Ming suzerainty. Garrisons were established to consolidate Ming sovereignty as far north as Nurgan, now Tyr in Russia.

Nurhaci

Nurhaci, a Jurchen, was born in the region of Jianzhou in 1559. His grandfathers on both sides of the family had been granted military titles by the Ming. As a young man, he traded in ginseng, mushrooms, and various furs in exchange for Chinese goods. He traveled to Peking to pay homage to the Ming court and received an honorary title for his family's support for the Ming. However, in 1583, as a result of a dispute among some Jurchen tribes, the Ming army massacred an entire village, killing over 2,000 people, including Nurhaci's father and grandfather. When Nurhaci demanded an explanation as to why his father and grandfather had been killed when they were loyal to the Ming, the Ming general simply answered: "It was a mistake."

Despite the Ming having returned his father's body for burial and compensating him with 30 horses and official titles as a gesture of reconciliation, Nurhaci was determined to take revenge. He knew that in order to become a powerful military force he must first unify the Jurchen tribes. It took Nurhaci the next 30 years, through warfare, threats, marriages and other alliances, to achieve this goal. By 1616, all the Jurchen tribes were united and Nurhaci declared himself khan of the state of Jin (referred to by historians as the Later Jin). He waited another two years, until, in 1618, he declared war on the Ming dynasty.

Nurhaci announced the "Seven Great Grievances," in which he listed all the wrongs the Ming court had done to him and his people. The Ming dynasty, which was in its last stages due to decades of incompetent government, was not in a position to bring the recalcitrant Jurchens, who were far north of the Great Wall, to heel.

During the four decades of the process of the unification of the Jurchen tribes, Nurhaci accomplished three crucial cultural, military, social, and economic tasks. He built a stable social and economic territorial base, established the Eight Banner military system, and created a written form specifically for the Jurchen language. Before this, Jurchen was an oral language only, having lost the ancestral written script of the Jin dynasty some time in the fifteenth century. For official communications, Mongolian or Chinese script was used. In 1599, however, Nurhaci ordered scholars to modify the Mongol script so that it could be used to write Jurchen. Later, diacritics were added to make it correspond to the Manchu language more precisely.

The Establishment of the Qing

From 1618, when Nurhaci declared war on the Ming, there were seven major battles fought over control of the Liaodong area. Nurhaci won all of them. After his death in 1626, his son Hongtaiji continued the military expansion. In 1636, he changed the name of the dynasty from Jin to Qing. The new term "Manchu" was coined to describe the citizens of the new state which, while predominantly Jurchen, included Mongols, Koreans, Sibes, Daurs, and Chinese residing in Qing territory. They did not all share the same

culture, language or life style, although the Jurchens provided a core. They were united only by their acceptance (by force or otherwise) of the newly emerging leadership.

In 1638, Hongtaiji conquered Korea and forced the king to change Korea's loyalty from the Ming to the Manchus. Internal chaos in Ming China, in particular the capture of the capital by the rebel Li Zicheng and the suicide of the last Ming emperor, resulted in the passes in the Great Wall being essentially undefended. In 1644, a year after Hongtaiji's death, the Manchus seized the opportunity to march on the Ming capital and take it with little resistance.

After proclaiming a new emperor and establishing their military supremacy in China, the Manchus turned their attention to Central Asia, which had never been a part of Ming territory. With a series of ambitious military campaigns, astute diplomacy, and economic investment, they defeated their major rivals, the Zungar Mongols. They brought under their control all of eastern Turkestan, which they renamed Xinjiang (the new territories), as well as all of Mongolia. In addition, they gained a dominant influence in Tibet. These frontier conquests brought about the geographical and political entity we know today as China.

ABOVE **The Imperial Palace at Liaoning, Shenyang,** although much smaller in scope, was built on the same principles as the Forbidden City in Beijing.

Kangxi and Yongzheng

The reign of Kangxi (1662–1722) consolidated Manchu rule in China and expanded the empire to its largest scale, second only to the Yuan under the Mongols. Kangxi's son, the Yongzheng emperor, laid the foundation for a further 60 years of prosperity.

Hongtaiji died of a cerebral hemorrhage in 1643, just one year before the Manchus breached the Great Wall. Thus, it was not Nurhaci nor his son Hongtaiji who became the first Qing emperor, but Shunzhi.

The First Two Emperors

Shunzhi was six years old when he was installed as emperor. This was engineered by his strong-minded mother, Empress Dowager Xiaozhuang, who was a descendant of a brother of Genghis Khan (Chinggis Khan). Throughout his life he lacked the leadership qualities of his father and grandfather and the regent, his uncle Dorgon, dominated decision making until his own death.

Shunzhi is remembered more for his passionate love affair than for his political merit. He was deeply in love with his half brother's consort and when she died, he was inconsolable and

wanted to abandon his throne to become a monk. The following year, he died of smallpox, aged 24. It was his second son, not the first, who inherited the throne as he had already had smallpox and was immune from the fate of his father. Smallpox was lethal to the Manchus and Tibetans as they had less resistance to this deadly disease in China than in their homelands. Shunzhi's second son, who was called the Kangxi emperor, reigned for 61 years. He was the longest ruling and one of the greatest emperors in Chinese history.

As a boy emperor, Kangxi had four regents appointed by his dying father to assist him in government. The strongest, Oboi, became dangerously dominating. Kangxi demonstrated his patience, political skill and intelligence from a very young age when, as a 15-year old, he put into effect a series of events that led to Oboi's arrest and eventual execution.

BELOW **Emperor Kangxi,** seen here beside the imperial palace moat on his return to Beijing *c.*1670, was free from the control of his regents from about the age of 16.

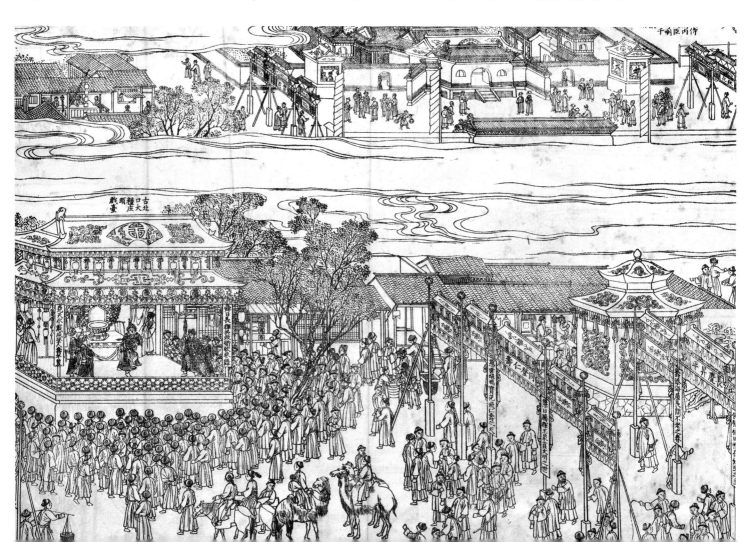

Consolidation of Rule Under the Qing

In the past, parts of China had been conquered many times by its northern neighbors. After the Mongols, the Manchus were the second non-Han Chinese ethnic group to claim the "Mandate of Heaven" to rule all of China. The Manchus, however, made up less than two percent of the entire population. The most urgent task for Emperor Kangxi, therefore, was how to consolidate Qing rule in such a vast territory and how to win the "hearts and minds" of the Chinese population.

When Kangxi's rule began, China was not entirely under the control of the central government. The Three Feudatories, Shang Kexi, Geng Jinmao and Wu Sangui controlled the geologically difficult southwest, including Yunnan, Guizhou, Guangdong, and parts of Hunan and Sichuan—a region as large as France and Spain put together. Both Shang Kexi and Geng Jinmao were Chinese bannermen who had surrendered to the Manchus in 1633. Wu Sangui, who had formerly been a Ming general, contributed to the final entry of the Manchu army through the Great Wall. The three leaders had been granted the status of Prince by the Qing Court, and their sons were married to daughters of Manchu nobles, with Wu's son marrying Emperor Shunzhi's sister.

More importantly, Shang, Geng and Wu had been awarded land and positions that essentially made them independent rulers of the region. They were in charge of every aspect of government— both military and civil—including the collection of taxes. They kept their trade monopolies while at the same time repeatedly making demands on Beijing for subsidies. When the price of keeping their loyalty became too high, Kangxi attempted to persuade Wu to leave his power base in Yunnan by moving him to a position in Beijing. However, Wu broke from the Qing in 1673 and declared his own dynasty. A year later, in 1674, Geng revolted and two years after that, Shang joined the rebellion. The inevitable war, from 1673 to 1681 almost succeeded in destroying the Qing, but after eight years Kangxi finally prevailed.

Kangxi then turned his attention to Taiwan, which, in the early seventeenth century was occupied by its native population together with European traders and Japanese and Chinese pirates. When pirate and trader, Zheng Chenggong, expelled the small Dutch settlement in the north of the island in 1662, the Ming court in its dying days had made him an official, and Taiwan remained the base for Ming loyalists intent on regaining power in China. In the early 1660s Kangxi's regents had tried unsuccessfully to force Taiwan into submission. While Kangxi was busy with the war against the Three Feudatories, he had little time to pay attention to Zheng and the Ming loyalists in

ABOVE **A statue of Zheng Chenggong** stands on Fuding Rock, on Gulang Island, where he established a base. Zheng is considered a Chinese national hero.

LEFT **Kangxi** achieved stability within his empire. by means of warfare against enemies both inside and outside China's borders. His actions are recorded here on fine porcelain.

Taiwan. Two years after the war, however, Kangxi launched a successful attack on Taiwan which was then integrated into Chinese territory. By the time he was 30 years old, Kangxi had accomplished consolidation of Qing rule throughout all of China.

Territorial Expansion

Despite Kangxi's consolidation of Qing rule, there were still threats from the northern frontiers. In the northeast, the Qing faced a threat from the Russians, who at that time were expanding into Siberia. A skirmish broke out at Albazin on the Amur River, and Kangxi sent in troops. After a brief military conflict, both sides preferred a peaceful solution which, in 1689, resulted in the Treaty of Nerchinsk that determined the border between the Russian and Chinese empires. This was the first time China had signed a treaty with a foreign power on equal terms. It was also the last until recent time. Treaties that followed were a series of "unequal treaties," that began with the one after the Opium War.

The Zunghars, a west Mongolian tribe, controlled a large area which now includes Mongolia, Qinghai and parts of Xinjiang. In order to prevent a possible alliance between the Russians and the Zunghars, Kangxi waged war on the Zunghar leader, Galdan, leading the troops into battle himself three times. Galdan was defeated and died the next year, in 1697. Soon after, however, other Zunghar leaders emerged and occupied Tibet and, in 1720, Kangxi decided to invade Tibet. Qing forces entered the Tibetan capital, Lhasa, from

RIGHT **Johann Schall von Bell,** a German Jesuit missionary, was imprisoned by Kangxi's regents for "propagation of an evil religion." On reaching his majority, Kangxi declared the sentence void.

two different directions and a new Dalai Lama, chosen by the Qing government, was installed. The Qing had now secured its frontiers with the Russians, Mongols, and Tibetans. The territorial expansion of the Qing had reached an unprecedented scale.

Winning the Hearts and Minds of the Han

As emperor of a multicultural dynasty, Kangxi had to deal with many different ethnic groups. In order to keep the Mongols and Tibetans in the Qing alliance, the court favored Tibetan Buddhism and formed marriage alliances with Mongol princes. On the other hand, in order to win the support of the Chinese, especially scholars, the court illustrated moral leadership in terms of Confucian values.

The Qing had largely adopted the previous Ming administrative system, and the traditional Chinese examination system was reinstalled as early as the Shunzhi period. Kangxi started to recruit Chinese scholars from the Yangzi River delta area which was not only the richest area in China, but had also produced many of China's finest scholars and high ranking officials over several centuries. Thus, Kangxi brought the Confucian establishment into his administration. Kangxi also emphasized his dedication to the Confucian virtue of filial piety by his long-term devotion to his grandmother, the Empress Dowager Xiaozhuang.

Kangxi made special efforts to demonstrate his patronage of Chinese scholarship. The most famous works compiled during his reign were the *Kangxi Dictionary*, and the *Complete Poems of the*

Tang Dynasty. Through his political skill and genuine commitment to Confucian values, he was able to turn resentment toward the Manchus among the Chinese elite and the population at large into acceptance and, eventually, into loyalty to the Qing dynasty.

Christian Missions

Emperor Kangxi had a great intellectual interest in pursuing new knowledge, particularly Western scientific knowledge brought to China by European Jesuits. As a result he had a good number of Jesuits serving in his court as artists, scientists, and engineers.

Kangxi initially had a relaxed attitude towards Christianity, and cathedrals and churches were permitted to be built in the capital and provinces. However, a dispute developed between the Dominicans and the Jesuits as to whether Chinese folk religion or Confucian rites were in conflict with Christian teaching. When Pope Clement XI decided in favor of the Dominicans, Kangxi was furious and banned Christian missions in China. However, he retained Jesuits at court, largely in secular functions.

Kangxi did not manage the issue of his succession as well as he did other matters. His 40 consorts produced 20 daughters and 36 sons, of whom 24 survived childhood, making a formidable number of contenders. Manchus did not traditionally, name their successor, and succession often fell to a brother, or a son or other member of the family, not necessarily the eldest. However, Kangxi named his 18-month-old son as his heir apparent in 1697. Years later, Kangxi came to believe that this son was unfit for the throne. He stripped him of his status of Crown Prince and put him under house arrest. Some years later, he reinstated this son, only to demote him soon after. All this created fierce rival factions among the princes, and deep divisions in the court. Plots led to arrests and executions.

When Kangxi died, his fourth son, who had never before seemed a keen contender in the race, inherited the throne, claiming that Kangxi

YONGZHENG'S REFORMS

Yongzheng undertook a monumental reform of the state tax system, transforming Qing fiscal policy to provide a reliable revenue stream at the local and national levels. The old system focused entirely on providing sufficient revenues for the central state, and the management of local government expenses was entirely up to local officials, which created opportunity for corruption. The new system allowed local officials to have a clear idea of how much money was available to them so that they did not have to rely completely on "squeeze" to carry out projects such as road maintenance and granary construction. During the later years of Kangxi's reign, some fundamental problems, such as tax reform, land survey and reclamation, had been neglected. Without Yongzheng's reforms and improvements to the bureaucracy, the prosperity of the following reign, that of Qianlong, would not have been possible.

had appointed him on his deathbed. He became known as Emperor Yongzheng (reigned 1723–1735). Yongzheng 's right to accession was considered dubious, and there was a popular rumor that he had forged Kangxi's will in order to steal the throne from his brother. The evidence for such allegations was provided by his ruthless treatment of his rival brothers and their associates after his succession. However, as an emperor, Yongzheng proved to be incorruptible, diligent, and competent. Measured by the amount of the correspondence between the emperor and his officials, his workload during the 13 years of his reign was far greater than the combined workload of his father in his 61-year reign and his son in his 60-year reign. Unlike his father's rather Daoist approach of minimal interference in the workings of the state, Emperor Yongzheng was extremely aggressive in targeting problems, and ruthlessly attempted to rid the empire of widespread government corruption.

LEFT **This etching of Kangxi** by Jesuit Bishop Alphonse Favier (1837-1905) is a copy of an original Chinese portrait. The etching was published in Favier's *Péking, Histoire et Description*.

The Qianlong Emperor

During the eighteenth century, the Qing expanded its territory even further, and the Qianlong emperor (reigned 1736–1795) became a great patron of Chinese culture and art. Qianlong represented himself as a "Universal Monarch," a ruler for all ethnic groups in China and beyond.

In order to spare his chosen son a succession struggle, Yongzheng secretly named Qianlong (1711–1799) as his heir apparent soon after his own succession to the throne in 1723. At the age of 12 years, Qianlong had been introduced to his grandfather, Kangxi, who was very impressed by the boy's brightness, maturity, and mastery of the Chinese classics. Qianlong was known to have become the favorite of his grandfather, and this later became part of Qianlong's political capital, and supported the legitimacy of his inheritance.

After his father's death, Qianlong became emperor with little opposition. He vowed his rule would not exceed the reign of his grandfather's 61 years. Should he be fortunate enough to live longer than 60 years, he would abdicate as a gesture of filial piety. In fact, he lived to the age of 89, and was reluctant to hand over power to his son. After formally abdicating, he continued to reign behind the scenes until his death. Late in his life, Qianlong was pleased to call himself "an old man with a perfect life."

BELOW **Qianlong,** who was an enthusiastic poet and essayist, published more than 40,000 poems and 1,300 prose texts in the course of his lifetime.

Military Campaigns

Qianlong's proudest and most frequently mentioned achievement was a series of wars he fought during his reign. Known as the Ten Perfect Campaigns, they were fought to suppress rebels, such as those in Taiwan and the Jinchuan Tibetans in western Sichuan, in order to secure or extend the northwest and southwest borders.

The two campaigns fought against the Zunghar Mongols (1755–1757) were the most significant. His grandfather and father had waged battle after battle against the Zunghars, but the most they had been able to achieve was a temporary peace, and every new leader of the Zunghars brought new challenges for the Qing. Qianlong, however, destroyed the Zunghars once and for all. He secured both the northern and western borders and diminished Mongol influence in Tibet. Much of the Zunghar territories were incorporated into Xinjiang.

The next campaign (1758–1759) was against the Turkish speaking Islamic population, the ancestors of the modern Uighurs. In 1764, Qianlong stationed a garrison of troops from central Manchuria, at the far eastern border, to defend the new frontiers. These troops were the ancestors of the Sibe, a people who are still living in that area today and who still speak a language very close to Manchu. This vast area of central Asia was included in the Qing Empire, and has remained a part of the territory of successive Chinese states.

The campaign against the Gurkhas in Nepal was undertaken to eliminate external influence in Tibet. An emerging strong state in Nepal, with British support through the East India Company, invaded southern Tibet in 1788. In 1791, the Qianlong emperor dispatched an army of 10,000 troops to the area. The war ended with the victory of the Qing in 1793.

Patron of Chinese Learning

Qianlong manifested different images to many different ethnic groups. To the Tibetans, he presented himself as a reincarnation of Manjusri, one of the most important bodhisattvas of Tibetan Buddhism. To the Han Chinese, he was a scholar and patron of Chinese learning and art.

The *Complete Library of Four Treasures* (*Siku Quanshu*) was his most outstanding cultural monument, and the largest single publishing project in Chinese history. Started in 1772, it took 20 years to complete. The four treasures represent the major categories of traditional Chinese knowledge: classics, history, philosophy, and literature. Nationwide, a total of 13,254 books

his officials selected certain words and sentences from poems and articles to charge the authors or possessors with sedition or other crimes. Offenders, and even their family members and relatives, could be killed for such crimes. Several years after the literary inquisition, the emperor secretly put in place a similar campaign to censor drama scripts. This proved to be more difficult because the authorship of such traditional dramas could often not be determined.

The rationale behind such a campaign has never been clearly understood, as there was no threat to the legitimacy of Qianlong's rule and no single event in the political and intellectual history of the 1770s that could be said to have triggered the campaign.

Art Collector Extraordinaire

Qianlong had a taste for grandeur. What ever he did, was done in a spectacular way. As a passionate and indefatigable art collector, he built a vast imperial collection of different kinds of artifacts including jade, ancient bronzes, seals, paintings, calligraphy, and ceramics. Some historians say that Qianlong was obsessed with surrounding himself with material treasures; others say he saw himself in the role of preserver and restorer of the Chinese cultural heritage. Whatever his reason was, Qianlong acquired the great private collections of the seventeenth century, and integrated their treasures into his own collection.

LEFT **Qianlong** took pride in his military achievements. This portrait of the emperor in ceremonial armor was painted by Jesuit and court painter to three emperors, Giuseppe Castiglione.

BELOW **This white jade seal,** inscribed *Tai Shang Huang Di* (Father of the Emperor), was carved on the occasion of Qianlong's abdication.

were collected and thousands of scholars were involved. Over four million pages were transcribed by thousands of copyists. Even to this day, the *Four Treasures* is still an extremely valuable resource for scholars.

The *Four Treasures* project also had a hidden agenda, however; it enabled Qianlong to carry out a nationwide campaign of censorship that lasted from 1772 to 1788. All books collected from scholar families were examined. Any that contained sensitive or offensive anti-Manchu sentiments had to be handed over to the court. Even books that had been selected for inclusion in the *Four Treasures* went through a censorship process, sometimes being altered or having certain passages deleted.

On occasions, particularly where criticism of the Qing dynasty was suspected, the emperor and

Tours to the South

Following in the steps of his grandfather, Qianlong made six tours to Jiangnan in south China. These tours served a political purpose as well as Qianlong's personal interest in seeing the whole empire. They were part of the strategy of spreading influence over all of China, particularly in the Jiangnan region where anti-Manchu sentiment was strongest, at least during the early years of the Qing. However, these exercises

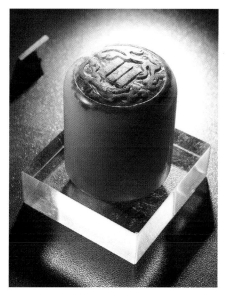

RIGHT **The Manchu style** of dress was forced on the Han, and Qianlong even wrote a book to ensure compliance, titled *Illustrated Precedents for the Ritual Paraphernalia of the Imperial Court.*

were extremely extravagant, far exceeding the tours of inspection of his grandfather who had been more interested in such matters as water conservancy projects, particularly the troublesome dykes along the Yellow River. However, local officials, merchants, and ordinary people had to bear the heavy burden of Qianlong's travels. Some areas needed years to recover financially from one of his tours.

There was no lack of criticism of these tours from his officials, but he simply dismissed them and punished his critics. After his abdication, however, he told a court official that should his successor want to make any southern tours, he should be stopped.

Initial Encounter with the British Empire

The Qianlong emperor had a tireless appetite for self-congratulation. When the first British diplomatic mission to China, led by Lord Macartney, arrived in Beijing in 1793, the dynasty was still superficially at the height of its power. China had never known any equal foreign relations or diplomacy except for the border treaty with Russia. Relations with foreign states came under the "tributary system", and although Britain was not a traditional tributary state, its envoys nevertheless announced their intention of presenting gifts on the occasion of the emperor's birthday. This greatly appealed to the vanity of the 83-year-old Qianlong.

King George III of Great Britain formally wrote to the Emperor of China requesting an exchange of ambassadors and reciprocal trading rights. This was the normal practice among the countries of Europe. Qianlong's reply, which is now held in Windsor Library, is often quoted as evidence of his pomposity and surreal sense of reality. The letter included the following:

You, O King, live beyond the confines of many seas, nevertheless, impelled by your humble desire to partake of the benefits of our civilization, you have dispatched a mission respectfully bearing

A CASE OF CULTURAL MISUNDERSTANDING

Many people think that the refusal of the British to perform certain subordinate rites, such as the three kneelings and nine prostrations (kowtow), contributed to the failure of the 1793 mission. Another factor, however, also influenced the outcome—the gifts presented to the emperor and how they were interpreted by both sides. These carefully chosen presents were meant to represent the latest and greatest European scientific achievements and craftsmanship, and to provide a basis for trading relations in the future. However, Qianlong was offended by such gifts. Tributary states should present token gifts, and the celestial dynasty would bestow more valuable ones in return. This meant Qianlong had to deride these gifts as useless baubles, despite the fact that he already had in his collection a large number of European clocks, and that the British presents were treated with great care.

LEFT *Approach of Emperor Qianlong of China to British Ambassador, Lord George Macartney, 1793* was painted by Willian Alexander, an artist who accompanied Macartney.

萬國來朝

your memorial. Your Envoy has crossed the seas and paid his respects at my Court on the anniversary of my birthday. To show your devotion, you have also sent offerings of your country's produce...your Ambassador and his deputy have come a long way with your memorial and tribute, I have shown them high favor, and have allowed them to be introduced into my presence. To manifest my indulgence, I have entertained them at a banquet and made them numerous gifts...

All requests from the British concerning the expansion of trade, the sending of an ambassador to Peking, and many other matters were refused. As Britain was preoccupied with the Napoleonic Wars, there was no reaction. It was only after the Napoleonic threat was over that they once more turned their attention to China.

The Empire in Decline

During the last two decades of Qianlong's reign, state affairs were essentially controlled by his most trusted court official, Heshen, who was from a relatively undistinguished Manchu family. Once Qianlong noticed him, however, his career took a spectacular turn. Qianlong promoted him

to the Imperial Guard in 1775, and the next year promoted him to the Grand Council. There were constant attempts by court officials to expose his various wrongdoings and general corruption, but such accusations were not pursued. As long as Qianlong was alive, Heshen was untouchable.

It remains a puzzle why a clever ruler like Qianlong would tolerate Heshen's outrageous behavior. Popular rumors hinted at some sort of homosexual relationship, but there is no evidence for this. The day after Qianlong died, the new emperor arrested Heshen and confiscated all his wealth and he was executed soon afterwards. The amount of wealth he had accumulated is legendary, and, as far as the people of Beijing could see, it all ended up in the new emperor's pocket.

During the later years of Qianlong's reign there was serious social unrest; the White Lotus Rebellion being particularly troublesome. The last poem Qianlong wrote the day before his death expressed a wish to see the White Lotus exterminated. This, however, took his heir, the Jiaqing emperor, a decade to accomplish. The golden period of the Qing had lasted more than a century, but had essentially come to an end before the death of Qianlong. After this, the empire went into rapid decline.

The Eight Banner System

The Banners

Nurhaci divided the Jurchens into four banners, or armies. As other tribes were conquered, he created new divisions. Their banners were the same colors as the original four but with red borders (a white border was used for the red banner) around them.

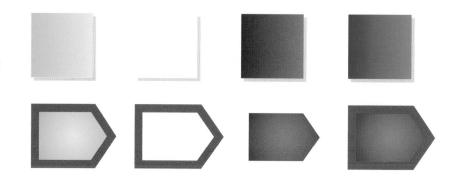

A Talented Administrator

Nurhaci created the banner system that grew into a powerful force for uniting the different peoples of the Qing empire.

Nurhaci created the banner system as an administrative organization, initially for military purposes, and his successors extended it. From the late 1620s, allied and conquered Mongol tribes were incorporated into the banner system, along with smaller ethnic groups, such as the Oroqon, Evenki, and Daur. Chinese in Manchu-controlled territory were also distributed under the Manchu banners.

By 1642, the system had grown to eight banners, into which the whole of the Manchu population was divided. The eight banners were: Plain Yellow, Bordered Yellow, Plain White, Bordered White, Plain Red, Bordered Red, Plain Blue, and Bordered Blue.

The status of bannerman was permanent. Bannermen had guaranteed administrative or military positions and received a graded but standardized salary. During the Qing dynasty, the bannermen were mainly defenders of the capital—where roughly half of them lived with their families—or the provinces, where some 18 garrisons were established. After Beijing, the largest of the banner garrisons were in Xi'an and Hangzhou. Sizable banner populations were also placed in Manchuria, and at strategic points along the Great Wall, the Yangzi River, and Grand Canal.

At the beginning of the Qing dynasty, there were 250,000 bannermen. The three "upper" banners (Plain Yellow, Bordered Yellow, Plain White) were directly responsible to the emperor, and the five "lower" banners were responsible to the imperial princes. Eventually, however, all the banners were placed under the direct control of the emperor.

After the conquest of China proper, the Qing empire needed a larger force than that provided by the Eight Banners army. The state started recruiting soldiers from the former Ming army and Chinese population. To distinguish them from the Eight Banners, they were called the Green Standard Army, because of the color of their flag. Units were located primarily in the northwest, along the coast, and in southern China. The Green Standard Army command structure was weak because officials were rotated constantly to prevent close ties forming between commanders and soldiers. In addition, their weapons and supplies were inferior. Despite this, they were a major force in suppressing rebels, such as the Three Feudatories, during the Kangxi era.

The Eight Banner army had strict rules intended to prevent bannermen losing their fighting vigor, but as the garrison troops became established in the cities, bannermen soon became accustomed to the comforts of urban life. By the mid-eighteenth century, Qianlong was greatly

alarmed at the extent to which the bannermen were losing their culture, language, and military skill. Their traditional skills in both archery and horsemanship had been eroded almost to the point of extinction, and most of them could no longer speak their native language. Toward the end of the Qing dynasty, the decline of traditional cultural heritage had enveloped the whole of the Manchu population, including the emperors, who were becoming more Han than Manchu.

By the early to mid-1800s, both the Eight Banners and the Green Standard Army had declined to such an extent that the government could no longer rely on them. In their place, regional armies, such as the Hunan (Xiang) and Huai Armies, were organized by local gentry or officials, and, starting with the suppression of the Taiping rebellion, it was essentially these armies that defended the dynasty against internal rebellions and the various Western incursions.

The New Style Army

In 1862 the Banner armies were no longer a strong force, and it was the Ever Victorious Army, made up of Chinese soldiers trained and led by Westerners, that fought the Taiping at the Battle of Cixi.

Bannermen in the Twentieth Century

By the twentieth century, the expression *baqi zidi*, "the sons and brothers of the Eight Banners," had come to mean someone who was useless, good for nothing, and lazy. The prohibition on bannermen engaging in any sort of civilian occupation was originally based on military considerations, and the bannermen were supported financially by the state. This meant that they were unable to support themselves in any civilian capacity. After the revolution, some of the Manchu aristocracy had land or valuable private collections of antiques which provided a means of support, and some were able to succeed in the new society as writers or artists. Most, however, were impoverished and had no means of supporting themselves in the new civilian society, except to become beggars or rickshaw pullers.

Economic Efficiency

Through the introduction of new crops and the more efficient utilization of land,
the Qing government tried to cope with an unprecedented population explosion,
from 100 million in the 1660s to 300 million by the mid-eighteenth century.

ABOVE **Rice farming** was
central to Chinese food
production in the south,
and irrigation technologies
that would improve culti-
vation were in demand.

The tension between the growing population and scarcer land became increased during the reign of Qianlong (reigned 1736–1795). Sweet potato and maize were introduced from America during the Ming dynasty, and were first planted in south China. Because the sweet potato does not require much rainfall or fertile soil, it was regarded as a famine crop.

New Crops

A long Confucian tradition regarded the discovery and promotion of famine crops and plants as the social responsibility of the scholar—official class. Xu Guangqi, a famous Ming official and scholar, compiled the *Comprehensive Guide to Agricultural Management* in which he summarized his experimental knowledge about new crops, particularly sweet potato. Attempts were made during the Kangxi period to plant sweet potato in northern China, but its principal area of production remained south China, mainly in Canton and

Fujian. During the Qianlong period, when population pressure reached an alarming level, provincial officials tried to encourage peasants to plant sweet potato to alleviate food shortages. Sweet potato was distributed to the peasants during famine by the government.

Less popular was maize, a hardy plant with the same advantages as the sweet potato. Long after its introduction in Canton, it was planted only in the most marginal land and only by the poorest peasants. Both maize and sweet potato gradually became a major food supply in less resourced agricultural regions, including the north and northwest parts of China. Peanuts also became increasingly important, as did cash crops such as tobacco which competed with rice and sugar cane for a share of the arable land. Cotton was widely grown, especially in the Yangzi delta region.

Although most of the "new" crops had been known in China since the Ming, they were not widely planted until the increase in population made it necessary to develop new sources of food. Their spread northwards was as a result of official policy, including the personal involvement of the emperor himself.

New Farming Techniques

Rotation of crops became more widespread as demand for food increased. Sweet potato and maize could be rotated and intercropped with other plantings, such as tobacco and winter wheat, and new types of rice from Southeast Asia with much shorter growth cycles could be planted. In particularly poor areas with little arable land, many hills and mountains, and insufficient rainfall, peasants could still harvest only one grain crop a year. However, they could sometimes rotate between wheat and millet. In Shandong, Hebei, Henan and Shanxi it was even possible to harvest three crops every two years by planting sorghum, rice, maize, millet, oats,

and buckwheat, and intercropping with green beans, soybean, and winter wheat.

In the more developed Yangzi delta area, peasants produced two crops a year, either by planting two crops of rice, or by planting rice in the spring followed by other grains or industrial crops like cotton after the initial crop. Further south, in Canton and Fujian, a cycle of three annual harvests was common—two rice crops a year plus a crop of wheat or various beans. This scale of multiple harvesting was unprecedented, and led to unforeseen consequences.

Migration into the Frontiers

More efficient utilization of land and new crops alone were not sufficient to cope with the rise in population. The government's solution was to encourage migration within the country, moving people from densely populated provinces to more remote areas such as Xinjiang (called the "New Territories"), including the Ili valley region, the prime agricultural lands of the Zunghar Mongols. This led to resistance, and suppression followed.

Eventually, the Qianlong Emperor was in a position to encourage migration of people from China proper into the western regions. The first people to migrate were Han bannermen and their families, followed by other Han Chinese, and the Chinese Muslims, the Hui. Qianlong had hoped that it would be those from the most densely populated provinces, such as Sichuan, who would

move to Xinjiang, but most were from Gansu, a sparsely populated and impoverished province through which the old Silk Road passed. Xinjiang also became a place of political banishment.

In order to preserve the Manchu way of life and maintain the well-being of the local population, Manchuria itself was deemed off limits for Chinese migrants. This did not stop poor peasants from north China flooding into the area, despite frequent warnings from the government.

Consequences of Population Growth

Mongolia was another area that was supposed to be protected from Chinese migration, however, the policy was ineffective there as well. Chinese from northern Shaanxi migrated into the western part of Inner Mongolia, and the population of Inner Mongolia increased from 1.885 million in 1776 to 2.29 million in 1820. The large number of Chinese peasants moving into basically non-agricultural areas changed the nature of the local economy and way of life. Deforestation and the over-cultivation of the grasslands for agriculture greatly damaged the already fragile environment and speeded up the desertification of northwest China. It also intensified the scarcity of water.

Paradoxically, the Qing government introduced new crops and farming techniques, encouraged migration to outlying areas, and implemented generous taxation policies in order to alleviate the population problem, but these very measures actually created a greater population growth. In the long term, the impact of migration into frontier areas was to have serious political and environmental consequences which even today continue to be serious issues for China.

The Dream of the Red Chamber

A Lot to Lose

According to recent research, Prince Gong's mansion (above) may have been the residence of Cao Xueqin before the family was bankrupted by Emperor Kangxi's frequent visits.

Still a Best Seller

This handwritten edition of *The Dream of the Red Chamber*, from a private collection in Beijing, is one of the many copies of the novel that have been circulating for over 200 years, and which are highly sought after by collectors today.

The *Dream of the Red Chamber*, which is also known as *A Dream of Red Mansions* or *The Story of the Stone*, was written in the middle of the eighteenth century during the reign of Qianlong and is one of the four masterpieces of the pre-modern Chinese novel. Its author, Cao Xueqin (1715–1763), was a Chinese bannerman whose family, having surrendered to the Manchus, was recruited as bondservants in the Plain White Banner.

Cao Yin, the grandfather of Cao Xueqin and a childhood friend of the Emperor Kangxi, was appointed by the emperor to the post of Jiangning Textile Commissioner. It was a position held only by the emperor's most trusted men and was highly profitable. During four of Kangxi's six tours to southern China, the Cao family had the privilege of hosting the emperor. Extravagant expenses, however, resulted in Cao Yin becoming bankrupt and he borrowed large sums of money from public funds to cover his debts. Despite frequent warnings from Kangxi, he was never able to repay the misused government funds.

As soon as Yongzheng came to power, determined to eradicate corruption, he targeted the Cao family. The fact that the Caos had sided with the rival faction during the succession struggle may have had something to do with this. Cao's family residences and all their other property were confiscated. Cao Xueqin was 18 when he witnessed this dramatic reversal in the fortunes of his family. He was to live the rest of his life in poverty, earning a meager living selling his paintings, writing poetry, and working on his novel. Before he died, he had completed only the first 80 chapters. It is widely believed that the last 40 chapters were compiled from Cao's unfinished manuscripts by another author, Gao E.

The Dream of the Red Chamber is a complex novel. On one level it is the story of ill-starred love and tragedy; in a broader sense, it is the story of the decline of a once great house. For the social historian and student of traditional Chinese culture, the novel is a treasure trove of information of a culture long past, but which in many ways is still alive in the deeper levels of the complex life of modern China. The basic philosophical theme of the novel is Buddhist/Daoist; that is, while our lives have moments of glory and disgrace, happiness and despair, they are in reality no more than a dream in an elaborate construction of the red dust of the world of ambition and vanity— hence the name of the novel.

The main character, Jia Baoyu, is the human incarnation of a stone left over when the goddess Nuwa repaired the vault of Heaven. His fate and that of the 12 major female characters is determined in some other world, and is merely played out in this one. In a climax that is reminiscent of *Romeo and Juliet*, Jia Baoyu marries one of his cousins, but not the one he loves. When he discovers this he runs to his true love, only to find that she has just died of a combination of ill health and a broken spirit. He faints, recovers and appears to participate in the red dust of the world, but eventually becomes a Buddhist monk and disappears into the unknown.

A Modern Interpretation

The great classic Chinese novel, *The Dream of the Red Chamber,* has been widely popular for over 200 years. One of its modern reincarnations is as a 50-episode television drama.

An English Translation

Like Shakespeare's plays, *The Dream of the Red Chamber* is considered a great classic and has become a special field of scholarship. Several complete and abridged English translations are available. One of these, the *Story of the Stone*, was translated by two Sinologists, the first 80 chapters by the famous Sinologist David Hawkes, and the next 40 by John Minford, an equally competent Sinologist of a younger generation. This gives English readers the same feeling that Chinese readers have; the two parts seem to be subtly different, but it is hard to explain where the difference lies.

A Role in a Classical Drama

There was fierce competition at auditions in Beijing to win a role in the television drama, *The Dream of the Red Chamber.* First broadcast in 2008, the series was a remake of a 1987 television adaption of the same novel.

Controlling Trade

From the eighteenth to the nineteenth century, the growing demand in Europe for tea caused an increasing trade deficit, especially in Britain. China's single, open-port restriction added to the Western traders' frustration.

RIGHT **The design on this porcelain plate** features Indonesian Wayang puppets and a globe of the world. It was designed for trade with the Rajahs of Java.

During the Ming dynasty, luxury goods from China, such as silk, porcelain, and lacquerware had been introduced to Europe, even though trade between China and Europe was periodically obstructed by Ming emperors who tried to impose stricter controls on trade. As long as there was a demand in the market and enough profit, however, these restrictions were never really effective. Enterprising merchants from Fujian sailed outside Chinese territory onto the high seas and continued to trade illegally in porcelain with Europe despite being regarded by the government as smugglers. In 1553, the Portuguese were finally given permission to build storage sheds on Macao and then, in 1557, permitted to establish a trade settlement there.

Chinoiserie

Demand for luxury Chinese goods in European markets encouraged the development of new Chinese designs, particularly in porcelain. In particular, chinoiserie porcelain was developed. The designs portrayed an imaginary China to cater for the European rococo taste for delicacy combined with frivolousness. Most common decorative motifs were floral designs, waterscapes, birds, insects, human figures, architecture, and geometric and crosshatched borders.

The Canton System

In 1684, the Kangxi emperor allowed four cities, including Canton, to do business with foreign traders. In 1757, however, he designated Canton as the only city where foreign merchants could trade. The Canton system forbade foreigners from trading directly with their Chinese customers. Instead, the official Chinese merchant guild acted as a government agency and monopolized European imports in much the same way as the East India Company monopolized trade at the other end of the trade route. The Canton system also put a limit of only one trading period a year, during the winter. Even during this period, the foreign traders were permitted to reside only in special quarters along the banks of the Pearl River, outside Canton's city walls. These quarters were known as Thirteen Factories (*Shisanhang*). At that

BELOW **The area in Canton** (now Guangzhou) which was known as the Thirteen Factories was sometimes referred to by local Chinese as the "Barbarian Houses."

time the word "factory" was used to mean a trading house. The term "Thirteen Factories" derived from the late Ming, and did not represent the number of foreign companies that existed in the Qing era. The Thirteen Factories area remained the primary center for Western trade until the Opium War in 1840.

Tea Drinking in Europe

Unlike silk and porcelain, export of tea to Europe was nonexistent until the sixteenth century. The Portuguese were the first to develop a taste for tea, and the Dutch and the French followed. Tea drinking among the upper classes in England came later, after King Charles II of England married Catherine of Braganza of Portugal in 1662. She brought her taste for tea with her and it quickly became fashionable. As it was very expensive, its consumption became a symbol of wealth.

After a direct trade route was created between Canton and Britain, the price of tea fell, and it became more popular and eventually cheaper than beer, soon replacing it as the national drink. In poor households as much as in polite society, tea became a common beverage and replaced silk as China's primary export. From five chests of tea in 1684, tea imports rose to 400,000 lb (181 metric tons) by 1720, and reached 23,000,000 lb (10,433 metric tons) by 1800.

Consequences of the Trade Deficit

Increasingly frustrated both with the growing trade deficit and with the Canton system, the powerful East India Company requested that King George III send a delegation to China to negotiate more favorable trading conditions. The Company was to be entirely responsible for the cost of the venture. The delegation, led by Lord Macartney, reached China in 1793. With his father, who was both secretary to Macartney and second in command, was a 13-year-old boy, Thomas Staunton. Thomas had learned to speak some Chinese during the journey. The emperor was so amazed, that he took a silk purse from his belt and presented it to him. This was the first of Staunton's encounters with China.

The Napoleonic Wars occupied Britain for the next few years, but in 1816 the government sent another delegation to China with the same goal of negotiating trade conditions. This delegation was led by Lord Amherst, and Thomas Staunton was appointed second commissioner. On this occasion they had to deal with Qianlong's son, the Jiaqing emperor. China's image in Europe as an exotic and enlightened empire had waned by this time, and signs of decline were evident. The British were unwilling to compromise, and the Chinese were even more recalcitrant. The delegation left without even an audience with the Jiaqing emperor.

China monopolized the world tea market and as late as 1871 supplied eighty-six percent of the world's consumption. Tea was paid for in silver and Britain had incurred a massive trade deficit. Its silver reserves had fallen dramatically. The country had been on the gold standard since the 1900s, and was forced to buy silver from continental Europe to pay the Chinese. Some way had to be found to tip the balance of trade in Britain's favor. That way was opium.

With the Chinese government resisting trade in opium, military confrontation was inevitable. After serving the East India Company for years, Thomas Staunton had become a Member of the British Parliament. In 1840, during a debate on how Britain should deal with the confiscation of British opium by the Chinese, it was Staunton who led the charge calling for war.

ABOVE **Tea picked in the hills** was brought downstream in sampans. After drying and packing in wooden chests, it was transported to foreign tea clippers.

The Opium Wars

The Opium Wars were initially clashes between China and Britain over the opium trade. As the result of the two wars, British and other Western powers gained significant commercial privilege and territory in China, and the opium trade was eventually legalized.

Toward the end of the eighteenth century, the British trade deficit with China reached an alarming level. In the 1760s, Britain paid China three million taels of silver. By the 1770s, this had reached 7.5 million, and in 1780 it was 16 million. The East India Company began selling opium in China as a way to reduce their deficit.

Opium, which was imported from British colonies in India, was the only alternative form of payment other than silver that was acceptable to the Chinese merchants. The Chinese government had banned opium as early as 1729, and allowed the importation, for medicinal purposes, of only 200 chests at a time. However, in 1773, 1,000 chests were imported, and this increased to 13,131 chests in 1828. By 1832 as many as 23,570 chests were being imported annually, an amount that could sustain the addiction of about two million Chinese. The sale of opium reversed

the trade deficit, and by 1820, two million taels of silver were flowing out of China. By the 1830s, this had reached nine million taels.

Attempts to Stop the Opium Trade

Alarmed by the silver flowing out of China, and the dramatic rise in opium addiction, the Qing government attempted to put a halt to the opium trade. Lin Zexu was appointed as an Imperial Commissioner to deal with the matter. He wrote an official letter to Queen Victoria requiring that the trade in opium be stopped. Charles Elliott, the Chief Superintendent of Trade and British Minister to China at that time, refused to forward the letter to the queen.

In 1839, Lin Zexu forced Charles Elliott to hand over all stocks of opium, some 20,000 chests each worth about £120. In the popular imagination, Lin burned the opium, but this is

BELOW **British ships smuggling opium** into China at Linton, near Canton, are depicted in this nineteenth-century engraving by John William Huggins. After unloading, the opium was sent up the coast by small craft.

not so. His men mixed the opium with lime and salt (a process which took 500 men 22 days) and flushed it into the sea. Lin then held a ceremony at Humen, near Canton, to appease the spirits for polluting their territory with foreign mud.

The Opium War

The British government, joined by the East India Company, decided on war in retaliation for Lin's action in Humen. The British Government was willing to meet all costs of a war. Consequently, in June 1840, the British dispatched 15 ships, four steam-powered gunboats, and 25 smaller boats, together with some 4,000 soldiers. With Lin Zexu defending the mouth of the Pearl River, the British fleet continued to sail north, to Xiamen and beyond.

The next year, the British defeated the Chinese army at Ningbo and other ports along the coast. Zhenjiang (Chin Kiang Foo), the last fortified city on the Yangzi, was taken by the British on the morning of July 21, 1842. When the British entered the city, they found the streets were deserted, and the houses filled with corpses. The 1,600 Manchu bannermen, badly equipped and trained, had defended the city desperately. Facing defeat, many of them killed their wives and children and then hanged themselves rather than surrender to the foreigners.

This battle was so crucial to the outcome of the war that the Madras Artillery (the present-day 127 Battery Regiment), who were the key force in the battle, were awarded the right to wear on all their appointments the insignia of a dragon with an imperial crown and the word "China." The regiment proudly named their

official battery day Chin-Kiang-Foo Day, which is still celebrated on July 21 every year.

Following their defeat, the Chinese government was forced to agree to the Treaty of Nanking. Lin Zexu was accused by the emperor of incompetency and of causing the war and and was exiled to Ili, in far west Xinjiang.

The Treaty of Nanking

On August 29, 1842, the Treaty of Nanking was signed aboard a British warship, and was ratified several months later by the Daoguang emperor and Queen Victoria. The treaty abolished the monopoly of the Canton system and China was required to open five ports to foreigners. The ports named were Canton (Guangzhou), Foochow (Fuzhou), Amoy (Xiamen), Ningpo (Ningbo), and Shanghai. The British were allowed to establish consulates in each treaty port and to communicate directly with Chinese officials instead of through the previous system of middlemen. France and the United States soon gained similar free trade rights. The Qing government agreed to hand over the island of Hong Kong to the British in order to provide their merchants with a harbor for unloading goods. The treaty also agreed to fixed tariffs on British goods.

LEFT **Smuggling of opium** continued even after 1839, when severe punishments, including death, were imposed for either smoking or trading in opium.

BELOW **The Treaty of Nanking**, taken to Britain for Queen Victoria's signature and seal, was later photographed and a framed "photocopy" given to the queen. The last page of the treaty appears below.

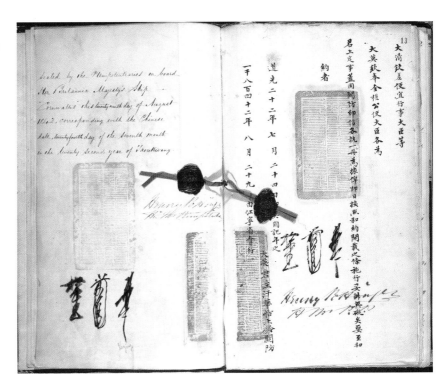

ABOVE **In 1841, the port of Canton was bombarded** by a large British expeditionary force which included steam-powered gunboats and thousands of British marines.

France, the United States, and Russia all received requests from the British to form an alliance. Although the United States and Russia supported Britain, they did not go as far as sending military aid. France, however, did—in part because of the execution of a French missionary by local authorities in Guangxi. British and French forces went on to capture Canton in late 1857 and maintained control of the city for almost four years. The governor of Guangdong and Guangxi, Ye Mingchen, was subsequently captured and sent to Calcutta as a prisoner of war, and later starved himself to death.

The treaty also set out reparation terms. The Qing government was to pay the British six million silver dollars for the opium that was confiscated by Lin Zexu, and three million in compensation for debts owed by the Chinese merchants associated with the Thirteen Factories. The biggest compensation was twelve million silver dollars for the cost of the war. On their part, the British agreed to withdraw troops from Nanking (Nanjing) and other places when the payment was received in full. The Treaty of Nanking was the first of a series of "unequal treaties."

The war was settled in 1858 by the Treaty of Tianjin. This stipulated that Britain, France, Russia, and the United States were to be allowed to establish diplomatic legations in Beijing. China was to open more ports to Western trade and to pay more indemnities to Britain and France. In the same year, the Aigun (Aihui) Treaty was signed between Russia and China to revise the border determined by the Treaty of Nerchinsk in 1689. This treaty gave Russia control over a port on the Pacific coast where Russia founded the city of Vladivostok in 1860.

The Arrow War and the Treaty of Tianjin

Often called the Second Opium War, the Arrow War was waged by Britain and France against China from 1856–1860. On October 8, 1856, Qing officials boarded the *Arrow*, a Chinese-owned ship that had recently been registered in Hong Kong. The ship's crew were suspected of piracy and smuggling, and Chinese officials arrested 12 Chinese crew members. The British representative in Canton demanded that the sailors be released on the grounds that the ship was British registered, and therefore protected by the Treaty of Nanking. The Chinese governor insisted that the arrested men were pirates and refused to release them. The British then launched an attack on Canton.

RIGHT **Before Lin Zexu resorted to destroying the opium,** he enacted laws to prevent its sale, and set up a treatment center to help addicts, under amnesty, to quit their habit.

The Looting and Burning of the Summer Palace

Before the ratification of the Treaty of Tianjin, some Qing officials in the court convinced Xianfeng, the "pleasure loving" emperor who

succeeded Daoguang, to resist the demands of the Western powers. In June 1858, Xianfeng ordered the Mongol general Senggelinqin to defend the Dagu forts in Tianjin. Senggelinqin brought from Inner Mongolia some 4,000 Mongolian cavalry. Lord Elgin, the newly appointed envoy, with a British naval force of 21 ships and 2,200 troops, sailed north for the ratification of the Treaty of Tianjin in Beijing. Senggelinqin allowed the envoys to continue the journey from Tianjin to Beijing, but refused to allow any of the armed foreign troops into the Chinese capital.

In the summer of 1860, 6,700 French and 11,000 British troops, and over 170 ships were dispatched from Hong Kong to Tianjin. They took Tianjin on August 3, 1860. The Chinese arrested and imprisoned the British diplomatic envoy and his entourage, some of whom were subsequently tortured, some of whom were murdered. The Anglo–French forces crushed Senggelinqin's elite Mongolian troops and marched into Beijing.

On September 21, 1860, Xianfeng and his entourage fled from Beijing to the Jehol (or Rehe) summer retreat, 125 miles (200 km) northeast of Beijing. The emperor's brother, Prince Gong, stayed in Beijing to deal with the devastation. Xianfeng remained in Jehol for over a year, with no intention of returning to the capital. As soon as he had settled in Jehol, Xianfeng called for the more than two hundred players of the palace theatrical and drama troupe to come from Beijing to entertain him. This is how he spent his days while the country was on the verge of collapse. Prince Gong and the court officials begged him to return to the capital many times, but Xianfeng refused and stayed in Jehol until his death.

On October 6, 1860, the British and French forces entered the Yuanmingyuan, ("The Garden of Perfect Brightness," also known as the Old Summer Palace) which they began looting. Yuanmingyuan was the preferred residence of several emperors and stored countless exquisite treasures. On October 18, Lord Elgin, the commander of the British troops, ordered that the Old Summer Palace be destroyed as a personal punishment to Xianfeng. Some 3,500 British troops took part in the pillage, and the fire took three days to consume the palaces. Charles George Gordon, who was later to gain fame as "Chinese Gordon" fighting the Taipings, was then a 27-year-old captain in the Royal Engineers. In a letter to his mother, he wrote: "You can scarcely imagine the beauty and magnificence of the palaces we burnt. It made one's heart soar to burn them; in fact, these palaces were so large, and we were so pressed for time, that we could not plunder them carefully."

The Impact of the Wars

The Treaty of Tianjin was ratified by Prince Gong on October 18, 1860. The Convention of Peking included the opening of Tianjin as a treaty port, free religious establishment in China, further land in Kowloon ceded to the British, and an increase of eight million taels to Britain and France. The opium trade was formally legalized. As part of the peace deal, the Russians forced the Qing to sign the "Supplementary Convention of Peking," in which Russia gained a further 300,000–400,000 square miles of land from China.

THE SACKING OF THE YUANMINGYUAN

Yuanmingyuan was the greatest garden in China. It took three generations of emperors—Kangxi, Yongzheng, and Qianlong—over one and a half centuries to bring it to the stage of elegance and opulence it was at the time of its sacking. European-style buildings, which were the work of the Jesuits Giuseppe Castiglione and Michel Benoist, had been added to please Qianlong's taste for exotica. In 1900, forty years after the sacking of Yuanmingyuan by British and French forces, Chinese plunderers, bandits, robbers and criminals of all types looted and damaged what was left of it during the Boxer Rebellion. The sacking of the Yuanmingyuan in 1860 remains a major symbol of foreign aggression and Chinese humiliation. The ruins of the garden have now become a "patriotic education" site and the government has started a controversial restoration plan.

ABOVE **In 1861, Victor Hugo wrote:** "There was, in a corner of the world, a wonder of the world; this wonder was called the Summer Palace. ... This wonder has disappeared."

The Taiping Rebellion

By the second half of the nineteenth century, rebellions had broken out all over China. Of these, the Taiping Rebellion was the most destructive. It was also a further blow to the already tottering dynasty.

ABOVE **Imperial Chinese troops,** equipped with Western weaponry, prepare for battle to retake the city of Tianjing from the Taipings.

Prior to the opium trade, the Chinese government had a considerable surplus of silver. Tax was paid by peasants in copper, which had a certain defined exchange rate with silver. As the amount of silver flowing out of China exceeded income, however, the exchange rate between the copper of the peasants and silver of the tax collector was subject to dramatic inflation, and this directly affected the ability of peasants to pay their taxes.

Rebellion in the North and South

The rapidly declining economic position of the peasant, famine, population pressure, scarcity of resources, government corruption, and heavy taxes, created a dangerous situation for the Qing government. Such situations had provoked many rebellions in the past, and were about to provoke uprisings yet again.

The initial impetus for the Nian Rebellion of 1853 to 1868 was the devastation caused when the Yellow River burst its banks in 1853 and 1855, flooding the land and causing a huge loss of life. Due to depleted finances, the government was unable to respond to this economic and human devastation and it was this lack of response that triggered the revolt. The Panthay Rebellion (1856–1873) started in Yunnan Province with fighting between the Hui (Chinese Muslims) and the Han Chinese migrants over mining resources. It then developed into an ethnic uprising against the state. A more serious revolt was the Muslim Rebellion in Xinjiang, Shaanxi and Gansu (1862–1877). This was a continuation of resistance to territorial conquests in the early- and mid-Qing.

The Kingdom of Heavenly Peace

The more devastating Taiping Rebellion (1851–1864) was unusual because of its basis in a peculiar form of Christianity. Hong Xiuquan, the founder of the Taiping Heavenly Kingdom, was from a modest peasant family near Canton. His ambition of climbing the social ladder diminished with repeated failure in the imperial examinations. After a third failure in the examination, he had a nervous breakdown. During this time he had a number of visions in which an old man told him that people had stopped worshipping him and were worshipping demons instead.

When Hong failed the examination for the fourth time, he began reading some Christian

RIGHT **Hong Xiuquan's ideology** was a mixture of pre-Confucian utopianism and a form of Protestantism. His followers were largely anti-Manchu and anti-establishment.

treatises he had brought home seven years earlier. He came to believe that the old man in his visions was God the Father, and that he himself was the younger brother of Jesus Christ. Hong formed a new religious sect dedicated to the destruction of idols. According to Hong, the Kingdom of Heavenly Peace would be established on the ruins of "foreign" Manchu rule.

The Rise and Fall of the Taiping

Hong Xiuquan and his followers began their uprising in Guangxi in 1850. The next year they established themselves in Jintian, where Hong proclaimed himself the Heavenly King. He led his forces into Hunan and Hubei, and then along the Yangzi River to Nanjing. The men of the Taiping Heavenly Kingdom army were devoted fanatics, willing to die in the cause of defending God against demon forces. The momentum of the rebellion increased and in 1853 Hong captured Nanjing, setting up his government there, and renaming the city Tianjing, the Heavenly Capital.

The policies of the Taiping were in many cases surprisingly modern. They included the abolition of private property, a classless society, equality between men and women, and the abolition of foot binding. Such social and economic reforms, combined with the Taiping's passionate anti-Manchu sentiment, attracted many people suffering under the dislocations and disasters of the mid-nineteenth century.

The Taiping made many military attacks on cities along the central Yangzi valley, and even (unsuccessfully) attacked Beijing. A long war, with its associated brutality and human cost, exhausted whatever popular support the Taiping had once enjoyed. They failed to consolidate their conquered territories, and had few capable officials. Hong himself became more and more deranged and took refuge in wine, women, and sensual pleasures. By 1864, Qing government forces were in a position to attack Nanjing. The Taiping's central military figure, Shi Dakai, fled. Hong, finally resigned to defeat, took poison before the Qing forces took Nanjing.

Reinforcements

The turning point in the battle against the Taipings was the addition of the Xiang Army of Zeng Guofan. This was originally a small-scale, self-protection militia formed by the local gentry and peasants. However, when the potential of such an organization became apparent, the

LEFT **Dubbed "Chinese Gordon" by the British,** General Gordon led the "Ever-Victorious Army," made up of Chinese peasants, and European and American volunteers.

central government encouraged this new addition to its military resources. Zeng's victory assisted his rise in the Qing government, initiating an unprecedented trend of Han Chinese to take up important positions in the court. Li Hongzhang and Zuo Zongtang followed the same path.

Western involvement also gave a significant boost to the Qing. Initially, Westerners, especially missionaries, saw the Taiping as Christians and were keen to support them. Their unorthodox form of Christianity, however, soon alienated the missionaries. The Taiping's opposition to opium was seen as a threat to Western interests.

The Taiping Rebellion coincided with the renegotiation of the Treaty of Nanking, and the Qing had little choice but to accede to Western demands in return for their support. Foreigners in Shanghai formed their own mercenary army, first led by Frederick Ward, an American, and then after his death by a British officer, Charles "Chinese" Gordon. Gordon's army, dubbed the "Ever Victorious Army," fought beside the Huai army of Li Hongzhang and captured several cities in the Yangzi area, including Nanjing. It is estimated that between 20 and 30 million people perished during the Taiping Rebellion.

Self-Strengthening

The Self-strengthening movement, from the 1860s to the 1890s, represented a long and painful response to the reality of international affairs, and an end to the self-aggrandizing illusions of the Chinese elite and the government.

Over a period of some 50 years, China had declined from the arrogance of the Qianlong emperor to a series of defeats and humiliations. The sense of both internal and external collapse was vividly demonstrated by Hu Linyi, the Governor of Hubei, a military man who made his name in the Xiang army fighting the Taiping. When he saw for the first time British steamboats speeding up the Yangzi River, "the shock of the new" was such that he fainted and fell off his horse. China had no way to match the might of the Western powers.

A group of the more realistic and enlightened officials at the imperial court came to terms with the need for drastic reform to avoid further defeats and eventual annihilation. Headed by Prince Gong, this group included Wenxiang, Zeng Guofan, Li Hongzhang and Zuo Zongtang, all of whom had come to prominence during the struggles against the Taiping. Despite strong opposition from some Manchu nobles, Prince Gong was able to institute some basic reforms.

Learning from the West

The basic idea of the reform was a modified version of *yiyi zhiyi* ("use barbarians to control barbarians")—the traditional way of dealing with barbarians, though in this case it was more a matter of using barbarian technology to defeat barbarians. It could be achieved, the reformists hoped, by learning the principles of Western technology, and the Western languages to access that knowledge. They would then be able to make their own cannon, guns, and steamboats. More conservative officials argued that this policy was tantamount to abandoning traditional culture for modern barbarism. The reformers insisted that their fundamental principles were still Confucian because the learning of Western technology was only for practical matters. China would remain Chinese, even if it adopted Western technology.

The government established the Zongli Yamen, a new institution similar to a Western Ministry of Foreign Affairs, to handle relations with the Western powers. This was a significant shift from its predecessor, the Lifanyuan, the "Barbarian Regulatory Authority"—a body which dealt with tributary states.

New schools were established for the study of foreign languages and other practical subjects. The Tongwenguan was founded in Beijing in 1862 and was followed by similar schools in Shanghai and Canton. Initially, the impetus for the establishment of these schools had been the Treaty of Tianjin which specified that only the English and French versions of the treaty would be considered authentic. China desperately needed its own interpreters. Gradually the Tongwenguan in Beijing developed into a broader educational institution, and evolved into Peking University.

The development of a military industry was paramount. From the 1860s onward, Zeng Guofan and Li Hongzhang established arsenals in several major cities, including the Jiangnan Arsenal in Shanghai, the Jinling Arsenal in Nanjing, the Tianjin Arsenal, and the Fuzhou Ship Yard.

The Failure of *Yiyi Zhiyi*

The first indication that the reforms were not sufficient to strengthen China to such a degree that it would be capable of dealing with threats from foreign powers, came in 1885 with a war

RIGHT **Members of the Zongli Yamen,** which was set up to deal with foreign relations, were told by more conservative officials that the agency would only be a temporary measure.

with the French over Annam (Vietnam) which was a traditional tributary state. More significant was the war with Japan (1894–1895) over Korea. In a similar way to China, Japan had been under pressure from the West and had undergone a process of modernization. However, unlike the modernizing efforts of China, which proved inadequate, the Japanese reform, known as the Meiji Reform, was eminently successful.

Korea was another traditional tributary state of China, but some reformist Koreans felt their interests would be better served by an alliance with the Western powers and an increasingly powerful Japan. Japan wanted to control Korea for security and economic reasons. In 1884, there were bloody coups and counter-coups in Korea between pro-Japan reformists and the pro-China government. From the early stages of the Meiji reform, Japan had been building its navy and, in 1894, the Japanese fleet defeated Li Hongzhang's Northern Fleet in one morning. The Chinese admiral in charge of the fleet, Ding Ruchang, subsequently committed suicide.

The war concluded with the signing of the Treaty of Shimonoseki, in which China recognized the independence of Korea, ceded the Liaodong Peninsula and Taiwan to Japan, and agreed to pay an indemnity of 200 million taels of silver. France, Germany, and Russia demanded, and got, 30 million taels of silver in lieu of the Liaodong Peninsula where they had strategic interests.

One Hundred Days' Reform

The terms of the Treaty of Shimonoseki were made public at a time when thousands of provincial graduates had gathered in Beijing for the triennial metropolitan examination. Kang Youwei, from Guangdong, organized a petition to the emperor which was signed by over 1,200 scholars from 18 provinces. The petition called for wide-ranging reform in education, the bureaucracy, the army, commerce, industry, banking, and many other areas. Kang later discussed his ideas personally with the young Emperor Guangxu, who accepted his proposals and issued a series of edicts announcing the new policies. The reforms lasted from the June 11 to September 21, 1898—just 104 days. The conservative faction panicked, and the Empress Dowager engineered a coup. The emperor was imprisoned in the Forbidden City until his death in 1908 (the day before the Empress Dowager herself died) and six leading reformists were publicly executed in the main street of the capital.

ABOVE **The launching of a warship at Jinling Arsenal, Shanghai,** was a momentous occasion for government officials who supported the *yiyi zhiyi* reforms.

BELOW **Kang Youwei** was an important participant in the campaign, now known as the One Hundred Days' Reform, to modernize China.

Peking Opera

A Classic Opera

Legend of the White Snake is a popular classic of the Peking Opera repertoire. This tragic love story, true to Peking Opera style, combines acrobatics, martial art, dance, song, and magic.

Chou Face Paint

In the Southern and Northern dynasties period, over 1,400 years ago, leading actors wore masks. These were later replaced with face paint so that audiences could see their facial expressions.

Peking Opera combines music, singing, dialog, dance, acrobatics, pantomime, and martial arts to depict different characters, circumstances, and emotions. Costumes, which are based on traditional Chinese dress—usually from the Ming dynasty—are intricate and highly colorful. Peking Opera is considered a national art form and is enjoyed by people from all walks of life.

Originally, stories in Peking Opera were mostly based on historical events and military heroes. During the 1960s, the repertoire was adapted to depict events from the communist revolution. Nowadays it includes wider themes, both historical and contemporary, even versions of *King Lear*, *Hamlet*, and *Macbeth*. Old operas are also modernised and sometimes changed to suit modern audiences.

A distinctive feature of Peking Opera is its symbolism. It employs stylized movements to indicate leaving or entering a room, opening or closing a door, climbing a mountain, or crossing a stream. Circling the stage with whip in hand suggests riding a horse. Holding an oar or paddle and doing knee bends indicates traveling on a boat. Four soldiers and four generals flanking both sides of the stage represent an army of several thousand.

Makeup also has an important role in defining the characters. For the painted face role, the color of makeup can indicate character or personality. For example, red indicates uprightness and loyalty; white, craftiness and cunning. Painted faces and subtle gestures, such as a slight eye movement or a small nod, transmit the experiences and emotions of the characters. Gestures are instantly recognized by regular opera goers. For example, the trembling of hands and body indicates extreme anger, while the flicking of a sleeve expresses disgust. Throwing a hand above the head and flicking back sleeves indicates the actor is astonished or surprised. Embarrassment is demonstrated by covering the face with one sleeve.

The more or less realistic backdrops which are used in Western theatres are not employed in Peking Opera. In bare and unadorned surroundings, the more stylized and abstract performances of Chinese opera, accompanied by loud and dramatic music, can have a very powerful effect on the audience.

Musical accompaniment is provided by percussion, wind, and stringed instruments. The main percussion instruments are gongs and drums of various sizes and shapes; the main stringed instrument is the "capital fiddle", the *jing hu*, supported by the *er hu*, or "second fiddle." The vocal parts of Peking Opera consist of both sung poetry, accompanied by music, and spoken recitatives which are chanted in a loud falsetto. The pronunciation and tonal patterns of the opera dialog are quite different from modern spoken Chinese.

The beginnings of Peking Opera can be traced to 1790, when four Anhui drama troupes arrived in Beijing to perform for the Qianlong emperor on the occasion of his eightieth birthday. This regional opera was a novelty in Beijing, and became very popular, although it was considered vulgar entertainment by the imperial court until it received patronage from the Empress Dowager Cixi. The Anhui troups stayed in Peking and over time their style, combined with other popular regional styles, gradually developed into the distinctive Peking Opera, which then spread throughout China.

Different Roles in Peking Opera

Peking operas feature four major roles, according to the sex and nature of the characters. These four roles are then subdivided to portray the characters needed for the story. All female roles are known as *dan* and were traditionally played by males. This tradition originated from the Qing ban on female performers. It continued until the last male *dan* retired from the stage at the end of the twentieth century. Male roles are called *sheng*: old men are *laosheng*, young men are *xiaosheng*, martial arts experts are *wusheng*, and so on. The final two roles are the *jing* (painted face), which portrays characters who are rough, boorish, and sometimes fierce; and the *chou* (clown). which is easily recognizable by the white face. Those familiar with Peking Opera are able to identify the main characters of the better-known operas by their various characteristic face paint and costumes.

Stories of the Empire

Tan Dun's opera *The First Emperor* is the story of how Qin Shihuang, in establishing a great empire, destroys the two people he loves—his daughter and his childhood friend.

Secession and Annexation

Despite continuous waves of defeats and humiliations, China never became a colony of any Western power. However, as its ability to defend itself continued to grow weaker, Western powers claimed various parts of China as their own particular concession or sphere of influence.

In the mid to late nineteenth century, the industrialization in Europe led Western nations to seek more sources of raw material and new markets. Their focus shifted from trade with, and indirect rule of, China to a desire for formal colonial control.

"Carving Up the Melon"

In China, Western powers were busy dividing China into "spheres of influence" or, to use the more vivid Chinese expression, "carving up the melon." Typically, various incidents, such as the murder of missionaries or the damage to foreign property, served as a pretext for further demands. These spheres of interest often involved holding leases for all railway and commercial privileges in a particular region. Some even claimed to own Chinese territory, such as the foreign settlements in Shanghai and other open port cities.

In 1885, France defeated China over control of Vietnam, and founded the French Union of Indochina. Soon after, the French demanded "rectification" of the frontier between China and Indochina. The French also laid claim to special rights in Guangzhouwan (present-day Zhanjiang), Yunnan, Guangxi, and the island of Hainan, as well as claiming a concession for a railway line from Tonkin to Yunnan.

In 1896, when Germany, France, and Russia, intervened against the Japanese attempt to annex the Liaodong Peninsula, they demanded special trading rights in return. In 1898, Britain occupied and took over control of the harbor at Weihaiwei in northern Shandong Peninsula, and forced the Qing government to agree to a 99-year lease, which the British continued to hold until 1930. By the end of the nineteenth century, the British controlled the Yangzi valley, the port of Weihaiwei, Kowloon, and Hong Kong. The Chinese government promised the British that rights would not be be granted in those regions to any power other than Britain, whether by lease, concession, or any other means.

The Germans, for their part, used the pretext of the murder of two of their missionaries to occupy the port city of Qingdao in the south of Shandong. The provincial capital, Jinan, soon came under German control. The Germans continued to lease Qingdao from 1897 to 1922, and claimed the rights to mining and railways in the areas nearby.

Rivalry Between Western Powers

In 1896, when Li Hongzhang was invited to St. Petersburg as the Chinese representative at the Coronation of Nicholas II, he agreed, in return for an alliance with Russia, that Russia would have the right to extend the Trans-Siberian Railway line to Vladivostok across northern Manchuria. Russia's aim was to have a direct link with Lüshun (Port Arthur), an ice-free port on the Pacific coast. In 1898, the Russians occupied Port Arthur, where they established a naval base, and signed a 25-year lease of the Liaodong Peninsula. They also claimed the right to build a railway from Port Arthur to connect with the Chinese Eastern line. In the far west, Russia was encroaching into Xinjiang from Kazakhstan, but there they clashed with the interests of the British Empire. The British were keen to gain control over Tibet as an extension of their colonies in India and Nepal. In 1876, they signed the Yantai Convention with China, which granted Britain the right to send a mission into Tibet. For the next few decades, the Tibetans violently resisted the British, but the British never gave up their efforts to establish a presence there.

Russia's influence in the Far East jeopardized Japanese ambitions in Manchuria. However, as Japan possessed Formosa (Taiwan) and the

BELOW **"Le gâteau des Rois des Empereurs"** (The cake of kings and emperors), a cartoon commenting on the European annexation of China, appeared in a French journal in 1898.

Pescadores Islands (Penghu) as a result of the Treaty of Shimonoseki, the coastal province of Fujian was within its reach. Through the Boxer Protocol, Japanese ships were able to operate along the Yangzi River and to establish manufacturing factories in all the treaty ports. The Japanese also demanded 230 million taels of silver as an indemnity, an amount that was three years of the total income of the Qing Empire. In 1904, Russia and Japan finally came into military conflict over Korea. Russia was defeated and Japan inherited the leases of Port Arthur and Dalian. This meant that Korea and southern Manchuria were now also within Japan's sphere of influence.

Open Door Policy

While other Western powers were occupied establishing their spheres of influence in China, the United States was concentrating on the Philippines and Guam. In 1899, the United States, which had not acquired any of its own territorial concessions in China, proposed what was termed an "open-door policy"; that is, commercial privileges in all treaty ports within and outside the various spheres of influence would be equally available to all foreign powers. Their justification was the protection of "China's administrative integrity"; though in reality, the European powers had administrative responsibility in their own spheres of interest. The US proposal would mean that America could enjoy the benefits of free trade without taking on any costly administrative responsibility. The relevant nations, except Russia, reluctantly agreed to the United States proposal, without any intention of enforcing it.

It was inevitable that such a situation would provoke a reaction in China; however, the Qing government was in no position to resist foreign demands. The reaction, when it came, was violent and bloody, and originated among the peasants of northern China. The unrest became known as the Boxer Rebellion.

ABOVE **Postures and dress** in this Japanese rendition of the surrender at Weihaiwei illustrate Japan's identification with Western powers.

BELOW **American diplomats** worked through the Zongli Yamen, the office that dealt with foreigners.

The Boxer Rebellion

The Boxer Rebellion of 1900 was a violent, anti-foreign, mass uprising in northern China. In retaliation, Western forces entered and looted the Forbidden City and other areas of Beijing. This was one of the final blows in the collapse of the dynasty just over a decade later.

ABOVE **The Boxers were a grass-roots organization** whose members viewed the rebellion as a righteous war against the corrupting influence of the West.

The economic and political exploitation of China by Western powers and Japan bred resentment all over China toward foreigners. In Shandong, British control of Weihaiwei and the German occupation of Qingdao, were particular local grievances. Toward the end of the nineteenth century, the region suffered a devastating flood, which resulted in widespread destruction of crops and subsequent starvation.

Origin of the Boxers

The Boxers began as a religious sect in Shandong and adjacent areas in Henan and Hebei. The Hebei areas, including Beijing, were then known as Zhili. Shandong had a long history of heterodox religions, and rebellions with a religious basis. In 1898, a secret society called the *Yihequan*, "The Society of Righteous and Harmonious Fists," emerged and attracted thousands of followers. The society practiced various martial arts and chanted magic spells which, they believed, made them invulnerable to bullets and physical pain. Westerners called this group the Boxers.

One of the first signs of unrest took place in a small village in Shandong province where there had been a land dispute between villagers and the Catholic Church. The local Chinese built a temple on land which the Catholic Church claimed had originally been the site of a church, abandoned after the Kangxi emperor expelled the earlier missionaries. When the local court ruled in favor of the Church, the angry villagers, led by the Boxers, attacked the church.

The presence of "foreign devils" became the focus of the Boxers' discontent, and their expulsion became their ultimate goal. Initially, they were suppressed by the Governor of Shandong, Li Bingheng, but the new Governor, Yuxian, a Manchu, tried to manipulate the Boxers into driving out the foreigners. As a result, the Boxers changed their anti-Manchu slogan of "Eliminate the Qing and Restore the Ming" to "Support the Qing, Eliminate the Foreigners." The movement spread quickly throughout northern China. Missionary settlements were attacked, churches burnt, and railway tracks and stations destroyed.

Chinese Government Attitudes Toward the Boxers

As far as the Chinese government was concerned, any secret society or organized mass movement had to be suppressed, as failure to do so could very well lead to a peasant rebellion. However, although the Boxers were initially suppressed, after Yuxian supported them their numbers grew quickly. In the spring of 1900, Boxers flooded into Zhili, and in June entered Beijing. By that time, the number of Boxers had reached four to five hundred thousand. Foreigners resident in the capital were alarmed and demanded that the Qing government take action.

The Guangxu emperor, supported by officials Zhang Zhidong and Yuan Shikai, held the view that the Boxers had to be suppressed immediately to avoid foreign military intervention. However, the Empress Dowager Cixi and a few Manchu princes hoped the Boxers might be more effective in getting rid of the foreigners than the Qing army. As it was a popular rebellion, not a government military action, the government could avoid responsibility for whatever they might do. Eight high ranking officials were executed for supporting the views of the Guangxu emperor, and the Boxers were welcomed into Beijing. They even set up altars in the Forbidden City.

By this stage there were at least 10,000 Boxers roaming the streets of Beijing. Prince Duan, who was an enthusiastic supporter of the movement, took over the *Zongli Yamen*, the Qing Ministry of Foreign Affairs. Upon recognizing the way things were going at court, some officials reversed their previous position, and expressed support for the Boxers. In the key region of Zhili, Governor General Ronglu, a Manchu noble and the Empress Dowager's most trusted official, also changed his initial anti-Boxer stance and invited them into Tianjin.

Boxer Atrocities

When the Boxers entered Beijing, they tried to destroy any trace of the foreigners. In Dashala, the major commercial street just outside the Qianmen Gate, they set fire to

LEFT **Riots and acts of sabotage,** including the cutting of railway and telegraph lines, began early in 1900 as anger against foreign influence grew.

a medicine shop selling foreign medicine. The fire got out of control and burned for 24 hours. Over a thousand shops with no foreign connections were destroyed. The square in front of Prince Zhuang's residence became the killing field of over a thousand Chinese Christians. Prince Zhuang was the Commander of the Metropolitan Infantry Brigade and was supposed to be in charge of the security of the imperial city and its inhabitants.

The Boxers were financially supported by the imperial court and rewards were offered for the

BELOW **English and French troops** began their attack on Beijing on June 28, 1900. In this print, the Boxers are depicted on the left and the allied troops on the right.

THE POWER OF THE EMPRESS DOWAGER

In 1899, the Empress Dowager Cixi decided that Guangxu, who had been under house arrest since the failure of the Hundred Days' Reform, should abdicate in favor of Prince Duan's son. She invited the foreign envoys to offer their congratulations. They declined, making it clear that they regarded Guangxu as the legitimate emperor. The Empress Dowager had to change her plan, and announced that Prince Duan's son would be Guangxu's successor. From then on the Empress Dowager regarded foreigners as supporters of the emperor, and therefore her personal enemies. This was one of the reasons she supported the vehemently anti-foreign Boxers. When she returned to Beijing in 1901, she changed her mind again. Prince Duan was sent into exile for his support of the Boxers, and his son was stripped of the title of Crown Prince. When it was clear that Guangxu was dying, the Empress Dowager nominated the two-year-old Puyi as Guangxu's successor. She herself died a few days later.

RIGHT **In January 1900, the Empress Dowager Cixi** issued an edict declaring that secret societies were part of Chinese culture, not criminals. This virtually gave official support to the Boxer movement.

BELOW **In the aftermath of the Boxer rebellion,** Chinese civilians, as well as officials, were accused as Boxers and executed. Among them was the murderer of the German envoy Klemens von Ketteler.

heads of foreigners. The city was in complete anarchy. Boxers and Qing soldiers went through the streets looting, burning, and raping.

The greatest atrocities to occur outside Beijing were in Shanxi and Zhili. Yuxian, the Governor of Shanxi, had supported the Boxers from the beginning. In late 1899, he was dismissed from his position of Governor of Shandong in response to the demands of the Western nations following the murder of two missionaries. During an audience with the Empress Dowager after his dismissal, he suggested that the court should summon the Boxers into Beijing. The Empress Dowager was so impressed that she immediately appointed him Governor of Shanxi. Yuxian then notified the missionaries in Shanxi that they and their families should come to the provincial capital, Taiyuan, for their own protection. He then ordered all 44 men, women and children be killed as they arrived. Altogether, he was responsible for the death of over 150 missionaries and their families, and carried out some of the executions personally.

The Siege of the Legation Buildings

In June 1900, the Boxers, who were now joined by elements of the Qing army, attacked foreign compounds in Beijing and Tianjin. The legations of Great Britain, France, Belgium, the United States, the Netherlands, Russia, and Japan were located in the Legation Quarter close to the Forbidden City. This area became a refuge for several hundred foreigners living in Beijing. The German Minister to China, Baron von Ketteler, was murdered on June 20 while on his way to see government officials. The next day, the Empress Dowager formally declared war against all the Western nations simultaneously.

The Legation Quarter remained under siege from June 20 to August 14, but the Boxers were poorly equipped and unable to break into the compound. The attitude of the Commander of the Chinese troops, Ronglu, was ambiguous. While obeying the Empress Dowager's orders to send Qing bannermen to attack the Legations, he did not issue them with artillery. On more than one occasion, he sent substantial food supplies to the compound as a gesture of goodwill.

Approximately 20,000 allied forces—from Italy, France, Britain, Germany, Austria-Hungary, the United States, Russia, and Japan—fought their way into Beijing from Tianjin. They entered Beijing on August 14, 1900. By the time the rebellion was finally quashed, 48 Catholic missionaries, 18,000 Chinese Catholics, 182 Protestant missionaries, 500 Chinese Protestant Christians, and 222 Eastern Orthodox Christians were dead. On the other side, it is estimated more than 50,000 Chinese were killed by foreign troops.

Just before the allied forces entered Beijing, the Empress Dowager Cixi fled the capital, disguised as a peasant. Emperor Guangxu's favorite consort, Zhenfei, had pleaded with Cixi to allow the emperor to stay in the capital to negotiate with the foreigners. As the Empress Dowager did not want to run the risk that the foreigners might reinstate Guangxu as the legitimate ruler of China in her absence, she ordered eunuchs to throw Zhenfei down a well. She then forced the unfortunate emperor to leave Beijing with her to go into temporary exile in Xi'an.

The Attitude of Regional Officials

Some regional officials believed that the policy of the court could only lead to catastrophe. Others, though not openly opposed to government policy, were still very concerned. Archival records reveal that Prince Chun, the brother of the Guangxu emperor and father of the last emperor, Puyi, was in a state of panic and several times secretly consulted fortune-tellers, each time asking the same question: Could disastrous consequences be avoided?

In an unprecedented act of defiance, many crucial regional officials refused to acknowledge the official declaration of war on foreigners. Two officials, Zhang Zhidong, Governor General of Hunan and Hubei, and Liu Kunyi, Governor General of Jiangsu, Jiangxi, and Anhui, initiated negotiations with the British to keep their regions free of Boxers. Soon, Li Hongzhang, the Governor General of Guangdong and Guangxi, and several other governors and governors general followed suit. As a result, southern China was spared from calamity. The governors actively communicated with diplomatic representatives of the Western nations and reached what came to be called an

"Agreement of Mutual Protection between Chinese and Foreigners." In contrast to the turbulent north, life carried on as usual in areas such as Shanghai and the cities along the Yangzi River. These were the areas where Western interests were most concentrated.

ABOVE **Boxer rebels were captured by allied troops** during the fighting and afterward. The group pictured here were brought in by the sixth US Cavalry.

The Boxer Protocol of 1901

The exiled imperial court stayed in Xi'an for more than a year. Li Hongzhang was called to Beijing to negotiate with the Western nations for a peace treaty. This treaty, which was known as the Boxer Protocol, was signed on September 7, 1901. Under the terms of the Protocol, China was required to pay, over a period of 39 years, an indemnity of 450 million taels of silver to the countries involved. Income from the Chinese customs service and the salt tax were to be the source of funds which would guarantee that the reparations were paid.

Western powers could now station their troops in Beijing to guard the legations and to maintain a clear corridor from the capital to the coast. The Protocol suspended imperial examinations for five years in areas where anti-foreign atrocities had taken place, and all arms imports into China were suspended. The Protocol also demanded the execution of ten top-ranking officials who were responsible for, or supported, the Boxer uprising. Yuxian was top of the list.

Imperial Examinations

For over 1,000 years, the imperial examination system served China as the means of selecting its officials. It ended in 1905 with the modernization of education.

RIGHT **Government officials** wore badges of office like this one on their gowns to identify their status.

BELOW **Passing the Country Magistrates Examination** meant a chance to wield great power as the role of magistrate included those of judge, police chief, resolver of disputes, and tax collector.

Prior to the Sui dynasty (581–618), officials were appointed based on recommendations from prominent aristocrats and existing government officials and all appointees belonged to the aristocrat class. In 605, the Sui emperor Yangdi introduced literary subjects as a means of recruiting at least a certain proportion of officials. A gradual increase in the percentage of recruits to the bureaucracy by examination developed during the Tang. By the Song, the procedure and content of the examination had become standardized, and the Song examination system served as the model during succeeding dynasties.

Social Mobility

In theory, any male adult, regardless of wealth or class, could become a government official and

rise through the ranks. In reality, however, the long process of studying required considerable financial resources. In addition, certain social groups, such as prostitutes, actors, and some regional outcasts, were excluded from the examination system, particularly during the Ming and Qing dynasties. As only about five percent of those who sat could pass the examination, many candidates tried more than once. Success in the imperial examinations brought social status, glory, and wealth. The importance given to the examination system and to the status it bestowed on those who passed can be seen in one aspect of the retaliation meted out by the Western nations after the Boxer Rebellion. The Metropolitan Examination Hall was burnt down, and the Boxer protocol demanded that provinces involved in the uprising were to suspend the examinations for five years.

Practice and Influence

There were three levels of degrees: county (and prefectural), provincial, and metropolitan. Graduates from the county or prefecture level earned the title of *xiucai*, "flourishing talent"; a provincial graduate gained the title of *juren*, "recommended man"; and a metropolitan graduate the title *jinshi*, "presented scholar." County and prefectural examinations were held every year, provincial and metropolitan examinations every three years. Among the "presented scholars", the three top positions were decided

by interview with the emperor. After successfully passing the provincial and metropolitan examinations, candidates were qualified for high official posts either in the provinces or the capital.

The examination usually took between 24 and 72 hours. Each prefecture, county, and province had a special examination hall, as did the capital. Interestingly, the site of the previous metropolitan examination hall in Beijing is now occupied by the Academy of Social Sciences and in provincial capitals there are still streets called *gongyuan*, derived from the location of examination halls. Each candidate occupied a small cubicle which they were not allowed to leave for the duration of the examination. The cubicles had two boards that could be placed together to form a bed, or at different levels to make a desk and bench. In order to achieve a fair outcome, candidates were identified by number rather than name. Examination papers were copied by professional copyists to prevent the disclosure of the identity of the candidate, and an evaluation of each paper had to be given by three different examiners.

The system impressed European thinkers, such as Voltaire, for its fairness and effectiveness. In Europe at that time social class and privileges were largely inherited without recognition for individual talent. In East Asia, the Chinese examination system influenced the method of recruitment of officials in Korea, Japan, and Vietnam. The Chinese system might even have played a role in the reform of the Civil Service in British India and later in Britain itslef as, from the late nineteenth century onward, recruitment of bureaucrats was at least partly decided by open competition in public service examinations.

The Abolition of the Examination System

A unified nationwide examination system was a very powerful and effective means of maintaining cultural unity and consensus on basic Confucius values. Neither the content nor the format of the examinations changed much at all for almost a thousand years, apart from a few exceptions such as examinations in the Yuan dynasty when the ruling class were Mongols, and the Taiping's, examinations which were based on the Christian Bible rather than the Confucian Classics. By the late Qing, despite pressures from the outside world, the examination system still focused on traditional Confucian Classics with no reference to the realities of the actual crises facing China.

The system became further compromised when a cash-strapped government began selling degrees to collect more revenue.

Education was one of the main priorities of the 1898 reform and became more urgent after the Boxer Rebellion. In 1905, prominent figures such as Zhang Zhidong and Yuan Shikai urged the court to abolish the traditional examinations and establish a new educational system. The Empress Dowager, who had thwarted the 1898 reform, now had no choice but to approve more radical policies. There were few of the hundreds of thousands of scholars who had spent their whole lives studying for the traditional examinations who could adjust to the new system. Their expectations and hopes for an official career suddenly disappeared. The impact of the abolition of the traditional examination system, dramatic and powerful as it was, was no more than a prelude to the 1911 (Xinhai) revolution and its consequences.

ABOVE **Up until the last examination in 1904,** steles were erected in the garden of the Temple of Confucius in Beijing to honor scholars who passed the imperial examination.

Revolution

The 1911 (Xinhai) revolution overthrew the Qing dynasty and ended an imperial dynastic system that went back to the unification of China in 221 BCE and the foundation of the first empire under the First Emperor of the Qin.

RIGHT **Sun Yat-sen** is often referred to as "Father of the Revolution." In 1912, he was named provisional president, but the position was soon snatched away.

Following the Boxer Rebellion, the Qing government was willing to accept much more radical measures than those that had been proposed by the One Hundred Days' Reform of 1898. However, it was a case of too little too late, and any attempt at reform within the government was unlikely to be effective. One reform that was undertaken was to create and train a Western-style army, armed with Western weapons and trained in Western methods. Another was to build a modern railway system. However, these apparently positive policies were to prove the means of the dynasty's final defeat.

Revolutionary Groups

Many anti-Manchu revolutionary groups emerged in the last decade of the nineteenth century. Most of them were organized by Chinese students in Japan or other Chinese living outside China.

The most famous of the revolutionaries is Sun Yat-sen (1866–1925). As he became increasingly troubled by the conservative Qing government, Sun left his medical practice to devote his time to the reform of China. Altogether he led ten attempts to overthrow the government and each time he failed. However, his

RIGHT **The new Imperial Army parades** with its Western equipment after being called out in October 1911 to deal with rebellion.

tireless efforts to promote revolutionary fervor within China, together with the rapidly deteriorating situation there, led to revolutionary sentiments becoming stronger, including those among the officers and troops of the New Army.

The Wuchang Uprising

The construction of railways, in line with new government policy, was in the hands of foreign companies using foreign funds. However, public opinion was that the newly constructed railways should be in Chinese hands. Consequently, the Qing government panicked and borrowed money from foreign banks to nationalize the railways, thus alienating many small Chinese investors in Hubei, Hunan, Sichuan, and Guangdong, as well as the foreign owners.

The Western powers made it clear that they would continue with railway construction within their spheres of influence whatever the Qing government did. This led to another wave of nationalism all over China, and a growing conviction that the Qing government could not possibly reform itself quickly or thoroughly enough to deal with the ever worsening situation. When particularly violent protests broke out in Sichuan, over the issue of nationalizing the railway, the Qing government sent the Hubei New Army, stationed in the Wuchang garrison in Wuhan to suppress the protesters. This left Wuchang undefended.

Revolutionaries in Wuhan had been planning an uprising for some time. When two of revolutionaries had an accident while manufacturing a bomb in Hankou on October 9, 1911, their hand was forced. As the government would be sure to investigate the accident, they decided to stage an insurrection the next day.

Republic of China Declared

The entire city of Wuchang was captured by the revolutionaries who then announced the establishment of the Republic of China Hubei Government. Many other provinces followed suit in proclaiming independence from the Qing. The government was in no position to respond. On December 2, Nanjing was captured by the revolutionaries and the whole Yangzi area was under their control. Nine days later, on December 11, representatives from 17 provinces met in Nanjing to discuss the establishment of a central government and to prepare for the election of a president. The Provisional Republic of China was established and Sun Yat-sen was named Provisional President. Although he had taken no part in the Wuchang uprising, he had been a leading figure in gaining support for the rebellion among overseas and local Chinese.

Aftermath of the Revolution

The question then arose, what should be done about the Qing court in Beijing. On January 3, Yuan Shikai, who, as a former court official and military commander had the trust of the Qing court, announced he could force the Qing to abdicate if he were offered the presidency of the Republic. Sun Yat-sen agreed. Yuan Shikai was able to persuade the Empress Dowager Longyu, the widow of Guangxu, to announce the abdication on February 12, 1912. Yuan Shikai became the second Provisional President on March 10.

Yuan subsequently declared Sun Yat-sen's political party, the Guomindang, an illegal organization, and not long after he invested himself as Emperor in a poorly attended ceremony at the Temple of Heaven. However, he faced fierce opposition and foreign powers withdrew their support. He died soon after.

In 1916 a royalist warlord, Zhang Xun, tried to restore the Qing dynasty, but that lasted only a few days. The Qing dynasty, which had ruled for over 260 years, had finally come to an end.

The Republic did not bring social order or prosperity to China. It was, however, certainly the beginning of a new era.

ARTICLES OF FAVORABLE TREATMENT FOR THE EMPEROR

On February 6, 1912, the National Assembly of the Nanjing Provisional Government passed a resolution regarding the "Favorable Treatment of the Great Qing Emperor." By this resolution, his title would remain; he would be treated with the courtesy due to a foreign monarch and be allocated 4,000,000 taels of silver for the expenses of the imperial family. He would remain in the Forbidden City until he could be transferred to the Summer Palace at some time in the future; the Qing ancestral temples and tombs would be protected and expenses incurred in the completion of Guangxu's tomb paid by the Republic. The private property of the imperial family would be protected, and palace employees and the Palace Guard would be provided for. Few of these promises were honored for more than a few years.

RIGHT **The bodies of Emperor Guangxu and his aunt,** Dowager Empress Cixi, were laid in state in the pavilion of Imperial Longevity after their deaths in 1908.

The Last Emperor

Aisin-Gioro Puyi (1906–1967) was the last emperor of the Qing and Chinese history. His journey from emperor to war prisoner in Russia and China, and finally to "ordinary citizen" in the People's Republic of China, is truly a legend.

Puyi was the son of Prince Chun, Emperor Guangxu's brother. In 1908, when the news reached Prince Chun's residence that his son, the two-year-old Puyi, had been chosen as the heir to the dying Guangxu, Puyi's grandmother, who had raised him, fainted. A few days after the announcement, Puyi became emperor and his father, Prince Chun, became regent.

Abdication and Expulsion

Just over three years later, following the declaration of the republic, Puyi abdicated—or rather,

the most senior member of the former ruling family, the widow of Guangxu, abdicated on his behalf. Inside the Forbidden City, but only inside the Forbidden City, Puyi retained the title of emperor. He grew up in the palace along with the four imperial consorts of his predecessors Tongzhi and Guangxu, and hundreds of eunuchs. Reginald Johnson, a British colonial officer, was appointed as his tutor.

Puyi dreamed of escaping to the West together with his younger brother Pujie, but that was not to be. In 1917, Zhang Xun, a loyalist general who was financed by Puyi's father, attempted a restoration of the Qing dynasty. This episode lasted only a few days, but encouraged anti-monarchist republicans in their belief that the Qing did not intend to honor the terms of the abdication. This gave them their justification for the expulsion of Puyi from the imperial palace in 1924. Another warlord, the Christian General Feng Yuxiang, was given the task of arranging for his departure.

The Sacking of the Emperor's Tomb

After being expelled from the imperial palace, Puyi first spent a short period in Prince Chun's residence and then in the Japanese legation. After that he lived in the Japanese concession in Tianjin, until the creation of the Japanese puppet state of Manchukuo in 1934.

One of the conditions for Puyi's abdication had been the protection of the imperial tombs. Despite this, the tombs were pillaged by the warlord Sun Dianying in 1928. The bodies of the Qianlong emperor and Empress Dowager Cixi were thrown out of their coffins, and priceless jewelry and other valuable items were stolen. Writing in his autobiography, *From Emperor to Citizen*, Puyi recalls:

> …the report of Sun Dianying's grave-robbery …gave me a shock worse than the one when I was expelled from the Palace. The royal clan and the former Qing officials were infuriated. Men of every faction…flocked to my house and expressed their hatred for the troops of Chiang Kai-shek.

BELOW **In 1908, Prince Chun** learned that Puyi, his two-year-old son, was to become emperor. Puyi's brother, Pujie, was still a baby.

RIGHT **On March 1, 1934,** former Emperor of China Henry Puyi was proclaimed emperor of Manchukuo, the newly founded Japanese state, but the role afforded him no power.

Qing veterans from all over the country sent funds for the restoration of the mausoleums.

Flight to Manchuria

Puyi's hatred of the Republic grew after the destruction of the tombs. His political alliance with Japan stemmed from his belief that Japan would help him to restore the Qing dynasty. After the Japanese invaded Manchuria in 1931, Puyi accepted their help to smuggle him out of China. The state of Manchukuo was formed in Manchuria and Puyi was given the title of chief executive of the new country. The Chinese government, however, branded Manchukuo a puppet state and accused Puyi of being a traitor to China.

In 1934, Puyi was given the title Emperor of Manchukuo. He soon discovered, however, that the real ruler, even of his personal life, was the Japanese military. Puyi resisted Japanese demands to marry a Japanese bride, but his brother, Pujie, agreed to an arranged marriage with a Japanese aristocrat. Puyi feared that the Japanese would replace him with his brother because of his greater cooperation, and his brother's heirs would be the ones to inherit the throne.

From Emperor to Citizen

When Japan surrendered to the allies in 1945, Puyi was captured and placed under house arrest in Russia. In 1946 he was brought to Tokyo to testify in the war crime tribunals. At the enquiry he denied having collaborated with the Japanese military of his own free will. He was sent back to China in 1950 and there served almost a decade in prison. He

was finally released at the end of 1959. After his release, Puyi lived much like an ordinary citizen. He had a job with a (generous) monthly salary, and remarried—this time to a Chinese nurse. He died of cancer in 1967 in the initial stages of the Cultural Revolution.

THE TRAGIC LIFE OF WANRONG, THE LAST EMPRESS

In 1922, at the age of 16, Wanrong (1906–1946), a Daur of the Plain White Banner, was chosen to be Puyi's wife. Her relations with Puyi, which had never been close, deteriorated to the point where she was utterly neglected and ignored. There were rumors that in Manchuria she had an affair with a member of Puyi's personal guard and became pregnant, and gave birth to a baby which, with Puyi's connivance, was immediately taken away and killed. No one was allowed to talk to her after that, not even her brother Runqi. In despair and isolation, her opium addiction grew worse. Puyi fled Manchukuo in 1945, but Wanrong was left behind. She was arrested along with others of Puyi's retinue by the Chinese communist army, and died in 1946 in Yanji prison, Jilin. No one knows where she was buried or how she met her death, but it is likely that opium withdrawal and malnutrition contributed.

RIGHT **In Tianjin,** relations between Wanrong and Puyi were cold.

Chronology

Historical dates before 500 BCE are often disputed; even the very existence of the Xia dynasty is a matter of contention. Dates for later periods and dynasties can vary depending on whether the beginning of a dynasty is considered to start from the time a ruler took power or from the adoption of a dynastic or reign title.

PLEISTOCENE ERA

1.7 million BP	Yuanmou Man (*Homo erectus*)
1.15 million–750,000 BP	Lantian Man (*Homo erectus*)
500,000–300,000 BP	Peking Man (*Homo erectus*)

NEOLITHIC PERIOD

c. **7000** BCE	Beginning of agriculture
c. **5000** BCE	Beginning of sericulture
c. **5000–3000** BCE	Yangshao culture
c. **3300–2200** BCE	Liangzhu culture
c. **3000–2000** BCE	Beginning of use of bronze
c. **2800–2200** BCE	Mythical Three Sovereigns and "Five Emperors"
c. **2500–1900** BCE	Longshan culture

XIA AUTUMN PERIOD

c. **2200–1700** BCE (trad.)	Erlitou culture
	Beginnings of Chinese bronze age

SHANG DYNASTY

c. **1600–1046** BCE	Oracle-bone writing
	Use of chariots
	Use of calendar

ZHOU DYNASTY

c. **1046–771** BCE	Western Zhou
771–256 BCE	Eastern Zhou
770–453 BCE	Spring and Autumn period
	Age of Confucius
	Sun Tzu writes *The Art of War*
453–221 BCE	Warring States period
	Casting of iron tools
	Age of "One Hundred Schools" of thinkers

QIN DYNASTY

221–206 BCE	First unified empire
	The Qin wall
	Standardization of weights, measures, and script
	"Burning of the books"
	Burial of terracotta army
	Expansion into Vietnam

HAN DYNASTY

206 BCE–CE **9**	Western Han dynasty
	Silk Road connects Luoyang to the Roman Empire
	Use of Confucian Classics as orthodox state teachings
	Expansion of empire into western Asia and Vietnam
	Sima Qian writes *Records of the Grand Historian*
CE **9–23**	Xin (Wang Mang) dynasty
CE **25–220**	Eastern Han dynasty
	Rise of "great families"
	Introduction of Buddhism
	Completion of *Shuowen jiezi* dictionary by Xu Shen
	Rise of Daoist religious movements
	Invention of paper
	Yellow Turban rebellion

THREE KINGDOMS

220–264	Wei dynasty
221–263	Shu Han dynasty
222–280	Wu dynasty
	Rise of distinct new phase of philosophical thought called "profound learning"
	Beginning of extended period of political disunity
	Beginning of the Nine Grades system for nominating potential officials

JIN DYNASTY

266–316	Western Jin dynasty
	Temporary reunification of China
317–420	Eastern Jin dynasty
	Age of poet Tao Qian
	Wang Xizhi writes his calligraphic masterpiece *Preface to Lanting Pavillion*

SOUTHERN DYNASTIES

	Spread of Buddhism
420–479	Liu-Song dynasty
479–502	Qi dynasty
502–557	Liang dynasty
557–589	Chen dynasty

NORTHERN DYNASTIES

	Spread of Buddhism
306–535	Northern Wei dynasty
534–550	Eastern Wei dynasty
535–557	Western Wei dynasty
550–577	Northern Qi dynasty
557–581	Northern Zhou dynasty

SUI DYNASTY

581–618	Reunification of China
	Completion of Grand Canal

TANG DYNASTY

618–907	Monk Xuanzang travels to India for Buddhist scriptures
	An Lushan Rebellion
	Expansion into western Asia
	Earliest printed texts
	Appearance of "regulated" (modern style) verse
	Regular civil and military examinations

FIVE DYNASTIES

	Subdivision of China
907–923	Later Liang dynasty
923–936	Later Tang dynasty
936–947	Later Jin dynasty
947–950	Later Han dynasty
951–960	Later Zhou dynasty

LIAO DYNASTY

916–1125	Steppe empire occupies northern provinces

SONG DYNASTY

960–1127	Northern Song dynasty
	Moveable-type printing invented
	Genesis of Neo-Confucian thought
	Lyrical poetry (ci) reaches height of its literary status
	Wang Anshi's reforms
1127–1279	Southern Song dynasty
	Retreat of court to the south
	Age of the great Neo-Confucian philosopher Zhu Xi
	Marco Polo sojourns in China

XI (WESTERN) XIA DYNASTY (1038–1227)

JIN DYNASTY (1115–1234)

YUAN DYNASTY

1279–1368	China integrated into eastern empire of the Mongols

MING DYNASTY

1368–1644	Return to Han rule
	Urban and commercial growth
	Zheng He's voyages
	Construction of the Forbidden City
	Golden age of literati culture
	Age of the Neo-Confucian philosopher Wang Yangming
	Portuguese establish permanent settlement in Macao

QING DYNASTY

1644–1911	Manchus rule China
	Expansion into Mongolia, Tibet, and western Asia
1716	*Kangxi Dictionary* completed
1791	*The Dream of the Red Chamber* published
1792	*Siku quanshu* compendium completed
1793	Macartney embassy to Beijing
1839–1842	First Opium War
1842	Treaty of Nanking
1850–1864	Taiping Rebellion
1856–1860	Second Opium War
1884	Sino–French War
1894–1895	First Sino–Japanese War
1895	Taiwan ceded to Japan
1898	Hundred Days' Reform
1900	Boxer Rebellion
1905	Abolition of civil examination system
1911	1911 (Xinhai) revolution

POST-IMPERIAL AGE

1912	Republic of China established
1919	May Fourth Movement
1921	Foundation of the Chinese Communist Party
1934	Long March and New Life Movement began
1937–1945	Second Sino–Japanese War
1949–	People's Republic of China

Further Reading

Origins: Prehistoric China

Chang, Kwang-chih. *The Archaeology of Ancient China*. Yale University Press: New Haven and London, 1986.

Crawford, G. "East Asian Plant Domestication." M.T. Stark (ed.). *Archaeology of Asia*. Blackwell: Oxford, 2006, pp77–95.

Fuller, D.Q., E. Harvey, and Ling Qin. "Presumed domestication? Evidence for Wild Rice Cultivation and Domestication in the Fifth Millennium BC of the Lower Yangtze Region." *Antiquity*, 81, 2007, pp316–331.

Garris, A., T. Tai, J. Coburn, S. Kresovich, and S. McCouch. "Genetic Structure and Diversity in Oryza sativa L..." *Genetics* 169, 2005, pp1631–1638.

Liu Li, *The Chinese Neolithic: Trajectories to Early States*. Cambridge University Press: Cambridge, 2004.

Lu, Tracey L-D. *The Transition from Foraging to Farming and the Origin of Agriculture in China*. B.A.R. International Series 774. Archaeopress: Oxford, 1999.

Shelach, Gideon. "The Earliest Neolithic Cultures of Northeast China: Recent Discoveries and New Perspectives on the Beginning of Agriculture." *Journal of World Prehistory* 14.4, 2001, pp363–413.

Underhill, Anne P. *Craft Production and Social Change in Northern China*. Kluwer Academic/Plenum Publishers: New York, 2002

Underhill, Anne P. "Current Issues in Chinese Neolithic Archaeology." *Journal of World Prehistory*, 11.2, 1997, pp103–160.

Zhang Chi. "The Rise of Urbanism in the Middle and Lower Yangzi River Valley." Peter Bellwood and Dianne Tillotson (eds.). *Bulletin of the Indo-Pacific Prehistory Association 16, The Chiang Mai Papers*, vol. 3, The Indo–Pacific Prehistory Association: Canberra, 1997, pp63–67.

Zhang, M. and Tang L.H. "Human selection of rice grains 5,000 years ago" (in Chinese). *Chinese Antiquities News*, 1995.

Zhao, Zhijun. "The Upper Liao River Valley as a Center for the Origin of Millet Cultivation." *Chinese Antiquities News*, 2006.

The "Three Dynasties": The Ancient Kingdoms

Allan, Sarah. "Erlitou and the Formation of Chinese Civilization: Toward a New Paradigm." *The Journal of Asian Studies* 66, Cambridge University Press, 2007, pp461–496.

Chen, Yan. *Maritime Silk Route and Chinese-Foreign Cultural Exchanges*. Peking University Press: Beijing, 2002.

Deady, Kathleen W. and Muriel L. Dubois. *Ancient China*. Capstone Press: Mankato, 2004.

Ebrey, Patricia Buckley, Anne Walthall, and James B. Palais. *East Asia: A Cultural, Social, and Political History*. Houghton Mifflin Company: Boston, 2006.

Fairbank, John King and Merle Goldman. *China: A New History; Second Enlarged Edition*. The Belknap Press of Harvard University Press: Cambridge and London, 2006.

Feng, Li. *Landscape and Power in Early China: The Crisis and Fall of the Western Zhou 1045–771 BC*. Cambridge University Press: Cambridge, 2006.

Keightley, David N. *Sources of Shang History: The Oracle-Bone Inscriptions of Bronze Age China*. University of California Press: Berkeley, 1978.

Keightley, David N. *The Ancestral Landscape: Time, Space, and Community in Late Shang China (ca. 1200 – 1045 B.C.)*. China Research Monograph 53, Institute of East Asian Studies, University of California Press: Berkeley, 2000.

Lee, Yuan-Yuan and Sinyan Shen. *Chinese Musical Instruments (Chinese Music Monograph Series)*. Chinese Music Society of North America Press, 1999.

Leeman, Bernard. *Queen of Sheba and Biblical Scholarship*. Queensland Academic Press Australia, 2005.

Li, Chu-tsing. "The Great Bronze Age of China." *Art Journal* 40(1/2), 1980, pp390–395.

Liu, L. and H. Xiu. "Rethinking Erlitou: Legend, History and Chinese Archaeology." *Antiquity*, 81(314), 2007, pp886–901.

Needham, Joseph. *Science and Civilization in China*, vol. 4, part 3. Caves Books, Ltd.: Taipei, 1986.

Sawyer, Ralph D. and Mei-chün Lee Sawyer. *Sun Tzu's The Art of War*. Barnes and Noble Inc.: New York, 1994.

Schirokauer and Brown. *A Brief History of Chinese Civilization*, 2nd edn. Wadsworth, a division of Thomson Learning, 2006, pp25–47.

Shen, Sinyan. "Acoustics of Ancient Chinese Bells." *Scientific American* 256, 1987, p94.

Sun, Guangqi. *History of Navigation in Ancient China*. Ocean Press: Beijing, 1989.

Sun, Yan. "Cultural and Political Control in North China: Style and Use of the Bronzes of Yan at Liulihe during the Early Western Zhou." Victor H. Mair (ed.). *Contact and Exchange in the Ancient World*. University of Hawai'i Press: Honolulu, 2006, pp215–237.

Sun, Yan. "Colonizing China's Northern Frontier: Yan and Her Neighbors During the Early Western Zhou Period." *International Journal of Historical Archaeology* 10(2), 2006, pp159–177.

Thorp, Robert L. "The Date of Tomb 5 at Yinxu, Anyang: A Review Article." *Artibus Asiae*, 43(3), 1981, pp239–246.

Wang, Hongyuan. *The Origins of Chinese Characters*. Sinolingua: Beijing, 1993.

Unification and Expansion: The First Chinese Empires

Brook, Timothy. *The Confusions of Pleasure: Commerce and Culture in Ming China*. University of California Press: Berkeley, 1998.

Bulling, A. "A Landscape Representation of the Western Han Period." *Artibus Asiae* 25(4), 1962, pp293–317.

Ebrey, Walthall, and Palais. *East Asia: A Cultural, Social, and Political History*. Houghton Mifflin Company: Boston, 2006.

Fairbank, John King and Merle Goldman. *China: A New History; Second Enlarged Edition* (2006). The Belknap Press of Harvard University Press: Cambridge and London, 1992.

Huang, Ray. *China: A Macro History*. An East Gate Book, M.E. SHARPE Inc.: New York, 1992.

Morton, W. Scott and Charlton M. Lewis. *China: Its History and Culture*. McGraw-Hill, Inc.: New York, 2005.

Mote, F.W. *Imperial China (900–1800)*. Harvard University Press, 1999.

Needham, Joseph. *Science and Civilization in China*, vol 4, part 2. Caves Books, Ltd.: Taipei, 1986.

Needham, Joseph *Science and Civilization in China*. vol. 5, part 7. Caves Books, Ltd.: Taipei, 1986.

Wright, David Curtis. *The History of China*. Greenwood Press: Westport, 2001.

Partition and Conflict: The Period of Division

Chang, Kang-i Sun. *Six Dynasties Poetry*. Princeton, 1986.

de Crespigny, Rafe. *Generals of the South: The Foundation and Early History of the Three Kingdoms State of Wu*. Canberra, 1990.

de Crespigny, Rafe. *Man from the Margin: Cao Cao and the Three Kingdoms*, 51st George Ernest Morrison Lecture in Ethnology. Canberra, 1990.

Dien, Albert E. *Six Dynasties Civilization*. Yale University Press, 2007.

Ebrey, Walthall, and Palais. *East Asia: A Cultural, Social, and Political History*. Houghton Mifflin Company: Boston, 2006.

Graff, David A. *Medieval Chinese Warfare*, pp300–900.

Holcombe, Charles. *In the Shadow of the Han: Literati Thought and Society at the Beginning of the Southern Dynasties*. University of Hawai'i Press. Honolulu, 1994.

Holzman, Donald. *Poetry and Politics: The Life and Works of Juan Chi A.D. 210-263*. Cambridge University Press, 1976.

Jenner, W.J.F. *Memories of Loyang: Yang Hsüan-chih and the Lost Capital (493–534)*. Oxford, 1981.

Knechtges, David (tr. 1982). *Wenxuan, or Selections of Refined Literature*, 3 vols. Princeton, 1982.

Miller, Roy Andrew. *Accounts of Western Nations in the History of the Northern Chou Dynasty*. University of California Press: Berkeley, 1959.

Pearce, Scott, Audrey Spiro, and Patricia Ebrey. *Culture and Power in the Reconstitution of the Chinese Realm, 200–600*. Cambridge, 2001.

Tian Xiaofei, Tian. *Beacon Fire and Shooting Star: The Literary Culture of the Liang*. Cambridge, 2007.

Wright, Arthur F. *Buddhism in Chinese History*. Stanford University Press: Stanford, 1959.

Great Changes: The Tang–Song Transition

Allsen, Thomas T. *Commodity and Exchange in the Mongol Empire: A Cultural History of Islamic Textiles* (Cambridge Studies in Islamic Civilization). Cambridge University Press: Cambridge, 1997.

Barfield, Thomas J. *The Perilous Frontier: Nomadic Empires and China*. Basil Blackwell: Oxford, 1989.

Bingham, Woodbridge. *The Founding of the T'ang Dynasty: The Fall of the Sui and the Rise of the T'ang*. Waverly: Baltimore, 1941.

Bol, Peter K. *"This Culture of Ours": Intellectual Transitions in T'ang and Sung China*. Stanford University Press: Stanford, 1992.

Buell, Paul D. and Eugene N. Anderson with Charles Perry. *A Soup for the Qan: Chinese Dietary Medicine of the Mongol Era as Seen in Hu Szu-hui's Yin-shan Cheng-yao* (Sir Henry Wellcome Asian Series). Kegan Paul International: London, 2000.

Buell, Paul D. *Historical Dictionary of the Mongolian World Empire*. The Scarecrow Press, Inc.: Oxford and Lanham, 2003.

Cahill, James. *Chinese Painting*. SKIRA, 1960.

Carswell, John. *Blue and White, Chinese Porcelain around the World*. Art Media Resources: Chicago, 2000.

Chaffee, John W. *The Thorny Gates of Learning in Sung China: A Social History of Examination* (new edition). State University of New York Press: Albany, 1995.

Chen, Jo-shui. "Empress Wu and Proto-Feminist Sentiments in T'ang China." *Imperial Rulership and Cultural Change in Traditional China*. University of Washington Press, 1994.

Chow, Kai-wing, On-cho Ng, and John B. Henderson. *Imagining Boundaries: Changing Confucian Doctrines, Texts, and Hermeneutics*. State University of New York Press: Albany, 1999.

de Bary, W. Theodore. *East Asian Civilizations: A Dialogue in Five Stages*. Harvard University Press: Cambridge, 1988.

Deng, Gang. *Maritime Sector, Institutions, and Sea Power of Premodern China*. Greenwood Press: Westport and London, 1999.

Dien, Dora Shu-fang. *Empress Wu Zetian in Fiction and in History*. Nova Science Publishers: New York, 2003.

Elman, Benjamin A. *A Cultural History of Civil Examination in Late Imperial China*. University of California: Berkeley, 2000.

Fitzgerald, C.P. *Son of Heaven*. Cambridge University Press: Cambridge, 1933.

Fitzgerald, C.P. *The Empress Wu*. Cheshire: Melbourne, 1955.

Forte, Antonino. *Mingtang and Buddhist Utopias in the History of the Astronomical Clock: The Tower, the Statue and the Armillary Sphere Constructed by Empress Wu*. Italian School of East Asian Studies: Rome, 1988.

Forte, Antonino. *Political Propaganda and Ideology at the End of Seventh Century China*. Italian School of East Asian Studies: Kyoto, 2005.

Gernet, Jacques. *A History of Chinese Civilization* (translated by J.R. Foster). Cambridge University Press: Cambridge, 1982.

Grousset, Rene. *Chinese Art and Culture* (translated by Haakon Chevalier). The Orion Press: New York, 1959.

Guisso, Richard. *Wu T'se t'ien and the Politics of Legitimation in T'ang China*. Western Washington University Press: Bellingham, 1978.

Hon, Tze-ki. *The Yijing and Chinese Politics: Classical Commentary and Literati Activism in the Northern Song Period, 960–1127*. State University of New York Press: Albany, 2005.

Humes, Robert P. and Conrad Schirokauer (eds.). *Ordering the World: Approaches to State and Society in Sung Dynasty China*. University of California Press: Berkeley, 1993.

Hymes, Robert P. *Statesmen and Gentlemen: The Elites of Fu-chou, Chiang-his, in Northern and Southern Song*. Cambridge University Press: Cambridge, 1986.

Johnson, David. *The Medieval Chinese Oligarchy*. The Westview Press: Boulder, 1977.

Lee, Hui-shu. *Exquisite Moments: West Lake and Southern Song Art*. China Institute Gallery: New York, 2001.

Mote, F.W. *Imperial China, 900–1800*. Harvard University Press: Cambridge and London, 1999.

Needham, Joseph, with Wang Ling and Lu Gwei-djen. *Science and Civilisation in China*, vol. 4: *Physics and Physical Technology*, part 3: *Civil Engineering and Nautics*. Cambridge University: Cambridge, 1971.

Pan, Yihong. *Son of Heaven and Heavenly Qaghan: Sui-Tang China and its Neighbors*. Center for East Asian Studies, Western Washington University: Bellingham, 1997.

Peterson, Charles. "Court and Province in Mid- and Late-T'ang." Denis Twitchett (ed.). *The Cambridge History of China*, vol. 3, *Sui and T'ang China*, pp589–906, Part I. pp464–560. Cambridge University Press: Cambridge, 1979.

Pulleyblank, Edward. *The Background of the An Lushan Rebellion*. Oxford University Press: London, 1955.

Rachewiltz, Igor de, Chan Hok-lam, Hsiao Ch'i-ch'ing, and Peter W. Geier (eds.). *In the Service of the Khan, Eminent Personalities of the Early Mongol-Yuan Period (1200–1300)*. Otto Harrassowitz: Wiesbaden, 1993.

Rossabi, Morris. *Khubilai Khan: His Life and Times*. University of California Press: Berkeley, 1988.

Rossabi, Morris. *Voyager from Xanadu: Rabban Sauma and the First Journey from China to the West*. Kodansha International: Tokyo and New York, 1992.

Rothschild, N. Harry. *Wu Zhao: China's Only Female Emperor*. Longman: New York, 2008.

Smith, Kidder, Peter Bol, Joseph Adler, and Don Wyatt. *Sung Dynasty Uses of the I Ching*. Princeton University Press: Princeton.

Smith, Paul. *Taxing Heaven's Storehouse: Horses, Bureaucrats, and the Destruction of the Sichuan Tea Industry, 1074–1224*. Harvard University Press: Cambridge and London, 1990.

Sullivan, Michael. *The Arts of China*, 4th edn. The University of California Press: Berkeley, Los Angeles, and London, 1999.

Tillman, Hoyt Cleveland, and Stephen H. West (eds.). *China under Jurchen Rule: Essays on Chin Intellectual and Cultural History*. State University of New York Press: Albany, 1995.

Tong, Jowen. *Fables for the Patriarchs: Gender Politics in Tang Discourse*. Rowman and Littlefield: Lanham, 2000.

Tsien, Tsuen-hsuin. *Science and Civilization in China*, vol. 5: *Chemistry and Chemical Technology*, part 1: *Paper and Printing*. Cambridge University Press: Cambridge, 1985.

Twitchett, Denis. "Hsuan-tsung (reign 712–56)." Denis Twitchett and John K. Fairbank (eds.). *The Cambridge History of China*, vol. 3: *Sui and T'ang China, 589–906 A.D.*, Cambridge University Press, 1979, part I, pp333–463.

Twitchett, Denis and John K. Fairbank (eds.). *The Cambridge History of China*, vol. 3, *Sui and T'ang China: 589–906 A.D.*, part I. Cambridge: Cambridge University Press, 1979.

Twitchett, Denis. *Financial Administration under the T'ang Dynasty*, 2nd ed. Cambridge University Press: Cambridge, 1970.

Wang, Gungwu. *The Structure of Power in North China during the Five Dynasties*. Stanford University Press: Stanford, 1963.

Wechsler, Howard. *Mirror to the Son of Heaven*. Yale University Press: New Haven, 1974.

Wechsler, Howard. *Offerings of Jade and Silk: Ritual and Symbol in the Legitimization of the T'ang*. Yale University Press: New Haven, 1985.

Wright, Arthur F. *The Sui Dynasty*. Alfred A. Knopf: New York, 1978.

Xiong, Victor Cunrui. *Emperor Yang of the Sui Dynasty: His Life, Times, and Legacy*. SUNY Press: Albany, 2006.

Xiong, Victor Cunrui. *Sui-Tang Chang'an: A Study in the Urban History of Medieval China*. Center for Chinese Studies, University of Michigan: Ann Arbor, 2000.

Yule, Henry and Henri Cordier. *The Book of Ser Marco Polo, the Venetian*, 3rd edn., 2 vols. Philo Press: Amsterdam, 1975.

Late Imperial China: The Ming and Qing Dynasties

Aisin-Gioro. *Pu Yi. From Emperor to Citizen* (trans. W.J.P. Jenner). Oxford University Press, 1987.

Bartlett, Beatrice S. *Monarchs and Ministers—The Grand Council in Mid-Ch'ing China 1723-1820*. University of California Press: Berkeley, 1991.

Berger, Patricia. *Empire of Emptiness—Buddhist Art and Political Authority in Qing China*. University of Hawai'i Press: Honolulu, 2003.

Chen Ru-hsi and Claudia Brown (eds.). *The Elegant Brush: Chinese Painting and the Qianlong Emperor 1735-1795*. Phoenix Art Museum: Phoenix, 1985.

Cranmer-Byng, J.L. (ed.). *An Embassy to China – Being the Journal kept by Lord Macartney during his Embassy to the Emperor Ch'ien-lung 1793-1794*. Longmans Green and Co. Ltd: London, 1962.

Crossley, Pamela Kyle. *The Manchus*. Blackwell: Massachusetts and Oxford, 1997.

Crossley, Pamela Kyle. "*Manzhou yuanliu kao* and the Formalization of the Manchu Heritage." *Journal of Asian Studies*, 46:4, 1987, pp761–90.

Crossley, Pamela Kyle. *A Translucent Mirror—History and Identity in Qing Imperial Ideology*. University of California Press: Berkeley, 1999.

Crossley, Pamela Kyle. *Orphan Warriors: Three Manchu Generations and the End of the Qing World*. Princeton University Press: Princeton, 1990.

Dickinson, Gary and Linda Wrigglesworth. *Imperial Wardrobe*. Ten Speed Press: Berkeley, 2000.

Elliot, Mark C. "The Manchu Language Archives of the Qing Dynasty and the Origins of the Palace Memorial System." *Late Imperial China* 22(1), June, 2001, pp1–70.

Elliott, Mark C. "The Limits of Tartary: Manchuria in Imperial and National Geographies." *Journal of Asian Studies* 59(3) August, 2000, pp603–646.

Elliott, Mark C. *The Manchu Way – The Eight Banners and Ethnic Identity in Late Imperial China*. Stanford University Press: Stanford, 2002.

Forêt, Philippe. *Mapping Chengde – The Qing Landscape Enterprise*. University of Hawai'i Press: Honolulu, 2000.

Guy, R. Kent. *The Emperor's Four Treasuries – Scholars and the State in the Late Ch'ien-lung Era*. Harvard University Press: Cambridge, 1987.

Hévia, James, L. *Cherishing Men from Afar – Qing Guest Ritual and the Macartney Embassy of 1793*. Duke University Press, 1995.

Jochim, Christian. "The Imperial Audience Ceremonies of the Ch'ing Dynasty." *Society for the Study of Chinese Religions Bulletin* no.7 Fall, 1979, pp88–103.

Kessler, Lawrence D. *K'ang-hsi and the Consolidation of Ch'ing Rule 1661-1684*. University of Chicago Press: Chicago, 1976.

Kuhn, Philip. *Soulstealers: The Chinese Sorcery scare of 1748*. Harvard University Press: Cambridge, 1990.

Metzger, Thomas A. *The Internal Organization of Ch'ing Bureaucracy – Legal, Normative, and Communication Aspects*. Harvard University Press: Cambridge, 1973.

Millward, James A, Ruth W. Dunnell, Mark C. Elliott, and Philippe Forêt (eds.). *New Qing Imperial History—The making of Inner Asian empire at Qing Chengde*. Rutledge Curzon: London and New York, 2006.

Millward, James A. *Beyong the Pass—Economy, Ethnicity, and Empire in Qing Central Asia, 1759–1869*. Standford University Press: Standford, 1998.

Naquin, Susan. *Millenarian Rebellion in China—The Eight Trigrams Uprising of 1813*. Yale University Press, 1976.

Perdue, Peter C. *China Marches West—The Qing Conquest of Central Eurasia*. The Belknap Press of Harvard University Press: Cambridge, 2005.

Rawski, Evelyn S. *The Last Emperors – A Social History of Qing Imperial Institutions*. University of California Press: Berkeley, 1998.

Spence, Jonathan D. *Emperor of China—Self Portrait of K'ang-hsi*. Jonathan Cape: London, 1974.

Spence, Jonathan D. *Treason by the Book*. Viking: New York, 2001.

Spence, Jonathan D. *Ts'ao Yin and the K'ang-hsi Emperor—Bondservant and Master*. Yale University Press, 1965.

Twitchett, Denis and John K. Fairbank (eds.). *The Cambridge History of China*, vol. 9: *The Ch'ing Empire to 1800* and vol. 10, *Late Ch'ing, 1800-1911*. Cambridge University Press: Cambridge, 1978.

Twitchett, Denis and John K. Fairbank (eds.). *The Cambridge History of China*, vol. 10, *Late Ch'ing, 1800–1911*, part 1. Cambridge University Press: Cambridge, 1978.

Ye Xiaoqing. "Ascendant Peace in the Four Seas—Tributary Drama and the Macartney Mission of 1793." *Late Imperial China* 26.2, 2005.

Ye Xiaoqing. "Imperial Institutions and Drama in the Qing Court." *European Journal of East Asian Studies* 2–2, Autumn, 2003.

Index

Plain page numbers indicate references in the body text. *Italicized* numbers indicate references in image captions, while **bold** numbers indicate references in colored feature boxes.

Acknowledgments

Global Book Publishing would like to thank Dannielle Viera for editing the index, as well as Loretta Barnard and Scott Forbes for their help during the conceptualization process prior to production.

Managing Director:	Chryl Campbell	Map Editor:	Alan Edwards
Publishing Director:	Sarah Anderson	Cover Design:	Kylie Mulquin
Art Director:	Kylie Mulquin	Designers:	Lena Lowe, Thomson Digital
Project Manager:	Sophia Oravecz	Junior Designer:	Althea Aseoche
Chief Consultant:	Dr John Makcham	Design Concept:	Alex Frampton, Stan Lamond
Contributors:	Dr Paul Buell, Duncan Campbell, Dr Rafe de Crespigny,	Cartographer:	John Frith
	Associate Professor Paola Demattè, Professor Edward	Graphics:	Althea Aseoche
	Farmer, Associate Professor Tze-ki Hon, Professor Anne	Picture Research:	Sarah Anderson, David Boehm, Oliver Laing,
	Behnke Kinney, Associate Professor Tracey Lie-Dan Lu,		Sophia Oravecz
	Jeffrey Moser, Associate Professor Scott Pearce,	Index:	Michael Ramsden
	Professor Yuri Pines, Associate Professor N. Harry	Proofreader:	Joy McCarthy
	Rothschild, Professor Gideon Shelach, Professor Richard	Production:	Ian Coles
	von Glahn, Professor Victor Xiong, Dr Xiaoqing Ye	Contracts:	Alan Edwards
Commissioning Editor:	Alan Edwards	Foreign Rights:	Kate Hill
Editors:	Maggie Aldhamland, Raewyn Glynn, Jody Lee,	Publishing Assistant:	Christine Leonards
	Catherine du Peloux Menagé		

Captions for Cover, Preliminary Pages, and Openers

Front cover: Fifteenth-century silk painting of two mandarins of the Ming dynasty
Back cover: Carved stone musician from the Buddhist cave temple at Yungang, Shanxi Province, China
Page 1: Ornate screen in Wangshi Garden, Jiangsu Province, China
Page 2: Terracotta statues, the first landing of the Great Wall of China, near Beijing
Pages 4–5: The Gate of Divine Military Genius, Forbidden City, Beijing, China
Pages 6–7: An imperial procession, watercolor on paper, Victoria and Albert Museum, London, United Kingdom
Page 9: Nineteenth-century painted textile of celebration with kites and fireworks

Pages 10–11: Ancient pagoda by the Three Gorges of the Yangzi River, Hubei Province, China
Pages 22–23: Skeleton and pottery from Liuwan tombs, Qinghei Province, China
Pages 56–57: Bronze head from the Shang dynasty, Sanxingdui Museum, Sichuan Province, China
Pages 106–107: Terracotta archer, Qin Shihuang Museum, Shaanxi Province, China
Pages 164–165: Section of the Great Wall of China, Hebei Province
Pages 186–187: *Chinese Poet Li Po Receiving Friends*, painted by Qiu Ying
Pages 276–277: *Saying Farewell Near Hsun Yang*, painted by Qiu Ying

Picture Credits

The Publisher would like to thank the copyright owners for permission to reproduce their images. Every attempt has been made to obtain permission for use of all images from the copyright owners. However, if any errors or omissions have occurred Global Book Publishing would be pleased to hear from copyright owners.

t = top; b = bottom; l = left; r = right; c = center
AA = Picture Desk/The Art Archive
AAAC = Ancient Art and Architecture Collection
AKG = AKG Images
CB = Corbis Australia
GBP = Global Book Publishing
GI = Getty Images
HIP = Heritage Image Partnership
IS = iStockphoto
LPI = Lonely Planet Images
NGS = National Geographic Image Collection
PL = Photolibrary
WF = Werner Forman Archive

Front Cover AA/Topkapi Museum Istanbul/Gianni Dagli Orti.
Back Cover AA/Musée Cernuschi Paris/Gianni Dagli Orti.

1c GI/Yann Layma/Stone, 2c GI/James Gritz/Photodisc, 5c GI/Martin Puddy/The Image Bank, 6–7t GI/Chinese School/The Bridgeman Art Library, 9c GI/The Bridgeman Art Library, 10–11c GI/China Span/Keren Su, 12t CB/Frank Krahmer/zefa, 13t GI/The Image Bank/Bruno Morandi, 13b CB/Zhuoming Liang, 14 CB/Pierre Colombel, 15t PL, 15b CB/Christie's Images, 16 AA/National Palace Museum Taiwan, 17t AA/Jan Vinchon Numismatist Paris/Gianni Dagli Orti, 17b AA/Bibliothèque Nationale Paris, 18 AKG, 19t CB/Lowell Georgia, 19b CB/Keren Su, 20 PL, 21t GI/National Geographic, 21b GI/Gallo Images/Travel Ink, 22–23 GI, 23 GI/Bruno Morandi/The Image Bank, 25t AAAC/Uniphoto, 25b GI/Chinese School/The Bridgeman Art Library, 26t CB/Bettmann, 26b CB/Bettmann, 27 CB/Dean Conger, 28 GI/Ira Block/National Geographic, 29t GI/National Geographic, 29b GI/National Geographic, 30t CB/Visuals Unlimited, 31t GI/Ira Block/National Geographic, 31b AA/Museo di Antropologia ed Etnografia Turin/Gianni Dagli Orti, 32 GI/Time & Life Pictures, 33tr Creative Commons CC-BY-SA-2.5, 33br GI/DEA/C. Sappa, 33l CB/Royal Ontario Museum, 34 AA/Freer Gallery of Art, 35t GI/Keren Su/Lonely Planet Images, 35b AAAC/Uniphoto, 36 GI/ China Tourism Press/The Image Bank, 37t GI/Foodcollection, 37 GI/Foodcollection, 38 AAAC/Uniphoto, 39t CB/Asian Art & Archaeology, Inc., 39b AAAC/Uniphoto, 40t AA/Genius of China Exhibition, 40b Creative Commons CC-BY-SA-2.5 41 CB/Lowell Georgia, 42 AAAC/Uniphoto, 43t AAAC/Uniphoto, 43b AAAC/Uniphoto, 44 GI/Bruno Morandi/The Image Bank, 45t GI/AFP, 45b AA/Genius of China Exhibition, 46t CB/Christie's Images, 46b AAAC/Uniphoto, 47bl AA/Genius of China Exhibition, 47r CB/Asian Art & Archaeology, Inc., 48 PL, 49t AA/Musée Guimet Paris/Gianni Dagli Ort, 49b HIP/The Museum of East Asian Art, 50l AAAC/Uniphoto, 50bl AAAC/Uniphoto, 51 AAAC/Uniphoto, 52t GI, 52b AAAC/Uniphoto, 53 CB/Asian Art & Archaeology, Inc., 54l AAAC/Uniphoto, 54br CB/Asian Art & Archaeology, Inc., 55 AKG/Bildarchiv Steffens, 56–57 GI/National Geographic, 57tl GI/Keren Su/China Span, 59t AAAC/Uniphoto, 59b AAAC/Uniphoto Japan, 60 AAAC/Uniphoto, 61t GI/Keren Su/China Span, 61b AAAC/Uniphoto, 62 AAAC/Uniphoto, 63t AA/Laurie Platt Winfrey, 63b AAAC/Uniphoto, 64 CB/Lowell Georgia, 65t PL, 65b PL, 66t GI/National Geographic, 66b NGS/O. Louis Mazzatenta, 67t GI/National Geographic, 67b AAAC/R. Sheridan, 68 GI/O. Louis Mazzatenta/National Geographic, 69t AA/ Shandong Provincial Museum/Laurie Platt Winfrey, 69b AKG/Werner Forman, 70t AA/Genius of China Exhibition, 71t AKG/Werner Forman, 71b CB/Lowell Georgia, 72 NGS/O. Louis Mazzatenta, 73t PL, 73b NGS/O. Louis Mazzatenta, 74 GI/David Evans/National Geographic, 75t AA/Musée Guimet Paris/Gianni Dagli Orti, 75b GI/O. Louis Mazzatenta/National Geographic, 76 AAAC/Uniphoto, 77t AA/Beijing Institute of Archaeology/Laurie Platt Winfrey, 77b NGS/O. Louis Mazzatenta, 78r NGS/O. Louis Mazzatenta, 78b AAAC/Ronald Sheriden, 79 PL, 80 GI/National Geographic, 81t AAAC/Uniphoto, 81b AAAC/Uniphoto, 82 AAAC/Uniphoto, 83t CB/Christie's Images, 83b AAAC/Uniphoto, 84 PL, 85t CB/Asian Art & Archaeology, Inc., 85b CB/Asian Art & Archaeology, Inc., 86 CB/Lowell Georgia, 87t AKG/Laurent Lecat, 87b AKG, 88 CB/Royal Ontario Museum, 89 AKG/Erich Lessing, 90t CB/Royal Ontario Museum, 90b AKG/Laurent Lecat, 91br AA/Musée Guimet Paris/Gianni Dagli Ort, 92b AA/Laurie Platt Winfrey, 93t AA/Musée Cernuschi Paris/Gianni Dagli Orti, 93b AA/Genius of China Exhibition, 94t NGS/Todd Gipstein, 94l HIP/The Museum of East Asian Art, 95 CB/Asian Art & Archaeology, Inc., 96 WF/Shaanxi Provincial Museum, Xian, 97t WF, 97b CB/Bettmann, 98 GI/Keren Su/China Span, 99tr WF/The Palace Museum, Peking, 99tl CB/Burstein Collection, 100t HIP/The British Library, 101t HIP/The Museum of East Asian Art, 101b HIP/The Museum of East Asian Art, 102t AA/Jan Vinchon Numismatist Paris/Gianni Dagli Orti, 102l AA/Jan Vinchon Numismatist Paris/Gianni Dagli Orti, 103t NGS/O. Louis Mazzatenta, 103b HIP/The British Library, 104 AA/Musée Cernuschi Paris/Gianni Dagli Orti, 105tl AKG/Erich Lessing, 105tr CB/Jerry Arcieri, 106–107 GI/National Geographic, 107tl

GI/The Bridgeman Art Library/Chinese School, 109t AA/National Palace Museum Taiwan, 109b GI/China Span/Keren Su, 110r GI/Chinese School/The Bridgeman Art Library, 110l CB/Asian Art & Archaeology, Inc., 111 CB/John T. Young, 112t AKG/Laurent Lecat, 112b GI/China Span/Keren Su, 113 AKG/Laurent Lecat, 114 PL, 115t PL, 115b PL, 116 CB/Keren Su, 117t CB/Liang Zhuoming, 117b GI/Rod Porteous/Robert Harding World Imagery, 118 GI/Keren Su/Stone, 119t AKG/Erich Lessing, 119b CB/Dean Conger, 120 AAAC/Uniphoto,121t GBP, 121b AAAC/Uniphoto, 122 PL, 123t AA/Bibliothèque Nationale Paris, 123b AAAC/Uniphoto, 124t AAAC/Dr S. Coyne, 124b GI/Jeremy Woodhouse/Photodisc, 125t GI/Keren Su/Taxi, 125b PL, 126 CB/Charles & Josette Lenars, 127t GI/The Bridgeman Art Library/Chinese School, 127b WF/National Gallery Prague, 128 CB/ Asian Art & Archaeology, Inc., 129t CB/Asian Art & Archaeology, Inc., 129b AA/British Library, 130b AKG/Erich Lessing, 131t AA, 131b AKG/Francois Guenet, 132l WF/Yang-tzu-shaw, Szechwan, 132b AA/Musée Cernuschi Paris/Gianni Dagli Orti, 133 PL, 134 NGS/O. Louis Mazzatenta, 135t AA/Musée Cernuschi Paris/Gianni Dagli Orti, 135b AAAC/Uniphoto, 136t GI/The Bridgeman Art Library/Chinese School, 136b CB/Asian Art & Archaeology, Inc., 137 GI/China Span/Keren Su, 138t CB/Bettmann, 138b CB/Asian Art & Archaeology, Inc., 139t CB/Asian Art & Archaeology, Inc., 139b AA/Musée Cernuschi Paris/Gianni Dagli Orti, 140 CB/Jose Fuste Raga, 141t PL, 141b CB/Jose Fuste Raga, 142 PL, 143t AAAC/Uniphoto, 143b PL, 144 PL, 145t CB/Asian Art & Archaeology, Inc., 145l PL, 146l CB/Asian Art & Archaeology, Inc., 146–147 GI/Lonely Planet Images/Krzysztof Dydynski, 147 HIP/Ann Ronan Picture Library, 148 AAAC/Uniphoto, 149t HIP/The Museum of East Asian Art, 149b HIP/The Museum of East Asian Art, 150t CB/Asian Art & Archaeology, Inc., 150b AKG/Laurent Lecat, 151 PL, 152 CB/Asian Art & Archaeology, Inc., 153t CB/Royal Ontario Museum, 153b PL, 154 AAAC/Uniphoto, 155t AKG, 155b AAAC/Uniphoto Press Japan, 156 GI, 157t AAAC/Uniphoto Press, 157b GI/Yann Layma/The Image Bank, 158 AKG, 159tl CB/Keren Su, 159tr GI/IMAGEMORE Co., Ltd., 160t HIP/The Museum of East Asian Art, 160l AAAC/Uniphoto, 161tl AAAC/R Sheridan, 161tr PL, 162t HIP/The British Library, 162b GBP, 163 AA/Bibliothèque Nationale Paris/Marc Charmet, 164–165 GI/National Geographic, 165tl GI/Keren Su/China Span, 167t AA/Musée Cernuschi Paris/Gianni Dagli Orti, 167b AA/Genius of China Exhibition, 168 AA/Genius of China Exhibition, 169t AA/Musée Cernuschi Paris/Gianni Dagli Orti, 169b AA/Genius of China Exhibition, 170 GI/Keren Su/China Span, 171t CB/Pierre Colombel, 171b AA/Eileen Tweedy, 172 CB/Lindsay Hebberd, 173tl Sanguo Pinghua, c. 1320 / Photo courtesy of Liu Ts'un-yan and Rafe de Crespigny, 173tr AA/Mireille Vautier, 174 WF, 175t AA/Genius of China Exhibition, 175b CB/Royal Ontario Museum, 176 GI/Keren Su/China Span, 177t CB/Liu Liqun, 177b CB/Royal Ontario Museum, 178 WF, 179t CB/Burstein Collection, 179b CB/Royal Ontario Museum, 180t CB/Burstein Collection, 180b AA/Musée Guimet Paris/Gianni Dagli Orti, 181 CB/Royal Ontario Museum, 182t HIP/The Museum of East Asian Art, 182b HIP/The Museum of East Asian Art, 183r CB/Burstein Collection, 184t CB/Asian Art & Archaeology, Inc., 184b CB/Michael S. Yamashita,185 CB/Wolfgang Kaehler, 186–187 AA/Private Collection Paris/Gianni Dagli Orti, 187tl GI/National Geographic/James L. Stanfield, 189t AA/National Palace Museum Taiwan, 189b AA/Musée Guimet Paris/Gianni Dagli Orti, 190t CB/Burstein Collection, 190b CB/Werner Forman, 191 AA/Musée Guimet Paris/Gianni Dagli Orti, 192t CB/Royal Ontario Museum, 192b CB/Royal Ontario Museum, 193 AKG/Erich Lessing, 194t CB/Burstein Collection, 195t AKG/Suzanne Held, 195b AA/Musée Guimet Paris/Gianni Dagli Orti, 196 GI/Demetrio Carrasco/Dorling Kindersley, 197t CB/Wolfgang Kaehler, 197b AA/Musée Guimet Paris/Gianni Dagli Orti, 198 HIP/The British Library - Institution Reference: Shelfmark/Page: Or. 2362, detail, 199tl AA/Bibliothèque Nationale Paris, 199r CB/Christophe Boisvieux, 200t AA/Musée Guimet Paris/Gianni Dagli Orti, 200b CB/Robert van der Hilst, 201 GI/AFP, 202 AKG/Erich Lessing, 203t AA/Imperial Household Collection Kyoto/Laurie Platt Winfrey, 203b CB/Royal Ontario Museum, 204 GI/The Bridgeman Art Library/Chinese School, 205t GI, 205b AA/Genius of China Exhibition, 206 GI/Riser/Peter Adams, 207t AA/Musée Guimet Paris/Gianni Dagli Orti, 207b HIP/The British Museum, 208t AA/National Palace Museum Taiwan, 208b GI/Time & Life Pictures, 209 GI/Robert Harding World Imagery/Gavin Hellier, 210t AA/Musée Cernuschi Paris/Gianni Dagli Orti, 210b CB/Christie's Images, 211 GI/Gallo Images/Travel Ink, 212 GI/Time & Life Pictures, 213t AA/Galerie Ananda Louvre des Antiquaires/Gianni Dagli Orti, 213b HIP/The British Library, 214 GI/Gallo Images/Travel Ink, 215t GI/Roger Viollet, 215b AA/Musée Cernuschi Paris/Gianni Dagli Orti, 216 AA/British Museum, 217tl AA/British Library, 217tr GI, 218 AA/Freer Gallery of Art, 219tl AA/British Library, 219r AA/Galerie Ananda Louvre des Antiquaires/Gianni Dagli Orti, 220 GI/China Span/Keren Su, 221t AA/Musée Cernuschi Paris/Gianni Dagli Orti, 221b GI/The Bridgeman Art Library/Chinese School, 222 CB/Pierre Colombel, 223t AA/Musée Guimet Paris/Gianni Dagli Orti, 223b CB/Werner Forman, 224 GI/National Geographic/David Evans, 225t CB/Christophe Loviny, 225b CB/Royal Ontario Museum, 226 AA/National Palace Museum Taiwan/Harper Collins Publishers, 227t AA/Private Collection Paris/Gianni Dagli Orti, 227b HIP/The Museum of East Asian Art, 228 HIP/The Museum of East Asian Art, 229t AA/Musée Guimet Paris/Gianni

Dagli Orti, 229b GI/AFP, 230t AA/Nelson Atkin's Museum Kansas, 230b AA/Private Collection Paris/Gianni Dagli Orti, 231 AKG/Archives CDA/St-Genes, 232t AA/Victoria and Albert Museum London/Sally Chappell, 232b HIP/The Museum of East Asian Art, 233 PL, 234 GI/China Span/Keren Su, 235t AA/National Palace Museum Taiwan, 235b AA/Genius of China Exhibition, 236 GI/Minden Pictures/Pete Oxford, 237t CB/Jonathan Blair, 237b PL, 238t WF, 238b GI/Hulton Archive, 239 GI/China Span/Keren Su, 240t AA/National Palace Museum Taiwan, 240b CB/Burstein Collection, 241t AA/National Palace Museum Taiwan/Harper Collins Publishers, 241b GI/AFP, 242t CB/Asian Art & Archaeology, Inc., 242b HIP/The Museum of East Asian Art, 243 A/Musée Cernuschi Paris/Gianni Dagli Orti, 244 AA/Musée Guimet Paris/Gianni Dagli Orti, 245t Wikimedia, 245b HIP/The Museum of East Asian Art, 246 GI/AFP, 247t GI/Photographer's Choice/Jeff Hunter, 247b CB/Royal Ontario Museum, 248 HIP/The Museum of East Asian Art, 249t CB/Christie's Images, 249b HIP/The Museum of East Asian Art, 250 AKG, 251t AKG, 251b HIP/The Museum of East Asian Art, 252 GI/National Geographic/James L. Stanfield, 253t AA/Museum of Fine Arts Boston, 253b HIP/The Museum of East Asian Art, 254 CB/Pierre Colombel, 255t CB/The Bridgeman Art Library/Chinese School, 255b AA/Museo Nazionale d'Arte Orientale Rome/Gianni Dagli Orti, 256 A/British Library, 257t GI/National Geographic, 257b AKG, 258t HIP/The British Museum, 258b CB/Christophe Boisvieux, 259 CB/Stapleton Collection, 260 AA, 261t CB/Royal Ontario Museum, 261b CB/Smithsonian Institution, 262 AA/Laurie Platt Winfrey, 263t CB/Smithsonian Institution, 263b CB/Craig Lovell, 264b AKG, 265t CB/Tiziana and Gianni Baldizzone, 265b CB/Asian Art & Archaeology, Inc., 266t AA/Topkapi Museum Istanbul / Gianni Dagli Orti, 267t HIP/The British Museum, 267b GI/Dorling Kindersley, 268 AA/Biblioteca Augusta Perugia/Gianni Dagli Orti, 269t AA/National Museum Damascus Syria/Gianni Dagli Orti, 269b CB/Bettmann, 270 CB/Stapleton Collection, 271t CB/Michael Freeman, 271b GI/Dorling Kindersley, 272tr CB/The Art Archive, 272l CB/Michael S. Yamashita, 273 AA/Bodleian Library Oxford, 274t CB/Lindsey Parnaby/epa, 274b AA/Musée Guimet Paris/Alfredo Dagli Orti, 275 CB/Jose Fuste Raga, 276–277 AA/Nelson Atkin's Museum Kansas/Harper Collins Publishers, 277tl GI/Yann Layma/The Image Bank, 279t CB/Brooklyn Museum, 279b AA/Percival David Foundation for Chinese Art/Harper Collins Publishers, 280 AA/Galerie Ananda Louvre des Antiquaires/Gianni Dagli Orti, 281t AA/Galerie Ananda Louvre des Antiquaires/Gianni Dagli Orti, 281b GI/The Bridgeman Art Library/Chinese School, 282 AKG, 283t GI, 283b HIP/The Board of Trustees of the Armouries, 284 CB/Liu Liqun, 285t AA/British Museum, 285b GI/National Geographic, 286 AKG/Bruce Connolly, 287t CB/Keren Su, 287b GI/The Image Bank/Tom Bonaventure, 288t GI/Ray Laskowitz/Lonely Planet Images, 288b CB/Free Agents Limited, 289t Gi/Gallo Images/Travel Ink, 289b GI/Michael S. Yamashita/National Geographic, 290t GI, 290b GI/AFP, 291 GI/AFP, 292 CB, 293t GI/Michael S. Yamashita/National Geographic, 293b CB/Philadelphia Museum of Art, 294 AA/British Museum, 295t GI/D. Normark/PhotoLink, 295r CB/Dean Conger, 296t Todd Gipstein/CORBIS, 296t CB/Burstein Collection, 297 CB/Werner Forman, 298 CB/Asian Art & Archaeology, Inc., 299t PL, 299b CB/Christie's Images, 300 AA/Musée Guimet Paris/Gianni Dagli Orti, 301t AA/Harper Collins Publishers, 301b AA, 302 GI/Asia Images/Martin Puddy, 303t CB/Burstein Collection, 303b AA, 304t AA/Musée Guimet Paris/Gianni Dagli Orti, 304b GI/Hulton Archive, 305 AA/Topkapi Museum Istanbul/Gianni Dagli Orti, 306l AA/Central Museum Taiwan/Harper Collins Publishers, 306r PL, 307t CB/Philadelphia Museum of Art, 307b CB/Asian Art & Archaeology, Inc., 308 AA/Museo Franz Mayer Mexico/Gianni Dagli Orti, 309 AA/Private Collection/Eileen Tweedy, 309b CB/Marc Garanger, 310t GI, 310b GI/The Bridgeman Art Library/Chinese School, 311 AA/Stephanie Colasanti, 312t PL, 312b CB/Todd Gipstein, 313 GI/Yann Layma/The Image Bank, 314 GI/Roger Viollet, 315t CB/Liu Liqun, 315b CB/Arte & Immagini srl, 316t HIP/The Museum of East Asian Art, 316l AKG, 317 AKG, 318 GI/Keren Su/China Span, 319t PL, 319b CB/YM/epa, 320t AA/British Museum/Eileen Tweedy, 320b AA/British Museum/Eileen Tweedy, 321 AA/Palace Museum Beijing, 322 Wikimedia, 323t AA/School of Oriental & African Studies/Eileen Tweedy, 323b AA/John Meek, 324 GI/The Bridgeman Art Library/Chinese School, 325t GI/AFP, 325b GI, 326t PL, 326b LPI/Linda Ching, 327t GI, 327b GI, 328t WF/Private Collection, 328b AKG/Sotheby's, 329 GI/George Chinnery/The Bridgeman Art Library, 330 AA/Eileen Tweedy, 331t AKG, 331b HIP/The National Archives, 332t CB/Bettmann, 332b CB/Wolfgang Kaehler, 333 AKG, 334t AA/Private Collection, 334b AKG, 335 AA/Royal Engineers Chatham/Eileen Tweedy, 336 CB, 337t CB, 337b CB, 338t CB/Robbie Jack, 338b GI/Keren Su/China Span, 339t GI/Asia Images/Martin Puddy, 339b GI/AFP, 340 AKG, 341t CB/Philadelphia Museum of Art, 341b CB/Bettmann, 342 HIP/The Print Collector, 343t CB/Stefano Bianchetti, 343b HIP/The British Library - Institution Reference: Shelfmark ID: Or 5896. Folio No: 11, 344t GI/The Bridgeman Art Library/Chinese School, 344b GI/Hulton Archive, 345 CB, 346t CB/Werner Forman, 346b AA/Bibliothèque Nationale Paris, 347 AKG/Erich Lessing, 348t AA/Private Collection/Marc Charmet, 348b GI/Hulton Archive, 349 AA/Gianni Dagli Orti, 350 CB/Hulton-Deutsch Collection, 351b CB/Bettmann, 351t CB.
Feature Spread Background Image IS.